D1116578

Realism with a Human Face

Hilary Putnam

Edited by James Conant

Harvard University Press
Cambridge, Massachusetts, and London, England
1990

Library of Congress Cataloging-in-Publication Data

Putnam, Hilary.
  Realism with a human face / Hilary Putnam ; edited by James
Conant.
    p. cm.
  ISBN 0-674-74950-2 (alk. paper)
  1. Realism. 2. Metaphysics. 3. Ethics. 4. Aesthetics.
5. Philosophy, American. I. Conant, James. II. Title.
B835.P87 1990   89-78131
149'.2—dc20   CIP

Be patient toward all that is unsolved in your heart and
try to love the *questions themselves* like locked rooms
and like books that are written in a very foreign tongue
. . . *Live* the questions now. Perhaps you will then gradually, without noticing it, live along some distant day
into the answer.

—Rainer Maria Rilke,
Letters to a Young Poet

Let us be human.

—Ludwig Wittgenstein,
Culture and Value

Preface

The essays that James Conant has selected for this volume represent a central part of the thinking I have been doing since I drew my now well-known (some would say "notorious") distinction between two kinds of realism ("metaphysical" and "internal") in a presidential address to the American Philosophical Association in 1976. Although they do not in any sense represent a giving up of the position I called "internal realism," I have chosen to emphasize a somewhat different aspect of that position than the one I emphasized in *Reason, Truth, and History*.

In *Reason, Truth, and History* I was primarily concerned to present a *conception of truth* alternative to both the classical metaphysical realist conception (truth as correspondence to "mind independent objects") and to relativist/positivist views. (My reasons for treating relativism and positivism as two sides of a single coin are discussed in "Why Is a Philosopher," Chapter 7 of the present volume.) According to my conception, to claim of any statement that it is true, that is, that it is true in its place, in its context, in its conceptual scheme, is, roughly, to claim that *it could be justified were epistemic conditions good enough*. If we allow ourselves the fiction of "ideal" epistemic conditions (as one allows oneself the fiction of frictionless planes in physics), one can express this by saying that a true statement is one that could be justified were epistemic conditions ideal. But this has opened me to a misunderstanding which I very much regret, and which Chapter 2 ("A Defense of Internal Realism") tries to set straight.

Many people have thought that my idealization was the same as Peirce's, that what the figure of a "frictionless plane" corresponds to is a situation ("finished science") in which the community would be in a position to justify *every* true statement (and to disconfirm every false one). People have attributed to me the idea that we can sensibly imagine conditions which are *simultaneously ideal* for the ascertainment of any truth whatsoever, or simultaneously ideal for answering any question whatsoever. I have never thought such a thing, and I was, indeed, so far from ever thinking such a thing that it never occurred to me even to warn against this misunderstanding when I wrote *Reason, Truth, and History,* although I did warn against it in the volume I published after that, *Realism and Reason.* But let me repeat the warning: There are some statements which we can only verify by failing to verify other statements. This is so as a matter of logic (for example, if we verify "in the limit of inquiry" that *no one ever will verify or falsify p,* where *p* is any statement which has a truth value, then we cannot decide the truth of *p* itself, even in "the limit of inquiry"), but there are more interesting ways in which quantum mechanics suggests that this is the case, such as the celebrated Case of Schrödinger's Cat. Thus, I do not by any means *ever* mean to use the notion of an "ideal epistemic situation" in this fantastic (or utopian) Peircean sense. By an ideal epistemic situation I mean something like this: If I say "There is a chair in my study," an ideal epistemic situation would be to be in my study with the lights on or with daylight streaming through the window, with nothing wrong with my eyesight, with an unconfused mind, without having taken drugs or been subjected to hypnosis, and so forth, and to look and see if there is a chair there. Or, to drop the notion of "ideal" altogether, since that is only a metaphor, I think there are *better and worse* epistemic situations *with respect to particular statements.* What I just described is a very good epistemic situation with respect to the statement "There is a chair in my study." It should be noted that the description of that epistemic situation itself uses material object language: I am "in my study," "looking," "the light is on," and so on. I am *not* making the claim that truth is a matter of what "sense data" we would have if we did such and such. Internal realism is not phenomenalism all over again. Even if what I were offering were a definition of truth (and, for a variety of reasons, it isn't), the point that it makes about truth operates *within* whatever type of language we are talking about; one cannot say what are good or better or worse epistemic conditions in quantum mechanics without using the language of quantum mechanics; one cannot say what are good or better or worse epistemic situations in moral discourse without using moral language; one cannot say what are good or better or worse epistemic situations in commonsense material object discourse without using commonsense material object language. There is no reductionism in my position; I am simply denying that we have in any of these areas a notion of truth that totally *outruns* the possibility of justification. What bothered me about statements of the sort I rejected, for example, "There *really are* (or 'really aren't') numbers," or "There *really are* (or 'really aren't') space-time points," is that they outrun the possibility of verification in a way which is utterly different from the way in which the statement that, say, there was a dinosaur in North America less than a million years ago might outrun the possibility of actual verification. These former statements are such that we cannot imagine how *any* creature with, in Kant's phrase, "a rational and a sensible nature" could ascertain their truth or falsity under *any* conditions.

Is this positivism? Am I not saying that statements that are "unverifiable in principle" are cognitively meaningless? What keeps this from being positivism is that I refuse to *limit in advance* what means of verification may become available to human beings. There is no restriction (in my concept of verification) to mathematical deduction plus scientific experimentation. If some people want to claim that even metaphysical statements are verifiable, and that there is, after all, a method of "metaphysical verification" by which we can determine that numbers "really exist," well and good; let them exhibit that method and convince us that it works. The difference between "verificationism" in *this* sense and "verificationism" in the positivist sense is precisely the difference between the generous and open-minded attitude that William James called "pragmatism" and science worship.

Although my view has points of agreement with some of the views Richard Rorty has defended, I do not share his skepticism about the very existence of a substantial notion of truth. In the Kant Lectures that constitute Chapter 1 of this volume, I try to explain not only how the metaphysical realist perspective has broken down in science itself, but also how Rortian relativism cum pragmatism fails as an alternative to metaphysical realism. Rorty's present "position" is not so much a position as the illusion or mirage of a position; in this respect it resembles solipsism, which looks like a possible (if unbelievable) position from a distance, but which disappears into thin air when closely examined. Indeed, Rorty's view is just solipsism with a "we" instead of an "I."

If some readers of my work have been worried about how I can distinguish my views from Rorty's, others have asked why we *should*

give up metaphysical realism. One school, represented by such "physicalist" philosophers as Richard Boyd, Michael Devitt, and Clark Glymour, has suggested that there is no problem about how words "hook
on to the world"; the glue is just "causal connection," they say. In
Chapter 5 I reply to this suggestion by trying to show that the notion
of "causality" on which these philosophers rely is not a physicalist
notion at all, but a cognitive one. Fundamentally, they are offering an
account of reference in terms of *explanation,* and explanation is as
much a cognitive (or "intentional") notion as reference itself. Another
school, represented perhaps by Daniel Dennett, agrees that intentional notions cannot be reduced to physicalist ones but contends that we
need only give up metaphysical realism with respect to the intentional
realm; we can still be hard-line metaphysical realists with respect to
physics. Still other philosophers (for instance, David Lewis) contend
that we should be metaphysical realists about both the intentional
realm and about physics; we just need to recognize the need for at
least one primitive notion not drawn from physics itself for the
description of intentional phenomena (for example, Lewis's notion of
a "natural" class).

What is wrong with these views, besides the inability of their metaphysical realism to do justice to the most fundamental physical theory
we have (quantum mechanics), is that they all fail to do justice to a
pervasive phenomenon that I call "conceptual relativity"; and if there
is any feature of my thought that is stressed throughout all the parts
of this book, it is the importance of conceptual relativity. The doctrine
of conceptual relativity, in brief, is that while there is an aspect of
conventionality and an aspect of fact in everything we say that is true,
we fall into hopeless philosophical error if we commit a "fallacy of
division" and conclude that there must be a part of the truth that is
the "conventional part" and a part that is the "factual part." A corollary of my conceptual relativity—and a controversial one—is the
doctrine that two statements which are incompatible at face value can
sometimes both be true (and the incompatibility cannot be explained
away by saying that the statements have "a different meaning" in the
schemes to which they respectively belong). I defend this controversial
corollary against Donald Davidson's objections in Chapter 6; but
examples of conceptual relativity occur in every part of this volume.
Indeed, it might be said that the difference between the present volume and my work prior to *The Many Faces of Realism* is a shift in

emphasis: a shift from emphasizing model-theoretic arguments against metaphysical realism to emphasizing conceptual relativity.

For me the importance of the debate about realism, relativism, positivism, and materialism has always been that one's position in metaphysics largely determines one's position about the nature and status of "values," and in our time the most popular versions of all these traditional positions have been used to support a "fact/value dichotomy." The essays in Part II of this volume concern ethics and aesthetics. They are largely, though not entirely, metaphilosophical in character; their aim is to show that the fact/value dichotomy is no longer tenable. This is argued in greatest detail in Chapter 11, "Objectivity and the Science/Ethics Distinction," but all of these essays except Chapter 14 are concerned to show that internal realism provides not just a more theoretically tenable but a more human way to view ethical and aesthetic disagreement. If the criticism of metaphysical error did not lead to a more human and a more sensible way to think about the issues that matter most in our lives, taking a stand on such hopelessly abstract issues would hardly have a point, in my view.

All of these ideas—that the fact/value dichotomy is untenable, that the fact/convention dichotomy is also untenable, that truth and justification of ideas are closely connected, that the alternative to metaphysical realism is not any form of skepticism, that philosophy is an attempt to achieve the good—are ideas that have been long associated with the American pragmatist tradition. Realizing this has led me (sometimes with the assistance of Ruth Anna Putnam) to make the effort to better understand that tradition from Peirce right up to Quine and Goodman. That effort is represented by the essays in Part III, many of which represent work that is still in progress. Both James Conant and I felt it was important to include this work in the present volume, because it represents the direction in which my interests are presently turning and also because we want the most significant tradition in American philosophy to be more widely understood in all its manifold expressions.

Hilary Putnam

Contents

Contents

Introduction by James Conant

The title of this volume, *Realism with a Human Face,* alludes to Alexander Dubcek's slogan "Socialism with a Human Face," which was the rallying cry of the Prague Spring of 1968. "Socialism" originally stood as the name for a dream of realizing some of humanity's most cherished aspirations. Yet somehow in the course of its development, Dubcek felt, what was called socialism in his country had turned into the enemy of everything it once stood for. The title Hilary Putnam has chosen for this volume proposes that the history of philosophical realism represents a parallel development. Having originally stood for the dream of realizing our natural human aspirations to knowledge and objectivity, "philosophical realism" now names an intellectual current that ultimately serves only to corrode our conviction in the possibility of attaining either. Putnam draws a distinction in the title essay of this volume between what he calls "Realism with a capital 'R'" (the currently regnant metaphysical image of the world in analytic philosophy) and "realism with a small 'r'" (our commonsense image of the world). He proceeds to argue that while claiming to serve as its representative, the former gives up on everything in which the latter believes. The Realist begins by offering to rescue us from the threat of philosophical skepticism and to vindicate our commonsense belief in the reality of the external world and the possibility of objectivity and truth, and ends by giving us back a world in which common sense no longer has a home; thus he begins by promising to save the world and ends by dehumanizing it. The essays collected in this volume argue that the cognitive values of objectivity and truth are only able to retain their sense within the framework of an overarching ideal of human flourishing. Hence, in attempting to wrench certain cognitive ideals from our overall conception of human flourishing, philosophical realism ends by undermining itself (and precipitating a

backlash of philosophical skepticism). In order to fulfill the philosophical program of providing an accurate and coherent account of
the nature of knowledge and objectivity, our image of knowledge and
objectivity must wear a human face.

In calling for "socialism with a human face," Dubcek's hope was to
rehumanize the movement in Czechoslovakia by confronting it with
the fact that it had betrayed its original motivations. In giving a similar name to his philosophical program, Putnam is evidently also calling for reform. The suggestion would appear to be that the time has
come to rehumanize philosophy, to call upon the prevailing currents
within this field of activity to attend to the gap between the present
condition of the subject and the human aspirations that philosophy
should (and once claimed to) represent. Like Dubcek's before it, Putnam's call for reform will no doubt strike some people as out of touch
with reality—just another instance of starry-eyed idealism rather than
a serious program. Hence the allusion might also appear to be an
unfortunate one in that Dubcek's attempted revolution is famous for
having ended in disaster. As I write, however, momentous changes
are taking place: enormous crowds are assembling in the streets and
public squares of Prague, brandishing placards that call for, among
other things, "a time when people can begin to live as human beings";
the Berlin Wall has come down—a structure that was once the single
most concrete symbol in our contemporary world of human aspiration divided against itself. The spark of Dubcek's vision is therefore
not only being rekindled in Czechoslovakia but has caught fire and is
presently spreading like a blaze across all of Eastern Europe. In the
light of these developments, it would appear that Putnam's title is an
apposite one.[1]

I came to know Putnam first as a teacher of philosophy. I attended
his classes at Harvard and was repeatedly struck by the following
peculiar feature of his pedagogic practice: he would usually motivate
the approach he wished to take to a contemporary philosophical issue
through a discussion of the work of some philosopher whom he
admired. One's first fleeting impression would therefore perhaps be
of someone unable to arrive at ideas of his own—an impression, however, that would vanish as one came to realize that Putnam's readings
of philosophers tended to be no less idiosyncratic than his own
approach to philosophical problems. The lectures for any given
course that Putnam gave were peppered with numerous, though often
puzzling, references to his current philosophical hero(es). An index of

how his readings of philosophical texts would tend to parallel developments in his own personal philosophical views is afforded by the following remark he made in one such course: "I find that as I keep getting clearer about these issues, Aristotle keeps getting clearer about them, too." Nonetheless, each decisive shift in Putnam's thought is generally accompanied by the concomitant abandonment of some (previous) philosophical hero and the inauguration of a new one—sometimes a thinker whom he had previously (and sometimes even famously) denounced. Thus the membership of Putnam's constellation of heroes, not unlike his own substantive philosophical views, tends to exist in a condition of perpetual flux; at any given point in his career, one has only to glance at the current membership of this constellation to ascertain the general philosophical direction in which he is (often quite rapidly) moving.

The present stage in Putnam's intellectual trajectory does not constitute an exception to this general rule of thumb. Scattered throughout the essays collected in the present volume, one finds the names of four philosophers in particular who are of interest in this connection: Immanuel Kant, Ludwig Wittgenstein, Stanley Cavell, and William James. Each of them is invoked at a critical juncture in the book; each functions as an exemplar of a particular aspect of the philosophical calling to which Putnam wishes to remain faithful. My aim in this introduction is to say something about what it is that Putnam admires about each of these philosophers. This endeavor has already been partially preempted by Putnam himself, since two of the essays collected here are devoted primarily to exploring the extent to which contemporary philosophers can still learn from the work of William James; therefore I have confined myself to a consideration of Putnam's relation to the other three of these figures. My aim in doing so is to say something of a general nature about the ways in which the work collected in the present volume represents a departure from Putnam's earlier work. I have tried, in particular, to shed light on the present character of Putnam's overall conception of philosophy and on what he (at least for the time being) thinks philosophy may reasonably hope to achieve.

Putnam's Kantianism

It should come as no surprise to readers familiar with Putnam's recent work that the pair of lectures that constitute the title chapter of this volume are dedicated to Kant. Still, some readers may be surprised by just how strong a claim Putnam is prepared to make for the contemporary relevance of Kant's work. Indeed, this volume opens with the following remark: "I hope it will become clear that my indebtedness to Kant is very large . . . For me, at least, almost all the problems of philosophy attain the form in which they are of real interest only with the work of Kant." This remark is as striking as it is sweeping—especially in view of the fact that in Putnam's first two volumes of philosophical papers there is no sustained discussion of Kant's work. At that stage Kant does not appear to constitute a significant influence on Putnam's own philosophical outlook; although his name makes an occasional appearance, it almost always stands for the figure that analytic philosophy was, in those years, forever distancing itself from: a deplorably influential dead German philosopher who held misguided views about the synthetic *a priori* nature of geometry and arithmetic. It is only in Putnam's last three books that Kant's name begins to stand for a figure from whom contemporary analytic philosophy still has much to learn. In the first of these books, Kant's attack on the correspondence theory of truth is identified as a pivotal chapter in the history of metaphysics;[2] the second book takes its bearings from the role of the concept of autonomy in Kant's moral philosophy;[3] and the third praises Kant's delicate treatment of the mind/body problem.[4] What happens in these books is not that Putnam undergoes a conversion to Kantianism; rather, his entire picture of Kant's achievement and its position in the history of philosophy is transformed. As Putnam's own philosophical views develop, his philosophical agenda increasingly comes to resemble the one he finds in Kant. The result is both an increasing interest in Kant and a deepening appreciation of the extent to which he succeeded in grasping and defining the problems that continue to plague contemporary philosophy. Kant's achievement, on this view, lies not primarily in the answers he provided but rather in the manner in which he pressed the questions. The aim throughout this volume is therefore not so much to defend or rehabilitate any specific solutions to standing problems that Kant himself tried to tackle, as to recapture an overall perspective on the character, structure, and interrelationship of the basic problems that have preoccupied modern philosophy.

In the first of the three books mentioned above, *Reason, Truth, and History,* Putnam credits Kant with being the first philosopher clearly to point the way toward the position in metaphysics[5] that Putnam himself seems now to favor: "Although Kant never quite says that this is what he is doing, Kant is best read as proposing for the first time, what I have called the 'internalist' or 'internal realist' view of truth."[6] The significance of Kant's example for Putnam in this regard is perhaps best summarized by saying that Kant offers the first serious attempt in the history of philosophy to explicate the concept of genuinely objective knowledge in a fashion that does not presuppose the coherence of the notion of an "absolute conception" of the world—the notion that there is some conception of the world that captures the way the world (already) is, in and of itself, independent of our particular (human) conceptions of it.[7] This Kantian quest for a coherent conception of what is "objective humanly speaking"[8]—a conception that avoids the twin perils of a relativism that denies the possibility of objective knowledge and of a metaphysical absolutism that transcends the limits of what is coherently conceivable—has emerged as perhaps the single most pervasive theme in Putnam's recent work. The essays collected in the present volume subserve this ideal in different ways. Those in Part I are concerned specifically with diagnosing the various sources of the traditional metaphysical picture of objectivity and showing that the abandonment of that picture does not require that we give up on the notion of objectivity itself. The essays in Part II argue that our everyday means of adjudicating practical disputes on matters of ethical and aesthetic controversy often represent what may be properly termed "objective resolutions of problematical situations"—and that *that* is "objectivity enough."[9] Thus the argument of the essays in Part II depends on the argument of those in Part I. The overarching claim is that the ways in which philosophers have attacked the possibility of genuine ethical or aesthetic knowledge have generally turned on their allegiance to a false (metaphysical) conception of objectivity. It is the burden of the essays in Part I to advance a critique of this traditional conception of objectivity. Putnam's so-called internal realism—or, as he prefers to call it here, "realism with a small 'r' "—aims to set forth a conception of objectivity that is more faithful to our actual (both everyday and scientific) practices of adjudicating conflicting knowledge-claims and achieving forms of rational consensus.

The doctrine of "internal realism" (of which Putnam discerns a version in Kant's work) has been summarized by Putnam in several different places and in a number of different ways. Many of the essays in this volume represent further attempts at its formulation from a variety of complementary perspectives. One such formulation sheds light on the relationship between Putnam's views and those of Kant:

> My own view is that the success of science cannot be anything but a puzzle as long as we view concepts and objects as radically independent; that is, as long as we think of "the world" as an entity that has a fixed nature, determined once and for all, independently of our framework of concepts . . . If we do shift our way of thinking to the extent of regarding "the world" as partly constituted by the representing mind, then many things in our popular philosophy (and even in technical philosophy) must be reexamined. To mention just two of them: (1) Locke held that the great metaphysical problem of realism, the problem of the relation of our concepts to their objects, would be solved by just natural scientific investigation, indefinitely continued. Kant held that Locke was wrong, and that this *philosophical* question was never going to be solved by empirical science. I am suggesting that on this subject Kant was right and Locke was wrong . . . (2) Since the birth of science thousands of years ago we have bifurcated the world into "reality"—what physical science describes—and appearance . . . I am suggesting that this is an error, and a subtle version of Locke's error. The "primary/secondary" or "reality/appearance" dichotomy is founded on and presupposes what Kant called "the transcendental illusion"—that empirical science describes (and *exhaustively* describes) a concept-independent, perspective-independent "reality."[10]

The importance of Kant's work for Putnam is connected not only to Kant's insight into the incoherence of the seductive idea of a "concept-independent, perspective-independent reality" but also to his appreciation of the ways in which certain forms of moral confusion are fueled by this species of metaphysical confusion.

In *The Many Faces of Realism,* the second of the three books alluded to previously, Putnam again looks to Kant—this time as an important source for "ideas that may be the beginning of a kind of 'internal realism' in moral philosophy."[11] Kant receives credit here for offering "a radically new way of giving content to the notion of equality"[12] through his "radical" and "deep"[13] explication of the concept of autonomy. What Putnam emphasizes most in this discussion is the intimacy of the connection revealed between ethics and metaphysics. Kant's views on moral philosophy flow naturally from his rejection of a metaphysically loaded conception of objectivity: "Kant's glory, in my eyes, is to say that the very fact that we cannot separate our own conceptual contribution from what is 'objectively there' is not a disaster . . . Similarly, I am suggesting, Kant rejects the idea that we have something analogous to the medieval 'rational intuition' with respect to moral questions. And again here he argues that this is not a disaster, that on the contrary it is a Good Thing. The whole Kantian strategy, on this reading . . . is to *celebrate* the loss of essence."[14]

Although there is little specific discussion of Kant's views on moral philosophy in the present volume, in Chapter 13 ("Taking Rules Seriously") Putnam does take recent Anglo-American moral philosophy to task for assuming "a derogatory attitude toward rules and toward the Kantian account" of the place of rules in moral reasoning.[15] Putnam points out that Kant does allow an important role for the pursuit of happiness in his moral scheme;[16] that, rather than devaluing the significance of happiness, Kant was concerned to keep its pursuit from being "allowed to degenerate into a consequentialist ethic;"[17] and that consequently there is room for considerably more harmony between Kantian and Aristotelian ethics than has hitherto generally been acknowledged.[18] Outside of his remarks in this one essay, however, Putnam devotes no further attention to the details of Kant's own moral theory. The feature of Kant's philosophy that resonates most in the present volume is the insistence on the interconnected character of metaphysical and ethical confusion. In particular, Putnam finds in Kant a concern with the way in which the metaphysical realists' picture of scientific objectivity leads to a devaluation of the objectivity of moral judgment. The pervasive attention to the ethical implications of prevailing metaphysical assumptions—and, in particular, to the subtle mutual influences exercised by prevailing conceptions of objectivity in philosophy of science and moral philosophy—represents perhaps the most significant sense in which the essays collected here constitute an important shift in the focus of Putnam's philosophical interests. It is not that these issues receive attention here for the first time in Putnam's work. However, as his conviction in their significance for philosophy (and in their impact on our culture as a whole) has deepened, they have come to assume an unprecedented degree of centrality. In this connection, I will simply note the extent to which the essays pervasively register the pressure of the following two questions: What are the moral (or political) implications of a given philosophical view (in metaphysics, epistemology, philosophy of mind, or philosophy of science)? How do our analyses in various areas of philosophy impinge on our understanding of our everyday practices of

ethical reflection and criticism? My suggestion is that the manner in
which these questions haunt the pages of this volume itself forms a
further significant affinity between Putnam and Kant.

In *Representation and Reality,* the third of the three books mentioned earlier, Kant's claim concerning the impossibility of giving a
scientific account of "schematism"[19] is acknowledged as an antecedent version of one of Putnam's central claims: namely, the inability of
a thoroughgoing physicalist or materialist view of the world to provide a coherent account of intentionality.[20] This feature of Kant's
influence also surfaces in a variety of ways in Putnam's most recent
work.[21] Putnam argues, for example, that Kant's thought marks a
decisive break with the Cartesian tradition: "Note that Kant does not
say there are two 'substances'—mind and body (as Descartes did).
Kant says, instead, that there are 'dualities in our experience' (a striking phrase!) that refuse to go away. And I think Kant was, here as
elsewhere, on to something of permanent significance."[22] What is of
permanent significance here is Kant's idea that the relation between
mind and body should not be pictured as a binary opposition, a dualism of two incommensurable kinds of entity, but rather as a *duality*:
two complementary poles of a single field of activity—the field of
human experience. Putnam goes on to suggest that the clock was
turned back and that philosophy of mind in the Anglo-American
world retreated for several decades to a pre-Kantian formulation of
the mind/body problem: "It was with the decline of pragmatism and
idealism and the rise of logical positivism that English-speaking philosophy reverted to its traditional, empiricist way of conceiving mind-
body issues."[23] Recent developments in the philosophy of mind (in
particular, the functionalism controversy), however, have had the sal-
utary effect, in Putnam's view, of finally bringing a variety of Kantian
"topics and concerns back into English-speaking analytic philosophy
in a massive way."[24]

The various passages quoted above offer some indication of the
magnitude of the achievement that Putnam wishes to claim for Kant's
contributions to philosophy—in metaphysics, moral philosophy, and
philosophy of mind—as well as the degree to which Putnam feels philosophical progress is to be attained by returning to Kant and recon-
sidering many of the traditional problems in the terms in which he
formulated them. That one of the leading figures in contemporary
Anglo-American philosophy should reach *this* conclusion is a devel-

opment worth pondering. I have attempted to indicate here that, despite the exceptional diversity of the topics that are taken up in this volume, one legitimate way of grouping their various concerns under a single heading is to note how they all tacitly participate in a single project: to inherit, reassess, and appropriate Kant's philosophical legacy, with the aim to take up philosophizing at the point at which he left off.

Given that in each of his last three books, Putnam has singled out a different aspect of Kant's view as playing a formative role in shaping his own work, the question naturally arises: What about *this* book? Is there a further Kantian problematic that emerges here and that can be recognized as now playing a decisive role in structuring Putnam's preoccupations? Or to shift the question slightly: Insofar as Putnam's reflections in these essays represent a further departure from his previously published work, do they in any way also represent a further step toward Kant? The frequency with which Kant's name recurs at critical junctures certainly encourages such a question. Yet it is difficult to specify the appropriation of any additional point of doctrine that would mark a further approach toward Kant. This is no doubt partly because the peculiarly Kantian flavor of many of these essays stems not from a new departure in Putnam's thought, but rather from the flowering of a tendency that has been maturing for some years. Earlier I specified one symptom of this process of maturation: the pervasive responsiveness of these essays to questions about how the formulation of issues in certain areas of philosophy (metaphysics, philosophy of mind, and philosophy of science) both determines and is determined by the formulation of (often apparently unrelated) issues in moral and political philosophy. Reflection on the nature of the relationship between these different branches of philosophy is the explicit topic of only a few of the essays in this volume.[25] Implicitly, however, this concern shapes almost all of them. Indeed, it would not be much of a distortion to summarize the underlying agenda of the volume as a whole in the following terms: Putnam wishes to draw limits to scientific reason in order to make room for ethics. Sacrificing the strictness of the parallel with Kant, it would be still more accurate to say: Putnam wishes to find a way to make sense of both our scientific and everyday practices of adjudicating disputes and arriving at truths in a way that also enables us to make the right kind of sense of our moral lives. Consequently, as with many of Kant's works, many of Putnam's essays in this collection that are overtly concerned with epistemology or metaphysics can be viewed, from a certain perspective, as exercises in moral philosophy.

Earlier we saw Putnam praising Kant's characterization of the mental and physical as constituting (not a dualism of substances but rather) a "duality of experience." The notion that these two poles constitute a *duality* is meant to indicate that neither pole is completely reducible to, nor completely separable from, its counterpart. The philosophical task here becomes one of doing conceptual justice to the intricacy of the relations of mutual interdependence and relative autonomy that obtain among the phenomena. For Kant, the field of experience is constituted by the *joint* exercise of the human faculties of understanding and sensibility. He writes: "To neither of these powers may a preference be given over the other. Without sensibility no object would be given to us, without understanding no object would be thought. Thoughts without content are empty, intuitions without concepts are blind."[26] The "duality" that Kant detects in the nature of human experience lies in the manner in which its constitution depends on the *interplay* of these two complementary faculties of sensibility and understanding, and the manner in which the character of human experience hence reflects their respective constitutive aspects of receptivity and spontaneity.

I would like to suggest that Putnam's most recent step forward toward Kant can be found in the extent to which his work increasingly registers the tension of yet another duality—one that Kant detects in the very nature of the enterprise of philosophical reflection itself. Kant characterizes it, in the section of the *Critique of Pure Reason* entitled "The Architectonic of Pure Reason," as a duality of two different concepts of philosophy—the scholastic concept of philosophy (*der Schulbegriff der Philosophie*) and the universal or cosmic concept (*der Weltbegriff*):

> Hitherto the concept of philosophy has been a merely scholastic concept—a concept of a system of knowledge which is sought solely in its character as a science, and which has therefore in view only the systematic unity appropriate to science, and consequently no more than the logical perfection of knowledge. But there is likewise another concept of philosophy, a *conceptus cosmicus,* which has always formed the real basis of the term 'philosophy,' especially when it has been as it were personified and its archetype represented

in the ideal of the *philosopher.* On this view, philosophy is the science of the relation of all knowledge to the essential ends of human reason.[27]

It emerges that the duality indicated here (as belonging to the nature of philosophical reflection) parallels the one that obtains between the moments of receptivity and spontaneity that characterize human experience, insofar as Kant goes on to suggest that it would be equally correct here to assert with respect to these two aspects of the field of philosophical activity: "To neither of these powers may a preference be given over the other." Thus the field of philosophical experience depends on the interplay of these two complementary concepts of philosophy.

The *Schulbegriff* (the scholastic concept) embodies philosophy's aspiration to the systematicity and the rigor of a science. Kant does not exactly say here that philosophy aspires to be a science, for it is neither exactly a science nor something alongside the other sciences; rather, he says that it aspires to "a system of knowledge which is sought solely in its character as a science." It is sought and valued as a science ("wird als Wissenschaft gesucht") for two reasons: first and foremost, because it strives to clarify the foundation of the other sciences (properly so-called) and to lay a groundwork for them; and second, because it provides a fertile breeding ground for scientific ideas.[28] Philosophy, pursued under the aspect of its *Schulbegriff,* will occasionally lay open to view new domains of inquiry and will thereby act as a midwife to new branches of science. Even the development of the methods of particular sciences—although these sciences themselves may be oblivious to this fact—can often be traced back historically to philosophical investigations into the sources and nature of the varieties of human knowledge. The crucial feature of the *Schulbegriff* of philosophy that Kant pauses over here, however, is its esotericism—the fact that it is the province of a few professionals. In this respect as well, philosophy can come to resemble a science: it requires of its practitioners a thorough knowledge of detailed matters of doctrine, method, and terminology. Its practice presupposes a mastery of all the elaborate tools and technicalities that come with any highly developed and specialized discipline. Philosophy's aspirations to clarity, rigor, and completeness exert a pressure for it to become a field in which a narrow class of specialists write only for one another. Insofar as philosophy aspires to gain a secure foothold in the academy, the forces of professionalization that prevail there will tend to ensure the ascendancy of the *Schulbegriff* over the *Weltbegriff*.

The high tradition of analytic philosophy—which traces its roots back to the seminal writings of Frege, Russell, and the Vienna Circle—represents perhaps the fullest realization of the aspiration of philosophy in its *Schulbegriff*. Russell inaugurated this development by calling for the application of the methods of the sciences (in particular the mathematical method of the logical construction of entities) to the questions of philosophy. Putnam's early mentors in philosophy, Hans Reichenbach and Rudolf Carnap, both began as followers of Kant and admirers of Russell, and in their mature years they continued (while scoffing at most of his views) to praise Kant for having clarified philosophy's relation to the natural sciences. They championed a conception of philosophy that they believed could be traced back to Kant: philosophy as the logical analysis of science. However, the ascendancy of the *Schulbegriff* reached what one might consider its metaphilosophical apotheosis in the work of Putnam's colleague and erstwhile mentor, W. V. O. Quine, who defends the (ultimately extremely un-Kantian) conclusion that philosophy simply *is* one of the empirical sciences.[29] For Quine, all philosophy worthy of the title falls squarely under the *Schulbegriff* of philosophy.[30]

In distinguishing between the *Schulbegriff* and the *Weltbegriff*, Kant refers to them as two *concepts* of philosophy. This suggests that, for Kant, it is not a matter of delineating two different kinds of philosophy but rather of discriminating two different poles of a single field of activity—the implication being not only that each of these concepts has a claim to the title of "philosophy," but that the philosophical enterprise itself can achieve full fruition only when pursued under the aspect of each. Hence, on this view, it would seem that in order for the subject to thrive, philosophy in the form of its *Schulbegriff* must flourish as well. It is this feature of Kant's conception of the subject that one could argue has been particularly enshrined in both the practice and the ideology of analytic philosophy. Few readers familiar with his previous work will be surprised to find Putnam vigorously espousing a latter-day version of this conception in one of his earlier writings: "If any further evidence were needed of the healthy state of philosophy today, it would be provided by the hordes of intellectuals who complain that philosophy is overly 'technical,' that it has 'abdicated' from any concern with 'real' problems, etc. For such complaints have always occurred precisely when philosophy was significant and vital! . . . The sad fact is that good philosophy is and always has been *hard,* and that it is easier to learn the names of a few philosophers than it is to read their books. Those who find philosophy overly 'technical' today would no more have found the time or the inclination . . . to read one of the *Critiques,* in an earlier day."[31]

Putnam comes by this particular affinity with Kant's conception of philosophy (namely, that in order for philosophy to flourish its *Schulbegriff* must flourish as well) through the philosophical culture in which he has been educated and to which he has contributed some of his own most important work. That is to say, the fact that Putnam has this much in common with Kant fails to distinguish him from most of his colleagues. What does distinguish his recent work, however, is the degree to which it has come implicitly to embody an insistence on the complementarity—rather than the opposition—of the two concepts of philosophy that Kant discriminates. I believe Putnam today would no longer be comfortable with the way in which the passage just quoted appears to endorse the equation of the following two complaints concerning his own philosophical culture: (1) "It has become too 'technical.'" (2) "It has 'abdicated' from any concern with 'real' problems." More specifically, I believe he would no longer be comfortable with pairing these two criticisms in a fashion that suggests that their relative degrees of justification are necessarily a straightforward function of each other. Although Putnam continues to remain a committed advocate of philosophy's *Schulbegriff,* he has become increasingly concerned to draw attention to how this commitment can lead (and has led) to a neglect of philosophy's *Weltbegriff.* For example, in Chapter 12 of the present volume we find the following charge: "Part of what makes moral philosophy an anachronistic field is that its practitioners continue to argue in . . . [a] very traditional and aprioristic way . . . They are proud of giving ingenious arguments—that is what makes them 'analytic' philosophers—and curiously evasive or superficial about the relation of the premises of these arguments to the ideals and practices of any actual moral community."

In the passage from *The Critique of Pure Reason* quoted earlier, Kant tells us that the *Weltbegriff* (the universal or cosmic concept) of philosophy is concerned with "the relation of all knowledge to the essential aims of human reason." He adds further: "The universal concept is meant to signify a concept relating to what must be of interest to everyone."[32] And he speaks of it as embodying an idea that "exists everywhere in the reason of every human being."[33] Philosophy, viewed under the aspect of this concept, is radically *exoteric*: both its sources and its aims are rooted in the very nature of what it is to be human. The sources of philosophy—and, in particular, the sources of philosophical perplexity—constitute the guiding topic of the second division of the *Critique of Pure Reason,* entitled "The Transcendental Dialectic." It emerges clearly in these pages that, for Kant, philosophy consists in the first order not primarily of a technical discipline reserved only for specialists, but of an elucidatory activity that aspires to illuminate those confusions of thought that ordinary human beings cannot escape entering into. Kant attempts to show that philosophical reflection derives from the natural human propensity to reason, and its problems stem from reason's equally natural propensity to transgress the limits of its own legitimate scope of employment: "Human reason has this peculiar fate that in one species of its knowledge it is burdened by questions which, as prescribed by the very nature of reason itself, it is not able to ignore, but which, as transcending all its powers, it is also not able to answer."[34] The *Weltbegriff* of philosophy is grounded in the fact that every human mind, by virtue of its sheer capacity to reason, harbors a philosopher. Each of us, as we reason, under the prodding of the philosopher within us (whether we wish to or not), concomitantly implicates himself or herself in the activity of philosophizing; and hence each of us is subject to the pressure of those questions that it lies "in the very nature of reason" both to pose to itself, and to be unable to answer, since "they transcend the powers of human reason." This is the province of what Kant calls *transcendental illusion*: "Transcendental illusion . . . exerts its influence on principles that are in no wise intended for use in experience, in which case we should at least have had a criterion of their correctness. In defiance of all the warnings of criticism, it carries us altogether beyond the empirical employment of the categories."[35]

The impact of this aspect of Kant's thought on Putnam's own metaphilosophical views is evident throughout the pages of this volume.[36] Equally pertinent, however, is the notion of a transcendental *dialectic* that Kant derives from his conclusions concerning the unavoidable character of transcendental illusion:

Transcendental illusion . . . does not cease even after it has been detected and its invalidity clearly revealed by transcendental criticism . . . This is an *illusion* which can no more be prevented than we can prevent the sea appearing higher at the horizon than at the shore . . . For here we have to do with a *natural* and inevitable *illusion* . . . There exists, then, a natural and unavoidable dialectic of pure reason—not one in which a bungler might entangle himself through a lack of knowledge, or one which some sophist has artificially invented to confuse thinking people, but one inseparable from human reason, and which, even after its deceptiveness has been exposed, will not cease to play tricks with reason and continually entrap it into momentary aberrations ever and again calling for correction.[37]

Kant views our recurrent state of philosophical confusion as an unwittingly self-imposed condition of intellectual entanglement that arises through our natural propensity to follow what we take to be "fundamental rules and maxims for the employment of our reason."[38] The form of entanglement in question here is therefore one that is imposed on the human mind by the human mind as a natural and inevitable symptom of the pressure of taking thought. It follows from this not only that some degree of philosophical confusion belongs to the natural condition of any creature endowed with reason, but that as long as the human animal wishes to enjoy the fruits of reason he must also expect to pay the price of repeatedly overstepping its limits. Hence as long as there are human beings there will be a need for philosophy. The idea that humanity has an enduring need for the vocation of philosophy is one that recurs in a number of the essays in the present volume—it is a region of Kant's thought in which Putnam sees deep affinities with certain strains in the teaching of the later Wittgenstein.

We saw earlier that the *Weltbegriff* of philosophy was radically exoteric in a second, intimately related sense as well: namely, through its activity of reflection on (as Kant puts it) "the essential ends of human reason." The object of all philosophical reflection, from the standpoint of its *Weltbegriff*, is that which relates to every rational being by virtue of his or her ability to reason, to that which must, as Kant says, "be of interest to everyone." The *Weltbegriff* represents philosophy's mandate to address, clarify, and illuminate those questions that naturally arise and come to perplex us in the course of exercising our capacities for deliberation and reflection. Kant begins the passage in which he distinguishes two concepts by speaking of a philosophy that is "merely scholastic"—merely scholastic because, insofar as the practice of philosophy confines itself to the satisfaction of the aspirations of its *Schulbegriff,* it fails to live up to what Kant terms "the ideal of the philosopher." The philosophical inquirer who neglects (or repudiates) the aspirations of philosophy's *Weltbegriff,* in Kant's view, betrays (or abdicates) the central responsibility of the vocation of philosopher: the responsibility to address the universal intellectual needs of his fellow reflective beings. If the practice of philosophy is not only pursued exclusively *by* specialists but, in addition, addresses itself exclusively *to* the needs and interests of specialists, then it should not properly be called "philosophy": "There is also the *Weltbegriff* which has always formed the real foundation of that which has been given the title [of philosophy]."[39] Kant amplifies the point in the paragraph that follows: "The mathematician, the natural philosopher, and the logician, however successful the two former may have been in their advances in the field of rational knowledge, and the two latter more especially in philosophical knowledge, are yet only artificers in the field of reason. There is a teacher, [conceived] in the ideal, who sets them their tasks, and employs them as instruments, to further the essential ends of human reason. Him alone we must call philosopher."[40]

Kant's idea here that the ideal of the philosopher should correspond to a certain ideal of the *teacher*—one who seeks to further the essential ends of humanity—is one that we will encounter again in considering the relation between Putnam's recent work and that of Cavell. The related idea that there is such a thing as the *responsibility* of philosophy—and that it is abdicated by the confinement of the pursuit of philosophy to the interests of its professional practitioners—is one that finds increasing resonance in Putnam's recent writings, as in the following passage: "Metaphysical materialism has replaced positivism and pragmatism as the dominant contemporary form of scientism. Since scientism is, in my opinion, one of the most dangerous contemporary intellectual tendencies, a critique of its most influential contemporary form is a *duty* for a philosopher who views his enterprise as more than a purely technical discipline."[41] This notion of a philosophical duty—a duty that binds every philosopher "who views his enterprise as more than a purely technical discipline"—is woven into the fabric of the arguments threaded through the essays in the present volume, controlling the focus and direction of analysis throughout. It constitutes a reasonable neighborhood in which to look for an answer to the question raised earlier—namely, what new Kantian dimension can be found in these essays that cannot be discerned as clearly in Putnam's earlier work? To view philosophy as no more than "a purely technical discipline" is to view it only under the aspect of its *Schulbegriff*—to ignore its calling to address the intellectual needs of our time. Kant's distinction between the *Schulbegriff* and the *Weltbegriff* of philosophy closely parallels the distinction between argument and vision that Putnam adapts from Burnyeat:

> I would agree with Myles Burnyeat who once said that philosophy needs vision *and* argument. Burnyeat's point was that there is something disappointing about a philosophical work that contains arguments, however good, which are not inspired by some genuine vision, and something disappointing about a philosophical work that contains a vision, however inspiring, which is unsupported by arguments . . .
>
> Speculation about how things hang together requires . . . the ability to draw out conceptual distinctions and connections, and the ability to argue . . . But speculative views, however interesting or well supported by arguments or insightful, are not all we need. We also need what Burnyeat called 'vision'—and I take that to mean vision as to how to live our lives, and how to order our societies. Philosophers have a double task: to integrate our various views of our world and ourselves . . . and to help us find a meaningful orientation in life.[42]

This emphasis on the philosopher's obligation to formulate an overall guiding vision that emerges in Putnam's recent work is particularly striking when one bears in mind the degree to which this notion of a philosophical duty runs against the grain of the traditional ideology of analytic philosophy. Of course, Putnam's commitment to philosophy's *Weltbegriff* does not, in and of itself, constitute a distinctively Kantian moment. This is a feature his work shares, for example, with currents in both pragmatism and continental philosophy. (Indeed, the emergence of this commitment in Putnam's own writings is unquestionably connected to his increasing interest in, and sympathy with, philosophers such as James and Kierkegaard.)[43] The characteristically Kantian moment here lies in the complementarity of Putnam's philosophical commitments: in the extent to which his recent philosophical work engages the aspirations of both the *Weltbegriff* and the *Schulbegriff* of philosophy and attempts to think productively in the tension that is the inevitable result of bringing them into each other's proximity. What is distinctive about so many of these essays is the cheerful and optimistic tone in which they carry off their attempt to sustain intellectual life in the atmosphere of that tension—a mood that differs significantly from the nihilistic tone that prevails in much contemporary philosophy on either side of the Atlantic.

The most characteristically Kantian aspect of *Realism with a Human Face* is, I am suggesting, its insistence on the *duality* of these two different concepts of philosophy—its insistence that the esoteric and exoteric aspects of contemporary philosophy constitute complementary moments in a single enterprise of reflection. Hence these pages are also pervaded by an insistence on the *unity* of philosophy: an opposition to any form of metaphilosophical dualism that takes philosophy's twin aspirations of rigor and human relevance as the hallmarks of two distinct and incommensurable kinds of philosophical activity. One could summarize the character of the dual nature envisioned here by performing the appropriate substitutions in Kant's famous aphorism concerning the relation between the concepts of the understanding and the intuitions of sensibility: the *Weltbegriff* of philosophy without the *Schulbegriff* is empty, and the *Schulbegriff* of philosophy without the *Weltbegriff* is blind.[44] These two alternatives—emptiness or blindness—represent the two forms of catastrophe that face the polar tasks of popularizing and institutionalizing the practice of philosophy. The former alternative awaits philosophy whenever—in its eagerness to achieve the sound of profundity and to assume the posture of the sage—it compromises its aspirations to perspicuity, clarity, systematicity, and rigor. (Hence all too often philosophers living in exile from the academy tend to be suspiciously eager to take reassurance from the fact that it has always been a mark of honor in philosophy to be opposed by those who claim to speak in the name of philosophy—to rescue the vocation of philosopher from its usurpers.) The latter alternative ensues whenever philosophy's practitioners, in their preoccupation with excavating some narrow slice of territory, lose sight of why it was that they had originally wanted to sink their spades into that particular plot of ground in the first place. (Thus philosophy in its professionalized form often purchases the security of a stable set of projects at the cost of severing contact with most people's original motivations to the subject.) Every attempt at philosophizing remains poised somewhere between these twin perils: the emptiness of pseudo-profundity and the barrenness of pedantry. The former danger has particularly haunted Continental philosophy in its least productive phases, whereas the latter has proved to be analytic philosophy's most characteristic form of infertility.

It is worth reflecting on the fact that Kant is the most recent common figure to whom these two traditions can trace themselves back. He represents the crossroads at which the history of Western philosophy branches. It is as if the task of inheriting his monumental legacy caused our philosophical culture to split into two unfriendly halves, so that the twin aspirations to philosophy that Kant had hoped, once and for all, to balance against each other entered instead into a state of continuous disequilibrium. The result is a philosophical cold war in which the *Weltbegriff* and the *Schulbegriff* each insists on its own respective sphere of influence, and each views the incursions of the other as acts of subversion. Indeed, each has its characteristic mode of intellectual terrorism. (Carnap accused Heidegger and his kin of uttering "pseudo-propositions" that were "devoid of cognitive content." Heidegger accused Carnap and his kin of dwelling in a state of "forgetfulness," oblivious to the "essential questions." Each represented the danger inherent in philosophy that the other most abhorred: charlatanry and philistinism. Each felt that his counterpart paid the price of the one danger because of his excessive fear of the other.) Hence it has become customary to speak of philosophy as having divided into two different "traditions." Kant might have been more inclined to think of this development as philosophy itself dividing into halves—as if each "tradition" had chosen to excel in expressing what the other repressed in the aspiration to philosophy.

In his recent writings, Putnam has been led to remark in a number of places on how the direction of his thought has impelled him "to think about questions which are thought to be more the province of 'Continental philosophy' than of 'analytical philosophy.'"[45] He has also become particularly fond of remarking on certain patterns of convergence that are beginning to emerge between these two cultures—sometimes favorably (for example, the affinities between Rawls's Kantian constructivism and the views of the Frankfurt School)[46] and sometimes unfavorably (for example, the parallel forms of pressure toward relativism in Rorty and Foucault;[47] or the parallels in Quine's and Derrida's theories of interpretation).[48] One of Putnam's motivations for returning to Kant, and for taking his philosophical bearings from Kant's formulations of the traditional problems, would appear to be to heal this rift: to find a piece of nonaligned ground, somewhere within earshot of both sides. Surely one precondition of clearing such a piece of ground is finding a way to bring Kant's two concepts of philosophy back into a stable equilibrium with each other. For the situation is still one in which each half of the contemporary philosophical world conducts itself as if it had been granted only one half of the Kantian inheritance, guaranteeing that philosophy everywhere would remain deprived of some part of its birthright. Putnam's increasing interest in the later work of Wittgenstein can be attributed in part to a conviction that, of the alternatives that have emerged thus far in the twentieth century, it comes closest to exemplifying a mode of philosophy that holds forth some promise of healing the rift which currently separates the analytic and Continental traditions of philosophy and which has left philosophy in our century divided against itself. Indeed, there are good reasons why Putnam might find in Wittgenstein—an Austrian, first schooled in his native country in the writings of Kierkegaard and Schopenhauer, who then came to study and eventually to settle in the Cambridge of Russell and Moore—someone who was uniquely placed to soothe the quarrel between the Anglo-American and Continental European philosophical cultures concerning which of the two concepts of philosophy should be granted ascendancy over the other. Putnam sees in Wittgenstein someone who succeeds in reconstituting the scaffolding of the Kantian architectonic, rejuvenating Kant's legacy to philosophy by fashioning a stable equilibrium between his two concepts of philosophy.

Putnam's Wittgensteinianism

A number of Putnam's earlier papers, including some of the most famous, have been devoted to attacking views such as the so-called criterial theory of meaning[49] and various conventionalist theories of mathematical truth[50]—views that both he and others have often dubbed "neo-Wittgensteinian." Against this background it can come as a surprise to find Putnam increasingly disposed in recent years to indulge in remarks such as the following: "In my view, Wittgenstein was simply the *deepest* philosopher of the century."[51] The apparent tension between Putnam's professed admiration for Wittgenstein in remarks such as this one and his recurring impatience with the forms of neo-Wittgensteinianism currently in vogue in philosophy of language and philosophy of mathematics can be perplexing. The appearance of a contradiction here, however, is eased somewhat by the discovery that Putnam also declares Wittgenstein to be "the most misunderstood" philosopher of the century.[52] This declaration issues not so much from a conviction that Wittgenstein's epigones have simply misrepresented his substantive philosophical *views*, as from a sense that they have misrepresented Wittgenstein as a philosopher who held views. On a number of occasions in the present volume, Putnam argues that Wittgenstein was not a philosopher who wished to put forward anything that could properly be termed a "philosophical view" of his own. In fact, he occasionally suggests that Wittgenstein should not even be thought of as wishing to put forward "arguments" in any traditional philosophical sense.[53] This raises the question: if it is not his philosophical views or his arguments, what is it about Wittgenstein that Putnam professes to admire? The answer would appear to be the *manner* in which Wittgenstein philosophizes: his means of arriving at insight into what fuels and what relieves the tensions of philosophical controversy. Wittgenstein, on Putnam's reading of him—unlike the neo-Wittgensteinians mentioned above—is not concerned to arrive at anything a traditional philosopher would consider a "solution" to a philosophical problem. It does not follow from this that he wishes to debunk the philosopher's questions: "Wittgenstein is not a 'debunker': the philosophical *search* fascinates him; it is answers that he rejects."[54]

It is at this point that we find perhaps the most striking mark of convergence between Wittgenstein's conception of philosophy and the one that informs Putnam's recent work: namely, the idea that it is the philosophical search itself that is of most interest in philosophy— the peculiar character of the questions that exercise philosophy—as opposed to any of the specific answers with which various thinkers have attempted to soothe the recurring insistence and mystery of the questions. Indeed, one aspect of the peculiarity of philosophy's questions lies in the very fact that they consistently tend to outlive the answers that are foisted upon them. Putnam begins Part Two of the title essay of this collection by invoking Wittgenstein in connection with the theme of "the death of metaphysics" and then goes on to issue the following summary statement of his own metaphysical credo:

> I take it as a fact of life that there is a sense in which the task of philosophy is to overcome metaphysics and a sense in which its task is to continue metaphysical discussion. In every philosopher there is a part that cries: "This enterprise is vain, frivolous, crazy—we must say, 'Stop!'" and a part that cries, "This enterprise is simply reflection at the most general and abstract level; to put a stop to it would be a crime against reason." *Of course* philosophical problems are unsolvable; but as Stanley Cavell once remarked, "there are better and worse ways of thinking about them."

To a reader primarily familiar with Putnam's early work, the most
surprising words in this entire volume may consist of Putnam's
remark here that "philosophical problems are unsolvable"—with the
sole exception, that is, of the even more surprising words that immediately precede this remark, namely, "*Of course!*" Does Putnam wish
us to take it as *obvious* that philosophical problems are unsolvable?
Then why should we occupy ourselves with them? Putnam is here
paraphrasing a passage in which Stanley Cavell says of the questions
of philosophy that "while there may be no satisfying answers to such
questions in *certain forms,* there are so to speak, directions to
answers, *ways to think,* that are worth the time of your life to discover."[55] To say that there are no satisfying answers to such questions
in *certain forms* is to say that part of how one makes progress with
such questions is by transforming them, by shifting the terms in which
they present themselves to us. The trickiness of this position lies in its
combining two perceptions that have traditionally competed with
each other: first, that philosophical problems do not admit of satisfying answers (at least in the forms in which they have usually been
posed), and second, that there is such a thing as philosophical progress (and that something of human importance hinges on its achievement). Cavell, in the passage in question, is summarizing what he
takes to be Wittgenstein's teaching concerning the character of the
questions that preoccupy philosophy. He makes this explicit, for
example, in the following remarks:

> [Wittgenstein's] philosophizing is about philosophy as something
> that is always to be received. Philosophy in him is never over and
> done with. The questions on his mind are perennially, How do phil-
> osophical problems begin? and How are they momentarily brought
> peace? When Wittgenstein says that he comes to bring philosophy
> peace, it's always a possible answer to say, "Listen to this tortured
> man. How can what he does be seen as bringing philosophy peace?
> If that's what he wanted, he certainly failed." But that assumes that
> what he wanted to do was to bring philosophy peace once and for
> all, as though it was to rest in peace. And some people are perfectly
> ready to take him that way, as showing that philosophy came to an
> end at some point in cultural time. Even he flickeringly thought that
> might be the case. But what I take him constantly to mean is that
> just as you don't know a priori what will bring philosophy peace,
> so you never know at any crossroads what will cause another begin-
> ning. His work cannot be exempted from—and is not meant to be

exempt from—such a view of what philosophy is, a view in which philosophy always lies ahead of him.[56]

On this reading of Wittgenstein, philosophy stands both for those questions that, in the forms in which they impose themselves, do not admit of satisfying answers *and* for the activity of searching out directions to answers, ways to think, that relieve us of the perplexity with which such questions can torment us. Philosophy, so understood, is not an activity that comes to an end.[57]

We can now see that in the passage by Putnam quoted above, he is summarizing a formulation of Cavell's which, in turn, is intended in part as a way of summarizing certain formulations of Wittgenstein's concerning the nature of philosophy's questions. Part of what Putnam takes from Cavell's reading of Wittgenstein here is the idea that any attempt to offer a straightforward solution to a longstanding philosophical problem constitutes a form of philosophical *evasion* insofar as it does not seek to come to terms with why it is that the purported "solution" is so unsatisfying to most people who are gripped by the question for which it was proposed as an answer—insofar, that is, as it does not seek in any way to contribute to our understanding of how it is that such problems persist in exercising the kind of fascination that they clearly do and clearly have for so many people for so many centuries. Putnam remarks elsewhere: "If philosophical investigations (a phrase made famous by another philosopher who 'changed his mind')[58] contribute to the thousands-of-years-old dialogue which is philosophy, if they deepen our understanding of the riddles we refer to as 'philosophical problems,' then the philosopher who conducts those investigations is doing the job right."[59]

Putnam aligns himself with Wittgenstein here by describing the work in which he aspires to engage as consisting of "philosophical investigations." Such investigations, rather than proposing solutions, aim to "deepen our understanding of the riddles we refer to as 'philosophical problems.'" The comparison of a philosophical problem with a riddle is itself one that derives from Wittgenstein: "For in riddles one has no exact way of working out a solution. One can only say, 'I shall know a good solution if I see it.'"[60] According to Wittgenstein, both a riddle and a philosophical question consist of a form of words still in search of a sense. The sense of the question, he suggests, is a borrowed one that can only be fixed once we have an answer in hand.[61] The form of words constrains the range of possible

answers but does not, in itself, uniquely determine the sense of the
question. In Wittgenstein's view, in order to answer straightforwardly
a question posed by such a form of words we must first specify a
language-game in which it has a home. Yet it is also internal to Wittgenstein's teaching that such an answer (which provides a comfortable home for the question) will generally not satisfy us, for the
answer will seem to drain the question of its original appearance of
profundity.[62] Philosophical problems, Wittgenstein writes: "have the
character of *depth*. They are deep disquietudes ... let us ask ourselves: why do we feel a grammatical joke to be *deep*. (And that is
what the depth of philosophy is.)"[63]

In order to preserve its character of depth, the question must preserve its likeness not only to a riddle, but to a riddle that still awaits
its solution. Each proposed answer that is imposed upon the question
threatens to rob it of some of its characteristically philosophical peculiarity. Riddles, unlike philosophical questions, are posed by someone
who has a specific, perfectly fitted answer already in view. A good
riddle is carefully tailored to match its preexisting answer. Philosophical questions are more like riddles with no preexisting answer, riddles
to which no answer quite fits—though various directions of answer
suggest themselves. Hence Putnam writes: "Philosophy is not a subject that eventuates in final solutions, and the discovery that the latest
view—no matter if one produced it oneself—*still* does not clear away
the mystery is characteristic of the work, when the work is well
done."[64] This will strike some readers as an astounding conclusion for
a philosopher like Putnam to reach. Yet, in some ways, it is a not at
all surprising development that the contemporary analytic philosopher most famous for both propounding and converting his colleagues to a wide range of different solutions to philosophical problems should now propound the conclusion that "philosophy is not a
subject that eventuates in final solutions." In the past, frustrated critics of Putnam's work have sometimes dismissively labeled him a
"moving target," referring to his infamous tendency to change his
mind.[65] As John Passmore, a historian of twentieth-century Anglo-
American philosophy, observes, Putnam can be considered the Bertrand Russell of contemporary philosophy in this respect.[66] Passmore
not only remarks that "Putnam shares Russell's capacity for changing
his mind as a result of learning from his contemporaries,"[67] but goes
on to complain that trying to characterize "Putnam's philosophy [in
particular, his swings between realism and anti-realism] is like trying

to capture the wind with a fishing net."[68] Indeed, this has often served as a rallying point for Putnam's critics, who have charged that his string of metamorphoses serves as evidence that in his philosophizing Putnam is unable to preserve a stable relation to his own convictions—as if a responsiveness to one's convictions could be measured by one's unwillingness to change. Nevertheless, some discussion of Putnam's work crops up in virtually every chapter of Passmore's latest book, entitled *Recent Philosophers,* as if it were undeniably the case that several of the most important recent philosophers all happened to be named "Hilary Putnam." Passmore himself remarks on the oddity of his procedure at one point: "Putnam's Russellian capacity for changing his mind makes him very useful for our purposes. He *is* the history of recent philosophy in outline."[69]

To many, however, this will still appear to be a dubious form of praise. For even if obstinacy is not an intellectual virtue, surely neither is fickleness—an inability to form genuine philosophical commitments. Is this Putnam's problem? Wolfgang Stegmüller, in a survey of contemporary philosophy not unlike Passmore's, puts a rather different face on this aspect of Putnam's work: "It is the coincidence of a variety of features, as fortunate as they are extraordinary, that have contributed to Putnam's occupying the central position that he does in intellectual discussion within the contemporary English-speaking world. Foremost among these is his infallible instinct for what, in the unsurveyable diversity of contemporary discussions, is genuinely *significant,* combined with his ability to arrange a confrontation with the issues in a fashion that consistently promises to advance our thinking in some new direction."[70] Stegmüller here portrays Putnam as someone who, far from blowing with the winds of current intellectual fashion, acts as the conscience of our philosophical culture, drawing attention to the strains in our commitments and driving wedges into the cracks in our contemporary dogmas—acting as a force that shapes, rather than merely conforms to, the prevailing intellectual agenda of the time. If there is anything to Stegmüller's assessment here, then a volume of Putnam's recent work should be of interest to anyone who seeks some glimpse not only of the direction in which philosophy "within the contemporary English-speaking world" is presently headed, but the direction which it might soon be about to take.

Putnam's remark that "philosophy is not a subject that eventuates in final solutions" would appear to suggest that his most recent

change is more than simply a change of mind. It does not simply mark
a conversion to some new philosophical position, one that is now
opposed to his previously held view, but rather a change of philosophical heart—a movement in an orthogonal direction: an aspiration to a broader perspective on his work as a whole. His search, it
would appear, is no longer simply directed toward arriving at a new
and more satisfying candidate for the next philosophical orthodoxy,
but rather is directed toward a more inclusive and a more historical
standpoint, one that allows him to survey and scrutinize the intellectual forces that have fueled the engine of his own philosophical development, provoking his series of conversions over the years—conversions that have in turn helped to usher in and usher out one form of
professional orthodoxy after another. The fact that his work over the
past few decades represents the history of recent analytic philosophy
in outline has helped to make the topic of the fragile and ephemeral
character of philosophical orthodoxy—as well as the cyclical alter-
nation between reigning forms of orthodoxy and heterodoxy—itself
a philosophical topic of increasing urgency and centrality for him.

Kant's name for this alternating cycle of orthodoxy and heterodoxy
is the dialectic between dogmatism and skepticism.[71] He argues that
the dogmatist's and the skeptic's respective pictures—one of Reason's
omnipotence and one of its impotence—are based on a common false
step. Indeed, this is the point at which Putnam sees an anticipation of
a Wittgensteinian theme in Kant's thought—as evidenced in the opening sentence of the *Critique of Pure Reason*: "Human reason has this
peculiar fate that in one species of its knowledge it is burdened by
questions which, as presented by the very nature of reason itself, it is
not able to ignore, but which, as transcending all its powers, it is also
not able to answer."

For Kant, as we saw earlier, this propensity of the human mind to
pose questions to itself that it is unable to answer is a natural and
inevitable concomitant of its capacity to reason. Hence, human beings
will always have a need for philosophy. A prevalent reading of Wittgenstein, recently popularized by Richard Rorty, attempts to distinguish him from Kant in this respect, viewing his work as undertaking
to quench the human need for philosophy once and for all. On this
reading, Wittgenstein is to be understood as teaching that all that
there is left for (the good) philosophers to do is to clean up the metaphysical mistakes that other (bad) philosophers have committed.
Putnam suggests at a number of points that such a reading of Wittgenstein depends upon a misunderstanding of the role of the meta-

physically inclined interlocutory voice that intervenes on almost every page of Wittgenstein's later writings. Rorty appears to follow the widespread tendency to interpret the presence of this interlocutory voice as a literary device for dramatizing the metaphysical temptations of some misguided other—someone not yet privy to Wittgenstein's vision of how matters stand—a voice that is ultimately to be brought to silence. It is to be sharply distinguished from Wittgenstein's own voice: the voice in his text that rounds on, corrects, and censors the interlocutory voice. Putnam appears to favor a reading in which the two voices that pervade Wittgenstein's later writing—Stanley Cavell calls them the voice of temptation and the voice of correctness[72]—are viewed as locked in an enactment of the Kantian dialectic of pure reason. On this reading, the insistence that drives each of these voices is understood as feeding on and sustaining the other. The antimetaphysical voice (which denies the theses that the metaphysician propounds) contents itself with propounding countertheses that only perpetuate, however unwittingly, the cycle of philosophical controversy. Putnam follows Cavell in holding that Wittgenstein's writing aspires to a further perspective—one that does not take sides in this dialectic of insistence and counterinsistence—one that seeks to bring the philosopher within himself a *moment* of peace. Yet it is important that this be consistent with Wittgenstein's holding that the voice of temptation is one that naturally and inevitably speaks up again—it can be brought to a moment of peace but never definitively silenced. On this reading, "the philosopher" whom Wittgenstein wishes to address is, *pace* Rorty, not primarily some subset of humanity that spends its working hours in university philosophy departments, but rather someone who might best be described as the philosopher in each and every one of us (including, preeminently, the philosopher in Wittgenstein himself).[73] In a famous section of his *Philosophical Investigations*, Wittgenstein writes: "The real discovery is the one that makes me capable of breaking off [coming to a pause] in philosophy when I want to.—The one that gives philosophy peace, so that it is no longer tormented by questions which bring *itself* in question."[74] The reference here to philosophy as an activity that the author wishes to be capable of breaking off implies that it is also one that will inevitably be resumed.

Wittgenstein's aim is thus to bring philosophy peace in each of its moments of torment, one by one, as they arise—not, however, to lay philosophy to rest once and for all, so that it may, in Cavell's words, "rest in peace" and never rise again. For Wittgenstein, as for Kant, philosophy is, on the one hand, the name of that inevitable form of intellectual entanglement that is a natural symptom of the pressure of our taking thought, and, on the other hand, the name of our equally inborn desire for intellectual clarity that ministers to us in our recurring crises of confusion. To undertake to lay the impulse to philosophy within ourselves to rest once and for all would be tantamount to renouncing our capacity for thought. Hence, "as long as reflective people remain in the world," as Putnam puts it, "metaphysical discussion will not disappear." Not only, on this view, is the impulse to philosophy a constitutive feature of the human, but the impulse to repudiate the philosopher within oneself—the dream of bringing philosophy to an end, not simply for the time being, but for all time—is itself a moment within philosophy. The impulse to repudiate the philosopher within oneself is paradigmatically philosophical, above all, in its human desire to repudiate one's own humanity.[75] Throughout the present volume, the reader will find Putnam suggesting that our philosophical "craving" for an unattainably high pitch of certainty (and the ensuing forms of all-consuming doubt that it precipitates) is rooted deeper in the human animal than has been hitherto generally acknowledged by those who undertake to propose "solutions" to the problems that our craving for philosophy spins off. The suggestion throughout appears to be that it is part of what it is to be human that one be subject to philosophical cravings that lead one to renounce the conditions of one's humanity. An examination of the character and sources of such cravings should therefore reveal something about what it is to be a human being. It follows further that the tendency in philosophical realism to wipe the human face off our image of the world and ourselves in it is itself a deeply human tendency. This adds a further twist to the title of this volume, for it would seem that, in this sense, every form of what Putnam calls "Realism with a capital 'R'" can be said to bear a human face (but then, in this sense, so can every form of totalitarianism be said to bear a human face).

The following theme pervades each of the essays that follow: The answers that philosophers have canvassed, and continue to canvas, as solutions to philosophy's problems are unable to provide satisfaction to most people (including most other philosophers) who are gripped by the questions of philosophy. A number of essays engage this theme by taking up the claim, most vigorously advocated in recent years by Richard Rorty, that we stand on the verge of a "post-philosophical culture" in which, once it dawns, the problems of philosophy will cease to exercise us any longer.[76] Part Two of the title essay of this volume primarily consists of an argument with Rorty over this issue. Its opening paragraph climaxes in Etienne Gilson's elegant aphorism: "Philosophy always buries its undertakers." Putnam is alluding here to Gilson's suggestion that a proclamation of the end of philosophy— something Rorty trumpets as the latest news—itself forms a constitutive and recurring moment *within* the history of philosophy—an integral phase of the dialectic which drives the subject onward—as if philosophy really would come to an end, that is, a standstill, if at every other juncture someone did not succeed in transforming and revitalizing the subject by calling, in the name of philosophy (that is, out of a faithfulness to philosophy's own aspirations), for the end of philosophy. Hence, having just completed an overview of the history of the subject from the medieval to the modern period, Gilson writes: "Now the most striking of the recurrences which we have been observing together is the revival of philosophical speculation by which every skeptical crisis was regularly attended. As it has an immediate bearing on the very existence of philosophy itself, such a fact is not only striking, it is for us the most fundamental fact of all. . . . The so-called death of philosophy being regularly attended by its revival, some new dogmatism should now be at hand. In short, the first law to be inferred from philosophical experience is: *Philosophy always buries its undertakers*" (his emphasis).[77]

Putnam concurs with Gilson here, summarizing his conclusion as follows: "A simple induction from the history of thought suggests that metaphysical discussion is not going to disappear as long as reflective people remain in the world." However, Putnam is not prepared to rest his case against Rorty on this simple induction from the history of thought. Writing half a century after Gilson, Putnam shares Rorty's sense that the traditional problems of philosophy have come to seem problematic to us in a way that no longer encourages the idea that some traditional form of philosophical speculation, as Gilson had hoped, will soothe our current skeptical crisis: "There is a sense in which the futility of something that was called epistemology is a sharper, more painful problem for *our* period—a period that hankers to be called 'Post-Modern' rather than modern" (Chapter 1, Part Two).

Nevertheless, Putnam is as wary of Rorty's scorn for traditional philosophical controversy as he is of Gilson's optimism that philosophy in its traditional form will continue to prosper. The second half of the title essay of this volume is devoted primarily to specifying his differences with Rorty and "the French thinkers he admires." In particular, Putnam focuses on "two broad attitudes" toward philosophical problems, both of which he claims are "gripping" for Rorty, and both of which he finds repugnant. He summarizes the first of these attitudes as follows:

> The failure of our philosophical "foundations" is a failure of the whole culture, and accepting that we were wrong in wanting or thinking we could have a "foundation" requires us to be *philosophical revisionists*. By this I mean that, for Rorty or Foucault or Derrida, the failure of foundationalism makes a difference to how we are allowed to talk in ordinary life—a difference as to whether and when we are allowed to use words like "know," "objective," "fact," and "reason." The picture is that philosophy was not a reflection *on* the culture, a reflection some of whose ambitious projects failed, but a *basis,* a sort of pedestal, on which the culture rested, and which has been abruptly yanked out. Under the pretense that philosophy is no longer "serious" there lies hidden a gigantic seriousness.[78]

Putnam's quarrel with philosophical revisionism is one of the motivating sources of his distinction between Realism with a capital "R" and realism with a small "r": "If saying what we say and doing what we do is being a 'realist,' then we had better be realists—realists with a small 'r.' But metaphysical versions of 'realism' go beyond realism with a small 'r' into certain characteristic kinds of philosophical fantasy" (Chapter 1, Part Two). It will emerge that to call such views characteristic kinds of fantasy is a very particular form of criticism— one that suggests that what these views require is a treatment that will prove therapeutic—that is, that will restore their sense of reality. Putnam defines Realism with a capital "R" (which he also calls "scientific realism" or "objectivism") as the set of views that depend upon the following two assumptions: "(1) the assumption that there is a clear distinction to be drawn between the properties things have 'in themselves' and the properties which are 'projected by us,' and (2) the assumption that the fundamental science—in the singular, since only physics has that status today—tells us what properties things have in themselves."[79]

Such views end by concluding that our commonsense view of the world (along with the commonsense "objects" that it "postulates" such as tables and chairs) embodies a false picture of reality (and hence that tables and chairs, strictly speaking, do not *really* exist).

Such views often, therefore, also tend to conclude that propositions that we ordinarily take to be true are, strictly speaking, false. What Putnam calls "realism with a small 'r'" opposes these conclusions and affirms our ordinary picture of the world and the everyday linguistic practices that it licenses. Putnam remarks in a number of places that what he thinks of as "realism with a small 'r'" is meant to bring out an important point of convergence that he finds in strains of both analytic and Continental philosophy (in particular, in the phenomenological tradition, as represented preeminently by Husserl, and in ordinary language philosophy, as represented preeminently by the later Wittgenstein): an unwillingness to hold our everyday intuitions about what is "reasonable" (or "true") hostage to our philosophical theories: "The strength of the Objectivist tradition is so strong that some philosophers will abandon the deepest intuitions we have about ourselves-in-the-world, rather than ask (as Husserl and Wittgenstein did) whether the whole picture is not a mistake."[80]

Putnam connects the label "realism with a small 'r'" with Wittgenstein's remark that in doing philosophy we tend to forget that trees and chairs—the "thises and thats we can point to"—are paradigms of what we call "real."[81] Putnam credits Husserl with tracing the source of our philosophical dissatisfaction with our commonsense picture of the world to the rise of modern science:

> Thus, it is clear that the name "Realism" can be claimed by or given to at least two very different philosophical attitudes . . . The philosopher who claims that only scientific objects "really exist" and that much, if not all, of the commonsense world is mere "projection" claims to be a "realist," but so does the philosopher who insists that there *really are* chairs . . .
>
> Husserl traces the first line of thought, the line that denies that there "really are" commonsense objects, back to Galileo, and with good reason. The present Western world-view depends, according to Husserl, on a new way of conceiving "external objects"—the way of mathematical physics . . . And this, he points out, is what above all came into Western thinking with the Galilean revolution: the idea of the "external world" as something whose true description, whose description "in itself," consists of mathematical formulas.[82]

The Realist, on the assumption that the scientific picture of the world represents "the One True Image" (or, as Putnam also likes to call it, "the God's-Eye View"), concludes that our commonsense image of the world is second-class. It begins to appear, indeed, to be in certain respects worse than second-class, if one endorses a further

assumption championed by some Realists: namely, that the scientific
and the everyday vocabularies for describing and understanding the
world embody *conflicting* "conceptual schemes." An allegiance to the
former vocabulary is then viewed as naturally entailing various forms
of disillusionment with beliefs and practices that depend upon the
latter. Putnam follows Wittgenstein in arguing that ordinary language
in itself embodies neither a theory of the world (that could so much
as conflict with scientific theory) nor an ontology (in the philosopher's sense) which commits the speaker to "postulating" the existence of a set of fundamental objects. Putnam sees Scientific Realism's
fixation on the achievement of modern science as leading to philosophical confusion in a further way as well, namely, through its fascination with the *methods* of science—in particular, those of reduction (exhibiting higher-level entities to be constructions of lower-level
entities) and formalization (revealing the hidden logical structure, or
lack thereof, of ordinary beliefs by rendering them in a formal language). In Chapter 7 Putnam diagnoses the tendency in modern philosophy to extrapolate the application of these methods beyond their
legitimate scope of application as a characteristic expression of the
pressure of certain philosophical cravings:

> I can sympathize with the urge to *know*, to *have* a totalistic expla-
> nation which includes the thinker in the act of discovering the total-
> istic explanation in the totality of what it explains. I am not saying
> that this urge is "optional" . . . But I am saying that the project of
> providing such an explanation has failed.
>   It has failed not because it was an illegitimate urge—what human
> pressure could be more worthy of respect than the pressure to
> *know*?—but because it goes beyond the bounds of any notion of
> explanation that we have.

The implication here is that "the pressure to know," which leads us
to legitimate forms of knowledge, is one that also leads us into metaphysical confusion. Since, even if it were possible, it would be self-
defeating for us to seek immunity from this pressure, we have no
choice but to try to be vigilant about when it pushes us beyond the
bounds of sense, stretching our ordinary concepts out to a point
where they cease any longer to have an application. Held up against
such a stretched-out philosophical concept of knowledge, our ordinary practices and beliefs appear too particular, too subjective, too
local, too perspectival. Putnam suggests that insofar as our analyses

of "Objective Knowledge," "Truth," and "Rationality" are tied to certain of these ideals—based usually on a metaphysical picture of what accounts for the success of science—the conclusion will inevitably be forthcoming that our ordinary claims to knowledge are not, strictly speaking, "true," nor are our everyday practices, strictly speaking, "rational." This forces a choice between our prephilosophical intuitions and the conclusions of our philosophical theories. If we opt for the latter, then it appears to follow that full philosophical honesty requires us to call for *revisions* in our ordinary practices. The first two steps, for Putnam, in countering this impetus to what he calls "philosophical revisionism" are to question the coherence of the ideals of objectivity and rationality that are being brought to bear on our ordinary practices, and to diagnose and do justice to the sources of their appeal. At many early junctures in the essays that follow, Putnam is often concerned at the outset merely to draw our attention to how deeply rooted in us "ideas of perfect knowledge" and "ideas of the falsity of everything short of perfect knowledge" are—how deeply such ideas "speak to us."[83] As a given essay progresses, the project in each case takes on a specific focus: to trace some particular contemporary form of philosophical dissatisfaction with our ordinary practices to its source in a disappointment over how those practices are unable to live up to the standard of a philosophical ideal that is being brought to bear on them. When the philosophical ideal turns out on closer examination to be an unattainable one, Putnam tries to show that rather than retracing our steps, we tend to opt for a strategy of despair: we lose confidence in our practices along with the ideals we brought to them. In whatever way a philosophical project of providing a foundation that holds out the promise of satisfying our philosophical cravings falls through, the tendency is then to conclude that the entire superstructure of ordinary practices and beliefs that the foundation was to support is bankrupt as well—to conclude, as Putnam expresses it, that "philosophy was not a reflection *on* the culture, a reflection some of whose ambitious projects failed, but a *basis,* a sort of pedestal, on which the culture rested, and which has been abruptly yanked out." The conclusion ensues that the genuine article (truth, objectivity, rationality) is unattainable. Putnam suggests, as a partial diagnosis, that what appeals to us about such philosophical views (that declare our ordinary practices to be merely second-class) is that they claim to demythologize our lives. Nothing satisfies us more, being the children of modernity that we are, than the thought that we cannot be duped. Only a view that holds out the promise of having completed the modern project of disenchanting the world, so that a moment of further disillusionment is no longer possible for us, will cater to our image of ourselves as immune to the temptation of self-deception. As Putnam says in Chapter 9, we want to believe that we have *seen through* how things appear to how they really are:

> Our modern revelation may be a depressing revelation, but at least it is a *demythologizing* revelation. If the world is terrible, at least we *know* that our fathers were fools to think otherwise, and that everything they believed and cherished was a lie, or at best superstition . . .
>
> I think that this consolation to our vanity cannot be overestimated. Narcissism is often a more powerful force in human life than self-preservation or the desire for a productive, loving, fulfilling life . . . We would welcome [a new view] . . . *provided* the new view gave us the same intellectual confidence, the same idea that we have a superior method, the same sense of being on top of the facts, that the scientistic view gives us. If the new view were to threaten our intellectual pride . . . then, I suspect, many of us would reject it as "unscientific," "vague," lacking in "criteria for deciding," and so on. In fact, I suspect many of us will stick with the scientistic view even if it, at any rate, can be *shown* to be inconsistent or incoherent. In short, we shall prefer to go on being depressed to losing our status as sophisticated persons.

Giving up our "status as sophisticated persons" requires allowing ourselves to be vulnerable to disappointment; hence we are only satisfied with absolute knowledge or no knowledge at all. We prefer the alternative of complete skepticism to the possibility of genuine knowledge with all the risks of fallibility it entails. In Chapter 8, entitled "The Craving for Objectivity," Putnam discusses the example of recent attempts in philosophy to reduce the highly informal everyday activity of interpretation to a set of formalizable rules and the ensuing wholesale skepticism about meaning and interpretation that has followed in the wake of the failure of such attempts. The essay concludes: "The contemporary tendency to regard interpretation as something second class reflects, I think, . . . a craving for absolutes—a craving for absolutes and a tendency which is inseparable from that craving, the tendency to think that if the absolute is unattainable, then 'anything goes.'" The title of this essay is derived from a famous passage in which Wittgenstein discusses what he calls the philosopher's "craving for generality." Wittgenstein also diagnoses this craving as arising in part through the philosopher's fixation on the methods of science: "Our craving for generality has another main source: our preoccupation with the method of science. I mean, the method of reducing the explanation of natural phenomena to the smallest number of primitive natural laws; and, in mathematics, of unifying the treatment of different topics by using a generalization. Philosophers constantly see the method of science before their eyes, and are irresistibly tempted to ask and answer questions in the way science does. This tendency is the real source of metaphysics, and leads the philosopher into complete darkness."[84]

Putnam's charge against Rorty and "the French thinkers that he admires" is not that they share this widespread philosophical preoccupation with the method of science, but that they falsely imagine themselves to have transcended the confusions engendered by this preoccupation—in particular, they fail to appreciate how much the manner in which they reject philosophical projects guided by such a preoccupation is still conditioned by the same craving which gave rise to such projects in the first place. In Putnam's view, the character of Rorty's disappointment with certain features of our culture reflects the strength of the hold that the philosophical craving for absoluteness continues to exert on him. It is his equation of objectivity with a certain metaphysical picture of objectivity that drives him to the misguided conclusion that the demise of this picture carries in its train implications for the integrity and security of our ordinary claims to knowledge. Putnam is alarmed by the *ethical* implications of Rorty's antimetaphysical stance, in particular, the moral it draws concerning how we should view our everyday lives—a moral that depends on a "misrepresentation" of "the lives we lead with our concepts."[85] Putnam follows Wittgenstein in proposing that philosophical progress will come from a closer examination of our everyday practices of entering and adjudicating claims about what is true and what is reasonable:

> Rather than looking with suspicion on the claim that some value judgments are reasonable and some are unreasonable, or some views are true and some false, or some words refer and some do not, I am concerned with bringing us back to precisely these claims, which we do, after all, constantly make in our daily lives. Accepting the "manifest image," the *Lebenswelt*, the world as we actually experience it, demands of us who have (for better or for worse) been philosophi-

cally trained that we both regain our sense of mystery . . . and our sense of the common (for that some ideas are "unreasonable" is, after all, a *common* fact—it is only the weird notions of "objectivity" and "subjectivity" that we have acquired from Ontology and Epistemology that make us unfit to dwell in the common).[86]

In saying that philosophy makes us "unfit to dwell in the common," Putnam follows Wittgenstein in viewing philosophy as an activity that places us not only at odds with what we ordinarily say and do, but also, what is more important, in a position from which we are unable to recover our sense of the ordinary. We become able to view the ordinary only through the lens of a philosophical theory: we lose our sense of the genuineness of our conviction in the reasonableness (or unreasonableness) or truth (or falsity) of certain actions or claims. Our former, prephilosophical conviction now appears to us to be only the consequence of our youthful, unreflective, metaphysical naiveté (and hence an effort at self-deception seems to be a necessary precondition of recovering such conviction). Thus the price of intellectual honesty appears to be the abandonment of many of our ordinary ways of talking and thinking. Putnam's summary statement of his disagreement with Rorty over this issue (in Chapter 1, Part Two) encapsulates the philosophical attitude that informs especially the essays concerned with specifically ethical and political matters in this volume: "I hope that philosophical reflection may be of some real cultural value; but I do not think it has been the pedestal on which the culture rested, and I do not think our reaction to the failure of a philosophical project—even a project as central as 'metaphysics'—should be to abandon ways of talking and thinking which have practical and spiritual weight."

Putnam links the hastiness with which Rorty draws revisionist implications from the failure of traditional philosophical projects with a second moment of hastiness—one that issues from the other of Rorty's "two broad attitudes": namely, the contempt with which Rorty dismisses long-standing philosophical controversies. Putnam suggests that this particular failing is, to some extent, characteristic of analytic philosophers: "Rorty's analytic past shows up in this: when he rejects a philosophical controversy, as, for example, he rejects the 'realism/anti-realism' controversy, or the 'emotive/cognitive' controversy, his rejection is expressed in a Carnapian tone of voice—he *scorns* the controversy" (Chapter 1, Part Two). Putnam's disagreement with Rorty here reflects a further difference in their respective interpretations of the teachings of the later Wittgenstein, as well as that of the major figures of the movement called Ordinary Language Philosophy (Austin, Bouwsma, Wisdom, and Ryle) whose philosophical methods most closely resembled Wittgenstein's. Rorty takes it that the work of these figures, and especially that of Wittgenstein, shows us that what we should do is simply *dismiss* the problems that have most exercised philosophers over the past few centuries. The feature of Rorty's attitude toward philosophical controversy that concerns Putnam here is evident in the following passages from Rorty's review of *The Claim of Reason* by Stanley Cavell:

> Austin, Bouwsma, Wittgenstein, Wisdom, and Ryle all suggested that we just shrug off the claims which Berkeley and Descartes and Moore made on us—that we teach epistemology as the history of some bad ideas. Now Cavell tells us that, unless we take these claims very seriously indeed, we shan't get the full benefit of what Wittgenstein and Austin (in particular) can do for us. We mustn't, he tells us, shrug off skepticism too easily, for then we may miss "the truth of skepticism" . . .
>
> But if [Cavell] . . . is not concerned about being professional, why worry about "American philosophical life"? The latter phrase can only refer to current trends in fashionable philosophy departments. Among intellectuals generally, Wittgenstein is in fact being read and used more and more. It is only within certain philosophy departments that he, and "Oxford philosophy," are *vieux jeu*. Such parochial matters should not concern Cavell . . . One would have expected him to conclude that Wittgenstein would be better served by *forgetting* "events within American philosophical life" than by recapturing them.[87]

This is the voice of a man who is angry about his education. He has come to the conclusion that the history of epistemology has been a "history of some bad ideas." His overwhelming emotion, when faced with the traditional problems of philosophy, is one of impatience—a desire to get on to something more fruitful. Rorty's interest in Wittgenstein therefore is an interest in someone who has managed to put this history behind himself—someone who will enable us to put this history behind ourselves, so that we may distance ourselves from the pain of its pointlessness. Thus he feels that there is an inconsistency in Cavell's being interested in Wittgenstein's work *and* in the problems that preoccupied the great historical figures and still preoc-

cupy "professional" philosophers: "What Cavell wants us not to miss
is, to be sure, as important as he thinks it is. But does he *have* to drag
us back through Berkeley and Descartes to see it?"[88]

What Rorty wants to know is why philosophers like Cavell and
Putnam do not simply confine themselves to stating what is *wrong*
with the traditional views. Why do they insist on motivating the issue
from within, dragging us back through the messy details of the traditional philosophical problems? Rorty feels their attachment to the
tradition is a mark of their unfaithfulness to Wittgenstein's teaching.
Putnam wishes to contest this reading of Wittgenstein. Rorty's reading
of Wittgenstein is both a fairly representative and a widely circulated
one—with the significant difference that Rorty celebrates what most
philosophers deplore in this version of Wittgenstein: namely, the conclusion that the problems of philosophy can be, and should be,
"shrugged off." Putnam's reading of Wittgenstein owes much to the
writings of Cavell. On Cavell's reading, Wittgenstein's primary philosophical virtue is precisely his *patience*—his willingness to head
straight into a confused tangle of issues and to crisscross back and
forth across the same piece of philosophical landscape until gradually
some perspicuous overview of the terrain can be achieved. Putnam
shares with both Rorty and Wittgenstein a deep distrust of analytic
philosophy's self-understanding of the integrity of its own projects.
He aligns himself with Cavell's reading of Wittgenstein and against
Rorty's, however, in order to justify an important presupposition of
the philosophical practice that pervades the essays collected here:
there is no substitute for (and hence philosophically no more pressing
task than) providing a detailed and convincing exposition of where
and how the central projects of analytic philosophy come apart on
themselves, and where and how they misrepresent our lives.

Wittgenstein has his interlocutor ask: "What is your aim in philosophy?" He responds: "To show the fly the way out of the fly-bottle."[89]
Rorty's recommendation appears to be that one should leave the fly
in the fly-bottle and get on with something more interesting. On Rorty's reading of Wittgenstein, the enlightened philosopher should simply dismiss the traditional problems and leave them to those who are
less enlightened. The implication would appear to be that these are
not necessarily *our* problems and that to be free of them all we need
to do is learn to lose interest in them. This suggests that we *can* "just
shrug off the claims which Berkeley and Descartes and Moore made
on us"—as if what we required in order to liberate ourselves from the

tangle of issues that has dominated the history of philosophy were primarily a sheer act of will. Contrast this with Wittgenstein's description of our relation to a philosophical problem: "A *picture* held us captive. And we could not get outside it, for it lay in our language and language seemed to repeat it to us inexorably."[90]

A philosophical picture holding us captive—this is roughly the opposite of something we can simply decide to "shrug off." The recognition that we are stuck does not by itself provide a means of liberation.[91] However, part of what Wittgenstein means by saying that a *picture* holds us captive is that we cannot recognize our picture of things as a picture—a fixated image that we have imposed—and it is our inability to recognize this that renders us captive. The fly is trapped because he does not realize that he is in a fly-bottle; in order to show him the way out, we first need to show him that we have an appreciation of where he thinks he is, that we are able to understand his view from the inside. In order to show the metaphysician anything, we need to take his questions seriously and register an awareness of what the world looks like from his point of view. On this reading of Wittgenstein, the central virtue of philosophy, as he conceives it, is responsiveness: a willingness always to make the other's questions real for oneself. This, however, is precisely the feature of Putnam's and Cavell's practice at which Rorty bristles: "One would have thought that, once we were lucky enough to get writers like Wittgenstein and Nietzsche who resist professionalization, we might get some criticism which *didn't* remain internal to philosophy."[92]

Rorty craves a critique of the tradition that remains *external* to philosophy. Wittgenstein's aim in philosophy was to *change* his readers and with them the tradition in which they participate—this is something that can only be undertaken from within the tradition.[93] Rorty is not interested in transforming the tradition, but rather in simply breaking with it. Hence his picture of the "edifying" philosopher is of someone who "can be *only* reactive," who "falls into self-deception whenever [he] tries to do more than send the conversation off in new directions."[94] Putnam is, above all, concerned to distance himself from this feature of Rorty's picture of "edifying philosophy," as he says in Chapter 1, Part Two: "I think that what is important in philosophy is not just to say, 'I reject the realist/antirealist controversy,' but to show that (and how) both sides *misrepresent* the lives we live with our concepts. That a controversy is 'futile' does not mean that the rival pictures are unimportant. Indeed, to reject a controversy without examining the pictures involved is almost always a way of *defending* one of those pictures (usually the one that claims to be 'antimetaphysical')."

A further important difference between Rorty's and Putnam's respective readings of Wittgenstein emerges here in Putnam's remark that what the philosophical critic needs to learn to do is to show how both sides of a typical philosophical controversy tend to "misrepresent the lives we live with our concepts." The point is not only that certain features of our everyday lives tend to become distorted when viewed through the lens of a philosophical theory, but, more important, that the nature and character of this distortion are themselves important subjects for philosophical reflection. The specific fashion in which our image of what it is to be human tends to be deformed under the equally specific pressures brought to bear upon it by the demands of our philosophical theories is itself deeply revelatory of part of what it is to be human—that is, to be subject to such cravings to deny one's humanity. Part of what Wittgenstein's work calls upon its reader to do is to acknowledge the attraction such cravings can exercise for him and hence also to recognize the depth of his resistance to such an acknowledgment. In his review of Cavell, it becomes clear that this is the feature of Cavell's interpretation of Wittgenstein that irritates Rorty the most, as well as the one that most separates his own vision of what philosophy should become from the one that Putnam entertains. Rorty says that what frustrates him about Cavell is his insistence that the philosophical questions that have exercised the tradition reveal "something important about *human beings*."[95] Putnam explicitly aligns himself with Cavell, and against Rorty, on this issue: "I think philosophy is both more important and less important than Rorty does. It is not a pedestal on which we rest (or have rested until Rorty). Yet the illusions that philosophy spins are illusions that belong to the nature of human life itself, and that need to be illuminated. Just saying, 'That's a pseudo-issue' is not of itself therapeutic; it is an aggressive form of the metaphysical disease itself" (Chapter 1, Part Two).

Putnam's last sentence echoes Wittgenstein's remark that "the philosopher's treatment of a question is like the treatment of an illness."[96] Part of what the treatment of an illness requires is compassion; only here we have to do with an illness one of whose symptoms is a form of uncompassionateness—obliviousness to the other. Putnam's observation that Rorty's terms of philosophical criticism offer no possibility for therapeutic progress harks back to Wittgenstein's famous comparison of his philosophical approach to therapy.[97] The pertinent feature of the analogy here is the role that the virtue of responsiveness plays in both. Wittgenstein says that only those words which occasion genuine self-understanding are the words we seek in philosophy: "We can only convince the other of his mistakenness [in philosophy] if he acknowledges [what we say] as genuinely expressing his feeling—if he acknowledges this expression as (genuinely being) the correct expression of his feeling. For only if he acknowledges it as such *is* it the correct expression. (Psychoanalysis.)"[98]

Eliciting the other's acknowledgment requires correctly identifying the sources of his philosophical insistence. The measure of the accuracy of a diagnosis is the degree of illumination it ultimately is able to afford one's interlocutor. It is a criterion of one's having arrived at the right words in philosophy that the other is able to recognize himself in those words—to recognize the accuracy of one's description of him as grounds for dissatisfaction with himself. "Just saying, 'That's a pseudo-issue' is not of itself therapeutic"; it will only infuriate him. Insofar as he truly is in the grip of a pseudo-issue, simply *denying* what he says will not constitute intellectual progress: the negation of a pseudo-proposition is also a pseudo-proposition. One does not free oneself from a metaphysical picture simply by asserting the negation of a metaphysical thesis. Unless one carefully examines the character of a given philosophical position's seductiveness to those who are attracted to it, as well as the character of the disappointment it provokes in those who reject it—what allows for it to appear initially so innocent and yet the implications of its failure so precipitous—one's gesture of rejecting the picture will inevitably represent a further form of participation in it and victimization by it. Our "antimetaphysical" rejection of one moment will prove to be, as Putnam says, "just another way of *defending*" another, often slightly more entrenched, moment in the metaphysical dialectic. There is a tremendous pressure to formulate our rejection in terms of a counterthesis and to latch firmly onto the ensuing formulation, convinced that it affords the only available refuge from the position from which we wish to escape. Hence each philosophical position bears the stamp of another—ironically, the one from which it most seeks to be free. As Putnam says in Chapter 16, "Very often, the problem in philosophy is that a philosopher who knows what he wants to deny feels that he cannot simply do so, but must make a 'positive' statement; and the positive statement is frequently a disaster."

This way in which we fixate on a counterthesis, Wittgenstein suggests, is one of the sources of "the dogmatism into which we fall so easily in doing philosophy."[99] A number of the essays collected here are specifically concerned to resist this temptation to lapse into one of a number of classical forms of counterassertion, to indicate a way out of the spiraling dialectic of insistence and counterinsistence; and these essays are often, in addition, concerned to indicate explicitly that their task is one of struggling against philosophical temptation.[100] The power and longevity of a given philosophical temptation are themselves something that calls for philosophical reflection. When particular philosophical theories are able repeatedly to resurrect themselves after their obituaries have been written several times over, it no longer suffices simply to rehearse the same old arguments. Putnam takes it as evident "that the brilliant thinkers who propound such theories are in the grip of an intellectual yearning worth taking seriously."[101] Part of the task of philosophical criticism, therefore, becomes to identify and isolate the source and character of the yearning. This requires the cultivation of a nose for what occasions philosophical fixation and, as in therapy, an ear for when someone is inclined to insist a little too loudly that something *must* be the case. Putnam writes: "It is just these philosophical 'musts,' just the points at which a philosopher feels no argument is needed because something is just 'obvious,' that . . . [one] should learn to challenge."[102] Precisely those claims that a philosopher finds most trivial are the ones we are to learn to look on with suspicion. In Wittgenstein's words: "The decisive movement in the conjuring trick has been made, and it was the very one that we thought quite innocent."[103]

The conception of philosophy that emerges from this—an activity isolating decisive moments in philosophical conjuring tricks—can seem to be a purely *negative* one.[104] Furthermore, given the outcome of the traditional agenda of analytic philosophy, it can seem as if the only space left for accomplishment in philosophy is occupied exclusively by such negative tasks. Putnam writes in Chapter 3:

> Analytic philosophy has great accomplishments, to be sure; but those accomplishments are negative. Like logical positivism (itself just one species of analytic philosophy), analytic philosophy has succeeded in destroying the very problem with which it started . . .
>
> But analytic philosophy pretends today not to be just one great movement in the history of philosophy—which it certainly was— but to be philosophy itself. This self-description *forces* analytic philosophers . . . to keep coming up with new "solutions" to the prob-

lem of the Furniture of the Universe—solutions which become more and more bizarre, and which have lost all interest outside of the philosophical community. Thus we have a paradox: at the very moment when analytic philosophy is recognized as the "dominant movement" in world philosophy, it has come to the end of its own project—the dead end, not the completion.

If one accepts this description of the outcome of the history of analytic philosophy, then the question naturally arises: is there a serviceable *positive* conception of philosophy that can inherit our aspirations to the subject?

Philosophy as the Education of Grown-ups

At a number of crucial junctures in the essays collected here, Putnam pauses to invoke the words of his Harvard colleague Stanley Cavell. This leads one to speculate on the significance of Cavell's work for Putnam. Regarding Cavell's most recent book, Putnam writes: "If there is one contemporary thinker whose work I could recommend to every sensitive and intelligent young person who is thinking about the future of philosophy . . . it is Stanley Cavell."[105] This suggests that, for Putnam, Cavell's work represents a place to begin thinking about the future of philosophy—a source of suggestions for ways to begin addressing the present condition of philosophy. We have already heard Putnam say that analytic philosophy, the tradition of philosophy in which he has worked most of his life, has come to a dead end. This suggests that the subject requires a change of direction—one that nevertheless represents a stage in the same journey.

Putnam writes that "the phenomenon called 'analytical philosophy' is best understood as part of the larger phenomenon of modernism" and that "the strains and conflicts in analytical philosophy reflect the strains and conflicts in modernism generally."[106] In what sense does the present condition of philosophy reflect the crossroads in the development of modern art that we call modernism? Cavell writes: "The task of the modernist artist, as of the contemporary critic, is to find what it is his art finally depends upon; it doesn't matter that we haven't *a priori* criteria for defining a painting, what matters is that we realize that the criteria are something we must discover, discover in the continuity of painting itself."[107]

If we put these passages from Putnam and Cavell together, we have the following suggestion: the task of the contemporary analytic philosopher is to find out what the practice of philosophy depends upon. It doesn't matter that we haven't *a priori* criteria for defining what philosophy is; what matters is that we realize that these criteria are something we discover through an examination of both our current practice of philosophy and the historical continuity of the subject. (Of course, this works in both directions: what we are presently willing to recognize as philosophy will influence the criteria elicited, and the criteria we elicit will give us an occasion to reflect on what we are willing to count as philosophy.) This suggests that it has only become necessary at this particular juncture in the *development* of "analytic philosophy" that it allow what philosophy is to become its own central question. For Cavell, this is in itself an indication that analytic philosophy represents a peculiar moment in the history of philosophy—one in which the distinction between philosophy and metaphilosophy achieves an illusion of clarity. Cavell writes: "If I deny a distinction, it is the still fashionable distinction between philosophy and meta-philosophy, the philosophy of philosophy. The remarks I make *about* philosophy (for example, about certain of its differences from other subjects) are, where accurate and useful, nothing more or less than philosophical remarks . . . I would regard this fact—that philosophy is one of its own normal topics—as in turn defining for the subject, for what I wish philosophy to do."[108]

If it is internal to philosophy that what philosophy is always remains a question for it, then the burden of modernism in the arts is that the arts have come to assume the condition of philosophy. If the phenomenon of "analytic philosophy" has only just come to recognize itself as part of the phenomenon of modernism, then it would seem to follow that there is a sense in which the institution we call "analytic philosophy" has only just come to acknowledge that it partakes of the condition of philosophy—it has only just come to know itself *as* philosophy. Analytic philosophy's own self-understanding has had, in particular, an investment in repressing its differences from science. Putnam argues that "the self-image and self-definition of analytical philosophy have too long been accepted uncritically."[109] He suggests that, according to its own self-definition, analytic philosophy has the following three salient characteristics: (1) it is nonideological; (2) it consists of piecemeal problem solving; (3) it can pursue its investigations independently of any concern with questions of value: "a concern with literature, the arts, culture, and the history of culture, [are] at best optional for an analytical philosopher."[110] All three characteristics serve to encourage the image of analytic philosophy as a cousin of the sciences. Putnam contests the accuracy of analytic philosophy's self-image on all three counts:

> The fact is that Carnap and the logical positivists were intensely ideological philosophers, even if their ideology did not take the form of *overt* politics or moralizing. The arguments that analytical philosophers discussed were sometimes piecemeal arguments, but very often they were produced by philosophers who were highly ideological in the sense that Carnap was. Without the motor of a certain amount of ideology which kept producing arguments that divided analytical philosophers into sides, analytical philosophy could hardly have kept going: it has already begun to lose shape as a tendency, with the demise of logical positivism. The fact that analytical philosophers were not interested in cultural history does not mean that they escaped being a part of it.[111]

Putnam's burgeoning interest in recounting various chapters in the recent history of analytic philosophy (which pervades the essays in this volume) is often in the service of highlighting the gap between analytic philosophy's own image of itself and the actual character of its practice and development. It also, however, serves a further aim: "to help us see analytical philosophy once again as a humanistic discipline, and its problems and themes as common problems and themes in the humanities."[112] Putnam's insistence that philosophy is one of the humanities is meant, first of all, to register the extent to which philosophy must raise for itself anew at each moment the question of what its aspirations should be, as well as how they are best to be achieved. Second, however, it is meant to underscore the significance of the fact that the philosophical endeavor is a literary one as well—an individual quest for a certain mode of *writing*:

> I propose that each philosopher *ought* to leave it more problematic what is left for philosophy to do, but philosophy should go on. If I agree with Derrida on anything, it is on this: that philosophy is writing, and that it must learn now to be a writing whose authority is always to be won anew, not inherited or awarded because it is philosophy. Philosophy is, after all, one of the humanities and not a science . . . We philosophers inherit a field, not authority, and that is enough. It is, after all, a field which fascinates a great many people. If we have not entirely destroyed that fascination by our rigidities or by our posturings, that is something for which we should be truly grateful.[113]

This suggests a further sense in which Cavell's work may be exemplary for Putnam: namely, in the way in which he writes philosophy—in the conception of philosophical authorship that his work embodies. This is not to say that Putnam admires Cavell's "style." The concept of style, Cavell himself has argued, has no clear application to modernist work.[114] A clear distinction cannot be drawn here between ways of writing and ways of thinking. This brings us back to a remark of Putnam's that we encountered earlier: "*Of course*, philosophical problems are unsolvable; but as Stanley Cavell once remarked, 'There are better and worse ways of thinking about them.'"[115] Putnam goes on in this essay to connect this point with the question of the future of philosophy—"the grand question 'After Metaphysics What?'"[116]—and to suggest that this is not a question that admits of a stable answer: "No one philosopher can answer that question. 'After metaphysics' there can only be *philosophers*—that is, there can only be the search for those 'better and worse ways of thinking' that Cavell called for."[117] To say that this question regarding the future of philosophy is one we should not evade—one that we must continue to take seriously, although it admits of no single satisfying answer—is simply to say that it is itself a philosophical question: a question *of*, not simply a question about, philosophy. Hence it is itself a question about which "there are better and worse ways of thinking."

The passage from Cavell that Putnam is referring to throughout these remarks is from his book *Themes out of School*. It is one that attempts to address the question "what makes philosophy philosophy?":

> I understand it as a willingness to think not about something other than what ordinary human beings think about, but rather to learn to think undistractedly about things that ordinary human beings cannot help thinking about, or anyway cannot help having occur to them, sometimes in fantasy, sometimes as a flash across a landscape; such things, for example, as whether we can know the world as it is in itself, or whether others really know the nature of one's own experiences, or whether good and bad are relative, or whether we might not now be dreaming that we are awake . . . Such thoughts are instances of that characteristic human willingness to allow questions for itself which it cannot answer with satisfaction. Cynics about philosophy, and perhaps about humanity, will find that questions without answers are empty; dogmatists will claim to have

arrived at answers; philosophers after my heart will rather wish to convey the thought that while there may be no satisfying answers to such questions in *certain forms,* there are so to speak, directions to answers, *ways to think,* that are worth the time of your life to discover.[118]

Having accepted the fact that the questions of philosophy, when they present themselves in certain traditional forms, do not admit of satisfying answers, we can see that the significance of this passage from Cavell lies in the path it glimpses between the prevailing alternative responses to this fact, namely, cynicism and dogmatism. In the distinction that Putnam draws between vision and argument, he remarks that philosophy cannot live on argument alone. Both the dogmatist and the cynic resist this conclusion. The dogmatist insists that he has argument(s) that can settle our questions in philosophy; the cynic, in his dissatisfaction with what argument can establish, affects an air of indifference, concluding that reason can shed no light on these questions. What we require in this situation, Cavell says, is not answers for our questions but "directions to answers"—a form of progress that does not culminate in the assertion of a thesis but in a change of perspective. Such writing must change the way its reader views the problems. In a review article on *Themes out of School* (which quotes this same passage from Cavell), Arnold Davidson offers the following reflection on the character of Cavell's own philosophical writing: "Cavell writes not primarily to produce new theses or conclusions, nor to produce new arguments to old conclusions, but . . . to excavate and transform the reader's sensibility, to undo his self-mystifications and redirect his interest. This is a distinctive mode of philosophizing, one which has its own special rigor, in which the accuracy of description bears an enormous weight. In aiming to transform a sensibility, one must capture it precisely, and if one's descriptions are too coarse, too rough or too smooth, they will hold no direct interest, seeming to have missed the mark completely."[119] Davidson goes on to describe the burden of Cavell's writing as one of diagnosing failures that are lapses, not of intelligence, but of "philosophical sensibility."[120] Earlier we saw Putnam equate what he called our need for "vision" in philosophy with a need for orientation. This, he says, echoing Davidson on Cavell, is "a matter of developing a sensibility": "Finding a meaningful orientation in life is not, I think, a matter of finding a set of doctrines to live by, although it certainly includes having views; it is much more a matter of developing a *sensibility*. Philosophy is not only concerned with changing our views, but also with changing our sensibility, our ability to perceive and react to nuances."[121]

This is a task philosophy shares with aesthetic and moral reflection: something one might call the task of *criticism*—the activity which aims, in Cavell's words, to "make its object available to just response."[122] If it is characteristic of philosophy that it leads us to doubt whether we know what we cannot help but know, it is equally characteristic of the activity of criticism that it elicits conviction by attaining a vantage point from which something we cannot help but know reappears to us, once again, as *obvious*.[123] But how can a claim be obvious if not everyone finds it obvious? When what is hidden to us lies right before our eyes, it is our conviction that it must lie elsewhere—somewhere hidden from view—that renders it invisible. This, according to Wittgenstein, is the structure of philosophical confusion. Hence Wittgenstein says that what we require in philosophy is not explanation but *description*. Wittgenstein's philosophical investigations, Cavell writes, are "investigations of obviousness."[124] Putnam suggests, at one point, that moral confusion has a similar structure: "When a situation or a person or a motive is appropriately described, the decision as to whether something is 'good' or 'bad' or 'right' or 'wrong' frequently follows automatically."[125] Everything depends here on achieving the "appropriate description," on one's ability to find the right words. "The sorts of descriptions that we need" in "situations requiring ethical evaluation," Putnam writes, "are descriptions in the language of a sensitive novelist."[126] Such descriptions seek to help us to *see* the world differently, to render what is right before our eyes visible to us.[127] They aim, Putnam argues, to engage and cultivate our sensibility—our capacity for vision. Philosophers, in regarding a capacity for argument as the touchstone of rationality, have tended to paint a distorted picture of moral reasoning, thereby contributing to a distorted image of what it means more generally to be reasonable. Rather than disparaging moral reasoning for not aligning well with the philosopher's narrow conception of reasoning, Putnam argues, we should learn to recognize it as paradigmatic of "reasoning in the full sense of the word," which "involves not just the logical faculties, in the narrow sense, but our full capacity to imagine and feel, in short, our full sensibility."[128]

The narrowness that characterizes the picture of moral reasoning Putnam opposes here parallels the narrowness in the picture of philosophical reasoning which his remarks about the role of vision in philosophy sought to redress: both narrow the space of the reasonable through their insistence that in order for someone to be *reasonably* convinced of something his conviction must be produced by a chain of argument. Philosophers tend to impose an unreasonable ideal of reasonableness upon us, one that requires the mutilation of our actual capacities for sustaining reasonable conviction. Putnam argues that the philosophical project of formalizing the activity of interpretation is an instance of this: "Not only is interpretation a highly informal activity, guided by few, if any, settled rules or methods, but it is one that involves much more than linear propositional reasoning. It involves our imagination, our feelings—in short, our full sensibility."[129]

If interpretation involves our full sensibility, then cultivating our capacities for interpretation involves cultivating our sensibility. A philosophical ideal of rationality that distrusts any form of conviction that is not based on argument will see such an appeal to sensibility as, at best, irrelevant to the enterprise of seeking truth. Such a view will concede that an appeal to sensibility can produce conviction, but not *rational* conviction. A temperamental bias in favor of certain truths is a merely subjective ground for conviction—something we should learn to overcome in the interest of truth. What the prevailing philosophical ideal of rationality occludes, according to Putnam, is that "temperament is subject to criticism."[130] Part of Putnam's recent interest in William James (as documented in the chapters devoted to him in this volume) is tied to the ways in which his work challenges this ideal of rationality through his claim that by obscuring the role played by sensibility in the attainment of philosophical conviction—placing it beyond the reach of criticism—philosophers have tended to make themselves the victims of their own individual temperaments. James writes:

> Of whatever temperament a professional philosopher is, he tries when philosophizing to sink the fact of his temperament. Temperament is no conventionally recognized reason, so he urges impersonal reasons only for his conclusions. Yet his temperament really gives him a stronger bias than any of his more strictly objective premises. It loads the evidence for him one way or the other, making for a more sentimental or a more hard-hearted view of the universe, just as this fact or that principle would. He *trusts* his temperament. Wanting a universe that suits it, he believes in any representation of the universe that does suit it.[131]

James concludes: "The history of philosophy is to a great extent that of a certain clash of temperaments."[132] Putnam describes this as "the most shocking claim that James makes"[133]—shocking, that is, to a "professional philosopher" who wishes to restrict himself in philosophy to criticizing questions of argument and principle. The implication that Putnam, following James, draws from the fact that temperament loads the outcome of a philosophical controversy for each of us is not that the philosopher should somehow learn to transcend the influence of his temperament, but rather that he should learn to take *responsibility* for it. This requires acknowledging the role that temperament plays in consolidating his conviction (hence a willingness to speak in the first-person singular) as well as subjecting it to criticism (hence a willingness to explore the character and sources of his experiences of philosophical compulsion). Insofar as every philosophical author aspires to elicit the conviction of his reader, this places as a condition on good philosophical writing that it seek to educate. This commits one, Putnam concludes, to a certain ideal of education: "Philosophy is not only concerned with changing our views, but also with changing our sensibility . . . Philosophers are, ideally, *educators*—not just educators of youth, but of themselves and their peers. Stanley Cavell once suggested as the definition of philosophy—'the education of grown-ups.' I think that is the definition I like best."[134]

The passage from Cavell that Putnam is referring to is from *The Claim of Reason*:

> In philosophizing, I have to bring my own language and life into imagination. What I require is a convening of my culture's criteria, in order to confront them with my words and life as I pursue them and as I may imagine them; and at the same time to confront my words and life as I pursue them with the life my culture's words may imagine for me: to confront the culture with itself, along the lines in which it meets in me.
>
> This seems to me a task that warrants the name of philosophy. It is also the description of something we might call education. In the face of the questions posed in Augustine, Luther, Rousseau, Thoreau . . . we are children; we do not know how to go on with them, what ground we may occupy. In this light, philosophy becomes the education of grownups.[135]

To claim that philosophy is the education of grown-ups is to suggest both that its audience is everyone and that its curriculum can never be definitively settled (no subject of human concern being in principle extracurricular to the interests of philosophical reflection). But how is education to proceed under these circumstances? Cavell writes: "In philosophizing, I have to bring my own language and life into imagination." Putnam echoes this in his remark that "what is important in philosophy" when treating a philosophical controversy "is to show that (and *how*) both sides *misrepresent* the lives we live with our concepts."[136] The implication is that the philosopher in each of us drives us out of communication with the person we ordinarily are in "the lives we live with our concepts." (Putnam follows Wittgenstein in also giving the name of "philosophy" to the activity that brings us *back* into communication with the lives we ordinarily lead.) Putnam argues in a number of the essays collected here[137] that analytic *moral* philosophy, in particular, has been haunted by a failure to bring our language and our everyday lives into imagination: "There is a weird discrepancy between the way philosophers who subscribe to a sharp fact/value distinction *make* ethical arguments sound and the way ethical arguments *actually* sound. (Stanley Cavell once remarked that Stevenson writes like someone who has *forgotten* what ethical discussion is like.)"[138]

The passage from Cavell's *The Claim of Reason* that begins by saying that in philosophizing one must bring one's own language and life into imagination is offered as a reflection upon Wittgenstein's famous remark that "to imagine a language means to imagine a form of life."[139] The imagining of one's form of life is the activity Cavell describes as the "convening of my culture's criteria"—a confronting of the culture with itself, "along the lines in which it meets in me." It involves mapping out for oneself the topology of the obvious, the points at which one's justifications run out. If one is not yet on familiar terms with philosophy this is apt to be an experience of either bafflement or chagrin; if one is, it is apt to be one of exhilaration or irritation. Of course, it is, and always will be, the birthright of every philosopher to continue to press his questions at this point. Part of the point of bringing the life I live into imagination is to recover a sense of the peculiarity of my questions, something a familiarity with philosophy can deaden. In focusing in imagination on where such questions can come alive for me, I clarify what weight they are able to bear in my life. Such reflections, Putnam indicates, will often uncover a point beyond which the philosopher's call for justification ceases to grip us. If I simply shape up to his questions as perfectly *ordinary* questions about what I am able to call into question (this, of course, may not be the way he wants me to shape up to them) then I may find that the doubt which he wishes to press appears to make no sense in the way in which he wishes to press it. Putnam writes: "These are cases in which I find I have to say: 'I have reached bedrock and this is where my spade is turned.'"[140]

Putnam is invoking here a passage from Wittgenstein's *Philosophical Investigations*:

> "How am I able to obey a rule?"—if this is not a question about causes, then it is about the justification for my following the rule in the way I do.
>
> If I have exhausted the justifications, I have reached bedrock, and my spade is turned. Then I am inclined to say: "This is simply what I do."[141]

This passage has been interpreted in very different ways by different commentators. Some have invoked it to support a reading of Wittgenstein in which justification is simply a function of consensus within a community—as if Wittgenstein were saying here: This is the right (justified) thing to do here because this is, after all, what *we* do. Putnam comments: "That Wittgenstein here uses the first person—where *my* spade is turned—is very important; yet many interpreters try to see his philosophy as one of simple deference to some 'form of life' determined by a community. On this see . . . Stanley Cavell's discussion in *The Claim of Reason*."[142] Putnam takes Wittgenstein's use of the first-person singular here to contest the consensus-theory reading of the passage; he takes it for granted that Wittgenstein is not an author who would be careless about such matters. Saul Kripke is the interpreter of Wittgenstein whom, above all, Putnam has in mind here as someone who tries "to see his philosophy as one of simple deference to some 'form of life' determined by a community." Kripke writes: "In Wittgenstein's own model . . . if the community all agrees on an answer and persists in its views, no one can correct it . . . If the corrector were outside the community, on Wittgenstein's view he has not the 'right' to make any correction."[143] According to this view, therefore, truth and warrant amount to nothing more than matters of brute *de facto* communal agreement. Putnam reports: "Cavell has suggested to me that this makes it sound as if Wittgenstein thought that truth and warrant are a matter of *etiquette*—wanting to find a justified (or a true) hypothesis is like wanting to use the same fork my 'cultural peers' use, on such a story. But Wittgenstein would not have thought *this* is a description of *our* form of life at all!"[144]

What would Wittgenstein have considered a description of *our* form of life? How does our form of life differ from a set of rules of etiquette? This question dovetails with another. How does philosophy involve the education of our sensibility? How are these two questions related? Both inquire after the character of what we take to be obvious and what we experience as compelling; both inquire against the background of our shared experience of necessity in everyday life and our inability in philosophy to achieve a shared sense of how deep such necessities go. In philosophy the fact that "this is what I do" appears to be a brute convention, floating free of any justificatory ground. Bringing our life back into imagination helps us to recover our sense of the extent to which we are and are not bound by such "conventions." The passage in *The Claim of Reason* that Putnam invokes in the quote given above addresses itself to this issue:

> The conventions we appeal to may be said to be "fixed," "adopted," "accepted," etc., by us; but this does not now mean that what we have fixed or adopted are (merely) the (conventional) *names* of things. The conventions . . . are fixed not by customs or some particular concord or agreement which might, without disrupting the texture of our lives, be changed where convenience suggests a change . . . They are, rather, fixed by the nature of human life itself, the human fix itself, by those "very general facts of nature" which are "unnoticed only because so obvious,"[145] and, I take it, in particular, very general facts of *human* nature . . . Here the array of "conventions" are not patterns of life which differentiate human beings from one another, but those exigencies of conduct and feeling which all humans share.[146]

Cavell says here that the "conventions" to which Wittgenstein wishes to draw our attention are not of a sort that differentiate human beings from one another. It follows that the concept of a "form of life" should not be understood just in broadly ethnographic terms as the set of rules or customs which distinguish one cultural group from another. Yet this is how the vast majority of commentators have tended to read Wittgenstein. Furthermore, certain passages appear to support their claim that Wittgenstein's idea of a form of life is meant to comprehend an ethnographic dimension. In a recent essay Cavell suggests that it is possible to distinguish two different directions in which Wittgenstein inflects his notion of a form of life, calling these "the ethnological or horizontal sense" of form of life and "the biological or vertical sense."[147] The former inflection encourages the idea that the sense of "agreement" at work in Wittgenstein's appeals to our "agreement in a form of life" is a conventionalized, or contractual, sense of agreement. The latter inflection of the idea of a form of life, however, contests this. Cavell writes:

> The idea [of a form of life] is, I believe, typically taken to emphasize the social nature of human language and conduct, as if Wittgenstein's mission is to rebuke philosophy for concentrating too much on isolated individuals . . . an idea of Wittgenstein's mission as essentially a business of what he calls practices or conventions. Surely this idea of the idea is not wrong, and nothing is more important. But the typical emphasis on the social eclipses the twin preoccupation of the *Investigations,* call this the natural, in the form of "natural reactions" (no. 185), or in that of "fictitious natural history" (p. 230), or that of "the common behavior of mankind" (no. 206). The partial eclipse of the natural makes the teaching of the *Investigations* much too, let me say, conventionalist, as if when Wittgenstein says that human beings "agree in the language they use" he imagines that we have between us some kind of contract or an implicitly or explicitly agreed upon set of rules (which someone else may imagine we lack).[148]

The stratum of conventionality that is at issue in this vertical inflection of the idea of a form of life is one—for us, as we stand now—that is pitched deeper than the level of the social. These are "conventions" from which, at present, we are not able to imagine freeing ourselves. But to picture the matter thus, imagining ourselves as shackled to contingencies, is to picture our form of life as a set of constraints that bind us and against which we chafe. Although this is not Kripke's reading of Wittgenstein, it is something like its mirror-image. Instead of viewing us as victimized by brute conventions, Kripke's Wittgenstein pictures us as enforcers of them, "licensed" to victimize one another. Not only do we bring our necessities into existence through our agreements, but these are conceived of as agreements from which we can, in principle, withdraw. Wittgenstein pauses at one point to ask himself whether this view (which is in essence the one Kripke attributes to him) is, indeed, one he wishes to encourage: "'So you are saying that human agreement decides what is true and what is false?'—It is what human beings *say* that is true and false; and they agree in the *language* they use. That is not agreement in opinions but in form of life."[149]

Kripke interprets Wittgenstein's use of agreement here on the par-

adigm of a contract from which, at any moment, we could, in principle, indecorously withdraw. (Kripke's view differs from a more traditional contractarian view in that agreement will not break down
through a withdrawal of consent but through a change in the inclinations to which we are subject. Agreement of the relevant sort arises
on Kripke's view because we happen to be inclined in the same ways.)
To say that human agreement decides what is true and what is false
is to say that these are things *on* which we agree and *to* which we
agree. Kripke here imposes on Wittgenstein's text a certain picture of
what (the relevant form of) agreement comes to. Wittgenstein contests
such a picture in the passage quoted above by saying that human
beings agree *in* a form of life. (The English words "agreement in" in
this passage translate Wittgenstein's German word *Uebereinstim-
men*.) Cavell comments: "The idea of agreement here is not that of
coming to or arriving at an agreement on a given occasion, but of
being in agreement throughout, being in harmony, like pitches or
tones, or clocks, or weighing scales, or columns of figures. That a
group of human beings *stimmen* in their language *ueberein* says, so
to speak, that they are mutually voiced with respect to it, mutually
attuned top to bottom."[150] Such agreement does not rest on *mere*
agreements or mere conventions. Talk of "mere conventions" immediately suggests the sorts of agreement which might, "without dis-
rupting the texture of our lives," simply be changed (or broken off)
"where convenience suggests a change." The agreement of which
Wittgenstein speaks, Cavell suggests, is not only not one that can be
abrogated at will, it is one concerning which we can form no coherent
conception of what it would mean to abrogate it. To withdraw from
the relevant form of "agreement" here would entail shedding one's
capacity to harmonize with others, becoming completely dissonant
with one's fellow beings. The attempt to imagine one's distancing oneself from one's form of life is, on this view, not a task that one is
obviously equal to. It is tantamount to envisioning one's withdrawal
from the human race and entering into a condition in which one is
stripped of the natural reactions and propensities that we share with
others and which permit us to lead a shared life.

To bring our form of life into imagination thus involves imaginatively exploring the limits of what is conceivable to us. In running up
against these limits, we expose to view the ground of what Cavell calls
our "mutual attunement" with others, and what Wittgenstein calls
our "agreement in judgment." The fact of such attunement rests on
the brute fact of our ability to see what another person sees, feel what

he or she feels, follow her lead, catch on to the direction in which he wishes to point. Our capacity to catch on in these ways is a necessary precondition of our being able to participate in civilization. Wittgenstein writes: "If a child does not respond to the suggestive gesture, it is separated from the others and treated as a lunatic."[151] Yet an exploration of the ground of our capacities for agreement with others will also yield moments of inexplicable dissonance with others, when we become opaque to one another. Hence, Putnam argues, any exploration of *our* mutual attunement in judgment must always be conducted in the voice of the first-person singular. Yet it will continue to be a voice that speaks in the name of *our* judgments, of *us*, and of what *we* are capable of sharing—where the "we" represents whoever is able to recognize himself or herself in the descriptions proffered. (It is a voice that claims to articulate what is obvious and yet invisible to us; hence it can seem to speak from a position of unforgivable arrogance.) Each time Wittgenstein reports that his spade is turned, he invites us to discover whether the same is not true for us. In reporting that he has reached bedrock—arrived at a moment of obviousness—his own aim is not to bully us with the assertion of a dogma, but rather to issue an invitation to us to gauge the range of our mutual agreement in judgments. Putnam writes: "Recognizing that there are certain places where one's spade is turned; recognizing, with Wittgenstein, that there are places where our explanations run out, isn't saying that any particular place is *permanently* fated to be one of these places, or that any particular belief is forever immune from criticism. This is where my spade is turned *now*. This is where my justifications and explanations stop *now*."[152]

There is a widespread tendency to read such moments in Wittgenstein as if they amounted to a declaration that justification simply amounted to an appeal to a brute fact of communal agreement (at least for the time being). In declaring that his spade is turned, however, Wittgenstein is not announcing the absence of justifications so much as a perplexity concerning what could count as a further justification here. His spade does not uncover a gaping void, it hits solid rock—it is turned back. He is standing on firm ground. He has reached a point at which it is no longer obviously possible to continue to dig any deeper. If pressed at such a point, nevertheless, to give a justification for what he does, Wittgenstein writes: "Then I am inclined to say: 'This is simply what I do.'"

Cavell finds that Kripke's interpretation of Wittgenstein can be understood as shifting the position of the idea of inclination here—as

if there were no significant difference between Wittgenstein's own formulation and something like the following: "Then I am licensed to
say: 'This is simply what I am inclined to do.'"[153] Once Kripke has
armed himself with such a formulation of Wittgenstein's remark, he
then goes on to interpret inclination as the fundamental court of
appeal for Wittgenstein. On this reading, Wittgenstein is seen to be
endorsing the idea that all justification amounts to is an appeal to the
presence of a community-wide inclination. On such a view, establishing norms of correctness simply amounts to determining whether any
(potential) member of a community shares the same inclinations to
respond in certain ways that the rest of the community has. The
nature of his inclinations is the ground upon which it is decided
whether he should be ruled in or ruled out of the community. Such a
conception of what validates our community's norms, Putnam argues,
cannot allow adequate room for the possibility of genuine progress.
Any modification of the norms of the community would amount to
nothing more than a mere change in the direction of our collective
inclinations; there would no longer be any meaningful sense, however, in which the change could be thought of as an *improvement*. In
a number of the essays collected here, Putnam follows Cavell in challenging the adequacy of Kripke's view of Wittgenstein's (or, as Putnam
prefers to call him, Kripkenstein's) account of the character of human
agreement (as well as in contesting the attribution on Kripke's part of
any such account to Wittgenstein). Against such a view, Putnam
writes: "From within *our* picture of the world . . . *we* say that 'better'
isn't the same as '*we* think it's better.' And if my 'cultural peers' don't
agree with me, sometimes I *still* say 'better' (or 'worse'). There are
times when, as Stanley Cavell puts it, I 'rest upon myself as my
foundation.'"[154]

The passage from *The Claim of Reason* that Putnam is alluding to
here turns out to be the one that immediately precedes the passage
that climaxes with the conclusion that philosophy can be thought of
as "the education of grownups." It begins by reflecting on the significance of the fact that Wittgenstein's parables in *Philosophical Investigations* are pervasively concerned to depict scenes of instruction; it
ends by reflecting on those moments in such scenes of instruction
when one's spade is turned:

Wittgenstein's stories using mathematical imagery . . . read, from a
step away, as though their characters are children. It is appropriate,
in writing so fundamentally about instruction, and in which a cen-

tral character is the child, that we have dramatized for us the fact that we begin our lives as children. Those tribes of big children can put us in mind of how little in each of us gets educated . . .

When my reasons come to an end and I am thrown back upon myself, upon my nature as it has so far shown itself, I can, supposing I cannot shift the ground of discussion, either put the pupil out of my sight—as though his intellectual reactions are disgusting to me— or I can use the occasion to go over the ground I had hitherto thought forgone. If the topic is that of continuing a series, it may be learning enough to find that I *just do*; to rest upon myself as my own foundation.[155]

The difference between ourselves and half-grown children is one of degree, not of kind. The asymmetry of our positions in the scene of instruction breaks down at a certain point. The philosophical hunger for justification is tied to a fantasy that this asymmetry could be prolonged indefinitely, that some equivalent of our parents will never cease to occupy a position of authority for us. There is a part of each of us that is horrified at the thought that we might play some role in determining what is right and wrong: we want to be instructed by authorities. Yet even at those moments when the child's source of authority finally runs out of things to say, when we come to a juncture at which we have to say to the child, "this is what we do," *that,* too, can provide instruction. By marking the limit at which his question begins to lose its sense, we help to teach the child the sense of those questions that can be asked about us and about what we do in the world and why we do it. Thus the child learns who we are and what a world is. We thus bear a terrifying responsibility for the shape of the world the child comes into. We initiate him into a (the, our) world; but there comes a point at which we exhaust our authority. Cavell continues: "But if the child, little or big, asks me: Why do we eat animals? or Why are some people poor and others rich? or What is God? or Why do I have to go to school? or Do you love black people as much as white people? or Who owns the land? or Why is there anything at all? or How did God get here? I may find my answers thin, I may feel run out of reasons without being willing to say 'This is what I do' (what I say, what I sense, what I know), and honor that."[156]

In the face of such questions, I am a child—a child in a world without grown-ups to educate me. In such a world, each of us is confronted with the task of occupying both the position of teacher and that of pupil. There comes a point at which *we* bear the responsibility for initiating ourselves into our world. In the face of the questions pressed by the child in us—a child that still requires education—and in the absence of a community of our elders, we are left wondering whether our questions even make sense. Still too much of a child to accede to a posture of authority with respect to our childlike questions, too much of an adult to simply ignore them, each of us struggles with the twin perils of becoming either a precocious child or a dismissive adult—either a dogmatist or a nihilist. In the face of this challenge, Cavell proposes that philosophy be understood as the task of living with these questions, that it stand as the name of our willingness to acknowledge the confused child in each of us. Our revulsion toward philosophy is a mark of our shame in the face of the incompleteness of our education. Our attraction to philosophy is a mark of our sensitivity to our own needs. We need to learn to overcome our shame at the childishness of the questions we are moved to ask; yet we also need to resist overindulging the child in ourselves, humoring his every whim. The difficulty in educating the child in oneself is in some ways the difficulty that all parents experience: to attend to him without spoiling him. Faced with the task of rearing ourselves, unsure of what authority we can lay claim to, what ground we may occupy, "in this light," Cavell writes, "philosophy becomes the education of grown-ups. It is as though it must seek perspective upon a natural fact which is all but inevitably misinterpreted—that at an early point in a life the normal body reaches its full strength and height. Why do we take it that because we then must put away childish things, we must put away the prospect of growth and the memory of childhood?"[157]

This is the definition of philosophy—the education of grown-ups—that Hilary Putnam says he favors most. If the presence of a confused and inquisitive child within each of us is a constitutive feature of our being human, then this definition has the virtue of securing a permanent role for philosophy in our lives. Even those who believe that the human being can, in principle, outgrow the child within himself should be willing to concede that there is no discernible limit to the extent of either his present confusion or his present propensity to inquire. Insofar as an acknowledgment of this fact excites in us an appetite for education, and insofar as such an acknowledgment is a precondition of a reflective life, surely Putnam is right to conclude that philosophical discussion "is not going to disappear as long as reflective people remain in the world."

In light of his endorsement of this definition of philosophy, what stands out most in the essays collected here is Putnam's insistence that *his* education not be allowed to come to an end, that it marks a betrayal of the philosophical calling to decide the question once and for all concerning what can or should belong to philosophy's curriculum—what it is that we grown-ups require in the way of education. I am thinking here not only of Putnam's unwillingness to allow his possibilities for philosophizing to be funneled by the constraints of his own original philosophical education (the resources of which he no longer finds equal to the tasks at hand) but of two further features of his practice that are in evidence in this volume as well. The first is his faithfulness to his original motivations to the subject—to what excited him about, to what attracted him to, and to what he hoped for from philosophy—at a point in the history of our culture when so many of philosophy's official practitioners have come to accept the idea that compromising their original sense of excitement and hope is simply an inevitable part of the cost of the professionalization of their subject. The second is Putnam's commitment to Kant's thought that the philosopher, in the ideal, should approximate the archetype of the *teacher*—someone who is able to minister to the youthful soul in each of us, who is able to preserve (in a fashion that does not deceive us) our fragile sense that both hope and excitement are not completely inappropriate responses to our condition. Although many of the essays in this volume are concerned with matters of detail regarding some specific controversy, some particular topic in contemporary philosophy, in each case the guiding concern is how the terms of the controversy in question have come to deform our overarching conception of human flourishing. To this extent, the conception of philosophy that informs these essays can be said to be, in many respects, a remarkably classical (though no longer an orthodox) one—one, that is, that harks back at least to Plato and Aristotle—which sees philosophy's fundamental task to lie in the quest for the good life.[158]

Part I

Metaphysics

1. Realism with a Human Face

Part One and Part Two of this essay were delivered individually as Kant Lectures at Stanford University in the fall of 1987.

Part One: Realism

In this essay I hope it will become clear that my indebtedness to Kant is very large, even if it must be "this side idolatry." For me, at least, almost all the problems of philosophy attain the form in which they are of real interest only with the work of Kant. Now, however, I want to do something which a *true* Kant lover might regard as virtually blasphemous: I want to begin this essay by meditating on a remark of Nietzsche's. I trust that the remark is one that Kant would not have been offended by.

In *The Birth of Tragedy* Nietzsche writes that "as the circle of science grows larger it touches paradox at more places." Part One of this essay will be a meditation on this wonderful aphorism. My interest is not in Nietzsche (although he is immensely interesting), nor in Nietzsche's text, but in the remark itself; which is to say that the remark, as I wish to understand it here, is entangled with the thought and experience of our own time, not Nietzsche's. The remark is about "the circle of science," however, and so I want to look at science, and at how the world can become more paradoxical as the circle of scientific knowledge enlarges. Nietzsche's remark could be illustrated with materials from just about any scientific field, but I want to consider just two examples here.

My first example is from an area which is familiar to a few, but highly esoteric stuff to most educated people: the field of quantum mechanics. It is not my purpose here to talk technicalities, so I will not try to describe the theory at all. What I will rather attempt to describe is a discussion which started almost as soon as quantum mechanics itself started and which is still going on—the discussion of "how to interpret" quantum mechanics.

Such discussions are not unprecedented in the history of science, but the *reasons* for the dispute are highly unusual. Let me try to state those reasons in a highly schematized form. The theory, as it was formulated by Bohr and also (somewhat differently) by von Neumann, applies to a dynamical system—say, a system of elementary particles, or a system of fields and particles. As in classical physics, the system can be quite small—one or two or three particles—or it can "in principle" be quite large. But—here is the curious feature which was *not* present in classical physics—any application of the theory requires that, *in addition* to the "system" being talked about, there be "apparatus" or an "observer" which is *not* included in the system. In principle, then, there is no "quantum mechanical theory of the whole universe."[1]

The wise men of the founding generation of quantum mechanics— men like Eugene Wigner—talked of a "cut between the system and the observer." The apparatus, which eventually makes the measurements which test the predictions of the theory, is said to be on the "observer's" side of the "cut." In Bohr's own version of the so-called Copenhagen Interpretation (which is actually a family of interpretations due to Bohr, von Neumann, Heisenberg, Wigner, and others, all different to a larger or a smaller extent), *every property of the system is considered to have meaning and existence only in relation to a particular measuring apparatus in a particular experimental situation.* In addition, the measuring apparatus is supposed to be satisfactorily describable (as far as its function in the experiment goes) using only the language and the mathematical formulas of classical physics (including special relativity). Thus, on Bohr's view, quantum mechanics does not make classical physics simply *obsolete;* rather, it presupposes classical physics in a way in which, for example, it would be absurd to claim that Newtonian physics presupposes medieval physics. The use of quantum mechanics to describe the "system" presupposes the use of a theory most people would consider incompatible with quantum mechanics—classical physics—to describe the apparatus!

This is paradoxical enough, but the dependence of quantum physics on classical physics (in Bohr's version of the Copenhagen Interpretation) is not the paradox I am trying to direct attention to.

Let me go back to a remark I made a moment ago: the remark that, in principle, there is no "quantum mechanical theory of the whole universe." It is part of the appeal of Newton's vision—and I speak of Newton's *vision* because Newton's physics had a peculiar *visualizability* that had an enormous amount to do with its impact on theology, philosophy, psychology, the whole culture—that it presents us with (what the seventeenth century took to be) a "God's-Eye View" of the whole universe. The universe is a giant machine, and if you are a materialist, then we ourselves are just subsystems in the giant machine. If you are a Cartesian dualist, then our bodies are just subsystems in the giant machine. Our measurements, our observations, insofar as they can be described physically, are just interactions *within* the whole shebang. The dream of a picture of the universe which is so complete that it actually includes the theorist-observer in the act of picturing the universe is the dream of a physics which is also a metaphysics (or of a physics which once and for all makes metaphysics unnecessary). Even dualists like Descartes dreamed the dream; they just felt we have to have an additional fundamental science, a fundamental science of Psychology to describe "the soul or the mind or the intellect," to carry out the dream completely. That dream has haunted Western culture since the seventeenth century. You could describe it as the dream of a circle of science which has expanded until there is nothing outside of itself—and hence, no paradoxes left for it to touch! Anyone who has ever done work, experimental or mathematical, with a *real* scientific theory must have felt this dream.

But Bohr's Copenhagen Interpretation gives up precisely this dream! Like Kant, Bohr felt that the world "in itself" was beyond the powers of the human mind to picture; the new twist—one Kant would never have accepted—is that even the "empirical world," the world of our experience, cannot be completely described with just *one* picture, according to Bohr. Instead, we have to make a "complementary" use of different classical pictures—wave pictures in some experimental situations, particle pictures in others—and give up the idea of a single picturable account to cover all situations.

Bohr's ideas were highly controversial, and remain so today. The first of the ideas that I mentioned—that quantum mechanics essentially presupposes the use of classical physics (to describe the measuring apparatus)—does not, I think, stand up. Von Neumann's classical work showed us how to analyze measurement in purely quantum mechanical terms.[2] But the "cut between the observer and the system" has proved more robust, and it is this cut and the idea of the relativity of physical concepts to the experimental situation that are the heart of the Bohr interpretation. Very few physicists today would understand "complementarity" as referring primarily to the complementary use of *classical* concepts, as Bohr did. In what follows, that aspect of Bohr's thought will not occupy us further.

To see how far opponents of the Copenhagen Interpretation are willing to go, let me describe a problem that was immediately raised in connection with the Copenhagen view(s), as well as an anti-Copenhagen response to the same problem, one that was, however, proposed many years later.

Suppose I have a system that is described as completely as quantum mechanics knows how to describe one. Descriptions, in quantum mechanics, are called "states,"[3] and a description that is as complete as the formalism allows is called a "maximal state" (also called a "wave function" or a "psi function"). For the sake of definiteness, imagine that the system is a radium atom about to undergo radioactive decay. Simplifying matters somewhat, let us say that at the future time t the atom may either be in the original state, call it A, or in a "decayed" state, B. (In other words, the atom may either have emitted or may have failed to emit one or more quanta of radiation.) The "indeterministic" character of the theory is *not* reflected in the mathematical formalism at all! Mathematically, the formalism—the famous Schroedinger equation—tells one that the atom will undergo a transition from its original state, call it A, into a new state $A^\#$. The fact that the atom may either have decayed (into state B) or not decayed (stayed in state A) is reflected *not* by the presence of a statistical element in the Schroedinger equation itself, as one would expect in the case of a normal stochastic theory, but rather by the fact that the new state $A^\#$ is, in a certain sense, a "superposition" of the two alternative possibilities A and B.

This feature of the theory was seized upon by opponents of the Copenhagen Interpretation from the beginning—and the opponents included Einstein as well as Schroedinger himself. "Aha!" they cried, "You see, the so-called 'superposition' of A and B is not really a complete description at all. When you say 'the system will be in state $A^\#$' what that means is that the system will *either* be in state A or in state B. Quantum mechanics is just not a complete description of physical reality. Its so-called 'maximal states,' such as $A^\#$, are only partial descriptions."

Defenders of the Copenhagen Interpretation[4] replied that the prediction that the atom will go into state $A^{\sharp}$ refers to what the atom will do when it is isolated—*a fortiori*, when *no* measurement is made. If a measurement is made at time t, then the measurement "throws" the system into either the state A or the state B. The deterministic transition

$$A \longrightarrow A^{\sharp}$$

governs the evolution of the isolated radium atom. (This transition is so "nonclassical" that any attempt to actually *picture* it is inappropriate, the defenders of the Copenhagen Interpretation say.) The stochastic transition

$$A^{\sharp} \longrightarrow \textit{either } A \textit{ or } B$$

governs the measurement interaction. (This stochastic transition is the famous "collapse of the wave packet.")

I must ask non-scientists to excuse what must sound like a lapse into technicality; what I am setting the stage for is not the exposition of the scientific theory, but rather the presentation of a surprising event in the recent history of science—one whose significance I shall leave it to the reader to judge.

The event I refer to is the appearance on the scene some years ago of the so-called Many-Worlds Interpretation of quantum mechanics. This interpretation, which was proposed by Everett and De Witt,[5] and for a time supported by John Wheeler, still has some enthusiastic proponents among quantum cosmologists. But it sounds more like something from the latest science fiction best seller than like a theory expounded by serious scientists.

What the theory says can be explained (informally, of course) with the aid of my little example of the atom which does or does not undergo radioactive decay. According to the Many-Worlds Interpretation, the *entire cosmological universe* is a "system" in the sense of quantum mechanics. Thus the "cut between the observer and the system" is simply rejected. This interpretation aims at restoring the feature of the Newtonian Weltanschauung that I referred to as its "God's-Eye View" of the world—restoring that feature at virtually any price. Moreover, according to this interpretation, the Schroedinger equation[6] is the only equation governing physical processes—the universe evolves *deterministically* according to this view; the indeterminism thought to be characteristic of quantum mechanics is also rejected. There is no "reduction of the wave packet." What happens in an experimental situation like the one described, according to the Many-Worlds Interpretation, is not that the universe makes an indeterministic "jump" into either the state A or the state B when the measurement is made,[7] but that the universe "splits" into two parallel worlds (mathematically, one of these is represented by the "relative state" A and the other by the "relative state" B). In one of these "parallel worlds" or "branches" the atom decays; in the other it does not.

But what about the observer, say *me?* Well, if I am the observer, then—according to Everett and De Witt and their supporters—I will have *two* "future selves" at the time *t*. Each of my future selves will, of course, think that it is the only "Hilary Putnam" and that its "branch" is the "whole world." But each of my future selves will be wrong. There will be two Hilary Putnams, one experiencing a "world in which the atom did not decay" and one experiencing a "world in which the atom decayed"!

As a philosopher, I am fascinated by the appearance of the Many-Worlds Interpretation as a cultural phenomenon. This is so similar to what we have seen over and over again in the history of metaphysics! A well-known poet (Derek Walcott) once riddled, "What is the difference between a philosopher and a ruler?" The answer was a pun: "A ruler will only stretch to one foot, but a philosopher will go to any length." But the pun contains a deep observation; it *is* part of our philosophical tradition that at least one kind of philosopher will go to any length to preserve what he regards as a central metaphysical principle, a principle that is "necessary" in the peculiar philosophical sense of "necessary." What is startling is to observe a metaphysical system as daring as any being born in the unexpected locus of a discussion among physicists about how to understand the deepest and the most accurate physical theory we possess.

Obviously, no one proposed anything as extreme as the Many-Worlds Interpretation until many other suggestions which are not as extreme had been tried out and rejected. And I cannot emphasize too strongly that only a small minority—an extremely small minority—of physicists feels any discomfort with the Copenhagen Interpretation to the present day. But there is and always has been a small minority—which included Einstein and Schroedinger, as I remarked—which does feel discomfort, and which tried and still tries to find a "God's-Eye View" to replace the "cut between the system and the observer."

At the beginning, opponents of the quantum mechanical orthodoxy looked for what were called "hidden variables." The idea was that quantum mechanics is an *incomplete* description of the physical world, and that if we found out how to complete it, by adding the missing parameters (the "hidden" ones), we would simultaneously get rid of the "objectionable" features—indeterminism, the clash with "realist" intuitions—*and* perceive that quantum mechanics is not giving us the ultimate physical processes, but only a kind of statistically average description of processes. The most famous attempt of this kind was made by David Bohm, whose interpretation has recently been revived and modified by J. S. Bell. The problems with this approach were summarized by Hans Reichenbach in his book on the foundations of quantum mechanics,[8] in the form of what he called a Principle of Anomaly. The principle says that there are, indeed, various ways of supplementing quantum mechanics with "hidden variables," but all of them require the postulation of instantaneous action at a distance, "clairvoyance" on the part of the "system" (that is, it acts, in certain situations, as if it "knew" which measurement was going to be made in the future), or other "causal anomalies." Although Reichenbach's attempt at a mathematical demonstration of this Principle of Anomaly cannot be accepted, an argument more recently offered by Bell shows that he is right. Since I am looking at the history of physics from a cultural, as well as from a logical, point of view, let me remark that the truth of the Principle of Anomaly accounts for the fact that, although there are, indeed, a number of hidden variable interpretations around, none of them convinces anyone but the inventor and (if he is lucky) up to six friends.

It is only in the light of the failure—or what the scientific community has perceived as the failure—of these many attempts to restore the God's-Eye View conception of physics while continuing to accept the framework of quantum mechanics that one can understand why anyone would even be tempted to try anything as metaphysically dramatic as the Many-Worlds Interpretation. In the Many-Worlds Interpretation there are no "hidden variables"—*every* fact is *completely* described by the "maximal state" of the whole Universe, with all its "branches." Of course, many facts are "hidden" from this particular "self." But no fact is hidden from God, or from any omniscient mind, since the omniscient observer knows the "state function of the whole Universe," and that state function codes *all* the information about *all* the "branches"—all the "parallel worlds." And it codes it in good old

everyday quantum mechanical language, the language of "states"—
there is no supplementation with "hidden variables" that are not
describable in the existing formalism.

Of course, this is a queer sense of "no hidden variables," at least
from a layman's point of view. *Whole parallel worlds and other selves
that I can't observe*—aren't *these* "hidden variables" with a ven-
geance? Not from the point of view of the Omniscient Quantum
Physicist—and it is the Omniscient Quantum Physicist's point of view
that this interpretation tries to capture.

Again, in this interpretation, there are no "nonlocal interactions"—
the splitting of the world into parallel worlds vitiates the proof of
Bell's Theorem—and, in particular, there is no "reduction of the wave
packet." The space-time structure is that of relativistic physics (which
is why it is cosmologists that are especially attracted to it). And the
logic is classical logic. Only one problem remains:[9] all this talk of
"other worlds" is, after all, only a *picture,* and the picture, if we
accept it, does nothing for us but give us metaphysical comfort. At
no point does this wild ontological extravaganza really change the
practice of physics in any way. It only reassures us that a God's-Eye
View is still possible.

Actually, it doesn't really do that. For, alas, we don't find that this
picture is one we can *believe.* What good is a metaphysical picture
one can't believe?

I began this essay with a quotation from Nietzsche. I hope that the
discussion I just reviewed illustrates the truth of the aphorism that I
took as the subject for my musings here: "As the circle of science
grows larger, it touches paradox at more places." *Indeed!* Quantum
mechanics is a beautiful example of the way in which increased
understanding can make the world a more paradoxical place.

I shall shortly place by the side of this example a very different
illustration of the same fact. But before I leave quantum mechanics,
let us consider for a moment the nature of the paradox involved. The
problem is often posed as a clash between our desire to interpret
quantum mechanics realistically and our desire to preserve the principle that one cannot send causal signals faster than light. But this
way of explaining what is paradoxical about the present state of our
understanding of quantum mechanics is too formalistic. Rather than
viewing the paradox as a "clash between realism and locality," I
myself prefer to go back to the discussion as it was when Bohr first
put forward his Copenhagen Interpretation.

Although von Neumann did not accept the claim that classical physics must be used on the "observer" side of the "cut between the system and the observer," he certainly agreed that there was such a cut, as did all the proponents of the Copenhagen Interpretation in that period. And I suggest that—as was, indeed, felt at the time—it was the need for and presence of such a cut that is the most paradoxical feature of the theory. "Locality" enters the discussion when we consider whether we can change or reinterpret the theory so as to avoid the need for the cut; but so do many other issues (can we change classical logic? can we change classical probability theory?[10] are "parallel worlds" intelligible?). Although the discussion in the last ten years has fixated on Locality and on Bell's Theorem, these issues are best considered as forming the technical background to the problem. What is paradoxical is the upshot, the need to recognize a cut between the observer and the system in any quantum mechanical description of physical reality. And we feel this to be a paradox precisely because what it means to have a cut between the observer and the system is, as I said at the outset, that a great dream is given up— the dream of a description of physical reality as it is apart from observers, a description which is objective in the sense of being "from no particular point of view." In short, I contend that it is the clash with "realism" in this sense that we consider paradoxical; our unwillingness to give up our belief in locality of course figures as well, in that physicists refuse to restore "realism" by just adopting some ad hoc nonlocal theory for the sake of satisfying our discomfort, but it should go without saying that ad hoc ways out of a paradoxical situation are not acceptable.

Logic and the God's-Eye View

My next example comes from logic—more precisely, from the response of modern logic to the most ancient of logical paradoxes, the puzzle of the Liar. Rather than consider the statement "All Cretans are liars" (uttered by a Cretan),[11] modern treatments begin with some such example as the following sentence:

(I) The sentence (I) is false.

I suppose someone might think that it is illegitimate to use "(I)" to name an expression which contains "(I)" itself as a proper part, but many forms of "self-reference" are quite harmless. (Consider: "Write down the sentence I am uttering in your notebook.") In any case, the suggestion that we throw self-reference out of the language turns out to be excessively costly; in fact, Gödel showed that as long as our language contains number theory, there will always be ways of constructing sentences that refer to themselves. So we shall stipulate that (I) cannot be denied the status of a proper sentence *merely* on the ground that it mentions itself. But then, it seems, we have a paradox.

We normally develop the paradox by observing that if the sentence (I) is true, then it must be false. But how do we do this? We have to accept the principle that *to say of a sentence that it is true is equivalent to asserting the sentence.* Tarski, the founder of the modern logical theory of these matters,[12] used "Snow is white" as his example of a typical sentence, and the requirement that any satisfactory treatment of truth must enable us to show that

"Snow is white" is true if and only if snow is white

has become a famous example in the philosophical as well as in the logical literature. Now, if we accept sentence (I) as having a truth-value at all (if it doesn't, then it is not in the scope of Tarski's theory), it follows by the principle just mentioned that

(i) "(I) is false" is true if and only if (I) is false,

and hence

(ii) "(I) is false" is true if and only if "(I) is false" is false

—which is a contradiction!

So far no inconsistency has actually resulted. We assumed that "(I) is false" has a truth value, and that assertion has now been refuted. We cannot consistently assert either that (I) is true or that (I) is false. But why should we *want* to assert either? Is it not natural to say that (I) is neither true nor false?

Indeed it is. But now another paradox arises to haunt us—the paradox Charles Parsons has called the Strong Liar. One form is:

(II) The sentence (II) is either false or lacks a truth-value.

The sentence (II) is paradoxical because, if we try to avoid the previous argument by denying that (II) has a truth-value, that is by asserting

(II) lacks a truth-value,

then it obviously follows that

(II) is either false or lacks a truth-value

—and the sentence (II) is one that we discover ourselves to have just asserted! So we must agree that (II) is true; which means that we have contradicted ourselves.

To Tarski it seemed—and this is the orthodox view among logicians to the present day—that in a properly regimented language we could avoid such paradoxes by giving up the idea that there is a universal and unitary notion of truth—that is, by giving up the idea that "is true" is the same predicate no matter what language we are speaking of. In addition, he maintained that if I say of a sentence in a language L that it is true or false, my assertion belongs to a different language—a "meta-language," call it meta-L. No language is allowed to contain its own truth-predicate. ("Semantically closed languages are inconsistent.")

Self-reference as such is not ruled out. There can be such a sentence as:

(III) The sentence (III) is not true-in-L,

but this sentence will not belong to L itself, but only to meta-L. Since it is not well-formed in L, it is, of course, true that it is not true-in-L. And since this is exactly what it *says* in meta-L, it *is* true in meta-L. By recognizing how truth is relative to language, we can see how (III) is nonsense (and not true) in the "object language" L and true in the meta-language meta-L, and this dissolves the paradox.

It remains to determine if Tarski has succeeded, or if he has only pushed the antinomy out of the formal language and into the informal language which he himself employs when he explains the significance of his formal work. In seeing this, the thing to keep in mind, I repeat, is that Tarski did *not*—as has sometimes been inaccurately claimed—ban self-reference as such. (As I remarked, the cost of banning all possible forms of self-reference from language is much too high.) Rather, he abandoned the idea that we have a unitary notion of truth. If each language has its own truth-predicate, and the notion "true-in-L," where L is a language, is itself expressible in a different language (a meta-language) but not in L itself, the "semantical paradoxes" can all be avoided. But in what language is Tarski himself supposed to be saying all this?

Tarski's theory introduces a "hierarchy of languages." There is the object language (this can be any language which is itself free of such "semantical" notions as reference and truth); there is the meta-language, the meta-meta-language, and so on. For every finite number *n*, there is a meta-language of level *n*. These languages form a hierarchy. Using the so-called transfinite numbers, one can even extend the hierarchy into the transfinite—there are meta-languages of higher and higher *infinite* orders. The paradoxical aspect of Tarski's theory, indeed of any hierarchical theory, is that one has to stand outside the whole hierarchy even to formulate the statement that the hierarchy exists. But what is this "outside place"—"informal language"—supposed to be? It cannot be "ordinary language," because ordinary language, according to Tarski, is semantically closed and hence inconsistent. But neither can it be a regimented language, for no regimented language can make semantic generalizations about itself or about languages on a higher level than itself.

This brings us to a philosophically important possibility: the possibility of denying that our informal discourse constitutes a "language." This position was taken by Bertrand Russell and recently revived by Charles Parsons in one of the most profound papers on the Liar paradoxes of recent decades.[13] According to this position, the informal discourse in which we say "Every language has a meta-language, and the truth predicate for the language belongs to that meta-language, not to the language itself" is not itself a part of any language, but a "speech act" which is *sui generis*.

The problem is that the inferences we draw from such "systematically ambiguous" statements (am I allowed to call them "statements"?) as

(V) Every language L has a meta-language ML

exactly resemble the inferences we draw from an ordinary universal statement such as "All men are mortal." Given the additional premise that L_1, L_2, L_3, . . . are languages, anyone who accepts (V) is immediately able to conclude that

L_1 has a meta-language ML_1
L_2 has a meta-language ML_2

in just the way that anyone who accepts "All men are mortal" is immediately able to conclude (given the additional premise that Tom, Dick, and Harry are men) that Tom is mortal, Dick is mortal, and

Harry is mortal. Yet, according to Parsons's suggestion, systematically ambiguous discourse is a primitive and irreducible kind of discourse, not to be understood on the model of other kinds of language use.

In spite of my great respect for Parsons, not to say for Bertrand Russell, I confess that I cannot understand this position at all. One could, after all, formally escape the paradox by insisting that all "languages" properly so-called are to be written with ink other than red, and reserving red ink for discourse which generalizes about all "languages properly so-called." Since generalizations about "all languages" which are printed in red ink would not include the Red Ink Language in which they are written (the Red Ink Language is *sui generis*), we cannot derive the Strong Liar or other semantic paradoxes. But this looks like a formalistic trick rather than an appealing, let alone a compelling, philosophical resolution of a conceptual difficulty. In what language do we express the fact that "Generalizations about the Non–Red Ink Languages do not include the Red Ink Languages in their scope"? Think it or say it but never write it in *ink?* (It cannot be written in a Red Ink Language without violating Tarski's strictures against "semantically closed languages," because it refers to all Red Ink Languages.) Or should we write it in pencil but not in ink, to avoid semantic closure? As Douglas Edwards asked some years ago (in his senior thesis at Harvard), "Can the Semantics of Systematically Ambiguous Discourse be Stated even in Systematically Ambiguous Discourse?"

Perhaps the real thought is that some forms of discourse can be understood without presupposing the notion of truth at all. But then, why not claim that *all* discourse can be understood without presupposing the notion of truth at all? (As Richard Rorty seems to do.) Or perhaps the suggestion is that these things cannot be "said" but can only be "shown." But the problem is that the things which we are "shown" when Systematic Ambiguity is explained to us are shown by being *said*. The idea that there are discursive thoughts which cannot be "said" is just the formalistic trick that I said I don't understand.

I do not wish to claim any particular originality for these reflections, apart from my particular formulation here. In a famous philosophical paper, Kurt Gödel made it quite clear that he did not think the semantic paradoxes had been solved (as opposed to the set theoretic paradoxes, which he did think had been solved). I have heard other logicians say that what we have done is push the semantic par-

adoxes out of the formalized languages we construct so that we don't
have to worry about them. But it is time to reflect on what this situation means.

First, let us reflect on the history of these puzzles. At least in a crude
form (for instance, the joke about the Cretan), they are very old. And
logic was quite a sophisticated business in Stoic times, in medieval
times, in Leibniz's time, as well as in the nineteenth century. Yet no
one seems to have regarded them as terribly serious business before
Russell. So the first problem we face, as we move away from the
technicalities, is: why have these puzzles recently become a subject
for such strenuous examination?

I am not a historian of science, so I will not attempt to answer this
question. It may be, however, that it required the formalization of
logic (which came to the center of world logical attention with the
appearance of Boole's logical investigations in the late 1840s), the
development of a logic of relations and of multiple generality, which
was the contribution of Peirce and Frege in the 1870s and 1880s, *and*
the idea of a single symbolic language adequate for the formalization
of all of science, which was the contribution of Frege in 1878 followed by Russell and Whitehead in the first decades of the present
century, to bring this problem to the forefront of logical attention.
(There still remains the problem of why it was Russell and not Frege
who did so, but I will not venture a conjecture about this.) If this is
right—and this is the way Russell views the matter—it is not until we
try to construct a totalistic symbolic language like that of *Principia
Mathematica* that the semantic paradoxes cease to look like mere
curiosities, or idle "brain teasers." What could have been regarded in
this way before suddenly threatens a whole logical system, the fruit
of decades of work by some of the greatest logicians of all time (I am
thinking of Frege, Russell, and Whitehead as engaged in a single collective enterprise here), with inconsistency. If the system is a formalization of our whole extant mathematical and deductive-logical
knowledge, that it should be inconsistent from the very start is intolerable. Some way has to be found to avoid this—even a device as
desperate as Russell's "Systematic Ambiguity" or Tarski's "Levels of
Language."

In short, what we have here is not a paradox which *first arises* as
the circle of science grows larger, as was the case with the cut between
the observer and the system in quantum mechanics, but rather a paradox which was already noticed (or almost noticed) but which looked

totally unimportant until the circle of science got big enough. In a sense, it was the importance of the semantic paradoxes that was the scientific discovery, not their existence.

The paradoxes themselves, however, are hardly less paradoxical than the solutions to which the logical community has been driven. For in giving up the idea that we can generalize about "all languages," in giving up the idea that we have a single unitary notion of truth applicable to any language whatsoever, we have arrived at a strange position—a position, I want to suggest, somehow reminiscent of the position we find ourselves in in quantum mechanics.

To bring out the analogy I have in mind, let us go back to the problem with the idea of Systematic Ambiguity. The problem may be put this way: if *you* construct a hierarchy of languages, then no paradox arises if I generalize over *your* whole hierarchy, provided I do not regard *my* "informal meta-language" as lying anywhere in *your* hierarchy of languages. In short, I can generalize over as large a totality of languages as I want (excluding totalities which include my own language or languages which themselves contain my own language), but the language in which I do the generalizing must always lie outside the totality over which I generalize. Substitute "the observer" for "I" in this formulation, and you get: There is always a cut between the observer's language and the totality of languages he generalizes over. The "God's-Eye View"—the view from which absolutely all languages are equally part of the totality being scrutinized—is forever inaccessible.

If we formulate the principle of the "cut between the observer and the system" in quantum mechanics by saying that the observer can take as large a totality as he wishes as the system (excluding totalities which include himself in the act of performing the measurement), but that he himself (or at least a part of himself) must always lie outside the system, then the analogy is complete. And it is more than a formal analogy; it is an *epistemic* analogy. The same notion of a "God's-Eye View," the same epistemic ideal of achieving a view from an "Archimedean point"—a point from which we can survey observers as if they were not *ourselves,* survey them as if we were, so to speak, *outside our own skins*—is involved in both cases. The same notion that ideal knowledge is *impersonal* is involved. That we should not be able to attain this ideal in practice is not paradoxical—we never expected really to attain it in practice. But that there should be *principled difficulties with the ideal itself*—that it should turn out that we can no

longer visualize what it would *mean* to attain the ideal—this is a fact
which constitutes for us, constituted as we are, the most profound of
paradoxes.

In the second part of this essay I shall discuss the significance all
this has for philosophy. I shall try to connect the failure of the ideal
of a God's-Eye View with the central problems of Western philosophy
from the time of Kant. I shall argue that the fashionable panacea of
relativism—even if it is given a new name, such as "deconstruction"
or even "pragmatism" (by Richard Rorty)—is not the only, or the
right, reaction to that failure. Since this is a Kant Lecture, let me say
that these issues were, of course, close to Kant's own interests, however much the outcome I have sketched here would have distressed
him. Kant was deeply torn between the idea that all knowledge is
partly our own construction and the idea that knowledge must yield
what I have called a "God's-Eye View." Yet the idea that there are
limits to knowledge, and that we find ourselves in "antinomies"—
another word for paradoxes—when we try to go beyond those limits
is also a Kantian idea. To Kant it looked as if what was beyond the
limits was "transcendent metaphysics"; today it begins to seem as if
part of what was once considered *within* the limits, within Kant's
"world of experience," cannot be fully brought under the Kantian
"regulative idea of Nature." ("Nature" for Kant included the notion
of a totally unified system of natural laws; a "cut between the observer and the system" would have been as distasteful to Kant as it was
to be, more than a century later, to Einstein.)

There is also a reason to mention Einstein at this point. Einstein
failed to carry through his project of overthrowing the Copenhagen
Interpretation and restoring the Kantian regulative idea of Nature.
But it would be wrong to view him as just a nostalgic reactionary (as
some quantum physicists came close to doing). There is a part of all
of us which sides with Einstein—which wants to see the God's-Eye
View restored in all its splendor. The struggle within ourselves, the
struggle to give up or to retain the old notions of metaphysical reality,
objectivity, and impersonality, is far from over.

Part Two: Relativism

The death of metaphysics is a theme that entered philosophy with
Kant. In our own century, a towering figure (some would say, *the*
towering figure in philosophy), Ludwig Wittgenstein, sounded that

note both powerfully and in a uniquely personal way; and he did not hesitate to lump epistemology together with metaphysics. (According to some of Wittgenstein's interpreters, what is today called "analytic philosophy" was, for Wittgenstein, the most confused form of metaphysics!) At the same time, even the man on the street could see that metaphysical discussion did not abate. A simple induction from the history of thought suggests that metaphysical discussion is not going to disappear as long as reflective people remain in the world. As Gilson said at the end of a famous book, "Philosophy always buries its undertakers."

The purpose of this essay is not to engage in a further debate about the question: "Is (or: "In what sense is") metaphysics dead?" I take it as a fact of life that there is a sense in which the task of philosophy is to overcome metaphysics and a sense in which its task is to continue metaphysical discussion. In every philosopher there is a part that cries, "This enterprise is vain, frivolous, crazy—we must say 'Stop!'" and a part that cries, "This enterprise is simply reflection at the most general and most abstract level; to put a stop to it would be a crime against reason." *Of course* philosophical problems are unsolvable; but as Stanley Cavell once remarked, "there are better and worse ways of thinking about them."

What I just said could have been said at virtually any time since the beginning of modernity. I also take it—and this too is something I am not going to argue, but take as another fact of life, although I know that there are many who would disagree—that the enterprises of providing a *foundation* for Being and Knowledge—a successful description of the Furniture of the World or a successful description of the Canons of Justification—are enterprises that have disastrously failed, and we could not have seen this until these enterprises had been given time to prove their futility (although Kant did say something like this long ago). There *is* a sense in which the futility of something that was called metaphysics and the futility of something that was called epistemology is a sharper, more painful problem for our period—a period that hankers to be called "postmodern" rather than modern.

What I want to do is lay out some principles that we should *not* abandon in our despair at the failure of something that was called metaphysics and something that was called epistemology. It will soon be evident that I have been inspired to do this, in large part, by a very fruitful ongoing exchange with Richard Rorty, and this essay may be viewed as yet another contribution to that exchange. For Rorty, as for the French thinkers whom he admires, two ideas seem gripping. (1) The failure of our philosophical "foundations" is a failure of the whole culture, and accepting that we were wrong in wanting or thinking we could have a foundation requires us to be *philosophical revisionists*. By this I mean that, for Rorty or Foucault or Derrida, the failure of foundationalism makes a difference to how we are allowed to talk in ordinary life—a difference as to whether and when we are allowed to use words like "know," "objective," "fact," and "reason." The picture is that philosophy was not a reflection *on* the culture, a reflection some of whose ambitious projects failed, but a *basis,* a sort of pedestal, on which the culture rested, and which has been abruptly yanked out. Under the pretense that philosophy is no longer "serious" there lies hidden a gigantic seriousness. If I am right, Rorty hopes to be a doctor to the modern soul. (2) At the same time, Rorty's analytic past shows up in this: when he rejects a philosophical controversy, as, for example, he rejects the "realism/antirealism" controversy, or the "emotive/cognitive" controversy, his rejection is expressed in a Carnapian tone of voice—he *scorns* the controversy.

I am often asked just where I disagree with Rorty. Apart from technical issues—of course, any two philosophers have a host of technical disagreements—I think our disagreement concerns, at bottom, these two broad attitudes. I hope that philosophical reflection may be of some real cultural value; but I do not think it has been the pedestal on which the culture rested, and I do not think our reaction to the failure of a philosophical project—even a project as central as "metaphysics"—should be to abandon ways of talking and thinking which have practical and spiritual weight. I am not, in that sense, a philosophical revisionist. And I think that what is important in philosophy is not just to say, "I reject the realist/antirealist controversy," but to show that (and how) both sides *misrepresent* the lives we live with our concepts. That a controversy is "futile" does not mean that the rival pictures are unimportant. Indeed, to reject a controversy without examining the pictures involved is almost always just a way of *defending* one of those pictures (usually the one that claims to be "antimetaphysical"). In short, I think philosophy is both more important and less important than Rorty does. It is not a pedestal on which we rest (or have rested until Rorty). Yet the illusions that philosophy spins are illusions that belong to the nature of human life itself, and that need to be illuminated. Just saying "That's a pseudo-issue" is not of itself therapeutic; it is an aggressive form of the metaphysical disease itself.

These remarks are, of course, much too general to serve as answers to the grand question "After Metaphysics What?" But no one philosopher can answer that question. "After metaphysics" there can only be *philosophers*—that is, there can only be the search for those "better and worse ways of thinking" that Cavell called for. In the rest of this essay I want to begin such a search by laying out some principles. I hope that this may eventually provoke Rorty to indicate which of the principles I list he can accept, and which ones his philosophical revisionism would lead him to scorn.

Warrant and Communal Agreement

I shall begin by laying out some principles concerning warranted belief and assertion. Since "justification" is a notion that applies to only certain sorts of statements,[14] I shall use John Dewey's technical term "warranted assertibility" (or just "warrant," for short) instead of the term "justification."

The first is the one with which Rorty is certain to disagree, and it sets the stage for all the others:

(1) In ordinary circumstances, there is usually a fact of the matter as to whether the statements people make are warranted or not.

Some of the principles that follow are likely to puzzle or disquiet various philosophers (including Rorty); but let me list the whole group before I deal with the "disquiets." Here are the others:[15]

(2) Whether a statement is warranted or not is independent of whether the majority of one's cultural peers would *say* it is warranted or unwarranted.

(3) Our norms and standards of warranted assertibility are historical products; they evolve in time.

(4) Our norms and standards always reflect our interests and values. Our picture of intellectual flourishing is part of, and only makes sense as part of, our picture of human flourishing in general.

(5) Our norms and standards of *anything*—including warranted assertibility—are capable of reform. There are better and worse norms and standards.

Although there is a tension—some will say, an unbearable tension—between these principles, I do not think I am the first to believe that they can and should be held jointly. From Peirce's earliest writing, they have, I believe, been held by pragmatists, even if this particular formulation is new. However, my defense of them will not depend on the arguments of particular pragmatist predecessors.

Let me begin my discussion with the first two principles: the existence of such a thing as "warrant" and its independence from the opinion of one's cultural peers. There is *one* way of defending these principles which is sure to provoke objections from antirealists and/ or nonrealists: that is to posit the existence of trans-historical "canons" of warranted belief which *define* warrant, independently of whether any given person or culture is able to state those canons. But that is not the way in which one should defend the independence of warrant from majority opinion. Rather than viewing the fact that warrant is independent of majority opinion as a fact about a transcendent reality, one should recognize that it is nothing but a property of the concept of warrant itself; or, since talk of "properties of concepts" has led some philosophers to overwork the analytic/synthetic distinction, let me say simply that it is a central part of our picture of warrant. To say that whether or not it is warranted in a given problematical situation to accept a given judgment is independent of whether a majority of one's peers would *agree* that it is warranted in that situation is just to show that one has the concept of warrant.

Indeed, that this is so is shown by the *praxis* of the Relativists themselves. They know very well that the majority of their cultural peers are not convinced by Relativist arguments, but they keep on arguing because they think they are *justified* (warranted) in doing so, and they share the picture of warrant as independent of majority opinion. But, it may be objected, surely the Relativist can reformulate his view so as to avoid this argument? Instead of claiming that he is describing our ordinary notion of warrant, the careful Relativist ought to say he is proposing a *better* concept. "Yes, this is a feature of our ordinary concept of warrant," the Relativist ought to admit, "but it is a *bad* feature."

But what can "bad" possibly mean here but "based on a wrong metaphysical picture"? And how can a Relativist speak of *right* and *wrong* metaphysical pictures? I am, of course, assuming the Relativist is a Relativist about *both* truth and warrant; a Realist about truth who happens to be a Relativist about warrant (there actually are such philosophers, I believe) can consistently hold that "I can't justify this belief, but I nonetheless believe that it is *true* that a statement S is warranted if and only if the majority of one's cultural peers would agree that it is warranted." Such a philosopher can hold without self-refutation that his own belief is true but not warranted; but there is a kind of pragmatic inconsistency about his position. The point I have just made is one that I have often made in the past: Relativism, just as much as Realism, assumes that one can stand within one's language and outside it at the same time. In the case of Realism this is not an immediate contradiction, since the whole content of Realism lies in the claim that it makes sense to think of a God's-Eye View (or, better, of a "View from Nowhere"); but in the case of Relativism it consti-tutes a self-refutation.

Let me now discuss the last of my five principles, and in particular the claim, which is the heart of that principle, that "there are better and worse norms and standards." And this time I *shall* discuss Rorty's position.

Superficially, it might seem that Rorty and I agree on this. He often speaks of finding better ways of talking and acting, ways that enable us to "cope better." Why shouldn't changing our norms and standards sometimes enable us to "cope better"? But in one crucial place[16] he says of reforms that they are not "better by reference to a previously known standard, but just better *in the sense that they come to seem clearly better than their predecessors.*" It is at precisely this point that I get the feeling that we do not agree at all.

The gloss Rorty puts on his own notion of "new and better ways of talking and acting"—*in the sense that they come to seem clearly better than their predecessors*—amounts to a rejection, rather than a clarification, of the notion of "reforming" the ways we are doing and thinking invoked in my fifth principle. Indeed, for many statements p it may well be the case that if those among us who want us to adopt standards according to which p is warranted win out, we will cope better in the sense that it will come to seem to us that we are coping better, and if those among us who want us to adopt standards accord-ing to which not-p is warranted win out, we will also cope better *in the sense that it will come to seem to us that we are coping better.* For example, since the community Rorty speaks of is normally all of Western culture, it could happen that a neofascist tendency wins out, and people cope better in the sense that *it comes to seem to them that they are coping better by dealing savagely with those terrible Jews, foreigners, and communists,* while if the forces of good win out it will also be the case that people cope better *in the sense that it comes to seem to them that they are.* Of course, Rorty himself would not feel "solidarity" with the culture if it went the first way. But the point is that *this* concept of "coping better" is not the concept of there being *better* and *worse* norms and standards at all. Just as it is internal to our picture of warrant that warrant is logically independent of the opinion of the majority of our cultural peers, so it is internal to our picture of "reform" that whether the outcome of a change is good (a reform) or bad (the opposite) is logically independent of whether it *seems* good or bad. (That is why it makes sense to argue that something most people take to be a reform in fact isn't one.) I believe, therefore, that Rorty *rejects* my fifth principle.

Is Rorty trapped in the same bind as the Relativist, then? Well, his views are certainly much more nuanced than are typical Relativist views. He has also changed them, often in ways I approve of. So I am not sure just what he is prepared to defend. But I shall take the risk of putting forward an amalgam of Rorty's published views as the view I *think* he holds now.

In *Philosophy and the Mirror of Nature* Rorty distinguished between "normal" and "hermeneutic" discourse. Discourse is normal when the culture is in agreement on the relevant standards and norms. Talk about tables and chairs is normal discourse in our culture; we all have pretty much the same ways of answering such questions as "Are there enough chairs for the dinner party tonight?" When there is unresolvable disagreement, discourse which attempts to bridge the paradigm-gap is forced to be "hermeneutic."

What happens when someone *criticizes* the accepted cultural norms and standards? Here, I think Rorty's answer is that I *can* say of the critic's views (I assume, for the sake of the example, that I agree with the critic in question) that they are "true," "more rational," or whatever seems appropriate, but these semantic and epistemic adjectives are really used *emotively*. I am "complimenting" the critic's proposals, not saying that they have particular attributes. In particular, when Rorty argues that his own views are more helpful philosophically, have more content, than the views he criticizes, he is engaged in hermeneutic discourse (which is to say, in rhetoric). But what is the purpose of his rhetoric?

It may be that we will behave better if we become Rortians—we may be more tolerant, less prone to fall for various varieties of religious intolerance and political totalitarianism. If that is what is at stake, the issue is momentous indeed. But a fascist could well agree with Rorty at a very abstract level—Mussolini, let us recall, supported pragmatism, claiming that it sanctions unthinking activism.[17] If our aim is tolerance and the open society, would it not be better to argue for these directly, rather than to hope that these will come as the by-product of a change in our metaphysical picture?

It seems more likely to me that, most of the time anyway, Rorty really thinks that metaphysical realism is *wrong*. We will be better off if we listen to him in the sense of having fewer false beliefs; but this, of course, is something he cannot admit he really thinks. I think, in short, that the attempt to say that *from a God's-Eye View there is no God's-Eye View* is still there, under all that wrapping.

To round out this part of the discussion, let me say a word about principle 3: the principle that says that norms and standards of warrant evolve in time. (Principle 4 is saved for discussion in a later section of this essay.) In one sense, the "historicity" of norms and standards is just a fact of life, but it is nonetheless necessary to have some picture of *how* norms and standards change. Although historians can do a far better job than I could hope to of painting such a picture, let me refer schematically to two important ways. (1) As Nelson Goodman has long emphasized, norms, standards, and judgments about particular cases often *conflict*. When this happens, we are often pushed to a special kind of philosophical reflection which we might call *reconstructive reflection*. Goodman's great contribution, I think, has been to urge that reconstructive reflection does not lose its value just because the dream of a *total* and *unique* reconstruction of our system of belief is hopelessly Utopian; we can learn a great deal from partial and even fragmentary reconstructions, and we can learn a great deal from reconstructing our beliefs in alternative ways. "Delicate mutual adjustment" of beliefs, norms, and standards to one another is a fertile source of change in all three. (2) There is a kind of *feedback loop:* relying on our existing norms and standards of warrant, we discover facts which themselves sometimes lead to a change in the pictures that inform those norms and standards (and thus, indirectly, to a change in the norms and standards themselves). The discovery of the anomalous phenomena which led to the successor theories to Newtonian physics—relativity and quantum mechanics—and of the post-Newtonian methodologies which went with those theories is an example in point.

The principle just discussed (the third in my list) was that our norms and standards are *historical objects*—they evolve and change in time; and the fifth, and last, was that our norms and standards can be *reformed*. The third and fifth principles must, of course, be understood as conditioning each other: the fact is not just that we *do* change our norms and standards, but that doing so is often an improvement. An improvement judged from where? From within *our* picture of the world, of course. But from within that picture itself, *we* say that "better" isn't the same as "*we* think it's better." And if my "cultural peers" don't agree with me, sometimes I *still* say "better" (or "worse"). There are times when, as Stanley Cavell puts it, I "rest on myself as my foundation."[18]

Realism with a Small "r" and with an "R"

The attempt to say that warrant (and truth) is just a matter of communal agreement[19] is, then, simultaneously a misdescription of the notions we actually have and a self-refuting attempt to both have and deny an "absolute perspective." Are we then forced to become "metaphysical realists"—at the end of the day, if not at the beginning? Is there no middle way?

If saying what we say and doing what we do is being a "realist," then we had better be realists—realists with a small "r." But metaphysical versions of "realism" go beyond realism with a small "r" into certain characteristic kinds of philosophical fantasy. Here I agree with Rorty.

Here is one feature of our intellectual practice that these versions have enormous difficulty in accommodating. On the one hand, trees and chairs—the "thises and thats we can point to"—are paradigms of what we call "real," as Wittgenstein remarked.[20] But consider now a question about which Quine, Lewis, and Kripke all disagree: what is the relation between the tree or the chair and the space-time region it occupies? According to Quine, the chair and the electromagnetic and other fields that make it up and the space-time region that contains these fields are one and the same: so the chair *is* a space-time region. According to Kripke, Quine is just wrong: the chair and the space-time region are two numerically distinct objects. (They have the same mass, however!) The proof is that the chair *could have occupied a different space-time region*. According to Quine, modal predicates are hopelessly vague, so this "proof" is worthless. According to Lewis, Quine is right about the chair but wrong about the modal predicates: the correct answer to Kripke is that if the chair could have

been in a different place, as we say, what that means is that a *counterpart* of this chair could have been in that place; not that *this very
chair* (in the sense of the logical notion of identity [=]) could have
been in that place.

Well, who is right? Are chairs really *identical* with their matter, or
does a chair somehow coexist in the same space-time region with its
matter while remaining numerically distinct from it? And is their matter really identical with the fields? And are the fields really identical
with the space-time regions? To me it seems clear that at least the
first, and probably all three, of these questions are nonsensical. We
can formalize our language in the way Kripke would and we can formalize our language in the way Lewis would, and (thank God!) we
can leave it unformalized and not pretend that the ordinary language
"is" obeys the same rules as the sign " = " in systems of formal logic.
Not even God could tell us if the chair is "identical" with its matter
(or with the space-time region); and not because there is something
He doesn't know.

So it looks as if even something as paradigmatically "real" as a
chair has aspects that are conventional. *That the chair is blue is paradigmatically a "reality," and yet that the chair [is/is not/we don't
have to decide] a space-time region is a matter of convention.*

And what of the space-time region itself? Some philosophers think
of points as location *predicates*, not objects. So a space-time region is
just a set of properties (if these philosophers are right) and not an
object (in the sense of concrete object) at all, if this view is right.
Again, it doesn't so much seem that there is a "view" here at all, as
yet *another* way we could reconstruct our language. But how can the
existence of a concrete object (the space-time region) be a matter of
convention? And how can the identity of A (the chair) and B (the
space-time region) be a matter of *convention?* The realist with a small
"r" needn't have an answer to these questions. It is just a fact of life,
he may feel, that certain alternatives are equally good while others
are visibly forced. But metaphysical realism is not just the view that
there are, after all, chairs, and some of them are, after all, blue, and
we didn't just *make all that up.* Metaphysical realism presents itself
as a powerful transcendental picture: a picture in which there is a
fixed set of "language-independent" objects (some of which are
abstract and others are concrete) and a fixed "relation" between terms
and their extensions. What I am saying is that the picture only partly
agrees with the commonsense view it purports to interpret; it has con-

sequences which, from a commonsense view, are quite absurd. There is nothing wrong at all with holding on to our realism with a small "r" and jettisoning the Big "R" Realism of the philosophers.

Although he was far from being a Big "R" realist, Hans Reichenbach had a conception of the task of philosophy[21] which, if it had succeeded, might well have saved Realism from the objection just raised: the task of philosophy, he wrote, is to *distinguish what is fact and what is convention ("definition") in our system of knowledge.* The trouble, as Quine pointed out, is that the philosophical distinction between "fact" and "definition" on which Reichenbach depended has collapsed. As another example, not dissimilar to the one I just used, consider the conventional character of any possible answer to the question, "Is a point identical with a series of spheres that converge to it?" We know that we can take extended regions as the primitive objects and "identify" points with sets of concentric spheres, and all geometric facts are perfectly well represented. We know that we can also take points as primitives and take spheres to be sets of points. But the very statement "we can do either" assumes a diffuse background of empirical facts. Fundamental changes in the way we do physics could change the whole picture. So "convention" does not mean *absolute convention*—truth by stipulation, free of every element of "fact." And, on the other hand, even when we see such a "reality" as a tree, the possibility of that perception is dependent on a whole conceptual scheme, on a language in place. What is factual and what is conventional is a matter of degree; we cannot say, "These and these elements of the world are the raw facts; the rest is convention, or a mixture of these raw facts with convention."

What I am saying, then, is that elements of what we call "language" or "mind" *penetrate so deeply into what we call "reality" that the very project of representing ourselves as being "mappers" of something "language-independent" is fatally compromised from the very start.* Like Relativism, but in a different way, Realism is an impossible attempt to view the world from Nowhere. In this situation it is a temptation to say, "So we make the world," or "our language makes up the world," or "our culture makes up the world"; but this is just another form of the same mistake. If we succumb, once again we view the world—the only world we know—as a *product.* One kind of philosopher views it as a product from a raw material: Unconceptualized Reality. The other views it as a creation *ex nihilo. But the world isn't a product. It's just the world.*

Where are we then? On the one hand—this is where I hope Rorty will sympathize with what I am saying—our image of the world cannot be "justified" by anything but its success as judged by the interests and values which evolve and get modified at the same time and in interaction with our evolving image of the world itself. Just as the absolute "convention/fact" dichotomy had to be abandoned, so (as Morton White long ago urged)[22] the absolute "fact/value" dichotomy has to be abandoned, and for similar reasons. On the other hand, it is part of that image itself that the world is not the product of our will—or our dispositions to talk in certain ways, either.

2. A Defense of Internal Realism

In December 1982 the American Philosophical Association sponsored a symposium on my book *Reason, Truth, and History* at the annual meeting of the Eastern Division. The papers of the critics, Hartry Field and Gilbert Harman, were published in the October 1982 issue of the *Journal of Philosophy*, but only a short abstract of my reply was included. What follows is my complete reply, which has not previously been published in full.

Great philosophical points of view which have permanent appeal cannot be expressed in a single sentence. This is one reason I feel justified in having taken the "metaphysical realist" to be a philosopher who accepts what Hartry Field calls "metaphysical realism₁" (the world consists of a fixed totality of mind-independent objects), *and* accepts "metaphysical realism₂" (there is exactly one true and complete description of the way the world is), *and* also accepts "metaphysical realism₃" (truth involves some sort of correspondence). These doctrines have been held by philosophers of every historical period, and one can think of a rich filigree of ideas, doctrines, and detailed arguments which flesh out these abstract theses in different ways.

These three sentences (taken from, or rather torn out of their place in, my book *Reason, Truth, and History*) have, in fact, no clear content at all apart from this rich filigree. What does it mean, apart from a philosophical tradition, to speak of "objects," let alone a "fixed totality" of *all* objects? What does it mean, apart from a certain philosophical controversy, to speak of "mind-independence"? Human minds did not create the stars or the mountains, but this "flat" remark is hardly enough to settle the philosophical question of realism versus antirealism. What does it mean to speak of a unique "true and complete description of the world"?

I can give this last phrase a sense, if I assume "metaphysical realism₁." For then there is a definite set I of individuals of which the world consists (say, the space-time points). And there is a definite set of all properties and relations (of each type, to avoid the paradoxes, but let us just consider the lowest type), call it P.

Consider an ideal language with a name for each member of I and a predicate for each member of P. (Perhaps Field, in his present nominalistic phase, would deny the existence of such a totality P; but then I don't know how to interpret his talk of *ways* of "carving out pieces of noumenal dough."[1] Such an ideal language is not a denumerable language (unless we take properties in extension, and then only if the number of individuals is finite), but it is unique (up to isomorphism), and the theory of the world—the set of true sentences, up to any definite type—is likewise unique. There may well be other ways of giving sense to the claim that there is "one true and complete theory of the world"; my point is only that the natural way of understanding "metaphysical realism$_2$" involves assuming "metaphysical realism$_1$."

Conversely, if we assume there is an ideal theory of the world, then the notion of a "fixed totality" of all individuals and a "fixed totality" of properties and relations of these individuals is naturally clarified by identifying the totality of individuals with the range of the individual variables and the totality of properties and relations (of each type) with the range of the predicate variables (of that type) in the theory. Metaphysical realisms *one, two,* and *three* do not have content standing on their own, one by one; each leans on the others and on a variety of further assumptions and notions.

Field and the "Redundancy Theory"

Let me explain Field's suggestion that one could be a metaphysical realist and accept the "redundancy theory" of truth. (This is how one could be a metaphysical realist and not accept the correspondence theory, according to Field.) On the redundancy theory, to say *"P" is true* is merely to affirm P. Since truth is not a property on this view, the claim that one can be a metaphysical realist and still hold this view of truth amounts to the claim that one can *say,* "There is a fixed totality of mind-independent things of which the world consists," while regarding that saying itself as true only in the sense of "immanent truth," that is, in the sense that (by calling it true one indicates that) it is a part of the total corpus that one accepts.[2] It is hard to see why such a view should qualify as being metaphysically realistic.

Field further appeals to work of mine in which I suggested separating the theory of truth from the theory of understanding. He suggests that a description of a speaker's "conceptual-role semantics," a description of the actual skill of producing sentences, assigning subjective probabilities to sentences, and so on, might be a complete theory of *understanding*. Finally, he rejects the idea that there is an objective notion of "degree of confirmation" or justification. He claims to be a metaphysical realist about that "mind-independent totality of objects" but a relativist about justification.

Thus, it is being claimed that one can deny that truth is a property, deny also that the sentences that we utter have any objective degree of inductive validity at all, and still claim that by virtue of uttering such *noises*, for that is all they are on such a picture, as "the world consists of a fixed totality of mind-independent objects" one has succeeded in being a metaphysical realist. If it is that easy, why should not even Richard Rorty agree to become a "metaphysical realist"?

The only reason that I can think of for denying that truth is a property is that one has bought into a physicalist or phenomenalist, or, in the case of some philosophers, a cultural relativist picture of reality which leaves no room for such a property. Having adopted such a picture, the philosopher feels compelled to say either that there is no such thing as truth, or, more commonly today, to "save" the word *true* by offering a disquotational theory. It is only commitment to one or another reductionist picture (whether the picture is called a "realist" or an "antirealist" picture does not matter) that leads anyone to think that truth is not a property. But notice that the very person who strongly denies that there is any such property as truth, and who waves his picture at us to call our attention to its various attractions, as, for instance, Richard Rorty does in *Philosophy and the Mirror of Nature*—notice that this very philosopher does not recognize that his picture is only a picture, but believes that in some deep pretheoretic sense his picture is the way the world is. That truth *is* a property— and a property which, unlike justification, or probability on present evidence, depends on more than the present memory and experience of the speaker—is the one insight of "realism" that we should not jettison. But Hartry Field shows signs of being inclined to jettison this insight, although he calls himself a "metaphysical realist" and says that I am a "nonrealist." Could it be that I am more of a realist— though not a "metaphysical" one—than Field, after all?

Justification and Reference

The level of abstractness of Field's and of Gilbert Harman's discussions is such that no reference to the practice by which we decide what any given word refers to—no reference to the practice of interpretation—ever intrudes. So let us look at some actual cases.

The term *phlogiston* did not in fact refer to anything. In particular, it did not refer to valence electrons, although I met a scientist once who did (half-jokingly) propose that we say, "There really is such a thing as phlogiston; it has turned out that phlogiston is valence electrons." Why do we regard it as reasonable of Bohr to keep the same word "electron" (*Elektron*) in 1900 and 1934, and thereby to treat his two very different theories, his theory of 1900 and his theory of 1934, as theories which describe the same objects, and regard it as unreasonable to say that phlogiston referred to valence electrons?

"Conceptual-role semantics" has no answer to such questions, for conceptual-role semantics knows no notion of synonymy at all. Bohr's subjective probability metric in 1900 was not Bohr's subjective probability metric in 1934. But this does not say whether the word *Elektron*, or any other German word, did or did not change its reference in Bohr's idiolect. If Field is right, and there is no objectivity to justification, then how can there be any objectivity to *interpretation?*

It seems to me that there are two options open to Field. He might say that there is a fact of the matter as to what is a good "rational reconstruction" of a speaker's referential intentions (and that treating *Elektron* as a "rigid designator" of whatever sort of entity is responsible for certain effects and approximately obeys certain laws is such a good "rational reconstruction"), but not an objective fact about justification in science and most of daily life. Or, alternatively, he might say that interpretation *is* subjective, but this does not mean that reference is subjective. The first option would involve him in the claim that deciding on a proper "rational reconstruction" of a speaker's semantic intentions is an activity isolated from full "general intelligence," full "inductive competence," and so forth. But how can the decision that something does or does not "approximately" obey certain laws (near enough, anyway)—the decision that electrons as we now conceive them "fit" the referential intentions of Bohr in 1900 but not the referential intentions of phlogiston theorists a little earlier—possibly be isolable from or different in nature from decisions about *reasonableness* in general? The second option would involve one in the claim that we have a notion of reference which is independent of the procedures and practices by which we decide that people in different situations with different bodies of background belief do, in fact, refer to the same things. This claim seems unintelligible. If that possibility is put forward seriously, then I have to throw up my hands!

Note that the point does not depend on recherché examples: we treat people two hundred years ago as having referred to what we today call "plants" (or to approximately the things we today call "plants") even though we disagree with people two hundred years ago over the essential properties of plants. Without an informal practice of discounting certain differences in belief ("charity in interpretation"), we could not say that the most common words of the language have kept even a part of their reference fixed across two hundred years. If all of this is supposed to be subjective, if translation practice is subjective, then I don't see that any intertheoretic, interlinguistic notions of reference and truth are left at all. But if it is supposed to be objective, then I want to ask why the notions of translation (a notion needed for even a disquotational theory of reference) and interpretation are in better shape than the notion of justification.

Gilbert Harman's View

Harman and I meet much more head on than Field and I do. Field is, so to speak, trying to scatter my fire, whereas Harman faces it and tries to throw it back in my face. Let me begin by asking how objective justification really is on Harman's view. Harman's examples of innate maxims presupposed by justification are the familiar maxims of conservativism, simplicity, and predictive power. But if each speaker has the "innate" knowledge that he or she ought to preserve past doctrine and preserve "simplicity," while having *no* objective standard of "simplicity" itself, or of the right kind of "conservativism," then justification is not going to be any more objective on Harman's account than it is on Field's account. If one opts for the view that justification is objective *just to the extent* that the great majority of speakers do, in fact, interpret these innate maxims the same way, and subjective where speakers disagree, then, depending on how high one sets the standard of "majority" agreement, and depending on the time, the place, and the culture, either one will discover that this very philosophical view is itself not justified, or one will find that many things—the infallibility of the Pope, for example—which we would not count as justified will turn out to be "objectively" justified in certain cultures. Philosophy itself is a field in which one believes that there is some right solution, or right dissolution or right discussion (or objectively better and worse discussion) of the problems, but in which this rightness (or better and worseness) does not consist in the possibility of an argument that will be satisfying to the majority. I find it a source of wonderment that philosophers, of all people, should be the ones to think that the fact that certain ideas are intrinsically controversial indicates that there is no being objectively right or wrong about those ideas. The argument that Harman gives for regarding ethical truth as relative[3] is precisely the argument that the man on the street gives for regarding *all of philosophy* as subjective.

I prefer to interpret Harman not as holding that it is only these desperately vague maxims of "coherence," "simplicity," and so on that are innate, but rather as holding, as his reference to Chomsky's competence/performance distinction suggests, that there is a detailed system of rules in the brain that interprets these vague-sounding maxims. On such a theory, what is justified is not necessarily what actual people say is justified, but rather is what an ideally "competent" member of the species would say is justified.[4]

The notion of "competence" was introduced by Chomsky in *Syntactic Structures*. The "competence" description, in Chomsky's sense, is a description that *conflicts* with the biological description. When I perform the experiment of trying to produce an infinite series of grammatical sentences (say, "There is one apple," "There are two apples," "There are three apples," . . . —this is something I have the "competence" to do, according to Chomsky) and fail, as I sooner or later must, this "performance error" is not due to any failure of my brain to live up to its biological "specifications." The brain is not built to use an infinite paper tape, or other form of infinite external memory, and would fail to go on producing these sentences forever even if it had such mechanical aids. In short, the competence description is like the description of the air as a perfect fluid—it may be, as Chomsky contends, the best description to use for the purposes of linguistic theory, as the description of the air as a fluid is the best description for certain purposes, but that does not mean that it is simply an account of the physicalistic facts. It is an *idealization*.

Chomsky promised us, in *Syntactic Structures*, that there would be a *normal form* for grammars and a mathematical simplicity function that would make all this precise. One would only have to look at the alternative descriptions of the speaker's competence, written out in the normal form, and measure the simplicity of each one, using the mathematical function to be provided, to see which one is "simplest." That one would then be, by definition, *the* description of the speaker's "competence." (Strictly speaking, Chomsky owes us another function as well—a function to measure the *goodness of fit* between a competence description and the actual performance. Chomsky seems to assume that what is a "performance error" is something that smart speakers will all know "intuitively.")

The idea that one can mathematicize the description of competence in linguistics has since been given up. At present, the idea that one particular idealization of a speaker's behavior represents his competence, rather than another, rests entirely on our intuitive notion of a "best idealization" or a "best explanation." To argue that the notion of justification is made physicalistic by identifying it with what people would say according to their competence description (in a much more ambitious sense of "competence" than even Chomsky has ever endorsed) is absurd.

My "Companions in the Guilt" Argument

Suppose we decided just to take such notions as "competence," or, perhaps, "best explanation," or, perhaps, "justification," as primitive. Since these notions are not physicalistic notions,[5] our "realism" would no longer be of the sort Harman wishes to defend. But why not go this route? someone might ask. Why not conclude, for example, that Brentano was right? That there are unreduced semantic properties? What can be wrong with an antireductionist metaphysical realism with primitive semantic notions, primitive notions of justification, and so on?

Well, in the first place, if nothing is wrong with it, then the question of why one should be a noncognitivist just in *ethics* becomes a serious one. The disagreement in ethical values that Harman points out is matched by disagreement in standards of justification and of explanation. That one should not, other things being equal, harm a benefactor is more universally accepted than is the relevance of *prediction* to the question of whether the earth came into existence five or six thousand years ago (as opposed to billions of years ago). This does not bother Harman, because Harman thinks that there are physical-istic facts (facts about "competence") which determine who is right in such a disagreement, but no physicalistic facts which determine who is right when there is ethical disagreement. Admitting objective ethical facts that are not reducible to physical facts would be a total violation of the spirit and content of physicalism. If the metaphysical realist has to break with Harman (and with Mackie) by admitting *any* unreduced and irreducible ethical or epistemological or intentional notions—has, say, to take as primitive such notions as "best ideali-zation" or "best explanation"—then the whole *raison d'être* of his sharp fact/value distinction is demolished. Our ideas of interpreta-tion, explanation, and the rest flow as much from deep and complex human needs as our ethical values do. If the objectivity of ethics is rejected on the ground that the distinction between a human need and a mere desire is itself a mere projection, a distinction without a real difference, then we have to be told why the same thing should not be true of the deep human needs which shape the notions of interpreta-tion, explanation, translation, and the like.

I can imagine a critic who would now say, "Very well, Putnam, I will concede that what is and is not a good interpretation, what is and what is not explanatory, what is and what is not justified, are in the same boat as what is and is not *good*. But I am willing to be a metaphysical realist about goodness too." What would I say to such a critic?

I would be pleased that my critic accepted my "companions in the guilt" argument. It was, after all, one of my main purposes in writing *Reason, Truth, and History* to get people to realize the very great strength that the companions in the guilt argument has. There are no serious reasons in support of ethical relativism which should drive a rational man, *moved by those reasons alone*, as opposed to the sway of the Zeitgeist, to be an ethical relativist but not a total relativist. And if a rebirth of a full-bodied, red-blooded metaphysical realism were the way to get people to accept the objectivity of ethics, then I would almost be willing to pay the price of letting that happen. But I don't think the metaphysical realist picture has any content today when it is divorced from physicalism.

The particular problem with physicalism that I emphasized in *Reason, Truth, and History* is that the question, "What singles out any one relation R as 'the' relation of reference?" has no answer. Har-man's response is that the world has a single causal structure.[6] But this doesn't help. For if my linguistic competence is caused by E_1, E_2, E_3, . . . , then it is true that it is caused* by $E_1{}^*$, $E_2{}^*$, $E_3{}^*$, . . . , where the * denotes the corresponding entity in a suitable nonstandard model. So I then ask, "Why is reference fixed by causation and not by causation*?" The only answer a physicalist can give me is, "because that is the nature of reference." To say that *nature* itself singles out objects and puts them into correspondence with our words is a claim that has no meaning that I can make out at all.

Consider, for example, one way in which it has been suggested that "nature" might do this. David Lewis has recently taken up the suggestion that there are certain classes of things "out there," "elite classes" as he calls them, which are intrinsically distinguished, and he suggests that it is a "natural constraint" on reference (that is, a constraint which is *built into nature*) that as many of our terms as possible should refer to these "elite classes."[7] This does not uniquely determine the reference of our terms: there are other desiderata, and there are sometimes trade-offs to be made between the desiderata, but this is supposed to be the constraint that makes language "hook onto" the world.

If God had decided that it was not the metaphysical realist's relation R but some nonstandard counterpart R^* that was to be the "singled out" relation of reference, then our experiences would have been the same, the sentences we would have believed would have been the same, and our successes and failures would have been the same. This is a part of the argument of *Reason, Truth, and History* that none of my critics has contested. It follows that Lewis's "natural constraint" is not brought into existence by our *interests;* rather, it has to be thought of as something that operates together with those interests to fix reference.

What Lewis's story claims is that the class of cats cries out for a label, while the class of cats* does not cry out to be named. Rather than solving the problem of reference, what the idea of a constraint built into nature and of "elite classes" does is to confuse the materialist picture by throwing in something "spooky."

The problem does not affect only reference relations; warrant relations, explanatory relations, cotenability relations (that one truth would still be true if another *weren't* true) all share the feature that they cannot be fixed by anything psychological, anything "in the head." Physicalism cannot say how they are fixed without falling back on medieval-sounding talk of "single causal structure," or "causal powers," or "natural constraints." Physicalism is a failure.

Antireductionist Metaphysical Realism

The question my imaginary interlocutor raised earlier was, "Why would I wish to reject a metaphysical realism which was antireductionist and free of any fact/value dichotomy?" My answer turns in part on the phenomenon of equivalent descriptions. (Equivalent descriptions are theories which are incompatible when taken at face value, or which have what at least seem to be quite different ontologies, but which are treated as notational variants in the actual practice of science. A more precise characterization is given in my book *Realism and Reason*, but this informal characterization, and the examples I shall mention, may perhaps make clear what I have in mind. As an example—one I shall return to shortly—one may think of the pair of theories consisting of the "nominalistic" physics presented by Field in his *Science without Numbers* and the "same" physical theory presented in a more standard way using the second-order theory of real numbers, or, equivalently, the third-order theory of natural numbers.)

An example I have often used in this connection is the pair of theories consisting of a version of Newtonian physics in which there are particles and forces acting on the particles but no extended "objects" between the particles (no "fields," according to the conception in which fields are not merely logical constructions), and the theory of Newtonian physics as it is done assuming the "electromagnetic field" and the "gravitational field" and treating these as genuine particulars.

The question of whether gravitation is an entity existing between bodies, or is a genuine "action at a distance," or has yet some other nature, came up repeatedly in the controversy between Newton and Leibniz. Newton's own reply was that the question is not a question for "experimental philosophy." The rejection of this sort of question, the question of whether some particular item in a workable scientific representation of the facts is really "out there" in the metaphysical realist sense, is *not* a rejection that springs in all cases from positivist preconceptions (it did not so spring in Newton's case, in fact), but is rather a rejection that is part of science itself, one that springs from the need to separate scientific and metaphysical questions. Now, what I think we have learned since Newton is that metaphysics is not a possible subject.

I may be wrong about this; perhaps Saul Kripke will show us how to do metaphysics. But to show us how to do metaphysics, Kripke, or whoever pulls off the stunt, will have to do something truly revolutionary. A metaphysical system will have to be rich enough to

embrace what is indispensable to discourse, including talk of reference, talk of justification, talk of values in general; and it will have
to be accompanied by some sketched-out story of how we can have
access to "metaphysical reality." To rely on "intuition" when the question is "whether the electromagnetic field is real" (whatever that is
supposed to mean), or "whether there are absolute space-time points"
(whatever that is supposed to mean), or "whether there really are
sets" (whatever that is supposed to mean) is to rely on what we don't
understand with respect to questions we don't understand.

The modern "metaphysical realist" is typically a philosopher who
does not even attempt such a revolutionary enterprise. Rather, he
treats single sentences, torn out of any real theoretical context, as
genuine philosophical questions, and he simply assumes that we have
some "handle" on the notion of *truth* as applied to such sentences.

Being "True" in the Realist's Sense versus Being Right

What I believe is that there is *a* notion of truth, or, more humbly, of
being "right," which we use constantly and which is not at all the
metaphysical realist's notion of a description which "corresponds" to
the noumenal facts. In that humble sense, there is no question of
choosing between Field's theory in *Science without Numbers* and the
more standard "mathematical" versions of the "same" theory. They
are both "all right." They are both *right*, if either is. From the point
of view of the notion of being "right" that does actual work in our
lives and intellectual practice, a mathematical theory which takes sets
as primitive and a mathematical theory which is intertranslatable
with the former, but which takes functions as primitive, may, similarly, both be right; from the point of view of life and intellectual practice, a theory which treats points as individuals and a theory which
treats points as limits may (in their proper contexts) both be right;
from the point of view of life and intellectual practice, a theory which
represents the physical interactions between bodies in terms of action
at a distance and a physical theory which represents the same situation in terms of fields may both be right.

Let me conclude by saying a little more about my own picture, for
I do have a picture. I don't think it is bad to have pictures in philosophy. What is bad is to forget they are pictures and to treat them as
"the world." In my picture, objects are theory-dependent in the sense
that theories with incompatible ontologies can both be right. Saying

that they are both right is not saying that there are fields "out there" as entities with extension and (in addition) fields in the sense of logical constructions. It is not saying that there are both absolute space-time points and points which are mere limits. It is saying that various representations, various languages, various theories, are equally good in certain contexts. In the tradition of James and Dewey, it is to say that devices which are functionally equivalent in the context of inquiry for which they are designed are equivalent in every way that we have a "handle on."

To prevent misunderstandings, I am not claiming that some perfectly good description of the world contains the sentence "There are no chairs in Manhattan," used in such a way that it could be rendered homophonically into standard English. Not *every* sentence changes its truth value on passing from one acceptable theory to some—or any—other acceptable theory. But to break the metaphysical realist picture, it is enough that the project of giving a "complete description of the world" without employing sentences which do have this kind of instability, this dependence on a theory for their truth-value, is an unworkable project.

If objects are, at least when you get small enough, or large enough, or theoretical enough, theory-dependent, then the whole idea of truth's being defined or explained in terms of a "correspondence" between items in a language and items in a fixed theory-independent reality has to be given up. The picture I propose instead is not the picture of Kant's transcendental idealism, but it is certainly related to it. It is the picture that truth comes to no more than idealized rational acceptability.

This kind of idealism is not a "verificationism" which requires one to claim that statements about the past are to be understood by seeing how we would verify them in the future. All I ask is that what is supposed to be "true" be *warrantable* on the basis of experience and intelligence for creatures with "a rational and a sensible nature." Talk of there being saber-toothed tigers here thirty thousand years ago, or beings who can verify mathematical and physical theories we cannot begin to understand (but who have brains and nervous systems), or talk of there being sentient beings outside my light cone, is not philosophically problematic for me. But talk of there being "absolute space-time points," or of sets "really existing" or "not really existing," I reject. When we claim that such a sentence as "There are absolute space-time points" is true, we are using the word *true* in a way that does not connect with a notion of warrant that we actually have or that I can imagine any being with "a rational and sensible nature" actually having.

Now, the picture I have just sketched *is* only a "picture." If I were to claim it is a *theory,* I should be called upon at least to sketch a theory of idealized warrant; and I don't think we can even sketch a theory of actual warrant (a theory of the "nature" of warrant), let alone a theory of idealized warrant. On the other hand, metaphysical realism is only a "picture." At a very abstract level, the debate between metaphysical realism and idealism is a standoff. Each side can truthfully say to the other, "You don't have a theory!"

In spite of this, I think that the idealist "picture" calls our attention to vitally important features of our practice—and what is the point of having "pictures" if we are not interested in seeing how well they represent what we actually think and do? That we do not, in practice, actually construct a unique version of the world, but only a vast number of versions (not all of them equivalent—I have focused on the case of equivalent descriptions simply as a dramatic case) is something that "realism" hides from us. That there is nothing wrong with vague predicates—all that is wrong is to be too vague in a given context—is another fact that "realism" ignores or misrepresents.[8]

The first of these facts, the pluralism of our practice, has been expressed by Nelson Goodman in a naughty way by saying that there are many worlds, not one. The second fact, the ultimacy of vagueness, was expressed to me in a recent conversation by Rogers Albritton by saying that there are vague objects.

Recognizing such facts as these is part of what might be called "rejecting 'realism' in the name of the realistic spirit." It is my view that reviving and revitalizing the realistic spirit is the important task for a philosopher at this time.

3. After Empiricism

If any problem has emerged as *the* problem for analytic philosophy in the twentieth century, it is the problem of how words "hook onto" the world. The difficulty with A. J. Ayer, who has tried, in his recent book, to sum up philosophy in the twentieth century is that there is no acknowledgment of the difficulty of this problem.[1]

A. J. Ayer's *Philosophy in the Twentieth Century* is pleasant and useful reading in its first half. One encounters William James, C. I. Lewis, Bertrand Russell, G. E. Moore, and such lesser Oxford figures as W. D. Ross and H. A. Pritchard, presented as they struck Ayer as a young man or as they influenced his philosophical life, and not just as he now regards them (although he tells us that as well). Ayer's description of the Wittgenstein of the *Tractatus* is likewise pleasant and useful to read. But beginning with the section on the later Wittgenstein the book becomes, for the most part, disappointing.

It is obvious that something happened in philosophy after the *Tractatus* with which Ayer is profoundly out of sympathy. And although he tries to present what happened conscientiously—and he is certainly fair-minded—he curiously fails to tell the reader *what* it is that he is unable to sympathize with; perhaps he does not know himself. The result is that a reader who had only this book to go by would have to see philosophy after the early Wittgenstein as, for the most part, a series of empty and confused ideas and arguments. Even the exposition becomes untrustworthy. My own views (with which Ayer concludes) are misrepresented (I do not hold that it is inconceivable that one could discover that water is not H_2O, as Ayer suggests), as are, for example, those of David Armstrong, the representative of contemporary materialism that Ayer chooses. (Ayer charges Armstrong with denying the existence of "appearances," that is, sense-data. But Armstrong is quite clear on this point: he believes in the existence of appearances,[2] but he does not take appearance-*concepts* as primitive and unanalyzable. Rather, he regards appearances as functionally characterized brain-events.)

If the book only half succeeds in its aim to be a sequel to Russell's *A History of Western Philosophy*, it succeeds better in giving a picture of Ayer as a philosopher. From the time he first appeared on the scene as *the* British exponent of logical positivism to the present moment, Sir Alfred Jules Ayer has been somewhat of a paradox—always against the fashion, always rebellious, yet also (and in a good sense) old-fashioned in his philosophical demeanor. Although his views have changed considerably since he wrote *Language, Truth, and Logic*, he continues to philosophize in the style and spirit of Bertrand Russell. If that style and spirit no longer speak to the concerns of practicing philosophers, that is, I suspect, a fact of cultural importance and not just an event for professional philosophers to note.

On the one hand, Ayer still bases his philosophy—he remains an empiricist—on sense-data, which he now prefers to call "sense-qualia." He answers Wittgenstein's famous doubts about the possibility of accounting for public language and public knowledge in terms of supposedly private objects by postulating a faculty he calls "primary recognition," which enables us to "straightforwardly identify" sense-qualia when they occur. Wittgenstein's treatment of skepticism about our ability to know other minds is seen as a "summary dismissal," rather than (as more appreciative readers of Wittgenstein would see it) as something which cannot be understood apart from the whole structure of Wittgenstein's philosophical work—which would make it just the opposite of "summary."

On the other hand, Ayer no longer holds to the positivist view that unverifiable statements are meaningless. (Statements about the distant past may be unverifiable, but according to Ayer, they are certainly meaningful.) Ayer has long since given up his former view that material objects are just a sort of logical fiction which we introduce to systematize our talk about sense-qualia. Like Russell in his later writings, Ayer now thinks that material objects are real things whose existence we are justified in inferring from the behavior of our sense-qualia.

There is even a hint—perhaps much more than a hint—of mind-body dualism in Ayer's current view. Ayer doubts that the statement that a sense-quale is "identical" with a brain-event is *intelligible;* and he further doubts that the evidence for a one-to-one correlation of sense-qualia and (some class of) brain-events is more than fragmentary. He avoids having to say either that human bodily motions are exceptions to the laws of physics or that human wishes and desires are epiphenomenal by postulating that some physical events—bodily behaviors—can have more than one causal explanation. The motion of my arm can be causally explained by events in my nervous system, but since it can also be causally explained by my wish to hand someone an ashtray, there is no question of this wish being something which I feel before the arm moves, but which does not "really" cause the arm to move.

I have indicated that practicing philosophers today feel a strong sense of *déjà vu* when they read this sort of thing. Ayer will reply that he is quite aware that his views are "out of fashion." But is a change of fashion really all that is in question? A change of fashion is certainly part of what is involved; as Ayer remarks, materialism is again in vogue, at least in American and Australian philosophy, and "sense-qualia" are out of vogue. But more is also involved. What analytic philosophers of almost any persuasion will regard as strange is that Ayer ignores an enormous amount of discussion of the issue of recognition of sense-qualia. Ayer has, so to speak, no interest in cognitive psychology. But a cognitive psychology of some sort—a theory of the mind—is what is needed to back his talk of "primary recognition." Thus, the possibility of misinterpreting one's sense-data is mentioned only in passing (they are qualitatively the same even if one misinterprets them, according to Ayer, who agrees with C. I. Lewis on this point). There are no entries under "corrigibility," "incorrigibility," or "privileged access" in the index of his book, although these are notions around which discussion has centered for the last forty years.

To see why this ought to be a problem for Ayer, let us recall that Ayer follows Hume in regarding causal statements as just a special class of regularity-statements. Certain sorts of regularities may be especially important and useful, and we may call them "causal" for that reason, but this should not mislead us, Ayer argues, into believing that the event we call the "cause" somehow *necessitates* the event we call the "effect." This is why Ayer can think that two such different events (in his view) as an electrochemical event in my brain and a desire to hand someone an ashtray can both cause the motion of my arm; why shouldn't the regularity-statements "When I wish to hand someone an ashtray my arm moves in such-and-such a way" and "When such-and-such an electrochemical event takes place in my brain my arm moves in such-and-such a way" both be true? ("How can two different events *both* bring about the motion of my arm?" is only a confused question on the Hume-Ayer view.)

Imagine now that someone misinterprets a sense-quale on a particular occasion. I myself once referred to a sweater as "blue" several times before someone pointed out that it was green. And it *was* green—it didn't even *look* blue; it's just that I persisted in calling it blue. I didn't even notice that I was using "blue" for green (or whatever was really going on) until another person corrected me. According to Ayer, such events don't matter; I still "recognized" the quale *green* even if I referred to it as "blue." What is this act of "primary recognition" that connects my mind to a universal?

According to Berkeley and Hume, I do not have such a thing as an "abstract idea" or a "general idea" of green. When a particular token—be it a green color-patch or a token of the word "green"— occurs in my mind, and is used as a symbol for the whole class of green sense-data, all that happens is that the token is associated with a certain class of other tokens to which it is similar or which are similar to one another. Ayer and Russell depart from Berkeley and Hume on this point—and with good reason. For they see that if I can think of a *particular* relation of "similarity," then I am able to recognize at least one universal. Thus universals cannot really be avoided in the way Berkeley and Hume wanted to do.

But a naturalistic theory of the mind must try to analyze "primary recognition" into something scientifically more intelligible—say, into straightforward causal processes. Here is where the trouble starts.

If a class A of events is highly statistically correlated with another class B of events (with, say, a correlation coefficient of .97), then any class A' of events which has almost the same members as A will also be correlated very highly with B. Thus there is no such thing as *the* class A of events with which a given class B is correlated. If the relation between occurrences of a sign, say the words "green sense-datum," and events (occurrences of a green patch in my visual field) were merely statistical correlation, then those words would be correlated with many different—at least slightly different—classes of events. There would be no such thing as *the* class of events associated with "green sense-datum," and no basis for saying that a particular event (imagine I utter the words "green sense-datum" when the sense-datum is really blue, and I fail to notice the slip) wasn't *really* associated with the words.

If one believes in non-Humean causation, then one can get around the problem by saying that the "right" class of events A is the class of events which exhibits whatever property objectively *brings about* utterances of the form "this is a green sense-datum" in the standard cases. Other classes A' may have a high statistical correlation with the occurrence of an utterance of this type, but that is irrelevant if the correlation is not truly causal.

But in the empiricist view, events do not have objective, perspective-independent "bringers-about." "Bringing about" is something we read into the world. "Bringing about" cannot be appealed to in explaining the nature of "primary recognition." On the other hand, mere statistical association is too weak a connection. The only remaining alternative is the one Russell and Ayer choose—to assume, or simply posit, a primitive, totally unanalyzed act of "primary recognition" which connects a sign directly to tokens that are not present to the mind performing the act (or, what comes to the same thing, connects the mind directly to one and only one "quality" of a token which is before it). This act of "primary recognition" is simply a mystery act, an occult sort of performance which establishes an intentional link between certain particulars and certain universals.

Perhaps it is no more of a mystery than Descartes's God, or Aristotle's Prime Mover (one needs *some* Archimedean point to avoid infinite regress, Ayer might claim), but a mystery nonetheless. For it has long been central to naturalistic psychology that the mind can interact with universals only through causal transactions involving instances of those universals, transactions which it is the business of psychology to analyze into elementary processes of a sort compatible with our scientific image of the world. But Ayer has no theory of the mind at all, nor is it clear that he has the building materials out of which such a theory—a theory of an organ with such capabilities as "primary recognition"—might be constructed. Is the mind supposed to be a collection of sense-qualia (as Hume thought)? Can a collection of sense-qualia engage in acts of primary recognition of universals? Ayer gives us nothing but matter and sense-qualia, and neither seems the sort of stuff that can perform such acts. It is strange that an empiricist and former positivist would feel so untroubled by the need to postulate a mysterious mental act.

Now that Ayer has become a realist about material objects, other problems occur which he does not notice, as well. The existence of material objects cannot really be a hypothesis which explains my sense-qualia, as Ayer thinks, unless I can *understand* this hypothesis.

To explain how I can understand it I must solve the problem which
so troubled Berkeley and Hume—I must succeed in somehow establishing a correspondence between the sign "material object" and
something which is *not* a "sense-quale." Clearly, no act of primary
recognition will help me here. Formerly Ayer would have been able
to say that "material object" only stands for a set of logical constructions out of sense-qualia anyway; now that he has given up his positivism, he does not have this way out. Unfortunately, he does not
appear to recognize the problem.

What is strange about this is that it was Russell (and the early Wittgenstein) who put this problem in the center of attention. Russell's
theory of material objects as a species of logical construction was part
of a comprehensive attempt to speak to this very problem. The distinction between what one can "say" and what one can only "show"
in Wittgenstein's *Tractatus* was an attempt to dissolve this problem
by removing it to the realm of the ineffable. Ayer describes Russell's
effort with loving care. But, after pointing out the many difficulties
with Russell's solution, he simply opts for the idea that the existence
of material objects is a causal hypothesis, without noticing that this
idea speaks to a different problem altogether.

It is because Ayer has changed problems altogether that he now
stresses the idea that philosophy is "theory of evidence." If the problem is *what is the evidence* that there is an external world in the
causal realist's sense, a world of mind-independent and discourse-
independent objects, and not *how can language or thought connect
with what is outside the mind,* then we are, indeed, in the province of
"theory of evidence" (if there is such a thing). But, as Russell and
Wittgenstein saw, the latter problem is prior to the former. It looks as
if, to solve the latter problem, one must either deny that material
objects are "outside the mind" (perhaps by constructing both the
"mind" and "material objects" out of something "neutral," which was
another of Russell's ideas) or postulate a mysterious relation of "correspondence" between what is in the mind and what is outside. If you
say, as Ayer in effect does, "Russell was wrong to treat material
objects as logical constructions; so I will treat them as inferred entities," you ignore, rather than solve, the problem which made Russell
want to treat them as logical constructions.

A way out, which Ayer ascribes to C. I. Lewis, is to say that the
"criterion for the reality of an object is the confirmation of the
hypothesis in which this reality is explicitly or implicitly affirmed."

But Ayer seems to be unwilling to go this far, although this is the sort of answer he himself gave in *Language, Truth, and Logic*. In any case, this answer, coupled with the claim that the "evidence" for the existence of material objects consists entirely of sense-qualia, amounts to the claim that all talk about material objects is just highly indirect talk about sense-qualia. This is the world-view of Berkelian idealism, pure and simple.[3]

But why should a theory which only a few philosophers have ever believed, the theory that the only objects whose existence is not of a highly derived kind are sense-qualia—that sense-qualia are the Furniture of the Universe—be more credible than the world-view of science and common sense?

In sum, Ayer lands himself in the following predicament: either he must return to subjective idealism or he must face the problem which has always been the nemesis of causal realism, the problem of the nature of the link between language and the world. (Even the nature of the link between language and sense-data not immediately present to the mind is a problem, for Ayer's view. Postulating an act of "primary recognition" is not providing an analysis of this link at all.)

The materialists to whom Ayer refers have a view on these matters, but it is not mentioned in his book. (Only their view on the mind-body problem is discussed, and that view is misrepresented, as I mentioned.) The contemporary materialist view, for what it is worth, is that the correspondence between signs and their objects is established by "causal connection." The difficulty mentioned before—that there are too many regularities and too many statistical tendencies for reference to be a matter of just regularities and/or statistical tendencies—is met by postulating that causality is more than a matter of regularities and statistical tendencies. Hume was just wrong; there are real "causal powers," real "abilities to produce" in the world, and these notions, these philosophers say, must be taken as primitive.

This view raises many problems, however, which I am sure Ayer would have pointed out had this issue been one he discussed. For one thing, the world-view of materialism is taken from fundamental physics—ignoring, however, the pervasive relativity of the state of a physical system to an "observer" which is characteristic of modern quantum mechanics. Materialists think of the whole universe as a "closed" system, described as God might describe it if He were allowed to know about it clairvoyantly, but not allowed to interfere with it. The states of the closed system succeed one another; which state will follow which is determined by a system of equations, the Equations of Motion of the system. The claim that the states do not merely follow one another (as prescribed by the Equations of Motion), but actually "produce" the states which follow them, introduces an element which physicists have long rejected as a metaphysical addition to the content of physics itself.

Even if one is not bothered by this (or thinks that the physicists have been too influenced by empiricism), a relation of "producing" which applies only to "states" of the whole universe will hardly clarify the meaning of "causes" as in "John's wild gesture caused the vase to fall off the mantlepiece." To explain the idea that John's gesture "produced" the falling of the vase without going back to the Hume-Ayer account (causality as regularities plus statistical tendencies), some materialists bring in such recherché objects as possible worlds and a relation of "nearness" between possible worlds (a genuine causal regularity is supposed to hold not only in the actual world but in non-actual worlds "near" to the actual world), while others just take the idea that some events "explain" other events as primitive.

The fact is that the God's-Eye View of the Universe as One Closed System—the metaphysical picture on which materialism is based—has no real room for "abilities to produce," a primitive relation of causation-as-explanation, or nearness-of-possible-worlds. This currently fashionable metaphysical talk is as incoherent from a consistent materialist view as it is from an empiricist view. On the other hand, the world of ordinary life—what Husserl called the "life-world" (Lebenswelt)—is full of objects which "produce effects" in other objects, of events which "explain" other events, of people who "recognize" things (and not only sense-qualia).

When the materialists get in trouble, what they do is forget their metaphysical picture and simply borrow whatever notions they need from the Lebenswelt, that is, from spontaneous phenomenology. (That they then dress up these notions from spontaneous phenomenology in a language which comes from medieval philosophy is a curious aberration.) But the whole point of having a metaphysical picture—a picture of the Furniture of the Universe—was to analyze the notions of our spontaneous phenomenology. Just as Ayer ignores the fact that there is nothing in what he gives us to start with—Humean sense impressions under the new name "sense-qualia"—to give us minds (let alone an act of "primary recognition" to put those minds in direct contact with universals), so the materialists ignore the fact that there is nothing in what they give us to start with—the closed system, its "states," and the Equations of Motion—to give us "abilities to produce," let alone a relation of "correspondence" between signs and objects.

In a way, Ayer's problem comes from Hume's project of analyzing causal talk into two parts: one part (the regularities) which is "objective," and one (the "necessity") which is nothing but a human projection (even if such projections are indispensable in practice). Both Ayer and the materialists are trying to carry out Hume's project of telling us what "really exists" (sense-qualia and their relations, in Ayer's view, until material objects got added on as a "causal hypothesis"; the closed system and its "states" in the materialist view), and what is only a "human projection." I want to suggest, as I think the later Wittgenstein was suggesting, that this project is now a total shambles. Analytic philosophy has great accomplishments, to be sure; but those accomplishments are negative. Like logical positivism (itself just one species of analytic philosophy), analytic philosophy has succeeded in destroying the very problem with which it started. Each of the efforts to solve that problem, or even to say exactly what could *count* as a solution to that problem, has failed.

This "deconstruction" is no mean intellectual accomplishment. We have learned an enormous amount about our concepts and our lives by seeing that the grand projects of discovering the Furniture of the Universe have all failed. But analytic philosophy pretends today not to be just one great movement in the history of philosophy—which it certainly was—but to be philosophy itself. This self-description *forces* analytic philosophers (even if they reject Ayer's particular views) to keep coming up with new "solutions" to the problem of the Furniture of the Universe—solutions which become more and more bizarre, and which have lost all interest outside of the philosophical community. Thus we have a paradox: at the very moment when analytic philosophy is recognized as the "dominant movement" in world philosophy, it has come to the end of its own project—the dead end, not the completion.

I now want to suggest that there is another way of reading the history of "philosophy in the twentieth century." In Ayer's reading, it all went somehow berserk after philosophers stopped talking about sense-data and about how sense-data are the "evidence" for everything we know. (Ayer professes to be optimistic, but on his description of the scene it is impossible to see why one should be.) I suggest that two things have happened. The first, which the first half of Ayer's book describes, consisted of a series of heroic attempts to solve the problems of traditional metaphysics. These attempts by Frege, Russell, Carnap, and the early Wittgenstein were called "attacks on metaphysics," but in fact they were among the most ingenious, profound, and technically brilliant constructions of metaphysical systems ever achieved. Even if they failed, modern symbolic logic, a good deal of modern language theory, and a part of contemporary cognitive science were all offshoots of these attempts.

The second thing that happened is almost unrecognized, even today. Beginning in the last decade of the nineteenth century, certain philosophers began to reject Hume's project—not just Hume's project with respect to causation, but the entire enterprise of dividing mundane "reality" into the Furniture of the Universe and our "projections." These philosophers have in common a rejection—a total root-and-branch rejection—of the enterprise mentioned, and a concern with the quotidian, with the *Lebenswelt,* with what a philosophy free of the search for a "true world" (Nietzsche's phrase!) might look like. I myself see Husserl as such a philosopher (Ayer's treatment of Merleau-Ponty, whom he chooses as his representative of phenomenology, is rendered worthless by Ayer's failure to understand that Merleau-Ponty rejects Ayer's entire *problématique*). Wittgenstein and Austin were such philosophers. Nelson Goodman is such a philosopher. Ayer does treat this last figure with a proper respect, but even here he cannot see quite *why* Goodman wants to be such a relativist—because Ayer has not seen the emptiness of his own resolution of the words-world problem.

The beginning of a philosophical movement which does not seek to divide our *Lebenswelt* into Furniture and Projections may itself be only a fashion, to be sure. But if this is the direction philosophical thought is going to take—and I rather hope that it is, because the old project deserves at least a respite, if not a permanent burial—then this is bound to affect the way in which the culture generally views almost all questions of general intellectual procedure. Much of our discussion—the discussion of whether values are "objective" or "subjective," for example—is still trapped in the categories fixed by Hume. Stanley Cavell suggests that a less distanced attitude toward the life-world (the only world we have, after all) may be a matter of some lasting moral importance. (He connects this with a way of reading Emerson and Thoreau.) Nelson Goodman has suggested that a rejection of the question "Is it the world itself or is it only a version?" may free us from "flat footed philosophy." He is not suggesting, as I understand it, that philosophers construct "worlds of worlds" irresponsibly; but he is suggesting that a recognition that philosophy is construction and not description of things-in-themselves is compatible with recognizing that the philosopher is responsible to evolving but genuine requirements of objectivity—requirements of "fit" with respect to his subject matter, and with respect to the self that he is both constructing and expressing.

What Ayer's book lacks is any sense of the way in which philosophy (like the arts) has become agonized, tormented by the weight of its past, burdened by predecessors whom it cannot escape. His tone is progressive throughout. But the fact that the key moves in Ayer's philosophy—postulating a primitive act of "primary recognition," and reviving causal realism (or more accurately, equivocating between causal realism and subjective idealism)—were in vogue before Kant even started to write the first *Critique* explodes this particular conception of "progress." The authors that Ayer discusses in the second half of his book have almost all, in one way or another, undermined these moves. If few of these authors ever come quite into focus, it is because he has to fit their work into his own picture of philosophical "progress." And he cannot, for they are all in another world.

4. Is Water Necessarily H₂O?

A. J. Ayer ended his *Philosophy in the Twentieth Century* with a criticism of both Saul Kripke's views and my own. He summed up the criticism in the closing sentences of the book: "I feel there to be more loss than profit in any . . . talk of essence or necessity or possible worlds. In my opinion, such talk is regressive, although currently in vogue. I should be more proud than otherwise if my opposition to it led to my being taken for an old-fashioned empiricist." I want to do two things here, namely, to discuss Ayer's criticism and to distance myself a bit more from Kripke than I have in the past. I say "discuss" and not "reply to." I think that Ayer's views are of deep interest, and what I propose to engage in will be reflection on those views rather than a polemical "reply." But the extent to which I am still recalcitrant will emerge in the course of my meditations.

Let me begin with what looks like a misunderstanding (in part, I think it *is* a misunderstanding, though not a straightforward one). Ayer obviously reads me as holding that it is *inconceivable* that water is not H₂O, and Ayer finds this view dotty. In fact, I have never asserted that it is *inconceivable* that water isn't H₂O, but only that it is *impossible* that it isn't H₂O; and most philosophers who have kept up with the discussion since Kripke published *Naming and Necessity* read that book as denying that there is any inference to be drawn from *p is conceivable* to *p is possible*. So (or so it seemed to me when I encountered this criticism by Ayer), Ayer just doesn't "get" what Kripke (and I) were driving at. But this reaction on my part was less than completely just.

I will explain why my reaction now seems less than completely just; but first another complication must be mentioned. Some years ago Ayer and I were at a conference in Florence,[1] and Ayer read a paper attacking Kripke's essentialism, to which I replied. The gist of my "minimalist" interpretation of Kripkean essentialism was subsequently incorporated in volume 3 of my *Philosophical Papers*;[2] but in that same place, I also began to worry about the flat claim that *it is metaphysically necessary that water is H$_2$O*. My worries have since deepened, and since the notion of "metaphysical necessity" is just what worries Ayer, philosophical honesty (as well as plain friendliness) requires that I "come clean." And I shall come clean—but rather late in this essay. And this is why I say that one of the things I will do is distance myself from Kripke more than I have in the past.

Conceivability and Metaphysical Possibility in Kripke

Although everyone—including me—read *Naming and Necessity* as denying the "conceivability implies possibility" inference, I am now not so sure we read it correctly. Kripke does advance the view that it is "epistemically possible" that water is not H$_2$O in the sense that we can imagine a world in which an "epistemic counterpart" of water—something which looks like water, plays the role of water, and about which (up to the present time) we have all the same well-confirmed information that we have in the actual world about water—turns out in the future (as a result of new information which we get in that world) not to be H$_2$O. But does this example show that *it is conceivable that water is not H$_2$O*, or only that *it is conceivable that stuff that resembles water should turn out not to be H$_2$O*? If only the latter, then Kripke, at least, may hold the view that Ayer finds dotty—the view that *it isn't conceivable* that water isn't H$_2$O.

I recall a conversation I had with Kripke many years ago in which I was describing a thought experiment. I was defending Quine's skepticism about analyticity, and I was trying to show that such analytic-seeming statements as "tigers are not glass bottles" aren't analytic. I proceeded in stages. First I argued (following a suggestion of Rogers Albritton) that glass bottles might turn out to be organisms (we discover their nervous system). Then, having made this astounding discovery, I suggested that we might later make the still more astounding discovery that *tigers are just the form that glass bottles take when frightened*. Kripke's comment on this thought experiment rather surprised me. He said, "I don't think you've shown that it's conceivable that tigers are glass bottles; I think you've shown that *it's conceivable that it could become conceivable*." (Perhaps Kripke had in mind a modal logic in which the "diamond"—the possibility operator—is interpreted as "conceivable" and in which "$\Diamond \Diamond p$ entails $\Diamond p$" is rejected.) At any rate—it now seems to me—it may be that Kripke *doesn't* think that "water isn't H$_2$O" is conceivable; it may be that he only thinks that *it's conceivable that it could become conceivable that water isn't H$_2$O.* (One piece of further evidence for this reading is that the famous argument at the end of *Naming and Necessity* against the theory that sensations are brain-processes rather obviously presupposes the principle that conceivability entails possibility.)

Physical Necessity and Metaphysical Necessity

To explain how I (and, I assume, most people) understood *Naming and Necessity*, it is easiest to begin with an analogy: the analogy between the metaphysical modalities (metaphysical possibility, impossibility, necessity) and the physical modalities (physical possibility, impossibility, necessity). The commonsense picture, I believe, is of physical necessity (and, hence, of physical possibility and impossibility) as something *nonepistemic.* The empiricist tradition rejects this commonsense picture, but I don't see how one can deny that it *is* the commonsense picture. The picture (like the commonsense picture of mathematical necessity) may or may not, in the end, *explain* anything—that is another question. But I think it undeniable that the man on the street thinks of physical necessity as something independent of our knowledge.

An example may help: a perpetual motion machine is "physically impossible." I think the commonsense picture is of this fact as something quite independent of whether anyone ever has known, does know, or will know this fact. Moreover, this fact is *not*—on the commonsense view, anyway—the same as the fact that no one ever has built, or will succeed in the future in building, a perpetual motion machine. The truth of the universal generalization:

(x) x is not a perpetual motion machine

is not the same fact as the truth of the statement

Perpetual motion machines are a physical impossibility.

There are—according to common sense—objective facts about what is *possible and impossible in the world.* We discovered that perpetual motion machines are a physical impossibility by discovering the First and Second Laws of Thermodynamics; but it would have been a physical impossibility even if these laws had never been discovered.

Now, for one who accepts this picture—and it is certainly the picture of the working scientist—it is simply obvious that the "conceivability" of a perpetual motion machine has nothing to do with its possibility. Perpetual motion machines may be conceivable, but they aren't physically possible. And, assuming high school chemistry,[3] water that isn't H_2O may be conceivable, but it isn't (physically or chemically) possible.

Now, what Kripke claimed to do in *Naming and Necessity*—and this is what generated all the excitement—was to discover another, stronger notion of *objective* (nonepistemic) necessity, a notion of objective necessity stronger than physical necessity. (In "The Meaning of 'Meaning'" I referred to it as "logical necessity." The difference in terminology may prove interesting.)

Rigid Designation

This stronger notion of necessity was explained in terms of the celebrated notion of "rigid designation." Let me try to explain this notion as clearly as I can. To begin with, we will be talking about situations in which we employ modal idioms, subjunctive conditionals, and other non-truth-functional modes of speech. In such situations, it is convenient to say that we are talking about various "possible worlds." This does *not* mean that we think possible worlds really exist (Kripke is very emphatic about this). Although Kripke's colleague David Lewis has advanced a metaphysics in which possible worlds have real existence, Kripke has repeatedly insisted that for him "possible worlds" are only hypothetical situations. Moreover, Kripke has also emphasized that his examples do not require the assumption of a totality of "all" possible worlds (although I think he believes there is such a totality); in a typical conversational situation we can take the "possible worlds" to be some set of mutually exclusive (but not necessarily exhaustive) hypothetical situations.

I shall now make a rather risky move; I shall try to explain the notion of rigid designation using a notion that Kripke himself very much dislikes, the notion of "sortal identity." I do this to avoid presupposing too many of Kripke's own metaphysical convictions at the outset. Consider such a puzzle as the following: would this table have been "the same thing" if one molecule had been missing from the start? One familiar way of dissolving the puzzle (though *not* one that Kripke accepts) is to say "the table would have been the same *table* but not the same *mereological sum of molecules.*" We can formalize this reply by relativizing identities to sortals, while rejecting "unrelativized" identity questions (for example, we reject the question, "Yes, but would the table have been the same, if 'same' means *the logical relation of identity* [" = "]?").

Now, suppose that while Nixon was still president of the United States, someone had said, "The president would never have become president if his mother had not encouraged him to aim high." The hypothetical situation envisaged is one in which an entity which is *person-identical* with the actual president at the time of the speech-act (that is, with Richard Nixon) fails to become president (and hence fails to be denoted by the definite description "the president"). Suppose, however, that the speaker had said, "The president might have been Hubert Humphrey." In this case, he is obviously *not* envisaging a situation in which Richard Nixon is identical with Hubert Humphrey; rather he is envisaging a situation in which the definite description "the president" denotes Hubert Humphrey.

In the same conversation, then, a definite description ("the president") can be used *either* to speak of whoever in the hypothetical situation is person-identical with the actual president *or* to speak of whoever in the hypothetical situation is the one and only president of the United States *in* the hypothetical situation. In the first use, the person denoted is the same (Richard Nixon) whether we are speaking of the actual world or of a hypothetical world; this is the "rigid" use. In the second use, the person denoted may not be the same, but the person denoted must satisfy the descriptive condition *in* the hypothetical situation (whether he satisfies the descriptive condition in the actual world or not). In the same way, in talk about hypothetical situations, "the table in this room" may mean *this very table* ("The table in this room might have been exported to China, in which case it would never have been in this house"), or it may mean whichever table fulfills the descriptive condition (*x is the one and only table in this room*) *in* the hypothetical situation—even if that table is not table-identical with the table that fulfills the descriptive condition in the actual world ("Your table might have been the table in this room").

The distinction between rigid and nonrigid uses is not restricted to *descriptions;* it is easily extended to substance names, for example. Thus, if I were to use the word "water" to refer to whatever stuff has certain observable characteristics *in* the hypothetical situation (regardless of its chemical composition), Kripke would say I was using the term "nonrigidly." (He would regard this as a very abnormal use of a substance term.) If I were to use it to refer to whatever stuff is substance-identical with the stuff that has those observable characteristics in the actual world, *whether or not it has them in the hypothetical situation,* then Kripke would say I was using the term "rigidly." The normal use of substance terms is the rigid use, according to Kripke.

But what is the criterion of substance-identity when we are speaking of hypothetical situations? It is at this point that I found a convergence between Kripke's views and my own. Starting in the 1950s, I had taken the position that the reference of natural kind terms and theoretical terms in science is typically fixed by a *cluster* of laws,[4] and I had later pointed out[5] that the connection between the cluster and the natural kind term or theoretical term cannot be represented by an ordinary analytic definition of the form:

> *x is water (or multiple sclerosis, or whatever) if and only if most of the following laws are obeyed (or approximately obeyed) by x:[list of laws] . . .*

I developed a more detailed view in "Is Semantics Possible?"[6] When I came to write a lengthier version ("The Meaning of 'Meaning'"),[7] I put the point in the following way: when we first think of "water," what we think of are the laws that we know (in a prescientific period, these may be low-level generalizations about observable characteristics); but if we were to travel to another planet, we could not determine once and for all whether some liquid that filled the lakes and rivers on that planet was water *merely* by asking whether it did or did not obey (or approximately obey) those laws or possess those observable characteristics. What would ultimately decide the question would be whether it *possessed the chemical composition—whether we knew that chemical composition or not—and whether it obeyed the laws—whether we knew all of them or not—*that the stuff we call "water" on Earth possesses and obeys. If the so-called "water" on Twin Earth turned out to consist of XYZ while the water on Earth turned out to consist of H₂O, then the correct thing for the scientist to say would be that "the stuff on Twin Earth turned out not to be water after all," even if at the beginning (before he discovered that water is H₂O) he knew of no property of Earth water which was not also a property of Twin Earth "water." Moreover, the fact that a scientist would talk this way (I claim he would, anyway) does not mean that he *changed the meaning of the word "water"* upon discovering that water is H_2O. It is not that he now uses "water" as a synonym for H_2O. *What he intended all along*—I claimed—was to refer to whatever had the "deep structure" of his terrestrial paradigms, and not to whatever had the superficial characteristics he knew about.

Even when it is a question of Earth alone, the idea that "water" is *synonymous* with a description in terms of clusters of (known) laws, observable properties, and the like is wrong. For if it turns out in the future that some bit of putative "water" does not have the "normal" chemical composition—the chemical composition that is shared by most of the paradigms—then it will be correct to say that that bit of stuff "turned out not to be water after all." The cluster of observable properties and known laws fixes the reference by enabling us to pick out paradigms; but those paradigms are *defeasible* paradigms. Future discoveries—discoveries of the "deep structure" common to most of the paradigms—may lead us to say that *some of the paradigms themselves were not really water.*

All this I still believe. But it is easy to see—I saw at the time, having learned of Kripke's work by 1973, when I wrote "The Meaning of 'Meaning'"—that there is a close relation between these ideas and Kripke's ideas. Far-away planets in the actual universe were playing the very same role in my own discussion that hypothetical situations ("possible worlds") were playing in Kripke's. In the terms I am using today (making use of the un-Kripkean notion of "sortal identity"), it is sufficient to take "has the same physicochemical composition and obeys the same laws" to be the criterion of "substance-identity" to see the relation. (Kripke himself mentions only composition and not laws, but this seems a defect of his version to me.) In my own example, discovering that the "water" on Twin Earth did not have the same composition as the water on Earth was discovering a failure of substance-identity.

It may help to present the theory in the form of an idealized model (which is what all theories of language are, after all). We picture the term "water" as becoming connected at some point in its history with the idea that substances possess a subvisible structure (speculations about atomic structure are quite old, after all). It is part of that picture that the subvisible structure explains why different substances obey different laws. (That is what makes *composition* important.) Thus, "has the same composition and (therefore) obeys the same laws" becomes the criterion of substance-identity. We picture "water" as acquiring a "rigid" use: as being used to denote whatever is substance-identical with (most of) the paradigms in our actual environment (limited both to the actual world and to the available part of the actual world).

Now suppose, for example, that after the discovery of Daltonian chemistry but before the discovery that water is H_2O, someone wrongly conjectures that water is XYZ. He would say that it is possible that water is XYZ, certainly. But what should we say *later, after* we have discovered that water is not XYZ but H_2O? If we really are using the term "water" rigidly, we ought to say that the "hypothetical situation in which water is XYZ" is misdescribed; any such hypothetical situation is properly described as one in which XYZ plays the role of water (fills the lakes and rivers, and so on) or (if that is impossible, because XYZ couldn't actually have those properties) as a situation in which an "epistemic counterpart" of XYZ is *warrantedly assertible* to be XYZ and to have those properties. What this means is that we will *now* be unwilling to say that *any* logically possible situation is "one in which water is XYZ." And that means that *it is impossible—metaphysically impossible—for water to be XYZ.*

But then what should we say if we later find out that we made a huge mistake? That water is XYZ after all and not H_2O? We should say that what we said before was wrong. Water was XYZ after all. *What was metaphysically impossible was that water was H_2O.* What we formerly believed could not possibly have been true.

This is what Ayer finds too paradoxical to be right. But notice that this "paradox" only arises in the case of the *rigid* use of terms. It is built into the rigid use (plus the given criterion for substance-identity) that our empirical discoveries may lead to revisions in what we are willing to call "water" in a given hypothetical situation. That is what makes the decision as to whether a given hypothetical case really is a case in which water is XYZ always subject to revision. In spite of the term "metaphysical possibility," no real metaphysics is involved over and above what was already involved in taking *physical* possibility to be an objective notion.

Why did I want to say that the conceivability of "Water may turn out *not* to be H_2O" does not imply the *logical possibility* (Kripke's "metaphysical possibility") that water is not H_2O? If water does turn out not to be H_2O, then of course it will have turned out to be *both* conceivable and possible that water is not H_2O. So that case does not help me to show that "conceivability doesn't entail possibility." (Nor does it help Ayer to show that it isn't necessary that water is H_2O—the claim that it is necessary that water is H_2O is a *defeasible* claim, according to my theory, and discovering that water is not H_2O in the *actual* world is what it takes to defeat it.)[8] What, however, if someone says "it is conceivable that water turn out not to be H_2O" and it turns out that water *is* H_2O? Consider a mathematical analogy. If I say, "There may turn out to be a mistake in this proof," and it turns out there was no mistake, was I wrong in holding that "it is conceivable that there is a mistake"? If "it is conceivable that there is a mistake" means "it is logically possible that there is a mistake," then it is not conceivable that there is a mistake in a mathematical proof unless there *is* a mistake in the proof. (If a proof is right, then it is logically necessary that it is right.) But that isn't what "conceivable" means. If an *epistemic counterpart* of this proof—a proof with respect to which I have the same evidence that it is a proof of this theorem—could be wrong, then it is right to say, "it is conceivable there is a mistake in the proof." And if an epistemic counterpart of H_2O could turn out to be such that we mistook it for H_2O up to now (everything we know of H_2O up to now at least appears to be true of it), but—in the hypothetical situation—it is discovered in the future that the counterpart is not H_2O, then it is right to say "it is conceivable that there is a mistake in our chemistry, conceivable that water is not H_2O." What is conceivable is a matter of epistemology (as I said earlier, I am not sure this is how Kripke would use the term "conceivable"), while what is possible is a matter of two things: the range of self-consistent possible situations[9] we have in mind *and* the conventions for describing those situations in our language. If we decide that what is not substance-identical with the water in the actual world is not part of the denotation of the term "water," then that will require redescription of some possible situations when our knowledge of the fundamental characteristics of water (the ones relevant to questions of substance-identity) changes. When terms are used rigidly, logical possibility becomes dependent upon empirical facts. But I repeat, no "metaphysics" is presupposed by this beyond what is involved in speaking of "physical necessity."

In fact, even without rigid designation there is some dependence of what we take to be "logical possibility" on empirical facts. A term may turn out not to be well defined for *empirical* as opposed to conceptual reasons. Thus, when we discovered that Special Relativity was correct, we also discovered that "simultaneous" is not as well defined as we thought it was in the actual world. But this means that whereas we previously thought that "it is possible that a radioactive decay on Mars and a radioactive decay on Venus happen simultaneously" described one definite possible state of affairs, we have learned that there are many different states of affairs that could be so described— learned this through empirical investigation.

Similar remarks apply (up to a point) to the case of personal identity and to the case of table-identity. If we accept that a hypothetical person is, say, Aristotle just in case the hypothetical person comes from the same fertilized egg (same atoms in the same arrangement) in the hypothetical situation as the actual Aristotle did in the actual world, or in case it is simply stipulated that the hypothetical person is Aristotle and nothing in the stipulations that govern the hypothetical situation contradict the "same fertilized egg" criterion of person-identity, then we can decide which counterfactual situations are situations in which Aristotle himself could have found himself and which ones are not. Aristotle could not have been Chinese or have had a different sex, but he could have failed to be a philosopher. If we accept that a hypothetical table is, say, this table just in case it consisted of at least 90 percent of the same atoms at the time of its making and the arrangement of those atoms did not differ from their arrangement in the actual table at the point of origin by more than a specified extent, then we can decide which counterfactual situations it makes sense to stipulate concerning this table. This is what I called my "minimalist" interpretation of Kripke. Whether this does justice to the depth of Kripke's metaphysical ambitions I now doubt; but it is worth noticing that *one* way (probably not the intended way) of reading Kripke is as a rational reconstructionist with a proposal for making sense of various identity questions across "possible worlds."

Why Kripke Rejects Sortal Identity

To leave matters here—which is where I left them when Ayer and I discussed these questions at the "Levels of Reality" conference in Florence so long ago—would, however, be unfair to Ayer, I now think. For I now agree with Ayer that Kripke intends something really "metaphysical" with his talk of Aristotle's "essence." And what I was doing at the Levels of Reality conference (and also in "Necessity and Possibility") was presenting a theory which was related to Kripke's, but which was stripped of metaphysical assumptions to the point where *Carnap* might have accepted it. (Carnap did believe there is a nonepistemic notion of physical necessity to be reconstructed, by the way.)

I had worries about this myself at the time. And when I was lucky enough to see a transcript of Kripke's unpublished lectures on "Time and Identity" (given at Cornell University in 1968) I saw just how far from a Carnapian "rational reconstructionist" Kripke really is. In those lectures Kripke categorically rejected the whole notion of sortal identity. Before sketching his argument, I would like to say a word about the "philosophical atmosphere" surrounding the notion of sortal identity. The notion has been used by philosophers who are concerned, at least some of the time, to reconstruct our "linguistic intuitions." Now, Kripke also talks about "intuitions" and gives great weight to them. What I was trying to do with my "minimalist" (re)interpretation of Kripke was to assimilate his *metaphysical* intuitions to the *linguistic* intuitions that other analytic philosophers talk about. This is what I now think cannot be done.

For someone who thinks the question is one of "linguistic intuition," sortal identity will appear as a convenient device. From such a point of view, anyway, the device presupposes criteria of substance-identity, person-identity, table-identity, and so on, but this will not appear to be a metaphysical problem. We just have to consult our intuitions and lay down a set of conventions which seem reasonable in the light of those intuitions. If two philosophers disagree about what are reasonable criteria of, say, person-identity across possible worlds, then (unless one of them thinks the other has a "tin ear," that is, no ear for the way we actually speak at all) they may well agree that "one can do it either way." In this view, the criteria for person-identity across possible worlds are, to some extent, to be *legislated* and not *discovered*. I do not mean to suggest that a philosopher who uses the device of sortal identity in his logical theories is *committed* to this quasi-"conventionalist" attitude, but only that that attitude seems, as a matter of fact, to be associated with the appearance of the device. And this attitude is precisely what Kripke dislikes.

Kripke thinks there is a *fact of the matter* as to whether Aristotle—"Aristotle *himself*," as he likes to say—*could have come from a different fertilized ovum*. We cannot *legislate* an answer to this question, much less say "we can do it one way in one context and another way in a different context, depending on what the *point* of the counterfactual talk is." There is (according to Kripke) a fact of the matter as to what it is to *be* Aristotle. Intuition is not just a mode of access to our culture's inherited picture of the world; it is a fundamental capacity of reason, a capacity that enables reason to discover "metaphysical necessity." This, I think, is what Ayer rejects (and I too think it should be rejected), and what I was trying to whitewash out of Kripke's text.

Consider the question of whether a hypothetical table 1 percent of whose matter differed at the moment of completion from the matter in this table would have been "this very table." No—first consider the question, "What—from a scientific philosopher's point of view—*is* a table, anyway?" Some "scientific philosophers"—for example, Wilfrid Sellars—would say that "tables" don't really exist, that there are objects which really exist and which answer to what the layman calls "tables," but the layman's "tables" are part of a hopelessly prescientific picture of the world. This view Kripke certainly rejects. For Kripke, it is hard to say if *electrons* are really "objects" (scientists tell us such weird things about them—perhaps we should just wait for the scientists to make up their minds), but tables and chairs (and, curiously, *numbers*) are certainly objects. Tables certainly exist. Other scientific philosophers—for example, Quine—would say that "tables" are on a par with electrons; they are theoretical entities just as electrons are. In fact, Quine proposes, tables should be identified with *space-time regions*. Still other philosophers—perhaps David Lewis would say this—would agree with Quine's attitude, but would identify tables with mereological sums of time-slices of elementary particles.

I am not forgetting that this essay is about Ayer's philosophy and not Kripke's; but Ayer's criticisms of Kripke's views are my take-off point. And I think that the difference between Kripke's views and Ayer's will come out most clearly if I go into just a bit more detail about Kripke's view at precisely this point. Kripke, first of all, thinks that objects have modal properties. (Remember, for Kripke modality is nonepistemic.) It is an objective (nonepistemic) fact about this table that *it could have been elsewhere*. But a space-time region obviously lacks this modal property; so the table is not any space-time region. Quine is wrong. (Quine, like Ayer, rejects these nonepistemic modal properties; so Kripke's argument does not impress him.) Of course, a "sortal identity theorist" would say that if the world had been such that "this" table was in a different place at least some of the time (occupied a different space-time region), then *it would have been the very same table but not the very same space-time region.* This is just what Kripke does *not* want to say.

Is the table a "mereological sum of time-slices of particles"? Well, the table has the modal property that *it could have consisted of different particles* (or so Kripke would argue). And a mereological sum of time-slices of particles obviously lacks this property. So David Lewis wrong. The table is not identical with any mereological sum of time-slices of particles. Of course, a sortal identity theorist would say that if the world had been such that "this" table consisted of different particles at least some of the time (its matter formed a different mereological sum of particle-slices), then *it would have been the very same table but not the very same mereological sum of time-slices of particles.* This is just what Kripke does *not* want to say.

What Kripke does want to say is that the table is *not identical* with the particles-and-fields that make it up. It is not identical with the space-time region (Quine takes the space-time region and not just the particles because he considers the electromagnetic and other fields to also be part of the table). And it is not identical with the particles (not identical with the mereological sum of time-slices of particles). The particles-and-fields that make it up are the *matter* of the table; but the table is not identical with its matter. If the table had been in a different place, it would have been *the very same* table. What does "the very same" mean? It means—Kripke says—precisely what "=" means in logic. It means *identity.* Identity is a *primitive logical notion,* Kripke claims, and it is a fundamental philosophical error to think it can or should be "explained." Kripke rejects the very idea of "criteria of identity."

The distinction between "the table" and its *matter* is, of course, reminiscent of Aristotle. But Kripke's view is very different from Aristotle's. According to Kripke, it is "essential" to the table that it consist of pretty much *this very matter (at least at its "origin"),* while for Aristotle the *particular* matter is never part of the essence of anything. (Also, it is doubtful if Aristotle ever recognized any such thing as an *individual* essence, as opposed to the essence of a kind.)

At any rate, since the table is not identical with its matter, the need for the dubious notion of sortal identity disappears. Instead of saying, "the hypothetical object you describe would be the same table, but not the same space-time region," one can simply say, "it would be the very same table, but it would not *occupy* the same space-time region." We can do everything we want with just the good old "primitive logical notion" of identity. (Kripke rejects the notion that the matter of the table is a mereological sum of time-slices of *anything*, by the way—he says that he doesn't know what a time-slice is, "unless it's the ordered pair of an object and a time," and objects certainly aren't sums of ordered pairs of themselves and times.)

For these reasons, the explanation I gave of rigid designation using the notion of sortal identity would be wholly unacceptable to Kripke. For example, instead of saying that the assignment of truth-values to counterfactual statements about "this table" requires the adoption of explicit or implicit criteria of table-identity,[10] Kripke would say that it requires an intuitive knowledge of what is "essential" to the table— an intuitive grasp of the limits of the possibilities in which the hypo- thetical object would bear the primitive logical relation " = " to the table I am pointing to. Criteria of table-identity are conceived of (by me, anyway) as to some extent *up to us*. Facts about " = " are not (in Kripke's view, anyway) at all up to us. Kripke is not doing rational reconstruction; he is engaged in (what he views as) metaphysical dis- covery.

Ayer would doubtless say that he cannot fathom what this sort of "metaphysical discovery" is supposed to come to. And I must admit that neither can I. The table can, after all, vary *continuously* across hypothetical situations (just imagine a series of hypothetical situa- tions such that in the n + 1st the table has one less molecule in com- mon with the table I am pointing to than it does in the nth). Is there supposed to be a fact of the matter as to when the hypothetical table stops being " = " (*identical*) with the table I am pointing to? Kripke might say that every possible border-line determines a different "essence," and that it is vague which essence our concept "this table" connects with, but then what are we being asked to "intuit"? A "fuzzy set" of essences, perhaps? If we can connect the description "this table" with different essences by adopting a different *convention*, then Kripke's view seems only verbally different from the quasi- conventionalist view; if not, then . . . ?

I myself have always been much more attracted to Kripke's ideas about natural kinds than to his ideas about individual essences (which I could understand, at best, only by regarding them as linguistic proposals for assigning truth-values to certain counterfactuals in a not implausible way). So let us return to natural kinds, and in particular to the example which Ayer took up, the "water is H$_2$O" example.

The "Identity" of Substances

I shall not consider further the question of how to *formalize* questions of substance-identity (that is, I shall not worry about whether the question concerns "sortal identity" or a unitary notion of identity). If it still seems to me that questions of the identity of chemically pure substances are much clearer than questions of the "identity" of the table in hypothetical situations, the reason is simply this: I accept (up to a point—I'll say what the limits are later) the commonsense picture of *physical* necessity. I accept, at least for ordinary scientific purposes, the idea that it makes sense to talk of laws of nature (physically necessary truths), and the idea that the search for such laws is a search for something objective (as objective as anything is). Given this picture, I would propose the following as a condition for the adequacy of any proposed criterion of substance-identity: the criterion must have the consequence that A and B are the same substance if and only if they obey the same *laws*.

I do not claim that there is no vagueness *at all* in this condition of adequacy.[11] The notion of "same laws" is, to be sure, somewhat vague. (I'll say in a moment how I got around this.) For·example, consider an ordinary sample of iron. By the standards of high school chemistry, it is "chemically pure." But it consists of different isotopes (these occur in fixed proportions—the same proportions—in all naturally occurring samples, by the way. Some philosophers who use isotopes as examples appear not to know this). Any naturally occurring sample of iron (which is sufficiently free of impurities) will exhibit the same lawful behavior as any other (unless we go to a quantum-mechanical level of accuracy). But if we use a cyclotron or some other fancy gadget from atomic physics to prepare a sample of iron which is mono-isotopic, that sample will—if the tests are sensitive enough—behave slightly differently from a "natural" sample. Should we then say that a hunk of iron consisting of a single isotope and a hunk of natural iron (consisting of the various isotopes in their normal proportions) are two different substances or one? Indeed, two naturally occurring samples may have tiny variations in the proportions with which the isotopes occur, and perhaps this will result in a slight difference in their lawful behavior. Are they samples of different substances? Well, it may depend on our interests. (This is the sort of talk Kripke hates!) But the fact that there is some component of interest relativity here, and, perhaps, some drawing of arbitrary lines, does not change the fact that *the degree of arbitrariness is infinitesimal compared to the arbitrariness in the "almost the same matter at the time of origin" criterion for identity of tables.*

Some of my readers will recall that in "The Meaning of 'Meaning'" I took *microstructure* as the criterion for substance-identity. But I pointed out that differences in microstructure invariably (in the actual world) result in differences in lawful behavior. (For example, *no other substance has the same boiling point at sea level or the same freezing point as H₂O*.) Since there is a standard description of microstructure, and microstructure is what determines physical behavior (laws of behavior), it seemed to me that the only natural choice for a criterion of substance-identity was the microstructural criterion. (In this way one also reduces the vagueness in the "same laws" criterion, although one does not completely eliminate it for the reasons just given.)

Another relevant point is that "possible worlds" were mentioned in "The Meaning of 'Meaning'" only in connection with the discussion of Kripke; my own ideas were presented in terms of a thought experiment that has already been mentioned: the thought experiment of imagining that we discover a superficially "terrestrial looking" planet. We were to imagine that a liquid on this Twin Earth superficially resembles water. How do we decide whether it really *is* water? Since the question only concerned *actual* substances, questions about "all possible worlds"—in particular, questions about worlds in which the *laws of nature can be different*—were not in my mind.

Even at this stage, my motivations were somewhat different from Kripke's. But I did not think through the consequences. Today I would add two qualifications to what I wrote in "The Meaning of 'Meaning.'" First of all, I would distinguish ordinary questions of substance-identity from scientific questions. I still believe that ordinary language and scientific language are interdependent;[12] but the layman's "water" is not the chemically pure water of the scientist, and just what "impurities" make something no longer water but something else (say, "coffee") is not determined by scientific theory. Second (and, in the present context, more important), I do not think that a criterion of substance-identity that handles Twin Earth cases will extend handily to "possible worlds."[13] In particular, what if a hypothetical "world" *obeys different laws?* Perhaps one could tell a story about a world in which H₂O exists (H still consists of one electron and one proton, for example), but the laws are slightly different in such a way that what is a small difference in the *equations* produces a very large difference in the *behavior* of H_2O. Is it clear that we would call a (hypothetical) substance with quite different behavior *water* in these circumstances?[14] I now think that the question, "What is the necessary and sufficient condition for being water *in all possible worlds?*" makes no sense at all. And this means that I now reject "metaphysical necessity."

Are Ayer and I now in total agreement on these matters, then? Well, up to a point we are. (But I warned at the beginning that there is a point at which I am still recalcitrant.) If the question about substance-identity in all possible situations can be dismissed (especially if the answer is required not to be a conventional stipulation but a metaphysical fact), then there is no need to make an issue about the "logical possibility" of water not being H_2O. If you have a hypothetical situation you want to describe that way, describe it that way—as long as it is clear *what* hypothetical situation you are describing. I won't insist (any more) that "it is conceivable that water may turn out not to be H_2O but it isn't logically possible that water isn't H_2O." But Ayer and I are still not in total agreement.

We are not in total agreement for two reasons. The first, which would take a much longer essay to discuss, is the difference in our theories of reference. I still believe that a community can stipulate that "water" is to designate *whatever has the same chemical structure* or *whatever has the same chemical behavior* as paradigms X, Y, Z, . . . (or as most of them, just in case a few of them turn out to be cuckoos in the nest) *even if it doesn't know, at the time it makes this stipulation, exactly what that chemical structure, or exactly what that lawful behavior, is.* But this still has some of the consequences Ayer objects to: I may discover that something that satisfied all the existing tests for water wasn't really water after all—not by discovering that it failed some qualitative criterion that I had in mind all along, but by discovering that *it doesn't obey the same laws that most of X, Y, Z, . . . do.* We didn't *know* those laws when we introduced the term "water," but we already had the *concept* of a physical law, and the concept of discovering a physical law,[15] and that is all we needed to formulate this notion of substance-identity.

The second disagreement is more fundamental than the first. The criterion of substance-identity which still seems fine to me (a little vagueness at the boundaries doesn't hurt, after all) presupposes the nonepistemic character of the notion of a "physical law." I still accept a notion of *objective nonlogical modality.* And this, I think, is where the real disagreement arises.

Empiricism and Necessity

The empiricist tradition has always been skeptical of the modalities. Although empiricist doubts have lately gone out of fashion, they should not, I think, be lightly dismissed. There *is* a prima facie difficulty about modality—a prima facie *epistemic* difficulty—and it runs very deep.

The difficulty, in its simplest form, may be stated thus: modal realists claim that we have knowledge about what is and is not possible. This is not believed to be a matter of pure logic, since knowledge of physical possibility is supposed to be synthetic knowledge. It must, then, somehow be based on observation. (No one any longer believes the laws of nature are *synthetic a priori*.) But how? *We only observe what happens in the* actual *world*. How, then, are we supposed to know what happens in nonactual "possible worlds"? (To appreciate the difficulty, try reading David Lewis's books with this in mind!)

Kripke's answer, that "possible worlds" are only hypothetical situations, and we know what is true in hypothetical situations because we *stipulate* them, may help with issues of metaphysical possibility (but there is the big problem of what is an *admissible* stipulation—the problem of criteria of identity across possible worlds is a small part of this big problem); but we are not now talking about "metaphysical" possibility but about *physical* possibility. We cannot just stipulate physical possibilities.

The answer that I myself find most attractive is the following: the distinction between what is and is not physically possible is not an external distinction imposed by philosophers; it is a distinction *internal* to physical theory itself. Just as in modern logic there are complicated devices for representing *logical* possibilities—state descriptions, and infinitary analogues of state descriptions ("models")—so in modern physics there are complicated devices for representing *physical* possibilities—phase spaces and Hamiltonians. A state of affairs is logically possible if it can be represented by a disjunction of state descriptions,[16] or more generally by a "model"; a state of affairs is physically possible if it can be represented by a wave function and a Hamiltonian. Physical theories have to agree with observation, but hypothetico-deductive inferences have led the scientist to accept as real many things that are not "observable." The machinery of "physical possibility" is just part of what we accept when we accept a modern physical theory as well confirmed.

Empiricists (including Ayer at the time he wrote *Language, Truth, and Logic*—a book that I, for one, still regard as a masterpiece, for all my disagreements with it) have sometimes replied by suggesting that physical theory itself is just highly derived talk about sense data. This is a bad move for the empiricist to make, however, since it plays into the modal realist's hands. The empiricist who makes this reply has now assumed the whole burden of proof—the burden of showing that some version of phenomenalism can be made to work—and the modal realist is off the hook.

A better reply—and the one Ayer would now make, if I am not mistaken—is the following: "There may indeed be a distinction of the kind you describe within physical theories, but that distinction is obviously *relative* to the physical theory you select. The question is not 'Can we make sense of possibility relative to Newtonian physics (or to Special Relativity, or to General Relativity, or to Quantum Mechanics, or to Supergravity, . . .),' but 'Can we make sense of an *unrelativized* notion of physical possibility?'." And this is indeed the question. For what I need to support my argument is a notion of substance-identity, *not* a series of notions (identity relative to high school chemistry, identity relative to quantum mechanics, identity relative to . . .). The nineteenth-century chemists who discovered that water is H_2O were not implicitly using the criterion that something is water if it has the same "nature" as (most of) the paradigmatic samples *relative to future quantum mechanics*, after all.

The empiricist can also tell a fairly convincing story about how the habit of speaking as if "possibility" were *non*-relative might have arisen. When something is possible/impossible relative to *the currently accepted* physical theory, it is natural to drop the relativizer. We say, "In Daltonian chemistry, transmutation of elements is impossible," because Daltonian chemistry is not the currently accepted theory on the subject. But if someone asks, "Is it possible to transmute elements?" today we might reply, "We have learned that it is, though not by purely chemical means—you need an atom smasher." This reply does not say "it is possible relative to contemporary physical theory," because it is understood that we are employing the best theory available. Thus possibility in an *epistemic* sense—possibility relative to our best available knowledge—gets spoken of as if it were some kind of knowledge-independent fact.

Indeed, one can see something like this happening in certain "vulgar" uses of the possibility concept. If someone told me that my neighbors Bernie and Marie had painted their house lavender, I would reply, "I don't believe it. They wouldn't paint their house such an ugly color. It's impossible." But I would be much less likely to say, "It is impossible for me to paint my house lavender." Instead I would say, "I hate lavender. I would never choose that color." What is happening here?

What is happening is that I represent the hypothetical situation in terms of most likely causal histories (Bernie and Marie deciding to paint their house lavender; my deciding to paint my house lavender). If the contemplated event is not unlikely to occur, I say "it is possible." (Note the explicitly epistemic "not unlikely.") If it is extremely unlikely, something interesting happens: I divide causal histories into those in which the event happens for reasons independent of *my* will and those in which the event happens because I will something I am not, in fact, likely to will. In the first kind of case, I may well say, "It's impossible." In the second kind of case I am much more likely to say, "I would never do that." Yet, obviously, there is no "objective" sense in which it is *impossible for Bernie and Marie to paint their house lavender but possible for me to do so.*

Moreover, suppose (Heaven forbid!) that Bernie and Marie *do* paint their house lavender. I wouldn't say, "Well, it was impossible that they would relative to my evidence then, but it is possible relative to my evidence now." Rather, I would say, "I was wrong." *I was wrong in saying it was impossible.* Even in a case like this, a case in which the "impossibility" spoken of is obviously epistemic, we speak *as if* possibility and impossibility were "tenseless" (and hence *non*-epistemic). Obviously, the fact that we speak the same way about physical possibility and impossibility cannot be given much weight.

Again, the modal realist may claim that the impossibility of, say, a perpetual motion machine *explains* the fact that every attempt to build one has failed. But we can deduce from the laws of physics (which can themselves be formalized without difficulty in a first-order extensional language) not only *that* there are no perpetual motion machines, but *how* and *why* each particular attempt to build one fails. The "deduction" of each law of physics L from the statement "it is impossible to violate L" adds no real explanatory content to these marvelously informative deductions; *what it adds is only meta-physical comfort.*

Physical Possibilities and Causal Powers

The power of this critique is undeniable. The best response, I think, is to undermine the original premise: the premise that what is at stake is knowledge of what happens in nonactual "possible worlds." Grant that premise, and the entire critique unfolds in the way we have just seen. An alternative way of looking at the situation is the following: think of talk of "physical possibility" and "physical impossibility" as a late refinement of ordinary causal talk. (Talk of "bringing about," talk of "dispositions," talk of abilities and capacities, all stem from this common root.) To say that something is impossible is to say that nothing has the capacity to bring it about. No system has the capacity to go on repeating its motions forever; this is the "impossibility of a perpetual motion machine of the first kind." Capacities and dispositions and other sorts of causal powers are possessed by things in the actual world; they are descriptions of what is the case in this world, not of what is (or isn't) the case in a variety of "nonactual worlds." Physics is concerned to describe the capacities of things—starting with the individual particles. Indeed, each physical magnitude, for example, *charge,* is associated with a set of causal powers from the day it is introduced into physical theory.

To this move, there is an ancient empiricist countermove. Causality itself, Hume argued, poses just the problem we have been discussing (and it is clear that Ayer agrees with Hume). If I say

A always brings about B,

the "objective" content of the assertion is that A-events are always followed by B-events. The supposition of something over and above the regularity—the assumption of a genuine "bringing about"—is just the assumption of something that is neither observable nor really explanatory.

The empiricist need not make the mistake of suggesting that he can *translate* causal talk into regularity talk. Like possibility talk, causal talk arises from a variety of "vulgar" ways of speaking and has a variety of uses. The sophisticated empiricist will keep the burden of proof on the side of the causal realist. *Show me what the notion of "bringing about" actually adds to the individual regularities we observe and their use in explanation and prediction,* he will say.

But the situation is a little different from the way it was with sophisticated "possibility" talk. No one supposes that we observe either physical possibility (except when it is actualized) or physical impossibility. But, as Anscombe has stressed,[17] our ordinary descriptions of what we observe are *loaded* with causal content. Ask someone what he saw, and he will talk about people *eating, drinking, moving* things, *picking up* things, *breaking* things, and so on, and every one of these verbs contains causal information. It isn't just that John's hand came to be in contact with the glass before the glass moved to the floor and separated into pieces; we say that John *broke* the glass. Moreover, even the statement that "the glass moved" uses notions of space and time; and ever since Kant, there have been strong arguments to the effect that assignments of space-time location are dependent on causal ascriptions. The Kantian view is, in this respect, an early forerunner of contemporary "holist" views of belief fixation. Kant can be interpreted (I think correctly) as holding that judgments as to how objects are distributed in space and judgments as to how objects send causal signals to one another are interdependent and are confirmed as a corporate body. (Michael Friedman has recently done a close study of Kant's *Metaphysical Foundations of Natural Science,* showing how Kant analyzes Newton's *Principia* in just this way.) If we cannot give a single example of an ordinary observation report which does not, directly or indirectly, presuppose causal judgments, then the empiricist distinction between the "regularities" we "observe" and the "causality" we "project onto" the objects and events involved in the regularities collapses. Perhaps the notion of causality is so primitive that the very notion of observation presupposes it?

Again there is an empiricist reply, but this time the reply does involve the empiricist in defense of a positive doctrine. The burden of proof cannot forever be shifted to the realist side. The famous empiricist doctrine of observation (which Ayer supports) is that *ultimately* there is a level of observation—an absolutely fundamental level—which is free of causal hypotheses. This is the level of sense qualities. When I observe that I have a particular sense experience, say a blue star against a white background, I observe something which is absolutely "occurrent," something which is independent of all alleged facts about "what causes what."

Whether this is right is, not surprisingly, the fundamental issue on which everything turns. I can hardly hope to do justice to it at the end of an essay. Many of the questions which have been raised in connection with it cannot even be discussed here. (For example, whether even sense qualities can really be described in a language which is

independent of our causally-loaded "thing language." And, for another example, the question—which was first raised by Kant—whether
the ascription of a *time order* to even sense qualities does not indirectly presuppose the objective material world and its causal structure.) But I shall single out one strain for discussion, because I am
especially interested in discovering what Ayer's response will be.

Causality and the Mind

From this point on, I shall focus on Ayer's own version of empiricism.
Ayer holds that we are directly acquainted with our "sense qualities."
By this he does not just mean that we *have* sense qualities; he means
that we can attend to them, give them names, and so on. Indeed, if
we could not name them, there would be a sort of epistemological
inconsistency in the position. ("I say we can't talk about X's." "Can't
talk about *what*?") This ability to have *knowledge* of our sense qualities is the epistemological foundation for every other sort of knowledge, in Ayer's view. As he himself puts it in *Philosophy in the Twentieth Century*, "Any check upon the use of language must depend
sooner or later on what I call an act of primary recognition" (p. 151).
But what conception of the mind does Ayer have, when he speaks of
"an act of primary recognition"? Isn't Ayer thinking of the mind as
distinct from its sense qualities, as something with *active powers?*

Perhaps not. In order to test the consistency of this pair of views
(View 1: *the objective content of our causal descriptions is the regularities that those descriptions encapsulate;*[18] View 2: *the mind has
the ability to be aware of and represent its sense qualities*), I should
like to employ a thought experiment (it may resemble the one Wittgenstein employed in the Private Language Argument, but the idea of
"in principle privacy" will play no part). Imagine a situation which is
epistemologically ideal from the point of view of a sense-quality
theorist. John is attending to his sense qualities, and he is describing
them in the vocabulary specified by the epistemologist. Moreover, his
reports are sincere. Suppose the epistemologist instructs him to use
"E" as a name for a particular sense experience (say, a blue star
against a white background), and to say "E" out loud when he has it.
What could it come to to say that John successfully represents the
sense experience in question by the sign "E"?

One wants to say that John doesn't *just* say "E" whenever the sense
experience in question occurs (in this context), but that its being E is

what *causes* him to say it, what "brings it about." But for Ayer, it seems, this can at most mean that other regularities obtain in John's behavior as well (for example, if asked "Why did you say 'E'?" John gives some "appropriate" reply, such as "Because that's what it looked like—a blue star on a white background"). The story in terms of sense qualities and regularities is *complete;* there is no need to supplement it with talk of "bringing about."

Let us grant, for the sake of argument, that it might just be an *ultimate* fact that in certain circumstances people do produce certain representations only when they have certain sense qualities (apart from occasional and inevitable slips). Is this all that Ayer means by saying that they recognize and describe those sense qualities? *Could* this be all it means?

I just mentioned "slips." In fact, slips are inevitable—slips of the mind as well as slips of the tongue—and one isn't always aware that one is making one. Suppose John occasionally, without noticing, says "E" when he is shown a *green* star on a white background. I assume that he is not at all blue-green color-blind, and that when this is pointed out to him (say, we point it out 50 percent of the time, and let his report stand the other 50 percent) he doesn't say, "Well, it looks blue to me," but rather says, "Oh my, I don't know what's the matter with me." In fact, he may even say, "Of course it looked green. I don't know why I said 'E.'"

This possibility—the possibility of error in one's *representation* of the sense experience—shows that one cannot take the hallmark of reference to a sense experience to be perfect correlation between the name and the experience (even under the special circumstances envisaged). But one might, I suppose, say that *nearly perfect correlation* is enough. Is nearly perfect correlation between occurrences of "E" and occurrences of a sense experience good enough to guarantee that the name *refers* to the experience?

It seems that it cannot be. For consider the whole class of cases in which John says "E" and does not subsequently retract his judgment. These may not all be occurrences of one sense experience (there will still be some slips, let us imagine, even though no one noticed them), but they will be cases of one *sense shmexperience;* that is, of a Goodmanesque predicate (apologies to Nelson Goodman!) such as "Is E and occurs at time t_1 or is E' and occurs at time t_2 or . . ."). Now what makes it the case that "E" does not refer to this *sense shmexperience* and not to the sense experience? Well, the epistemologist told John to use "E" as the name of a sense experience. *But what makes it the case that the epistemologist's term "sense experience" stands for sense experiences and not for sense shmexperiences?*

In effect we have gone from a species ("E") to a genus ("sense experience"). But the problem is the same. If the term ("E" or "sense experience") is correlated (very well but not perfectly) with a particular class or a particular class of classes, it is also correlated in the same way with many other slightly different classes. A unique association between a particular representation and a particular universal (first order or higher order) cannot be a matter of mere "very high correlation." The moral is: if all we are given to work with is sense experiences and "regularities," we will never get *reference*.

Perhaps Ayer's picture is different from this, however. Perhaps Ayer's picture is that there is a primitive *relation* R between the mind and the sense quality (*the universal itself,* not the instances). But is this relation itself something *observable?* Obviously it isn't a sense quality! If it is a *capacity,* on the other hand, and we can know without observation that we are exercising a capacity (I observe the sense-quality and I observe myself saying "E" and I know without observation that my saying "E" was an exercise of my capacity to report the sensation), then the argument that capacities (and causal powers in general) are *epistemically inaccessible* collapses. It is not, after all, as if we had any kind of serious scientific account of what the relation R is, or how it can connect us to universals (sense qualities), or how we observe that it *is* connecting us to universals.

Empiricism and Ayer

I hope to have conveyed that I find a great deal of power in the empiricist critique of our modal and causal notions. Not to feel the power of that critique, not to feel disturbed by it, is to miss much of what philosophy is about. Yet ultimately the critique succeeds too well. If we reject everything but sense qualities and regularities[19] as unnecessary metaphysical baggage, then even our ability to refer to sense qualities becomes mysterious; and just *positing* a primitive relation to do the job is no solution. Not *everything* the scrupulous empiricist regards as a human projection can really be so.

Empiricism is a mighty tradition, and Ayer is one of its foremost representatives in our time. To see the depth of the empiricist critique is, I think, to see the limits of our philosophical understanding. In this sense, empiricism performs an immensely valuable service. It is when empiricism turns from critique to construction that we become dissatisfied. Empiricism sees that our scientific picture of the world—the picture of the scientist as discovering what is physically necessary and what is impossible, as discovering the nature of substances and forces and processes—does not really provide the kind of philosophical security that one has wished for—that I myself have often wished for. But that picture, like the commonsense picture of things "bringing about" events, of things having "capacities" and "dispositions," is deeply interwoven with our practice—so deeply interwoven that our very notions of observation and reference rest on this picture. To give up the picture for the alternative picture—the desert landscape of sense qualities and regularities—associated with classical empiricism does not seem a real possibility to me. But I await Ayer's reply!

5. Is the Causal Structure of the Physical Itself Something Physical?

According to David Hume, thinking is just a matter of "association of ideas." According to many contemporary philosophers, understanding our words is a matter of grasping their "conceptual roles in the language."[1] Sometimes the conceptual role of the words in a language is thought of as something associated with the whole language, something not separable from the skills of confirming and disconfirming sentences in a language, deducing consequences from hypotheses stated in the language, and so forth—so that talk of the "conceptual role" of an isolated word or sentence would be, strictly speaking, incorrect—and sometimes it is thought of as something that a single word or single sentence can have.

In either case, insofar as mastering "conceptual roles" is learning what to believe (with what degree of confidence) under various conditions of prior belief and sensory stimulation, these accounts are still associationist. We are represented as probabilistic automata by such accounts—systems having "states" that are connected by various "transition probabilities" to one another and to sensory inputs and motor outputs. (Some authors suggest that we might be systems of probabilistic automata rather than single automata, but this does not affect the point I am making.) If you think of the states of these automata as "mental states" (possibly unconscious ones) and the transition probabilities as the "rules of association," then you will see that this is just a sophisticated and more mathematical version of Hume's "association of ideas." A big change is that it is not only conscious "mental states" that are associated; the connection between two conscious mental states may be mediated by a long string of unconscious associations of more than one kind. Another big change is that an "idea," in the sense of a concept, is identified with a program or program-feature rather than a single mental entity. Still, our theory of understanding, to the extent that one has been suggested, is a direct successor to Hume's.

Hume's account of causation, on the other hand, is anathema to most present-day philosophers. Nothing could be more contrary to the spirit of recent philosophical writing than the idea that there is nothing more to causality than regularity or the idea that, if there is something more, then that something more is largely subjective. One recent writer even speaks of his doctrine as belief in "non-Humean causation."[2]

I want to suggest that there is a certain absurdity in trying to hold on to an associationist account of understanding while believing in "non-Humean causation." Hume's problems with causation *ought to be* problems for contemporary philosophers, if they thought through their own doctrines.

To explain what I mean, I must first set aside the anachronistic suggestion that Hume thought one can define "A causes B" as "if A, then immediately afterwards B," or something of that kind. Hume was not a twentieth-century linguistic philosopher trying to translate sentences in ordinary language into an "ideal language," or a "conceptual analyst" in the style of Moore and Broad. What Hume held was that the circumstances under which we think or say that A causes B are characterized by certain objective properties (regular succession and the possibility of filling in intermediate causal links so that the causal action is via contiguity in space and time). He did not claim that we think or say "A causes B" *whenever* these properties are present. But he seems to have thought that what makes us regard some regularities (in which the contiguity conditions are satisfied) as noncausal or coincidental and others as causal is largely subjective: a matter of human psychology, not of something that is present in Nature in the latter class of cases and absent in the former. His important thesis was negative, not positive. He did not say that we can define "causes" in noncausal terms, much less attempt actually to do it, but he maintained that the idea that in some cases the cause does not merely precede the effect but actually (in some "thick" sense) necessitates the effect is totally unintelligible. (He explained the almost irresistible temptation to think something like this in terms of a theory of projection—we project our feeling of necessitation, which is itself an epiphenomenon of the habit of expectation we have built up, in Hume's view, onto the external phenomena.)

What I want to say is that once one has "bought" an associationist account of understanding, then the *other* famous Humean doctrines—the "idealist" doctrines as well as the "skeptical" doctrine about causality—are almost forced upon one.

To see why this is so, let us recall the antirealist arguments that I employed in *Reason, Truth, and History*—the model theoretic arguments about realism, in particular.[3] I showed that an ideal set of operational and theoretical constraints on sentence acceptance at most fixes the truth-value of whole sentences. If one is inclined to think that "survival value" somehow determines what sentences are true under which conditions, which sentences should be believed under which conditions of "sensory stimulation," which "motor responses" one should make when one believes which sentences, then, I argued, even if this is right, such "evolutionary" considerations cannot do better than (suitable) operational and theoretical constraints can do; again, only the truth-value of whole sentences gets fixed (in various actual and possible situations). This leaves the reference of most signs within the sentence underdetermined, in a very radical way. Even a function that specifies the truth-value of "a cat is on a mat" in all possible worlds does not suffice to rule out that "cat" refers to cherries in the actual world (chapter 2).

Robert Shope summed up my argument so well in his review[4] that I take the liberty of quoting him:

> Constraints, e.g., that "cat" be applicable to an object upon inspection, or, e.g., that our employing "cat" be linked to a causal chain of the appropriate type, will fail to provide a general account of reference. For invoking such constraints still fails to explain how the word "inspection" or the words describing that particular type of causal chain get their reference. This is because the set-theoretical technique [the one I employ in chapter 2] shows that the string of signs saying that the constraint is met . . . would remain true if the word 'inspection' had a different interpretation. So assumption of a metaphysical realist perspective leaves us in an epistemological impasse. It allows us no way of telling, on the basis of what is going on within our minds, whether the occurrence of the thought that the constraint is being conformed to indicates the *right* actual relation, R, holds between the word "inspection" in our thought and the world.

The standard "realist" response to this sort of argument is to say that all my argument shows is that what is "going on within our minds" does not fix the "right" reference relation, R. ("*You* know which one that is," says the metaphysical realist, in effect.) There are constraints built into physical reality (that is, into the external world) that single out the "right" reference relation. (David Lewis even uses the phrase "natural constraint" in this sense—to mean *not* a constraint that, when described by a string of signs, seems natural subjectively, but a constraint that is *imposed*—and, apparently, *interpreted*—by Nature herself.) What is wrong with this response?

What is wrong is that Nature, or "physical reality" in the post-Newtonian understanding of the physical, has no semantic preferences. The idea that some physical parameter, or some relation definable in terms of the fundamental parameters of physics, simply cries out for the role of mapping our signs onto things has no content at all. Consider, for example, the way in which Lewis himself suggests that Nature might interpret our signs for us. The "natural constraint" that (together with other constraints imposed by *us*) fixes the reference of our words is that certain words—the natural kind terms—should *refer to "elite" classes*.[5] What is "eliteness"? Lewis does not say. He just postulates that there must be a special family of sets, the "elite" sets, such that physical reality itself insists that (*ceteris paribus*) our natural kind terms have sets in that family as their extensions.

Donald Davidson, on the other hand, has suggested that whereas a set of "true sentences" is somehow fixed, it is not fixed by a relation of reference. Seeking a theory of the mysterious relation R that "hooks language onto the world" is just a mistake, Davidson thinks. Rather, *any* of the "reference-relations" whose existence I proved, any of the relations that maps signs onto things in such a way that the truth conditions come out right (up to logical equivalence)—call these *admissible* relations—is equally kosher.[6] On Lewis's view, there *must be* a singled-out R, otherwise physics itself is impossible. On Davidson's view there is no such relation, nor do we need one. Who is right?

It is easy to show that not only would we have the same experiences *in all possible worlds* on either theory, but that all physical events (events described in terms of the fundamental magnitudes of physics) would be the same. The same physical theory would be true on Davidson's view as on Lewis's. So the question—if it is an intelligible question—which of these two theories is right is certainly not an empirical question.

I myself find both views incoherent. Lewis's view requires us to believe that some sets of things *identify themselves* as "natural kinds"; Davidson's requires us to believe in a world of things in themselves that have no determinate relations to our language.

The way out that most materialists (metaphysical realists of the physicalist persuasion) prefer is to think of *causation* (understood in a "non-Humean" way) as the relation that (somehow) does the "singling out." *Causation*—real necessitation—has so much dignity, as it were, that it seems absurd that the existence of admissible relations that map the two-place predicate "causes" onto relations other than the *real* relation of causation (the one with all that dignity) should have any philosophical significance at all. The world has, as physicalists are fond of saying, a "causal structure," and the reference relation R is singled out from the huge set of admissible relations by that causal structure (somehow).

It is just at this point that three of Hume's concerns—the concern with understanding, the concern with causation, and the "idealism"—become relevant to our present-day discussion.

Let *causation** be the image of the term "causes" under any non-standard reference relation—any admissible relation R^* that is *not* the "right" relation (you know, R). (I am speaking within the metaphysical realist picture, of course—my own view is that the whole picture is a mistake.) Then, if God had picked R^* instead of R to be the "right" relation (or if "physical reality" had), all these physicalists would now be worshiping Causation* instead of Causation.

On the "conceptual role" theory of understanding—the theory that I described as a neoassociationism—there is *no* respect in which Causation* is any less appropriate a referent for the term "causes" than is Causation itself. The *-concepts fit the conceptual role semantics every bit as well as the R-concepts (the ones picked out by the "right" relation).

This is the problem the physicalist faces: his metaphysical realism makes him want to hang onto the image of language as "hooking onto" the world via a "right" relation R. His neoassociationist account of understanding, however, commits him to an account of how we understand *all* of our notions—including the notion of causation itself—which has nothing to do with R. The conceptual role semantics—the schedule of associations—fits cats*, mats*, causation* perfectly, in the sense that our inductive and deductive inferences are valid and invalid exactly as often whether "physical reality" picks R or R^* to put our terms in correspondence with things in the world. An associationist or neoassociationist account of understanding simply turns reference, conceived of as an explanatory relation between what is "going on in our minds," on the one hand, and mind-independent entities, on the other, into a bit of superstition. The materialist ends up looking like a believer in occult phenomena, such as magic, divine intervention, or inexplicable noetic rays running from referents to signs.

What I have just sketched (in modern dress) is how an association-ist theory of understanding naturally leads to skepticism about our ability to refer to a discourse-independent (or mind-independent) external world.

Criticizing this argument, Michael Devitt[7] and (independently) Clark Glymour[8] have suggested that the "right" reference relation is something they refer to as "causal connection." And they reject my charge that they are postulating an obscure or occult kind of "meta-physical glue" binding the term "causal connection" (or the term "ref-erence") to R. "Causal connection" is attached to R by causal con-nection, not by metaphysical glue, they write. But this is, in fact, just to say that R (causal connection) is *self-identifying*. This is to repeat the claim that a relation can at one and the same time be a physical relation and have the dignity (the built-in intentionality, in other words) of choosing its own name. Those who find such a story unin-telligible (as I do) will not be helped by these declarations of faith.[9]

There are, basically, two ways a metaphysician can go at this point. He may try to keep the idea that causation is just a physical relation in the sense of being definable in terms of the fundamental magni-tudes (field tensors, and so on) of physics. In this case he (1) abandons the attempt to explain how one physical relation should have the dig-nity—or intentionality—that enables it to fix reference, when anoth-er—causation*—does not. (Of course, causation* can be defined in terms of the fundamental* magnitudes just as causation can be defined in terms of the fundamental magnitudes, *if* causation *can be* so defined. And the fundamental* magnitudes, by virtue of the logical equivalences between statements about them and statements about the fundamental magnitudes, are represented by the same operators on Hilbert space as the fundamental magnitudes; it makes no differ-ence to *physics* whether we describe the world in terms of the fun-damental magnitudes or the fundamental* magnitudes.) (2) He takes on the task of carrying out a formidable reduction program.

The other way he can go is to say that causation is not definable in terms of the fundamental parameters of physics and to say that it has a special intentionality. (Perhaps this is what its "non-Humean" char-acter consists in. If A causes B then A *explains* B; and explanation is connected with reason itself.) This, as I understand him, is Richard Boyd's approach. Boyd would defend including such a mysterious relation as "non-Humean causation" in a materialist ontology by arguing that science itself needs to postulate such a relation.

As far as fundamental physics is concerned, I have already indicated why I think that such views are wrong. Quantum mechanics has no realist interpretation at all, which is why it is an embarrassment to materialists (generally they write as if quantum mechanics did not exist). But if we make quantum mechanics look classical by leaving out the observer and the observer's side of the cut between system and observer, or if we confine attention to pre–quantum mechanical physics, then the world looks like this: there is a closed system (in classical physics this could be the whole physical universe) that has a maximal state at each time (along each time-like hyperplane). There is a well-defined mathematical function that determines the state at all earlier and later times (depending on the characteristics of the system). The equations of motion (for example, the Dirac equation) enable one to determine this function. If one says, "The states do not merely succeed one another in the way the theory says; each state *necessitates* the succeeding states," then one is not reporting the content of classical physics, but reading in a metaphysical interpretation that physicists have long rejected as unnecessary. Even the time-directedness of causal processes disappears in fundamental physics.

When we come to sciences less fundamental than fundamental particle physics, say sociology or history, or even to evolutionary biology, or even to chemistry or solid-state physics, then, of course, we find that causation-as-bringing-about is invoked constantly, in the guise of disposition talk ("the gazelle's speed *enables* it to outrun the lion most of the time"), in the guise of counterfactuals ("the salt would have dissolved if the solution had not been saturated"), and in the guise of "causes"-statements ("the extreme cold caused the material to become brittle"). Even in fundamental particle physics such talk becomes indispensable when we *apply* the physics to actual systems that are (of course) *not* the whole universe-regarded-as-a-closed-system. But the *ontology*—the *Weltbild*—of materialist metaphysics is, remember, the ontology of the universe-as-a-closed-system-from-a-God's-eye-view; and it is precisely *this* ontology and this *Weltbild* that has no room for "non-Humean causation."

One way of reconciling the indispensability of causation-as-bringing-about in daily life and in applied science with the fact that *no* mysterious relation of "non-Humean causation" figures in the world picture of fundamental physics at all was suggested by Mill (and revived by John Mackie).[10] Fundamental physics implicitly defines a notion Mill called "the total cause" (at a given time). In post-Einsteinian physics, we might define the total cause at time t_0 of an event A (at a time subsequent to t_0) to be the entire three-dimensional space-time region that constitutes the bottom of A's light cone at the time t_0. Any aspect of this region that is sufficient to produce A (at the appropriate time t_1) by virtue of the Dirac equation (or the appropriate equation of motion) may also be called a "total cause" of A.

When we say that the extreme cold (at t_0) caused the material to be brittle (at t_1), then we do not mean that this was the total cause of the material's becoming brittle (even given the cold at t_0, the material would not have become brittle if a heater had been present and preset to turn on immediately after t_0, for example). What we do, according to Mill and Mackie, is *pick out* a part of the total cause that we regard as important because of its predictive and explanatory utility. If we discover that the cold was correlated with something that by itself provides an explanation of the material's becoming brittle, and the material will become brittle even in the absence of the cold if this correlated factor is still present, then we will change our inference-licensing practice and we will also select a different part of the total cause to call "the cause." Which is "the cause" and which a "background condition" depends on a *picking out*, an act of *selection*, which depends on what we know and can use in prediction; and this is not written into the physical system itself.

If we postulate a "non-Humean causation" in the physical world, then we are treating causation-as-bringing-about as something built into the physical universe itself: we are saying that the physical universe distinguishes between "bringers-about" and "background conditions." This seems incredible; after all, if heaters were normally set to turn on when a place got cold, then we might very well choose to say that the cause of the material's becoming brittle was that the heater malfunctioned and allowed the place to get cold (which is quite different from saying that the extreme cold at t_0—prior to when the heater would have turned on—is the cause). Like counterfactuals, causal statements depend on what we regard as a "normal" state of affairs, what we regard as a state of affairs "similar" to the actual, and so on. For example, when a heater is present, then we regard it as "normal" that it should turn on at the preset time, and this is a reason for singling out the "exceptional" part of the total situation—the heater's failing to turn on—as a "cause" and not as a "background condition." On the other hand, every concrete situation has infinitely many exceptional or improbable features, and we do *not* single out most of these, nor do we accept counterfactuals to the effect that had *they* been different, then the material would not have become brittle. Rejecting these counterfactuals, in turn, involves considering certain nonactual "possible worlds" as sufficiently "similar" (or better, sufficiently cotenable, in Goodman's sense)[11] with the actual world (in the light of which contrary-to-fact-supposition is being thought about) to serve as counterexamples to counterfactuals. Is all *this* supposed to be "built into physical reality"?

The view of those who answer "yes" seems to be a desperate attempt to combine a medieval notion of causation (a notion according to which what is normal, what is an explanation, what is a bringer-about, is all in the essence of things in themselves and not at all contributed by our knowledge and interests) with modern materialism. On the other hand, the view of those who answer "no" (and give the sort of reasons Mill and Mackie give) creates a new kind of dualistic cut between what is "really there" (the physical system with its "states" and the law determining how they succeed one another in time) and the referring, knowing, interested mind that picks out some aspect of what is really there as "the cause" when it finds it can use that aspect in predictions that are important for it, issues "inference licenses," considers nonactual situations as "similar to the actual" (or as similar as can be expected, given that the antecedent of a counterfactual is supposed to be true in them), and thus determines an *epistemic* distinction between a "cause" and a "background condition." How does this mind get to be able to *refer* to the mind-independent world? Answer "via the relation of causal connection," and you have slipped back to treating causation as something "out there" and not simply "epistemic."

Notice that Hume's project was to distinguish between what "really exists," in the metaphysician's sense (or what "really exists" *as far as we can know*) and what we "project." Notice further that both Mackie and Boyd *accept* Hume's project. Boyd says, in effect, "Causation really exists—none of it, not one bit, is a projection," and Mackie says, "Much of it is projection."

The reason I do not regard either the "yes" answer or the "no" answer to the question "Is causation-as-explanation built into physical reality?" as acceptable is that I find the whole notion of being "built into physical reality" or of "really existing" in the metaphysician's sense without content.

A first stab at another way of looking at the whole question might come from recalling that whether causation "really exists" or not, it certainly exists in our "life world." What makes it "real" in a *phenomenological* sense is the possibility of asking, "Is that really the cause?"—that is, of *checking* causal statements, of bringing new data and new theories to bear on them. If we say this, while leaving aside the problematic idea of "really existing," then we have a picture not too different from Wittgenstein's or Austin's, or, for that matter, Husserl's. The world of "ordinary language" (the world in which we actually live) is full of causes and effects. It is only when we insist that the world of ordinary language (or the *Lebenswelt*) is defective (an ontological "jungle," vague, gappy, and so on) and look for a "true world" (free of vagueness, of gaps, of any element that can be regarded as a "human projection") that we end up feeling forced to choose between the picture of "a physical universe with a built-in structure" and "a physical universe with a structure imposed by the mind," not to mention such pictures as a physical-universe-plus-a-mysterious-relation-of-"correspondence," or a physical-universe-plus-mysterious-"essences"; to choose, that is, between pictures that are at once terribly alluring and perfectly contentless.

To recapitulate: I have argued that materialism, which conceives of persons as automata, inherits Hume's problems. A neoassociationist theory of understanding (the probabilistic automaton model) renders it unintelligible that anything in the mind/brain can bear a *unique* correspondence to anything outside the mind/brain. (Of course, everything corresponds in *some way or other* to everything else; the problem is how any *one* correspondence can be singled out as "the" relation between signs and their referents.) In this sense, Hume's difficulties with objective reference to an external world are difficulties for the materialist too.

Moreover, if the physical universe itself is an automaton (something with "states" that succeed one another according to a fixed equation), then it is unintelligible how any particular *structure* can be singled out as "the" causal structure of the universe. Of course, the universe fulfills structural descriptions—in *some way or other* it fulfills every structural description that does not call for too high a cardinality on the part of the system being modeled; once again, the problem is how any *one* structure can be singled out as "the" structure of the system.

If we say that the structure of the physical universe is singled out by the *mind,* then we either put the mind outside the universe (which is to abandon materialism) or else we are thrown back to the first problem: the problem of how the signs employed by the mind can have a determinate "correspondence" to parts and aspects of the universe. If we say that the causal structure of the physical universe is "built into" the physical universe, then we abandon materialism without admitting that we are abandoning it; for all we do in this case is to project into physical systems properties (for example, being a "background condition," being a cause, being cotenable with the antecedent of a counterfactual) that cannot be properties of matter "in itself." In this sense, Hume's difficulties with objective necessitation are difficulties for the materialist too.

There are those who would say, "So much the worse for materialism," while keeping Hume's project (of dividing reality into what is "really there" and what is a human projection). But attempts to build a metaphysical system that is not materialist always appear as mere cultural curiosities. We cannot really go back to the Middle Ages or to Plato's time. If science does not tell us what is "really there" in the metaphysical sense, then neither does anything else. What has collapsed is the attempt to divide mundane reality, the reality of the *Lebenswelt,* into Real Reality and Projection.

II

Up to now I have looked mainly at efforts by philosophers who are both physicalists and metaphysical realists (call them "materialists"). Now, I wish to begin by looking at some very influential writings by a philosopher who is a physicalist but *not* a realist—W. V. Quine. Quine regards the counterfactual idiom as hopelessly subjective and (for this reason) to be shunned in scientific work. On the other hand, he has no objection to individual disposition predicates, for example, *soluble,* and employs them freely in his own philosophy of language. How does he reconcile these views?

Quine employs two ideas: one well understood but of limited applicability, and the other very ill understood, even by Quine's many admirers. The first is the idea of a *natural kind.*[12] A natural kind is, for example, the class of things with a given microstructure, for example, the soluble things. (Quine assumes that there is what he calls a "chemical formula" for solubility.) Quine's basic claim is that we can identify the dispositional property (solubility) with the corresponding microstructure.

One reason this idea is of limited applicability is that many dispositions cut across natural kinds. Being *poisonous,* for example, cannot be identified with the possession of any one microstructure (membership in any one natural kind) because there is no such one microstructure (no such one natural kind). (The stimulus meanings of sentences are dispositions, in Quine's view[13]—the most important dispositions there are, for Quine's philosophy of language—and Quine himself points out that there is no *one* microstructure that is common to all human brains with a given speech-disposition.)

This is not the feature of Quine's account that I wish to concentrate on, however. The second idea that Quine uses needs a little explaining. This is the idea that truth and reference are "disquotational." A dispositional predicate—say "soluble"—can stand for a nondispositional microstructural property, in Quine's view, *even if we cannot say which one.* Our question is, how does this come about?

The problem that Quine might seem to face is the following. If what associates a particular microstructure M with the predicate "is soluble" is the fact that M *explains* the event of this substance dissolving when it is put in water, the event of this other substance dissolving when it is put in water, and so on, then we need a notion like "explanation" to describe the association in question. But Quine does not regard explanation as a precise notion (he has balked in print at talk of "laws," for example, and he detests counterfactuals), and he certainly would not admit "explains" as a primitive notion in his ideal language (the "first-class conceptual system").

Of course, there are other possibilities one might try. One might say that what associates the microstructure M with the predicate is the fact that *scientists* have identified the microstructure in question with solubility, or will in the future. But what if we are dealing with a disposition whose microstructural basis scientists will never discover? The human race may become extinct in the next hundred years; but Quine would still let us talk of "the stimulus meaning of 'Lo, a rabbit,'" and would say that this stimulus meaning was a dispositional predicate that applied to a class of organisms—the class of all organisms in a certain *disjunction* of microstates—even though it is virtually certain that we could not discover the description of that disjunction in a hundred years (or ever). One might talk about what scientists would discover if investigation continued indefinitely, but this would be to employ a counterfactual (with a very vague and problematic antecedent, to boot). What is often missed by readers of

Quine is that this is no problem at all for him, given his view of language (but for reasons that are unacceptable to realists).

We have been speaking as if reference were a relation between things in a mind-independent world and bits of language. But this is a picture that Quine rejects. For Quine, truth is "immanent truth"— that is, to say *"Snow is white" is true* is to reaffirm "Snow is white" and not to ascribe a mysterious property called "truth" to "Snow is white." Similarly, we might say that for Quine reference is "immanent reference"—to say *"Cat" refers to cats* is to say only that cats are cats,[14] and not to say that a mysterious relation called "reference" obtains between the word "cat" and cats. Any definition of reference that yields the truisms " 'Cat' refers to cats," " 'Electron' refers to electrons," and so on, will do. We do not have to *first* "put the words in correspondence with objects" and *then* utter these statements to declare which objects our words correspond to; our Skinnerian schedule of conditioning enables us to use the words (which is all understanding them involves, in Quine's view), and the truisms just mentioned give a way of *adding* the word "refers" to our language, which ensures that it will have the property we want—that we can use the word "refers" to give a disquotational definition of truth (for the sublanguage that does not contain "semantic" words).

Now, since the question "How does language hook onto the world?" is a *pseudoquestion* on this view (because languages "hook onto the world" only *relative* to a translation manual into *my* language, and *my* language hooks onto the world "transparently," via the disquotational account of reference and truth), the question that *is* a question for a correspondence theorist—"How do dispositional (or any other) predicates 'hook onto' the right objects and properties?"—is also a pseudoquestion. If my evolving doctrine contains the sentence "Having the same stimulus meaning as 'Lo, a rabbit!' is being in any microstructure in a certain (unspecified) set S," then, according to my evolving doctrine, it is *true* that the predicate "has the same stimulus meaning as 'Lo, a rabbit!' " is true of all and only those things that have a microstructure in some set S of microstructures, whether we shall ever be able to define S or not. The realist objection, "Yes, it is true *according to your doctrine,* but is it really true?" is only intelligible as a request to reexamine my doctrine *scientifically*. As a philosophical request to explain how this *can* be true if no such set S has been (or ever will be) "singled out," it is unintelligible; the doctrine Quine calls "Ontological Relativity" is supposed to show that *that* sort of philosophical request is impossible to meet.

In sum, if the theory that microstructures *are* what dispositions turn out to be is a "good" theory (scientifically speaking), then it becomes true—or as true as anything is, in a Quinian way of thinking—as soon as we adopt it. The work of actually *reducing* dispositions one by one to (disjunctions of) microstructures is unnecessary. We have all the advantages of "theft over honest toil."

The price one pays for Quine's solution to the metaphysical problem is abandoning the idea that truth is a substantial notion, the idea that truth-or-falsity is a genuine parameter with respect to which we appraise one another's utterances and writings. When I say that I am trying to decide whether what you have said or written is true, then, in Quine's view, all I mean is that I am making up my mind whether to "assent." But this is to give up what is right in realism. The deep problem is how to keep the idea that statements are true or false, that language is not mere noise and scribbling and "subvocalization," without being driven to postulate mysterious relations of correspondence. Quine's view is not the cure for metaphysical realism but the opposite pole of the same disease.

III

John Mackie's *The Cement of the Universe* does not pretend to offer definitive solutions to the problem I have discussed, but it does present the different strands of the problem of causation in a remarkably sensitive way. Dealing in chapter 8 with the crucial question, in what sense there is an objective "causal link" to be found in Nature, Mackie suggested that this link consists in certain kinds of qualitative and structural persistence and continuity. An example may help to explain what he had in mind.

Consider simple cases of collision, say a baseball bat striking a baseball. In these cases, something quite specifiable "persists," namely the momentum of the bat. One can treat this momentum as an enduring quantity (a vector quantity: one possessing a direction as well as a magnitude), and its "persistence" is described by the law of the conservation of momentum.

Unfortunately, there does not appear to be any *one* quantity that is conserved in every case of what we describe as causation. To explain how Mackie would probably meet this objection, let us look at a different sort of case. Suppose the valve on a boiler sticks and the boiler explodes. This is not a case of a quantity "persisting" from the sticking to the explosion, nor of something changing continuously from the sticking to the explosion. Indeed, from an "objective" point of view it might well seem that the valve plays no more of a part in the production of the explosion than any piece of the boiler of comparable surface area. Yet we describe the sticking of the valve as the "cause" of the explosion, and not the presence of X, where X is an arbitrary small piece of the boiler.

What Mackie would do in such a case is to distinguish between the "neolithic" (his term) statement that the sticking of the valve caused the boiler to explode, which he regards as having an epistemic element and hence as not "simply true," and the "law of working" that is exemplified in the case described. The law of working would simply be that the increase in the temperature of the steam produces a continuous increase in the pressure of the steam against the boiler until the appropriate coefficient of strength of the material of the boiler is exceeded. (A second law of working would describe the flying apart of the material when this limit is reached.) An ordinary language counterfactual (which is *not* "simply true") tells us that steam would have escaped (bringing down the pressure—and hence exemplifying yet another "law of working") if the valve had not stuck. The "neolithic" statement is epistemic in the way the counterfactual is epistemic, but the success of all this talk that is "neolithic" and "not simply true" is explained by something that is objective and in nature—that is, the continuous changes of temperature and pressure described by the several "laws of working." It is *these* that constitute the "causal link" (which Mackie equates with the "necessitation").

Even if Mackie could specify the different sorts of statements he is prepared to count as "laws of working," and thereby indicate what sorts of "structural and qualitative" persistence and continuity should count as "causal links," very little of what philosophers call "causal connection" turns out to be objective on such a story. "Causal theories" of this and that typically assume that statements to the effect that X brought about Y are "simply true," in Mackie's phrase, and this is just what Mackie is prepared to give up.

Indeed, it is not clear to what philosophical problem Mackie's theory actually speaks. He suggests that he is speaking to Hume's problem, but how? True, temperature and pressure increase continuously when a boiler explodes. But temperature* and pressure* (the images of the terms "temperature" and "pressure" under any admissible nonstandard reference relation) also increase continuously; indeed "the temperature increased" and "the temperature* increased" have the same truth-value not just in the actual world but in all possible worlds. Yet it seems sticky to say that the objectivity of the causal nexus consists in the continuity of the increase of temperature* and in the continuity of the increase of pressure*. In some places Mackie uses frankly epistemic considerations to decide what is and what is not the right sort of persistence: it would be *surprising,* he argues, if a particle that has moved in a straight line ceased to do so in the absence of a force. But this appeal to what we find "surprising" undercuts the whole enterprise of answering Hume.

IV

The idea that we have found the Furniture of the Universe when we get down to such things as the conservation of energy and momentum (and, in classical physics, of matter) represents the idea I have already criticized, the idea that the world picture of fundamental physics is metaphysically "complete." This picture and the dualist picture of the mind "imposing" a structure on the material world, "singling out" conditions as background conditions and events as "bringers about," employing counterfactual conditionals and "neolithic" causal statements as inference licenses, and so forth, are made for each other.

We might be saved from this particular sterile clash of views if we paused to reflect that science itself, and not just "ordinary language," is deeply pluralistic in its ontology. Physics may—sometimes—present the world in the language of functional dependence, but evolutionary biology, for example, explains evolutionary survival in terms of "neolithic" causal and dispositional concepts. Gazelles survived because they could outrun lions and other predators; that is a perfectly good "scientific explanation," and it claims, among other things, that gazelles would not have escaped if they had not run so fast. The causal structure of the world is not physical in the sense of being built into what we conceive of as physical reality. But that doesn't mean that it is pasted onto physical reality by the mind. It means, rather, that "physical reality" *and* "mind" are both abstractions from a world in which things having dispositions, causing one another, having modal properties, are simply matters of course. Like all matters of course, causality can be seen as either the most banal or the most mysterious thing in the world. As is so often the case, each of these ways of seeing it contains a profound insight.

6. Truth and Convention

The "internal realism" I have defended[1] has both a positive and a negative side. Internal realism denies that there is a fact of the matter as to which of the conceptual schemes that serve us so well—the conceptual scheme of commonsense objects, with their vague identity conditions and their dispositional and counterfactual properties, or the scientific-philosophical scheme of fundamental particles and their "aggregations" (that is, their mereological sums)—is "really true." Each of these schemes contains, in its present form, bits that will turn out to be "wrong" in one way or another—bits that are right and wrong *by the standards appropriate to the scheme itself*—but the question "which kind of 'true' is really Truth" is one that internal realism rejects.

A simple example[2] will illustrate what I mean. Consider "a world with three individuals" (Carnap often used examples like this when we were doing inductive logic together in the early 1950s), x_1, x_2, x_3. How many *objects* are there in this world? Well, I *said* "consider a world with just three individuals," didn't I? So mustn't there be three objects? Can there be nonabstract entities which are not "individuals"? One possible answer is "no." We can identify "individual," "object," "particular," and so on, and find no absurdity in a world with just three objects which are independent, unrelated, "logical atoms." But there are perfectly good logical doctrines which lead to different results.

Suppose, for example, like some Polish logicians, I believe that for every two particulars there is an object which is their sum. (This is the basic assumption of "mereology," the calculus of parts and wholes invented by Lesniewski.) If I ignore, for the moment, the so-called "null object," then I will find that the world of "three individuals" (as Carnap might have had it, at least when he was doing inductive logic) actually contains *seven* objects:

World 1

x_1, x_2, x_3

(A world à la Carnap)

World 2

$x_1, x_2, x_3, x_1 + x_2, x_1 + x_3, x_2 + x_3,$
$x_1 + x_2 + x_3$

("Same" world à la Polish logician)

Some logicians (though not Lesniewski) would also say that there is a "null object" which they count as a part of every object. If we accepted this suggestion, and added this individual (call it O), then we would say that Carnap's world contains *eight* objects.

Now, the classic metaphysical realist way of dealing with such problems is well known. It is to say that there is a single world (think of this as a piece of dough) which we can slice into pieces in different ways. But this "cookie cutter" metaphor founders on the question, "What are the 'parts' of this dough?" If the answer is that $x_1, x_2, x_3,$ $x_1 + x_2, x_1 + x_3, x_2 + x_3, x_1 + x_2 + x_3$ are all the different "pieces," then we have not a *neutral* description, but rather a *partisan* description—just the description of the Warsaw logician! And it is no accident that metaphysical realism cannot really recognize the phenomenon of conceptual relativity—for that phenomenon turns on the fact that *the logical primitives themselves, and in particular the notions of object and existence, have a multitude of different uses rather than one absolute "meaning."*

An example which is historically important, if more complex than the one just given, is the ancient dispute about the ontological status of the Euclidean plane. Imagine a Euclidean plane. Think of the points in the plane. Are these *parts* of the plane, as Leibniz thought? Or are they "mere limits," as Kant said?[3] If you say, in *this* case, that these are "two ways of slicing the same dough," then you must admit that what is a *part* of space, in one version of the facts, is an abstract entity (say, a set of convergent spheres—although there is not, of course, a *unique* way of construing points as limits) in the other version. But then you will have conceded that which entities are "abstract entities" and which are "concrete objects," at least, is version-relative. Metaphysical realists to this day continue to argue about whether points (space-time points, nowadays, rather than points in the plane or in three-dimensional space) are individuals or properties, particulars or mere limits, and so forth. My view is that God himself, if he consented to answer the question "Do points really exist or are they mere limits?" would say "I don't know"; not because His omniscience is limited, but because there is a limit to how far questions make sense.

One last point before I leave these examples: *given* a version, the question "How many objects are there?" has an answer, namely "three" in the case of the first version ("Carnap's world") and "seven" in the case of the second version ("the Polish logician's world"). Once we make clear how we are using "object" (or "exist"), the question "How many objects exist?" has an answer that is not at all a matter of "convention." That is why I say that this sort of example does not support cultural relativism. Of course, our concepts are culturally relative; but it does not follow that the truth or falsity of what we say using those concepts is simply "determined" by the culture. But the idea that there is an Archimedean point (or a use of "exist" inherent in the world itself) from which the question "How many objects *really* exist?" makes sense is an illusion.

Nor does it help, in general, to talk about "meanings" or "truth conditions." Consider again the two sentences (I am referring to the same example as before):

(1) There is an object which is partly red and partly black.
(2) There is an object which is red and an object which is black.

Observe that (2) is a sentence which is true in both the Carnapian and the Polish logician's version if, say, x_1 is red and x_2 is black. (1) is a sentence which is true in the Polish logician's version. What is its status in the Carnapian version?

Let me introduce an imaginary philosopher whom I will call "Prof. Antipode." Professor Antipode is violently opposed to Polish mereology. He talks like this: "I know what you're talking about if by an object you mean a car, or a bee, or a human being, or a book, or the Eiffel Tower. I even understand it if you refer to my nose or the hood of my car as 'an object.' But when philosophers say that there is an 'object' consisting of *the Eiffel Tower and my nose,* that's just plain crazy. There simply is no such object. Carnap was talking just fine when he said to you 'consider a world with just three objects'—I ignore Carnap's regrettable tendency to what he called 'tolerance'—and it's crazy to suppose that every finite universe contains all the objects those Poles would invent, or, if you please, 'postulate.' You can't create objects by 'postulation' any more than you can bake a cake by 'postulation.'"

Now, the language Carnap had in mind (we were working together on inductive logic at the time, and most often the languages we considered had only one-place predicates) probably did not contain a two-place predicate for the relation "part of"; but even if it did, we can imagine Professor Antipode denying that there is any object of which x_1 and x_2 are both "parts." "If there were such an object, it would have to be different from both of them," he would say (and here the Polish logician would agree), "and the only object different from both of them in the world you showed us is x_3. But x_3 does not overlap with either x_1 or x_2. Only in the overheated imagination of the Polish logician is there such an additional object as $x_1 + x_2$". If we add "Part Of" to Carnap's little language, so that sentence (1) can be expressed in it, thus:

(3) (Ex) (Ey) (Ez) (y is Part Of x & z is Part Of x & Red(y) & Black (z))

then, true to his anti-Polish form, Professor Antipode will say that this sentence is false. "Whether you say it in plain English or in fancy symbols," he growls, "if you have a world of three nonoverlapping individuals, which is what Carnap described, and each is wholly red or wholly black, which is what Carnap said, then there cannot be such a thing in that world as an 'object which is partly red and partly black.' Talking about the 'mereological sum of x_1 and x_2' makes no more sense than talking about the 'mereological sum of my nose and the Eiffel Tower.'"

Professor Antipode, it will be seen, is a staunch metaphysical realist. He *knows* that only some objects are parts of other objects, and that to say that for *every* pair of objects there is an object of which they both are parts (which is an axiom of mereology) is just "rubbish." (In the world Carnap imagined) (1) is false and (2) is true, and there's the whole story.

Carnap himself would have taken a very different attitude. Carnap was a conceptual relativist (that is, in part, what his famous Principle of Tolerance is all about), and he would have said that we can choose to make (1) false (that is, we can choose to talk the way Professor Antipode talks) *or* we can choose to make (1) true—to talk as the Polish logician talks. There is even—and this is very important—there is even a way in which we can have the best of both worlds. We keep Carnap's version as our official version (our "unabbreviated language"); we refrain from adding Part Of as a new primitive, as we did before, but we introduce Part Of as a *defined* expression (as "abbreviated language," or, as Quine often puts it, as a *façon de parler*). This can be done, not by giving an *explicit* definition of Part Of, but by giving a scheme which translates the Polish logician's language into Carnap's language (and such a scheme can easily be given in a recursive way, in the case of the kind of first-order language with finitely many individuals that Carnap had in mind). Under such a scheme, (1) turns out to say no more and no less than (2).

(To verify this, assuming that "red" and "black" are predicates of Carnap's language, observe that the only way a Polish logician's object—a mereological sum—can be partly red is by containing a red atom, and the only way it can be partly black is by containing a black atom. So if (1) is true in the Polish logician's language, then there is at least one red atom and at least one black atom—which is what (2) says in Carnap's language. Conversely, if there is at least one black atom and at least one red atom, then their mereological sum is an "object" [in the Polish logician's sense] which is partly red and partly black.)

Although the formal possibility of doing this—of "interpreting" the Polish logician's version in Carnap's version—is easy to establish, as a result in mathematical logic, the philosophical significance of this fact, of the interpretability of the second language in the first, is more controversial. An objection—an objection to the idea that this kind of interpretability supports conceptual relativity in any way—might come from a philosopher who pursues what is called "meaning theory." Such a philosopher might ask, "What is the point of treating (1) as an abbreviation of (2) if it doesn't, in fact, have the same *meaning* as (2)?" Meaning theorists who follow Donald Davidson might argue that, although (1) and (2) are "mathematically equivalent" (if, like the Polish logician, and unlike Professor Antipode, we are willing to count the axioms of mereology as having the status of logical or mathematical truths), still, sentence (2) is not a sentence one would ordinarily offer as an explanation of the truth-conditions of sentence (1); or at least, doing so would hardly be in accordance with what is called "translation practice." And a "meaning theory," it is said, must not correlate just *any* extensionally or even mathematically correct truth-conditions with the sentences of the language the theory describes; the sentence used to state a truth-condition for a sentence must be one that might be correlated with that sentence by "translation practice." Whatever one is doing when one invents reductive definitions that enable one to explain away talk about "suspicious" entities as a mere *façon de parler,* it obviously isn't just "radical translation."

One suggestion as to what one *is* doing comes from a classic article by Quine.[4] In "On What There Is" he suggested that the stance to take in a case such as the one I have been describing—in a case in which one language seems more useful than another, because it countenances entities which (although philosophically "suspicious") enable us to say various things in fewer words, and in which the at-first-blush "richer" language is formally interpretable in the at-first-blush "poorer" language—might be to say (this is a stance Professor Antipode might adopt): "Sentence (1), asserting as it does the existence of mereological sums, is literally false. But if one wants to go on talking like the Polish logician while rejecting his undesirable ontological commitments, one can do that. One can responsibly take the view that the Polish logician's story is only a useful make-believe, and yet employ its idioms, on the ground that each of the sentences in that idiom, whatever its 'meaning,' *can* be regarded—by fiat, if you like—as merely a convenient abbreviation of whatever sentence in the 'unabbreviated language' it is correlated with by the interpretation scheme."

To give another example, one long familiar to students of mathematical philosophy, Frege and Russell showed that number theory is interpretable in set theory. This means that, if one wants to avoid ontological commitments to "unreduced numbers" (to numbers as objects over and above sets)—and if one does not mind commitment to *sets!*—one can treat every sentence of number theory, and, indeed, every sentence in the language which uses a number word, as a mere abbreviation for another sentence, one which quantifies over sets, but not over any such entities as "numbers." One need not claim that the sentence of number theory and its translation in set theory have the same "meaning." If they don't, so much the worse for our intuitive notion of a "number"! What this kind of interpretation—call it *reductive interpretation*—provides is evidence against the real existence of the unreduced entities, as anything over and above the entities countenanced by the language to which we are doing the reducing. The moral we should draw from the work of Frege and Russell is not that there is a conceptual *choice* to be made between using a language which countenances only sets and one which countenances set *and* numbers, but that—unless the numbers are in fact identical with the sets with which we identified them—there is no reason to believe in the existence of numbers. Talk of numbers is best treated as a mere *façon de parler*—or so Quine maintains.

It is easy to see why Professor Antipode should like this line. In the case of the two versions we have been discussing, the reductive interpretation is syncategorematic; that is, it interprets sentence (1) (and likewise any other sentence of Carnap's language) as a whole, but does not identify the individual words in (1) with individual words and phrases in (2); nor does it identify "mereological sums" with any objects in the language to which the reducing is being done. (1) as a whole is "translated" by (2) as a whole; but the noun-phrase "object which is partly red and partly black" has no translation by itself. In this case the moral of the translation—the moral if Professor Antipode imitates Quine's rhetoric—is slightly different. We cannot say *either mereological sums are identical with the entities with which we identified them or they don't really exist* (because the "translation," or relative interpretation of the Polish logician's language in Carnap's language, didn't identify "mereological sums" with *anything;* it just showed how to translate sentences about them syncategorematically). The moral is, rather, *mereological sums don't really exist, but it is sometimes useful to talk* as if *they existed.* Of course Professor Antipode would be delighted with *this* moral!

I do not mean to give the impression that the possibility of reducing entities away by a formal translation scheme is always decisive evidence that they don't really exist, according to Quine. Sometimes we have the choice of either doing without one batch of entities, call them the *A* entities, or doing without another batch, call them the *B* entities—the reduction may be possible in either direction. In such a case, Occam's Razor doesn't know whom to shave! Or the reducing language may itself seem suspicious (some people think *sets* are very suspicious entities). But, when the reducing language (the prima facie "poorer" language) is one we are happy with, and the reduction does not go both ways, it is clear that Quine regards this as very strong evidence for denying the real existence of the unreduced entities.

Carnap, on the other hand, rejected the idea that there is "evidence" against the "existence" of numbers (or against the existence of numbers as objects distinct from sets). He would, I am sure, have similarly rejected the idea that there is evidence against the "existence" of mereological sums. I know what he would have said about this question: he would have said that the question is one of a choice of a language. On some days it may be convenient to use what I have been calling "Carnap's language" (although he would not have *objected* to the other language); on the other days it may be convenient to use the Polish logician's language. For some purposes it may be convenient to regard the Polish logician's language of mereological sums as "primitive notation"; in other contexts it may be better to take Carnap's language as the primitive notation and to regard the Polish logician's language as "abbreviations," or defined notation. And I agree with him.

It will be seen that there are a number of different stances one could take on the question of the *relation* between (1) and (2). One could say:

(a) The two sentences are mathematically equivalent.
(b) The two sentences are logically equivalent.
(c) The two sentences are neither logically nor mathematically equivalent.
(d) The first sentence is false and the second true (Professor Antipode's position).
(e) The two sentences are alike in truth-value and meaning.
(f) The two sentences are alike in truth-value and unlike in meaning.
(g) The second sentence can be used as an abbreviation of the first, but this is really just a useful "make believe."

My own position—and my own internal realism—is that there is no fact of the matter as to which of *these* positions is correct. Taking the original dispute up into the "metalevel" and reformulating it as a dispute about the properties—mathematical or logical equivalence, synonymy, or whatever—of linguistic forms doesn't help. None of these notions is well defined enough to be a useful tool in such cases. Suppose, for example, I follow the apparently innocent route pioneered by Donald Davidson, and say that the test for meaning is to see what we get when we construct a theory of the language which is (i) recursively presented (in the style of a Tarskian truth definition), and (ii) in accord with translation practice.[5] Obviously, I shall have to admit that it violates standard translation practice to give (2) as a translation of (1).[6] This settles the truth-value of (e) above; (e) is false, whether the sentences are alike or unlike in truth-value, since they are not the same in meaning.

Suppose we follow Davidson farther, and accept the central Davidsonian tenet that if I regard a sentence in an "alien language" as meaningful (and I claim to know what it means), then I must be able to give (or would be able to give, if I were sufficiently self-conscious about my knowledge) a *truth-condition* for that sentence in my "own" language (one which follows from a "meaning theory" which is in conformity with the "constraints on translation practice"). If my "own" language is Carnap's, and we accept that *no* "truth-condition" for (1) statable in Carnap's language will satisfy the constraints on translation practice any better than (2) did, then the conclusion is forced: the Polish logician's language is *meaningless*. We have arrived at a strong metaphysical result from what looked like a bit of ordinary language philosophizing (aided with a bit of Tarskian semantics) about the notion of "meaning"!

Of course, we might simply adopt the Polish logician's language as our own language to begin with. But what we cannot do, according to Davidson, is regard both choices as genuinely open.

It seems to me that the very assumption that there is such a thing as the radical interpreter's "own" language—*one* language in which he can give the truth-conditions for *every* sentence in *every* language he claims to be able to understand—is what forces the conclusion. As long as one operates with this assumption, conceptual relativism will seem unintelligible (as it does to Davidson).[7] But if one recognizes that the radical interpreter himself may have more than one "home" conceptual scheme, and that "translation practice" may be governed by more than one set of constraints, then one sees that conceptual relativity does not disappear when we inquire into the "meanings" of the various conceptual alternatives: it simply reproduces itself at a metalinguistic level!

7. Why Is a Philosopher?

The great founders of analytic philosophy—Frege, Carnap, Wittgenstein, and Russell—put the question "How does language 'hook on' to the world?" at the very center of philosophy. I have heard at least one French philosopher say that Anglo-Saxon philosophy is "hypnotized" by this question. Recently a distinguished American philosopher[1] who has come under the influence of Derrida has insisted that there is no "world" out there for language to hook on *to;* there are only "texts." Or so he says. Certainly the question "How do texts connect with other texts?" exerts its own fascination over French philosophy, and it might seem to an American philosopher that contemporary French philosophy is "hypnotized" by *this* question.

My aim in recent years has not been to take sides in this debate about which the question should be, for it has come to seem to me that both sides in this quarrel are in the grip of simplistic ideas—ideas which do not work, although this is obscured by the fact that thinkers of genius have been able to erect rich systems of thought, great expressions of the human metaphysical urge, on these shaky foundations. Moreover, it has come to seem to me that these ideas are intimately related, that the great differences in style between French (and more generally continental) philosophy and Anglo-Saxon philosophy conceal deep affinities.

Relativism and Positivism

To engage in a broad but necessary oversimplification, the leading movement in analytic philosophy was logical positivism (not from the beginning of analytic philosophy, but from 1930 to about 1960). This movement was challenged by "realist" tendencies (myself and Kripke), by "historicist" tendencies (Kuhn and Feyerabend), and by

materialist tendencies. I will not take the risk of identifying the leading movement in French philosophy today, but if logical positivist
ideas were for a long time (thirty crucial years) at the center of
"Anglo-Saxon" philosophy, *relativist* ideas were (and perhaps continue to be) at the center of French philosophy. This may seem surprising
because philosophers in all countries regularly remark that positivist
and relativist ideas are self-refuting (and they are right to do so). But
the fact of self-contradiction does not seem to stop or even slow down
an intellectual fashion, partly because it is a fashion, and partly for
the less disreputable reason that people don't want to stop it as long
as interesting work is being produced under its aegis. Nevertheless, in
my recent work[2] I have been trying to stop these fashions because
they begin to threaten the possibility of a philosophical enterprise that
men and women of good sense can take seriously.

Relativists do not, indeed, generally go quite all the way. Paul Feyerabend *is* willing to go all the way, that is, as far as to refuse to admit
any difference between saying "It is raining" and "*I think* it is raining"
(or whatever). For Feyerabend *everything* he thinks and says is merely
an expression of his own subjectivity at the instant. But Michel Foucault claims that he is not a relativist; we simply have to wait for the
future structuralist Copernican Revolution (which we cannot yet predict in any concrete detail) to explain to us how to avoid the whole
problem of realism versus relativism.[3] And Richard Rorty[4] simultaneously denies that there *is* a problem of truth (a problem of "representation") at all and insists that some ideas do, and some do not,
"pay their way."

If there is such a thing as an idea's paying its way, that is, *being
right*, there is, inevitably, the question of the *nature* of this "rightness." What makes speech more than just an expression of our
momentary subjectivity is that it can be appraised for the presence or
absence of this property—call it "truth," or "rightness," or "paying
its way," or what you will. Even if it is a culturally relative property
(and what relativist really thinks that relativism is only *true-for-my-
subculture?*), that does not exempt us from the responsibility of saying *which* property it is. If being true (or "paying one's way" as an
idea) is just being successful by the standards of one's cultural peers,
for example, then the entire past becomes simply a sort of logical
construction out of one's own culture.

It is when one notices this that one also becomes aware how very
positivist the relativist current really is. Nietzsche himself (whose

Genealogy of Morals is the paradigm for much contemporary relativist-cum-poststructuralist writing) is at his most positivist when he writes about the nature of truth and value. It seems to me that what bothers both relativists and positivists about the problem of representation is that representation—that is to say, intentionality—simply does not fit into our reductive post-Darwinian picture of the world. Rather than admit that that picture is only a partial truth, only an abstraction from the whole, both positivists and relativists seek to content themselves with oversimplified, in fact with patently absurd, answers to the problem of intentionality.[5]

Logical Empiricism and the Realist Reaction

In the United States, these relativist and historicist views were virtually ignored until the 1960s. The dominant currents in the forties and fifties were empiricist currents—the pragmatism of John Dewey and (much more) the logical empiricism transported to the United States by Rudolf Carnap, Hans Reichenbach, and others. For these latter philosophers the problem of the nature of truth took a back seat to the problem of the nature of confirmation.

The primary kind of *correctness* and *incorrectness* that a sentence possesses was thought to be the amount of inductive support the sentence receives on the basis of the evidence as the speaker perceives and remembers that evidence. For Quine, who has many affinities to these philosophers, although he must be counted as a postpositivist, *truth* is not a property at all; "to say a sentence is true is merely to reaffirm the sentence." (Quine also says that the only truth he recognizes is "immanent truth"—truth from within the evolving doctrine. Note how very "French" this sounds!) But if truth and falsity are not properties at all—if a sentence is "right" or "wrong" in a *substantive* sense only epistemically (only in the sense of being confirmed or disconfirmed by the present memories and experiences of a speaker)— then how do we escape from solipsism? Why isn't this picture *precisely* the picture of solipsism-of-the-present-instant? (To say that it is only a *methodological* solipsism is hardly a clear answer. It sounds as if saying that there are past times, other speakers, and truths which are not confirmed right now is correct "speaking with the vulgar" but not really the right standpoint thinking as a philosopher.)

Perhaps on account of these questions, by the end of the 1960s I began to revive and elaborate a kind of realism (joined by Saul

Kripke, who I learned in 1972 had been working along similar lines). Our realism was not simply a revival of past ideas, however, because it consisted in large part in an attack on conceptions which had been central to realism from the seventeenth century on.

The Theory of Direct Reference

The seventeenth century thought of concepts as entities immediately available to the mind, on the one hand, and capable of fixing reference to the world, on the other. On this picture, the concept *gold,* for example, is in the mind of any speaker (even if he uses a Greek word, or a Latin word, or a Persian word) who can refer to gold; the "extension," or reference, of the word "gold," or "chrysos," or whatever, is determined by the concept. This picture of language is both individualistic (each speaker has the mechanism of reference of every word he uses in his own head) and aprioristic (there are "analytic truths" about the natural kinds we refer to, and these are "contained in our concepts").

It is not hard to see that this picture does violence to the facts of language use and conceptual thought, however. Few speakers today can be certain that an object is gold without taking the object to a jeweler or other expert. The reference of our words is often determined by other members of the linguistic community to whom we are willing to defer. There is a *linguistic division of labor* which the traditional picture entirely ignores.[6]

Kripke pointed out[7] that this linguistic division of labor (or "communication" of "intentions to refer," in his terminology) extends to the fixing of the reference of proper names. Many people cannot give an identifying description of the prophet Moses, for example. (The description "the Hebrew prophet who was known as 'Moses'" is not even correct; in Hebrew, Moses is called "Mosheh," not Moses.) This does not mean that those people are not *referring* when they speak of "the prophet Moses"; we understand that they are referring to a definite historical figure (assuming Moses actually existed). Experts today can tell us that that figure was called (something like) "Mosheh," but that is not an identifying description of Moses. There might have been Hebrew prophets who have been forgotten who were called "Mosheh," and the actual "Mosheh" might have had an Egyptian name which became corrupted to "Mosheh" centuries later. The "right" Mosheh or Moses is the one at the end of a *chain,* a chain leading backward in time. Or, to put it the right way around, the "right" Moses—the one we are referring to—is the one at the *beginning of a history*, a history which causally underpins our present uses and which is knitted together by the intention of speakers to refer to the person whom previous speakers referred to.

We may use descriptions to indicate to whom or to what we mean a word to refer, but even when those descriptions are correct they do not become *synonymous* with the word. Words acquire a kind of "direct" connection with their referents, not by being attached to them with metaphysical glue but by being used to name them even when we suppose the identifying description may be false, or when we consider hypothetical situations in which it is false. (We have already had an example of this: we can refer to Moses as "Moses" even when we know that this was not the name he actually bore. And I can explain which Richard Nixon I mean by saying "the one who was president of the United States" and then go on to imagine a situation in which "Richard Nixon was never elected president of the United States." I repeat, calling these cases "cases of direct reference" is merely denying that the name—"Moses" or "Richard Nixon"— is synonymous with a description: "the Hebrew prophet named 'Moses'" or "the president of the United States named 'Richard Nixon.'" The mechanisms by which this "direct reference" is established are just the opposite of direct, involving chains of linguistic communication and division of linguistic labor as they do.)

A second way in which the seventeenth-century model of reference as fixed by concepts in individual minds does violence to the facts is, perhaps, more subtle. The reference of our words is determined (in some cases) by the nonhuman environment as well as by other speakers. When I speak of "water" I mean to be speaking of the liquid that falls as rain in *our* environment, the one that fills the lakes and rivers *we* know, and so forth. If somewhere in the universe there is a Twin Earth where everything is much as it is here *except* that the liquid that plays the role of "water" on Twin Earth is not H_2O but XYZ, then that does not falsify *our* statement that "water is H_2O." What we refer to as "water" is whatever liquid is of the composition, and so on, of *our* paradigmatic examples of water. Discovering that composition or the laws of behavior of the substance may lead scientists to say that some liquid which a layman would take to be water is not really water at all (and the layman would defer to this judgment). In this way, the reference of the terms "water," "leopard," "gold," and so forth is partly fixed by the substances and organisms themselves. As the pragmatist Charles Peirce put it long ago, the "meaning" of these terms is open to indefinite future scientific discovery.

Recognizing these two factors—the division of linguistic labor and the contribution of the environment to the fixing of reference—goes a long way toward overcoming the individualistic and aprioristic philosophical Weltanschauung that has long been associated with realism. If what a term refers to depends on other people and on the way the entire society is embedded in its environment, then it is natural to look with skepticism at the claim that armchair "conceptual analysis" can reveal anything of great significance about the nature of things. This kind of "realism" goes with a more fallibilistic spirit in philosophy. However, the traditional problems connected with realism are thereby considerably sharpened.

Brains in a Vat

The new realism gives up the idea that our mental representations have any *intrinsic* connection with the things to which they refer. This can be seen in the example of Twin Earth mentioned earlier: our "representations" of water (prior to learning that *water is H_2O/water is XYZ*) may have been phenomenologically identical with the Twin Earthers' "representations," but according to the "theory of direct reference" we were referring to H_2O (give or take some impurities) all along, and the Twin Earthers were referring to XYZ all along. The difference in the reference was, so to speak, "sleeping" in the substance itself all along, and was awakened by the different scientific discoveries that the two cultures made. There is no magical connection between the phenomenological character of the representation and the set of objects the representation denotes.

Now, imagine a race of people who have been literally created by a mad super-scientist. These people have brains like ours, let us suppose, but not bodies. They have only the illusion of bodies, of an external environment (like ours), and so on; in reality they are brains suspended in a vat of chemicals. Tubes connected to the brains take care of the circulation of blood, and wires connected to the nerve endings produce the illusion of sensory impulses coming to the "eyes" and "ears" and of "bodies" executing the motor commands of these brains. A traditional skeptic would have used this case (which is just the scientific version of Descartes's demon) to show that we may be radically deceived about the existence of an external world at all like the one we think we inhabit. The major premise in this skeptical argument is that the race we just imagined is a race of beings who *are* radically wrong in their beliefs. But are they?

It certainly seems that they are. For example, these people believe: "We are not brains in a vat. The very supposition that we might be is an absurd philosopher's fantasy." And obviously they *are* brains in a vat. So they are wrong. But not so fast!

If the Brain-in-a-Vatists' word *vat* refers to what *we* call "vats" and the Brain-in-a-Vatists' word *in* refers to spatial containment and the Brain-in-a-Vatists' word *brain* refers to what we call "brains," then the sentence "We are brains in a vat" has the same truth-condition for a Brain-in-a-Vatist as it would have for one of us (apart from the difference in the reference of the pronoun *we*). In particular, it is (on this supposition) a true sentence, since the people who think it are, in fact, brains spatially contained in a vat, and its negation, "We are not brains in a vat," is a false sentence. But, if there is no intrinsic connection between the word *vat* and what are called "vats" (any more than there is an intrinsic connection between the word *water* and the particular liquid, H_2O, we call by that name), why should we not say that what the word *vat* refers to in Brain-in-a-Vatish is phenomenological appearances of vats and not "real" vats? (And similarly for *brain* and *in*.) Certainly the *use* of *vat* in Brain-in-a-Vatish is dependent on the presence or absence of phenomenological appearances of vats (or of features in the program of the computer that controls the "vat reality"), and *not* on the presence or absence of real vats. Indeed, if we suppose that there aren't any real vats in the mad scientist's world except the one that the brains are in, then it seems as if there is no connection, causal or otherwise, between actual vats and the use of the word *vat* in Brain-in-a-Vatish (except that the brains wouldn't be able to use the word *vat* if the one real vat broke—but this is a connection between the one real vat and *every* word they use, not a differential connection between real vats and uses of the word *vat*.)

This reflection suggests that when the Brains-in-a-Vat think "we are brains in a vat" the truth-condition for their utterance must be that they are *brains-in-a-vat in the image,* or something of that kind. So this sentence would seem to be *false*, not true, when *they* think it (even though they are brains in a vat from *our* point of view). It would seem that they are *not* deceived—they are not thinking anything radically false. Of course there are truths that they cannot even express; but that is, no doubt, true of every finite being. The very hypothesis of "radical deception" seems to depend on the idea of a predetermined, almost magical, connection between words or thought-signs and external objects that Transcendental Realism depends on.

Indeed, symbolic logic tells us that there are many different "models" for our theories and many different "reference relations" for our languages.[8] This poses an ancient problem: *if there are many different "correspondences" between thought-signs or words and external objects, then how can any one of these be singled out?*

A clever form of this problem (which, of course, goes back to the Middle Ages) is due to Robert Nozick (unpublished communication). Let C_1 and C_2 be two different "correspondences" (reference relations, in the sense of model theory) between our signs and some fixed set of objects. Choose them so that the same sentences come out true no matter whether we interpret our words as "referring" to what they correspond to in the sense of C_1 or as referring to what they correspond to in the sense of C_2. That this can be done—that there are alternative ways of putting our signs in correspondence with things which leave the set of true sentences invariant—was emphasized by Quine in his famous doctrine of Ontological Relativity.[9] Now, imagine that God arranged things so that when a man uses a word he refers to the things which correspond-C_1 to that word (the things which are the "image" of the word under the relation C_1) while when a woman uses a word she refers to the things which correspond-C_2 to that word. Since the truth-conditions for whole sentences are unaffected, no one would ever notice! So how do we know (how can we even give sense to the supposition) that there *is* a determinate correspondence between words and things?

There are many quick answers to this question. Thus, a philosopher is likely to say, "When we come to learn the use of the word *vat* (or whatever), we don't merely associate the word with certain visual sensations, certain tactile sensations, and so forth. We are *caused* to have those sensations, and the beliefs which accompany those sensations, by certain external events. Normally those external events involve the presence of vats. So, indirectly, the word *vat* comes to be associated with vats."

To see why this answer fails to speak to what puzzles us, imagine it being given first by a man and then by a woman. When the woman says this she is pointing out that certain ones of a speaker's beliefs and sensations are in a certain relation—the relation $effect_2$—to certain external events. In fact, they are caused$_2$ by the presence$_2$ of vats$_2$. When a male philosopher says this, he is pointing out that the same beliefs and impressions are caused$_1$ by the presence$_1$ of vats$_1$. Of course, they are both right. The word *vat* is "indirectly associated" with vats$_2$ (in the way pointed out by the woman) and also "indirectly associated" with vats$_1$ (in the way pointed out by the man). We still have not been given any reason to believe in the One metaphysically singled out correspondence between words and things.

Sometimes I am accused (especially by members of the materialist current in analytic philosophy) of caricaturing the realist position. A realist, I am told, does not claim that reference is fixed by the connection in our theory between the *terms* "reference," "causation," "sensation," and so on; the realist claims that reference is "fixed by causation itself." Here the philosopher is ignoring his own epistemological position. He is philosophizing as if naive realism were true for him, or, equivalently, as if he and he alone were in an *absolute* relation to the world. What *he* calls "causation" really is causation, and *of course* there is somehow a singled-out correspondence between the word and one definite relation in his case. But how this can be so is just the question at issue.

Internal Realism

Must we then fall back into the view that "there is only the text"? That there is only "immanent truth" (truth *according to* the "text")? Or, as the same idea is put by many analytic philosophers, that "is true" is only an expression we use to "raise the level of language"? Although Quine, in particular, seems tempted by this view (supplemented by the idea that a pure cause-effect story is a complete scientific and philosophical description of the use of a language), the problem with such a view is obvious. If the cause-effect description is complete, if all there is to say about the "text" is that it consists in the production of noises (and subvocalizations) according to a certain causal pattern; if the causal story is not to be and need not be supplemented by a normative story; if there is no substantive property of either warrant or truth connected with assertion—then there is no way in which the noises that we utter or the inscriptions we write down or the subvocalizations that occur in our bodies are more than expressions of our subjectivity. As Edward Lee put it in a fine paper on Protagoras and Plato,[10] a human being resembles an animal producing various cries in response to various natural contingencies, on such a view, or better, a plant putting forth now a leaf and now a flower. Such a story leaves out that we are *thinkers*. If such a story is right, then not only is representation a myth; the very idea of thinking is a myth.

In response to this predicament, the predicament of being asked to choose between a *metaphysical* position on the one hand and a group of *reductionist* positions on the other, I was led to follow Kant in distinguishing between two sorts of realism (whether Saul Kripke, whose work I alluded to earlier, would follow me in *this* move I rather doubt). The two sorts I called "metaphysical realism" and "internal realism."[11] The metaphysical realist insists that a mysterious relation of "correspondence" is what makes reference and truth possible; the internal realist, by contrast, is willing to think of reference as internal to "texts" (or theories), *provided* we recognize that there are better and worse "texts." "Better" and "worse" may themselves depend on our historical situation and our purposes; there is no notion of a God's-Eye View of Truth here. But the notion of a right (or at least a "better") answer to a question is subject to two constraints: (1) *Rightness is not subjective*. What is better and what is worse to say about most questions of real human concern is not just a matter of *opinion*. Recognizing that this is so is the essential price of admission to the community of sanity. If this has become obscured, it is in part because the tides of philosophical theory have swept so high around the words *subjective* and *objective*. For example, both Carnap and Husserl have claimed that what is "objective" is the same as what is "intersubjective," that is, in principle public. Yet this principle itself is (to put it mildly) incapable of "intersubjective" demonstration. That anyone interested in philosophy, politics, literature, or the arts should really equate being the better opinion with being the "intersubjective" truth is really quite amazing! (2) *Rightness goes beyond justification*. Although Michael Dummett[12] has been extremely influential in advocating the sort of non–metaphysical-realist and non-subjectivist view of truth that I have been putting forward, his formula that "truth is justification" is misleading in a number of ways, which is why I have avoided it in my own writings. For one thing, it suggests something which Dummett indeed believes and I do not: that one can *specify* in an effective way what the justification conditions for the sentences of a natural language are. Second, it suggests something on which Dummett's writing is rather ambiguous: that there is such a thing as *conclusive* justification, even in the case of empirical sentences. My own view is that truth is to be identified with idealized justification, rather than with justification-on-present-evidence. "Truth" in this sense is as context-sensitive as *we* are. The assertibility conditions for an arbitrary sentence are not surveyable.

If assertibility conditions are not surveyable, how do we learn them? We learn them by acquiring a practice. What philosophers in the grip of reductionist pictures miss is that what we acquire is not a knowledge that can be applied as if it were an algorithm. The impossibility of formalizing the assertibility conditions for arbitrary sentences is just the impossibility of formalizing human rationality itself.

The Fact-Value Dichotomy

If I dared to be a metaphysician, I think I would create a system in which there were nothing but obligations. What would be metaphysically ultimate, in the picture I would create, would be what we *ought* to do (ought to say, ought to think). In my fantasy of myself as a metaphysical super-hero, all "facts" would dissolve into "values." That there is a chair in this room would be analyzed (metaphysically, not conceptually—there is no "language analysis" in this fantasy) into a set of obligations: the obligation to think that there is a chair in this room if epistemic conditions are (were) "good" enough, for example. (In Chomskian language, one might speak of "competence" instead of "obligation": there is the fact that an ideally "competent" speaker would say (think) *there is a chair in this room* if conditions were sufficiently "ideal.") Instead of saying with Mill that the chair is a "permanent possibility of sensations," I would say that it is a *permanent possibility of obligations*. I would even go so far as to say that my "sense-data," so beloved of generations of empiricists, are nothing but permanent possibilities of obligations, in the same sense.

I am not, alas! so daring as this. But the reverse tendency—the tendency to eliminate or reduce everything to description—seems to me simply perverse. What I do think, even outside of my fantasies, is that fact and obligations are thoroughly interdependent; there are no facts without obligations, just as there are no obligations without facts.

This is, in a way, built into the picture of truth as (idealized) justification. To say that a belief is justified is to say that it is what we ought to believe; justification is a normative notion on the face of it.

Positivists attempted to sidestep this issue by saying that which definition of justification (which definition of "degree of confirmation") one accepts is conventional, or a matter of utility, or, as a last resort, simply a matter of accepting a "proposal." But proposals presuppose ends or values; and it is essential doctrine for positivism that the goodness or badness of ultimate ends and values is entirely subjective. Since there are no universally agreed upon ends or values with respect to which positivist "proposals" are *best,* it follows from the doctrine that the doctrine itself is merely the expression of a subjective preference for certain language forms (scientific ones) or certain goals (prediction). We have the strange result that a completely consistent positivist must end up as a total relativist. He can avoid inconsistency (in a narrow deductive sense), but at the cost of admitting that all philosophical propositions, including his own, have no rational status. He has no answer to the philosopher who says, "I know how you feel, but, you know, positivism isn't *rational in my system."*

Metaphysical realists attempted to deal with the same issue by positing a total logical cleavage between the question of what is *true* and the question of what is *reasonable to believe.* But what is *true* depends on what our terms *refer to,* and—on any picture—determining the reference of terms demands sensitivity to the referential intentions of actual speakers and an ability to make nuanced decisions as to the best reconstruction of those intentions. For example, as noted in Chapter 2, we say that the term "phlogiston" did not refer to anything. In particular, it did not refer to valence electrons, although a famous scientist (Cyril Stanley Smith) once joked that "there really is such a thing as phlogiston; it turns out that phlogiston is valence electrons." We regard it as reasonable of Bohr to keep the same word, "electron" *(Elektron),* in 1900 and in 1934, and thereby to treat his two very different theories, his theory of 1900 and his theory of 1934, as theories which described the same objects and unreasonable to say that "phlogiston" referred to valence electrons.

Of course, a metaphysical realist might be a realist about reasonableness *as well as* a realist about truth. But that is, in a way, my point: neither a positivist nor a metaphysical realist can avoid absurdities if he attempts to deny any objectivity whatever to the question of what constitutes *reasonableness.* And *that* question, metaphysically speaking, is a typical *value* question.

The argument I have just briefly sketched (it is developed at length in my book *Reason, Truth, and History*) has been called a "companions in the guilt" argument. The structure is: "You say [imagine this addressed to a philosopher who believes in a sharp fact-value dichotomy] that value judgments have no objective truth-value, that they are pure expressions of preference. But the reasons that you give—that there are disagreements between cultures (and within one culture) over what is and is not valuable; that these controversies cannot be settled "intersubjectively"; that our conceptions of value are historically conditioned; that there is no "scientific" (reductive) account of what value *is*—all apply immediately, and without the slightest change, to judgments of justification, warrant, reasonableness—to epistemic values generally. So, if you are right, judgments of epistemic justification (warrant) are also entirely subjective. But judgments of coreferentiality, and hence of reference and truth, depend on judgments of reasonableness. So instead of giving us a fact-value *dichotomy*, you have given us a reason for abandoning epistemic concepts, semantic concepts, indeed, abandoning the notion of a *fact* altogether." Put more simply, the point is that no conclusion should be drawn from the fact that we cannot give a "scientific" explanation of the possibility of values until we have been shown that a "scientific" explanation of the possibility of reference, truth, warrant, and so on, is possible. And the difficulties with the correspondence theory suggest that to ask for this latter is to ask for a we-know-not-what.

Why Am I Not a Relativist?

My failure to give any metaphysical story at all, or to explain even the possibility of reference, truth, warrant, value, and the rest, often evokes the question: "But then, why aren't you a relativist too?" I can sympathize with the question (and even with the querulousness which often accompanies it) because I can sympathize with the urge to *know*, to *have* a totalistic explanation which includes the thinker in the act of discovering the totalistic explanation in the totality of what it explains. I am not saying that this urge is "optional," or that it is the product of events in the sixteenth century, or that it rests on a false presupposition because there aren't really such things as truth, warrant, or value. But I am saying that the project of providing such an explanation has failed.

It has failed not because it was an illegitimate urge—what human pressure could be more worthy of respect than the pressure to *know?*—but because it goes beyond the bounds of any notion of explanation that we have. Saying this is, perhaps, not putting the grand projects of Metaphysics and Epistemology away for good—what another millennium, or another turn in human history as profound as the Renaissance, may bring forth is not for us today to guess—but it is saying that the time has come for a moratorium on Ontology and a moratorium on Epistemology. Or rather, the time has come for a moratorium on the kind of ontological speculation that seeks to describe the Furniture of the Universe and to tell us what is Really There and what is Only a Human Projection, and for a moratorium on the kind of epistemological speculation that seeks to tell us the One Method by which all our beliefs can be appraised.

Saying "a moratorium on those projects" is, in fact, the opposite of relativism. Rather than looking with suspicion on the claim that some value judgments are reasonable and some are unreasonable, or some views are true and some false, or some words refer and some do not, I am concerned with bringing us back to precisely these claims, which we do, after all, constantly make in our daily lives. Accepting the "manifest image," the *Lebenswelt,* the world as we actually experience it, demands of us who have (for better or for worse) been philosophically trained that we both regain our sense of mystery (for it *is* mysterious that something can both be *in* the world and *about* the world) and our sense of the common (for that some ideas are "unreasonable" is, after all, a *common* fact—it is only the weird notions of "objectivity" and "subjectivity" that we have acquired from Ontology and Epistemology that make us unfit to dwell in the common).

Am I then leaving anything at all for philosophers to do? Yes and no. The very idea that a poet could tell poets who come after him "what to do" or a novelist could tell novelists who come after him "what to do" would and should seem absurd. Yet we still expect philosophers not only to achieve what they can achieve, to have insights and to construct distinctions and follow out arguments and all the rest, but to tell philosophers who come after them "what to do." I propose that each philosopher *ought* to leave it more problematic what is left for philosophy to do. If I agree with Derrida on anything it is on this: that philosophy is writing, and that it must learn now to be a writing whose authority is always to be won anew, not inherited or awarded because it is philosophy. Philosophy is, after all, one of the humanities and not a science. But that does not exclude anything—not symbolic logic, or equations, or arguments, or essays. We philosophers inherit a field, not authority, and that is enough. It is, after all, a field which fascinates a great many people. If we have not entirely destroyed that fascination by our rigidities or by our posturings, that is something for which we should be truly grateful.

8. The Craving for Objectivity

Count Alfred Korzybski used to claim that to say of anything that it is anything—for example, to say of my car that it is an automobile—is to *falsify*, since (to stick to the example of my car) there are many automobiles and my car is not identical with all of them, nor is it identical with the Platonic Idea of an automobile. As part of the pseudoscience that he created, the pseudoscience of "General Semantics," he recommended that one should use the word *et cetera* as often as possible. In his view, it would be highly therapeutic to say, "That is an automobile, *etc.*," and not, "That is an automobile," in order to keep in mind that the "that" referred to (my car) has infinitely many properties besides those mentioned in my statement.

That everything we say is false because everything we say falls short of being everything that could be said is an adolescent sort of error; it is the burden of this essay to suggest that this adolescent error haunts the entire subject of interpretation.

It must be conceded that the error has deep roots. Talk of "otherness," "exotopy," and "incommensurability" would not be as widespread as it is if the ideas of perfect knowledge, of falling short of perfect knowledge, and of the falsity of everything short of perfect knowledge did not speak to us. What those roots are is a matter for speculation. Certainly there is the desire for what psychoanalysts call "fusional" relationships. It is commonplace to say that the tragedy of life is that we are "alone," that such relationships are impossible; but perhaps as one grows older one comes to feel that separateness is a blessing as well as a curse. I really don't know what I'd *do* with a "fusional" relationship. Second, there is the epistemological worry which Stanley Cavell has brilliantly described in a recent book,[1] the worry that one may simply not be getting the other right, that one may be deceived by a facade or be misreading all the clues. As Cavell points out, the classic epistemological problem, whether one can know what goes on inside another mind, can be a very real existential problem. And even if one makes the leap of trust and manages to understand another person more than superficially, and the further leap which allows one to trust one's perception that one *is* understanding the other more than superficially, one knows that what one understands is only a part of something infinitely complex. Human nature (whether in the individual case or in the abstract) is simply not *surveyable*. Yet to conclude that if one does not know, acknowledge, share everything there is to know, acknowledge, share about another, then one cannot truly interpret what the other says, is just to repeat Korzybski's mistake in a different form.

"Enough is enough, enough isn't everything," John Austin wrote, and that applies to interpretation as much as to justification. There is an ultimate separateness that really exists. To identify *that* with a situation that crops up in interpretation (incommensurability) or with a trope that crops up in literature (exotopy) is to confuse background for foreground. Enough is enough, enough isn't everything.

But there are other routes to the notion of incommensurability than the Romantic ones. A somewhat oversophisticated route to the same erroneous conclusion is the following: traditionally, interpretation was thought of as a process or act by which the mind was able to relate words and sentences to objects in the world. Avicenna, writing in the tenth century, claimed that to think that any belief is true is just to relate that belief to objects, for example.[2] But the idea that we sometimes compare our beliefs directly with unconceptualized reality, or think about objects sometimes by thinking our thoughts and sometimes by thinking our thoughts and "relating" those thoughts to objects (according to Avicenna, this would be the difference between merely entertaining a proposition and thinking that the proposition is true) has come to seem untenable. Access to the world is *through* our discourse and the role that discourse plays in our lives; we compare our discourse with the world as it is presented to us or constructed for us by discourse itself, making in the process new worlds out of old ones; and a psychological act of comparing our discourse with things as they are in themselves has come to have the status of a "mystery act." The writings of contemporary philosophers on ontological questions, of Heidegger as much as of Wittgenstein or Quine, have undermined our confidence in the notion of an object and have caused us to see reference itself as relative to scheme of interpretation. With reference indeterminate, and with our capacity to relate thought and object directly banished to the status of a "mystery act," the very category of an object has begun to crumble for contemporary thought. And as the category of an object crumbles, so—it has seemed to some thinkers—must the notion of *interpretation* crumble as well.

What this last line of thought overlooks is that the notion of interpretation as correlation with objects in themselves is not the only notion of interpretation available to us. If interpretation cannot be meaningfully thought of as mediated by a correlation between the words or thought-signs to be interpreted and neutral, discourse-independent objects, it still remains the case that we can seek to correlate discourse with discourse; or if perfect correlation is impossible, then we can at least seek to construct a meaningful commentary on one discourse in another without first passing through the supposed discourse-independent objects.

Here, too, there is a problem. Frege thought that words and sentences were correlated not only to objects but also to concepts, to *senses*. But it is not only the idea of discourse-independent objects that has crumbled under philosophical critique; Wittgenstein and Quine have savaged the idea that the question "Do A and B have the same meaning?" is a question which has any context-independent answer. Bereft of Fregean "senses" as well as of discourse-independent objects, we are left without either *Sinn* or *Bedeutung*.

Still, *enough is enough, enough isn't everything*. We *have* practices of interpretation. Those practices may be context-sensitive and interest-relative, but there is, given enough context—given, as Wittgenstein says, the language in place—such a thing as *getting it right* or *getting it wrong*. There may be some indeterminacy of translation, but it isn't a case of "anything goes." The appeal that incoherent ideas often have is greatly reinforced when the incoherent idea rests on a sophisticated background of a paradoxical kind. Such is the situation with the idea that there are "incommensurable" discourses, discourses that represent concepts and contents that we, imprisoned as we are in our discourse, in our conceptual frame, can never fully understand.

Incommensurability in the Philosophy of Science

According to Hegel, the whole of existence flows from the supposition that Being is identical with Nothing. What flows from the incoherent idea of "incommensurable" discourse? Let us study the development of one of the most ingenious contemporary philosophers and historians of science, Thomas Kuhn.

In the first edition of his book *The Structure of Scientific Revolutions*, Kuhn went all out. Not only the *concepts* of scientists who work with different paradigms, but also the objects to which they refer, are supposed to be incommensurable. The Copernican astronomer and the Ptolemaic astronomer "inhabit different worlds," Kuhn tells us. One goes from one paradigm to another by a "Gestalt switch."

Taken at face value, Kuhn represented a kind of latter-day Protagoreanism. In Kuhn's discourse, Protagoras's great maxim gets altered to read: *the paradigm is the measure*. And like Protagoras, Kuhn was vulnerable to Plato's arguments in the *Theaetetus*.

A few years ago Edward N. Lee gave us a wonderful reading of those arguments (*Tht.* 161–171).[3] There are several strands, Lee suggests: (1) "the peculiarly proprietary, self-protective and self-centered tone in which 'Protagoras' is made to take up his defense throughout Socrates' impersonations of him"; (2) "the fact that the content of Protagoras' great maxim, far from helping to distinguish man from other forms of life, in fact applies indiscriminately to the lowest common denominator of all sentient being—the sheer possession of some form of sentience, a capacity ranging from the gods down to the merest plant life." Both of these strands meet and fuse in (3), the "final image," according to Lee. That is the image of Protagoras's curious "return."

Protagoras is imagined to return—incredibly enough—by "popping his head up through the ground right there as far as to the neck." "But what is the meaning of the curious detail that Protagoras would rise up *just as far as to his neck*—that far and no further?" Lee asks. "Just as soon as one visualizes this bizarre scene, I believe, the point of the detail becomes clear: the 'returned' Protagoras is being depicted as a 'living creature rooted in the earth'—that is, he is being presented as a *plant*."

To show us in what way Protagoras is supposed to resemble a plant, Lee finds it useful to employ a different image: the image of the chess player who keeps his hand upon his piece. He may have made a move that appears to him to be a good move (one "valid for him," as it were), but he has not actually *made* the move. "Now," Lee writes, "the person systematically saddled with Protagoras' relativizers is like someone who can never remove his hand from his pieces.

Though he may say that he believes something, that it is true-for-him, he cannot say that it is true *simpliciter;* and though he cannot be refuted in such statements (read: made his move), he has not 'released' his opinion from the sphere of an expression of his subjectivity and placed it into a public arena of open and objective discussion (read: exposed his piece to capture)."

As Lee goes on to show, the image of Protagoras as a plant has deep affiliations with what he calls "Plato's spiritualistic phytology"—especially the metaphor for human nature as a "plant which is not earthly but heavenly" at *Timaeus* 90A. Aristotle makes a similar use of the plant metaphor in his defense of the Principle of Non-Contradiction in the *Metaphysics* when he writes that he can refute any opponent of that principle who will *say* something, but that *"if he says nothing, it is absurd to give an account of our views to one who cannot give an account of anything, in so far as he cannot do so. For such a man, as such, is from the start no better than a plant"* (1006a13–15; cf. 1008b10–12).

Plato is saying that on Protagoras's view it would not be possible for two people to disagree; and where the very possibility of disagreement between speakers is ruled out, so is, equally, the possibility of agreement. Even the possibility of *repeating* what another said is ruled out, in any sense that goes beyond repeating the mere noise. For if Jones says "Snow is white," he means "Snow is white is true for me," and that is not something I can say and mean as *he* means it. Even if I say, "Snow is white is true for Jones," what *that* means is "Snow is white appears true to Jones is true for Hilary Putnam," and that is certainly not what *Jones* meant. We might say that Protagoras was the first deconstructionist. We turn out to be mere facts of nature making our noises and our subvocalizations (just as an animal goes through its natural life growling or grumbling, or just as a plant goes through its natural life putting out now a leaf and now a flower). When Donald Davidson suggests that if we couldn't interpret a conceptual scheme, then we would have no basis for calling it a *conceptual* scheme, he is simply restating Plato's argument against Protagoras.

Davidson adds the observation that interpretative practice always requires us to attribute to the speaker a substantial number of true beliefs and reasonable desires. If I attribute to you as absurd a belief as one could attribute to another, say the belief that you have built a perpetual motion machine, or the belief that the earth is flat, or the belief that all government expenditure on welfare is morally wrong, I thereby credit you with the concepts of a machine, of the earth, of flatness, or of welfare; and I could not credit you with these concepts if my "translation scheme" did not make a great many of your more mundane beliefs about what is and is not a machine, what is and is not the earth, what is and is not flat, what is and is not a case of giving someone welfare, agree with mine. All disagreement presupposes an indefinitely large fund of shared beliefs. As Davidson puts it, in interpretation we seek to make others come out "believers of truth and lovers of the good."[4]

The conclusion Davidson draws from all this is that an interpreted conceptual scheme will necessarily turn out to be for the most part like our own, however violently it may contradict our own in its higher reaches. Kuhn seems to have anticipated some such criticism, for long before the argument was voiced so strongly by Davidson, Kuhn had begun to revise (or reinterpret) his own doctrines. He did this by playing down the psychological machinery. We no longer find Kuhn speaking of Gestalt switches; more and more we find him talking about anomalies, predictions, simplicity, and the rest.[5] The idea that paradigm shifts are just things that happen has been replaced by the idea that it can be *justified* to start looking for a paradigm to replace one's existing paradigm, and it can be justified to decide that one has found a good paradigm to serve as the replacement.

I do not wish to suggest that this was merely a fallback position. The new position had substantial merit on its own. The idea that there is a notion of justification which is transcultural and, as Kuhn puts it, "nonparadigmatic"—not simply a creature of the local epistemology and the standards of the time—is a right and important one. To deny it is to land oneself in the commonest sort of self-refuting relativism. If one says (as Rorty recently has)[6] that rightness is simply a matter of what one's "cultural peers" would agree to, or worse, that it is defined by the "standards of one's culture" (Rorty compares these to an algorithm), then the question can immediately be put: Do the standards of Rorty's culture (which he identifies as "European culture") really require Rorty's "cultural peers" to assent to what he has written? Fortunately, the answer is negative. Extreme versions of relativism are inconsistent in more than one way, as Plato saw. It is important to recognize, as Kuhn came to do, that rationality and justification are presupposed by the activity of criticizing and inventing paradigms and are not themselves defined by any single paradigm. Kuhn's move away from relativism is one that I hail.

But—here's the rub—it must be recognized that *justified* and

rational are words like any others. We do have paradigms of justification, even if they don't *define* the required nonparadigmatic sense
of justification. We do have images of knowledge; we do have more
or less elaborate methodological doctrines. These change from time
to time. There have been revolutions in methodology as there have
been revolutions in everything else. What Kuhn is doing is allowing
selected exceptions to his own doctrine of incommensurability. What
he is saying is that, whereas we cannot equate either the meaning or
the reference of the word *electron* as used by Bohr in 1900 with the
meaning or the reference of the word as used by Bohr in 1934, even
if Bohr himself kept the same word, nevertheless we can equate the
meaning and reference of *reasonableness* and *justification,* or at least
partially equate them, across changes in our paradigms of justification as great as those which occurred between the tenth century and
the time of Newton. The "Principle of Charity," which, in all its various forms, is designed to allow us to say that some terms keep their
meaning and reference the same, or roughly the same, across a body
of theory change, is implicitly accepted by Kuhn in the case of the
notions of *justification* and *rationality* but not in the case of other
notions.

This leads to a pervasive incoherence in Kuhn's thought. If there is
a nonparadigmatic notion of justification, then it must be possible to
say certain things about theories independently of the paradigms to
which they belong. The notion of justification, like any other, depends
on a vast number of other notions. To tell whether a theory is justified
requires knowing that it is a *theory,* and, in general, what *sort* of a
theory it is. To know whether a theory is justified, I have to know
what sorts of perceptual reports it explains, and what sort of explanation it gives (for example, is it a *causal* explanation?). Hanson
thought that we cannot mean what someone living in the age of
Ptolemaic astronomy meant by saying "I see the sun rise" because
even the *perceptual* notion of a "sunrise" has been affected by the
shift from Ptolemaic to Copernican astronomy. But Hanson was
wrong. We can say *what* Ptolemaic astronomy was trying to explain,
and we can give a good description of how it went about trying to
explain it. Once one has allowed *interpretation* (for that is what it is
to allow charity in interpretation), it is utterly inconsistent to restrict
the practice of interpretation to a handful of our most abstract epistemological notions.

In a way, Kuhn has come to concede all of this. In more recent work one finds him expressing admiration for the work of Joseph Sneed and Wolfgang Stegmüller.[7] The notion of incommensurability still appears in his writing, but now it seems to signify nothing more than intertheoretic meaning change, as opposed to uninterpretability. According to Sneed and Stegmüller, who build on ideas that go back to Carnap, the theoretical terms in a theory refer to complex logical constructions out of the set of models of that theory, which in turn depend on an open set of "intended applications." I shall not go into details. But one point is worth mentioning: When two theories conflict, then, although the common theoretical terms generally have different meanings and a different reference on the Sneed-Stegmüller account (that is what "incommensurability" becomes), that does *not* mean that there is no "common language" in which one can say what the theoretical terms of both theories refer to. In fact, if we have available the "old terms," that is, the terms which existed in the language prior to the introduction of the specific new terms characteristic of the two theories, and enough set-theoretic vocabulary, we can express the empirical claim of both theories, and we can say what the admissible models of both theories are.

Kuhn still maintains that we cannot interpret the term *phlogiston* in the language that present-day scientists use; but what this in fact means is that we must use a highly indirect mode of interpretation, which involves describing the entire phlogiston theory, its set of intended applications, and its set of admissible models in order to say what *phlogiston* means. A serious residual difficulty still faces Kuhn: he has long maintained that the meaning of old terms (say, observation terms) is *altered* when new theories are constructed. But the whole assumption of Sneed and Stegmüller is precisely that this is *not* the case. Their sets of admissible models are well defined only if we can assume that the old terms have fixed meanings which are not altered by theory construction. It is precisely the aim of neopositivism to view scientific theories as constructed in levels in such a way that the terms of one level may depend for their meaning on the terms of a lower level, but not vice versa. Neopositivism denies that there is a two-way dependence between observation terms and theoretical terms, whereas Kuhn has long agreed with Quine that the dependence goes both ways.

Even if I cannot make full sense of Kuhn's current position, I think that I have said enough to indicate the general nature of the development. This might be summed up in three stages. Stage 1: There is a doctrine of radical incommensurability, that is, impossibility of interpretation. Stage 2: The doctrine is softened. We can, it turns out, say something about theories which are incommensurable with our own, and we can use some notions (justification, rationality) across paradigm changes. Stage 3: Something which is thought to be *better than* interpretation is embraced and propounded, namely, the *structural* description of theories.

Incommensurability in Literature

A strikingly similar set of ideas can be found in the writings of some well-known deconstructionist critics. Thus, in a recent paper by Paul de Man, we have the idea of radical "otherness" described in a way reminiscent of "stage 1" Kuhn.[8]

Bakhtin is criticized by de Man for reintroducing "the categorical foundations of a precritical phenomenalism in which there is no room for exotopy, or otherness, in any shape or degree." This is a striking charge, since exotopy is one of Bakhtin's central notions. De Man elaborates:

> When it is said, for example, that "the heteroglot voices create the background necessary for (the author's) own voice," we recognize the foreground-background model derived from Husserl's theories of perception and here uncritically assimilating the structure of language to the structure of a secure perception: from that moment on, the figure of refraction and of the light ray becomes coercive as the only possible trope for trope, and we are within a reflective system of *mise en abyme* that is anything but dialogical. It is therefore not at all surprising that, still in the same passage, Bakhtin modulates irrevocably from dialogism to a conception of dialogue as question and answer of which it can then be said that "the speaker breaks through the alien conceptual horizon of the listener, constructs his own utterance on alien territory against his, the listener's, apperceptive background." Again, there is no trace of dialogism left in such a gesture of dialectical imperialism that is an inevitable part of any hermeneutic system of question and answer.

De Man, speaking in his most authoritative tone of voice, pronounces a verdict: *"The ideologies of otherness and of hermeneutic understanding are simply not compatible, and therefore their relationship is not a dialogical but simply a contradictory one."* (He hastens to add that Bakhtin might himself have been engaged in a complex "trope" in this "contradiction": "It is not a foregone conclusion whether Bakhtin's discourse is itself dialogical or simply contradictory.")

The idea that there can be incommensurability so great that it is a logical blunder to think that any sort of communication could take place across it was immediately softened in the discussion (at the symposium at which de Man's paper was read) by the cheerful admission that "of course" there are better and worse interpretations of what an "other" says or thinks. Interpretation turns out not to be totally subjective after all. There is something very much like a transparadigmatic notion of rationality available to the literary critic, too.

What is more interesting than this (it is not very surprising that even deconstructionists draw back from the *abyme*) is that while interpretation is admitted someplace, it is admitted, as it were, grudgingly. (The tone suggests that interpretation is a *dumb* activity to engage in, not that it's impossible.) The moral of de Man's paper was that we should recognize an activity different from interpretation, one to which it was clear he gave some priority: the activity of analysis of tropes, or, as he called it, "poetics."

Interpretation and Absoluteness

We all realize that we cannot hope to mechanize interpretation. The dream of formalizing interpretation is as utopian as the dream of formalizing nonparadigmatic rationality itself. Not only is interpretation a highly informal activity, guided by few, if any, settled rules or methods, but it is one that involves much more than linear propositional reasoning. It involves our imagination, our feelings—in short, our full sensibility.

If one thinks of sociology of science and neopositivist set-theoretic description of theories as "real science" (like physics), then it may seem that Kuhn is suggesting that we replace our traditional (and, in his view, unsound) practices of interpretation with "scientific" procedures. If one thinks of poetics as a structuralist discipline (like Lévi-Straussian anthropology), then it may seem that de Man is doing the same (though with a different notion of what being "scientific" consists in). It would be easy, but I think wrong, to suspect Kuhn and de Man of a refusal to grant any sort of objective status to whatever cannot be reduced to "scientific" rules and procedures. This would be an incorrect interpretation because Kuhn and de Man are both far too sophisticated to be victims of what amounts to a vulgar fact/value dichotomy. They recognize that sociology of science and poetics are no more formalizable than interpretation is. They are not asking us to trade in our informal practice of interpretation for the kind of objectivity we have in physics.

What troubles people about interpretation, I think, is not its lack of methodology but its lack of *convergence*. Interpretations of bodies of thought, whether of the *Weltbilder* of scientific theories or of literary works, have always reflected the philosophical views, religious views, political views, literary crotchets, and so on, of their authors and of the times in which they were produced. Out-of-date scientific theories are often inspiring; out-of-date interpretations seem quaint.

If we think of the search for convergent description as a search for *absoluteness* (a term suggested by Bernard Williams), then we may say that what is missing in interpretation, as it is missing in morality, philosophy, ideology generally, is even the possibility of an absolute knowledge. But why should we be disturbed by the fact that every interpretation is at the same time a commentary? Interpretation is commentary-laden, after all, in the same way and for much the same reasons that observation is theory-laden. Common sense suggests that the fact that an interpretation presupposes a view is deplorable only if the view is deplorable. And the views of past interpreters have not always been deplorable. Instead of finding past interpretations quaint, I wonder if we might not find many of them enlightening if we learned to interpret the interpretations? Interpretations of complex systems of thought and of complex works of art are, after all, creations, and as worthy of interpretation as any other creations.

To leave the matter here, however, would be to reinstitute something suspiciously like a fact/value dichotomy. I am not content with Bernard Williams's contrast between the absoluteness of science and the "relativity" of the rest of the culture. In my own work, I have often emphasized that theories in a mature science typically include earlier theories as limiting cases. But it is important to notice that what they include as limiting cases are the *equations* of the earlier theories, not the *world-views* of these theories. There is no sense in which the world-view of Newtonian physics is a "limiting case" of the world-view of general relativity, or a "limiting case" of the world-view of quantum mechanics. There is no more evidence that science converges to one final world-view than there is that literature or morality converge to one final world-view.

Yet for all that, we do sometimes get things right. Newton got it right when he said that the tides are caused by the gravitational pull of the moon and the sun. He got it right, even though his statement has been reinterpreted in an age of general relativity and may have to be reinterpreted as long as there continue to be scientific revolutions in physics. Matthew Arnold (dare I say?) got some things right, even if he got many others wrong.

The contemporary tendency to regard interpretation as something second class reflects, I think, not a craving for objectivity but a craving for absolutes—a craving for absolutes and a tendency which is inseparable from that craving, the tendency to think that if the absolute is unobtainable, then "anything goes." But *enough is enough, enough isn't everything.* Craving absoluteness leads to monism, and monism is a bad outlook in every area of human life.

Part II

Ethics and Aesthetics

9. Beyond the Fact/Value Dichotomy

Several years ago I was a guest at a dinner party at which the hostess made a remark that stuck in my mind. It was just after the taking of the American embassy in Iran, and we were all rather upset and worried about the fate of the hostages. After a while, my hostess said something to the effect that she envied, or almost envied, the consolation that their intense faith in Islam must give the Iranian people, and that *we* are in a disconsolate position because "science has taught us that the universe is an uncaring machine."

Science has taught us that the universe is an uncaring machine: the tragic Weltanschauung of Nietzsche prefaced with "science has taught us!" Not since Matthew Arnold talked so confidently of "the best that has been thought and known" has anyone been quite so confident; and Arnold did not think that science was all, or even the most important part, of "the best that has been thought and known." Those who know me at all will surmise correctly that I did not let this claim about what "science has taught us" go unargued-against, and a far-ranging discussion ensued. But the remark stayed with me past that almost eighteenth-century dinner conversation.

Some months later I repeated this story to Rogers Albritton, and he characterized my hostess's remark as "a religious remark." He was, of course, quite right: it *was* a religious remark, if religion embraces one's ultimate view of the universe as a whole in its moral aspect; and what my hostess was claiming was that science has delivered a new, if depressing, revelation.

One popular view of what is wrong with my hostess's remark was beautifully expressed by Ramsey, who closed a celebrated lecture with these words:

> My picture of the world is drawn in perspective, and not like a model to scale. The foreground is occupied by human beings and the

stars are all as small as threepenny bits. I don't really believe in astronomy, except as a complicated description of part of the course of human and possibly animal sensation. I apply my perspective not merely to space but also to time. In time the world will cool and everything will die; but that is a long time off still, and its present value at compound discount is almost nothing. Nor is the present less valuable because the future will be blank. Humanity, which fills the foreground of my picture, I find interesting and on the whole admirable. I find, just now at least, the world a pleasant and exciting place. You may find it depressing; I am sorry for you, and you despise me. But I have reason and you have none; you would only have a reason for despising me if your feeling corresponded to the fact in a way mine didn't. But neither can correspond to the fact. The fact is not in itself good or bad; it is just that it thrills me but depresses you. On the other hand, I pity you with reason, because it is pleasanter to be thrilled than to be depressed, and not merely pleasanter but better for all one's activities.[1]

If one has seen a little more of life than the 22-year-old Ramsey who delivered this lecture, and if one has faced the beastliness of the world (not just the wars and the mass starvation and the totalitarianism—how different our world is from Ramsey's England of 1925!—but the beastliness that sensitive novelists remind us of, and that even upper-middle-class life cannot avoid), one *is* more likely to be depressed than "thrilled." Also, that Ramsey himself died when he was only 27 depresses *me*.

But notice—I think it comes out even in the bit of Ramsey's lecture that I quoted, and it certainly comes out in the phrase "science has taught us"—notice how sure we are that we are *right*. Our modern revelation may be a depressing revelation, but at least it is a *de-mythologizing* revelation. If the world is terrible, at least we *know* that our fathers were fools to think otherwise, and that everything they believed and cherished was a lie, or at best superstition.

This certainly flatters our vanity. The traditional view said that the nature of God was a mystery, that His purposes were mysterious, and that His creation—Nature—was also largely mysterious. The new view admits that our knowledge is, indeed, not *final;* that in many ways our picture will in the future be changed; that it can everywhere be superseded by new scientific discoveries; but that in broad outlines we *know* what's what. "The universe is an uncaring machine," and we are, so to speak, a chance by-product. Values are just *feelings*. As

Ramsey put it elsewhere in the same lecture, "—Most of us would agree that the objectivity of good was a thing we had settled and dismissed with the existence of God. Theology and Absolute Ethics are two famous subjects which we have realized to have no real objects."

I think that this consolation to our vanity cannot be overestimated. Narcissism is often a more powerful force in human life than self-preservation or the desire for a productive, loving, fulfilling life, as psychologists have come to realize: I think that, if someone could *show* that Ramsey's view is wrong, that objective values are *not* mythology, that the "uncaring machine" may be all there is to the worlds of physics and chemistry and biology, but that the worlds of physics and chemistry and biology are not the only worlds we inhabit, we would welcome this, *provided* the new view gave us the same intellectual confidence, the same idea that we have a superior method, the same sense of being on top of the facts, that the scientistic view gives us. If the new view were to threaten our intellectual pride, if it were to say that there is much with respect to which we are unlikely to have more than our fathers had—our fallible capacity for plausible reasoning, with all its uncertainty, all its tendency to be too easily seduced by emotion and corrupted by power or selfish interest—then, I suspect, many of us would reject it as "unscientific," "vague," lacking in "criteria for deciding," and so on. In fact, I suspect many of us will stick with the scientistic view even if it, at any rate, can be *shown* to be inconsistent or incoherent. In short, we shall prefer to go on being depressed to losing our status as sophisticated persons.

Such a new view is what I try to sketch and defend in my book *Reason, Truth, and History.*[2] I only sketch it, because it is intrinsic to the view itself that there isn't much more one *can* do than sketch it. A *textbook* entitled "Informal Non-Scientific Knowledge" would be a bit ridiculous. But I feel sure that it is, in its main outline, more on the right track than the depressing view that has been regarded as the best that is thought and known by the leaders of modern opinion since the latter part of the nineteenth century. This essay is, then, a short sketch of something that is itself a sketch.

W. V. Quine has pointed out that the idea that science proceeds by anything like a formal syntactic method is a myth. When theory conflicts with what is taken to be fact, we sometimes give up the theory and sometimes give up the "fact"; when theory conflicts with theory, the decision cannot always be made on the basis of the known observational facts (Einstein's theory of gravitation was accepted and Whitehead's alternative theory was rejected fifty years before anyone thought of an experiment to decide between the two). Sometimes the decision must be based on such desiderata as simplicity (Einstein's theory seemed a "simpler" way to move from Special Relativity to an account of gravitation than Whitehead's), sometimes on conservativism (momentum was redefined by Einstein so that the Law of the Conservation of Momentum could be conserved in elastic collisions); and "simplicity" and "conservativism" themselves are words for complex phenomena which vary from situation to situation. When apparent observational data conflict with the demands of theory, or when simplicity and conservativism tug in opposite directions, trade-offs must be made, and there is no formal rule or method for making such trade-offs. The decisions we make are, "where rational, pragmatic," as Quine put it.

Part of my case is that *coherence* and *simplicity* and the like are themselves *values*. To suppose that "coherent" and "simple" are themselves just emotive words—words which express a "pro attitude" toward a theory, but which do not ascribe any definite properties to the theory—would be to regard *justification* as an entirely subjective matter. On the other hand, to suppose that "coherent" and "simple" name *neutral* properties—properties toward which people may have a "pro attitude," but there is no objective rightness in doing so—runs into difficulties at once. Like the paradigm value terms (such as "courageous," "kind," "honest," or "good"), "coherent" and "simple" are used as terms of praise. Indeed, they are *action guiding* terms: to describe a theory as "coherent, simple, explanatory" is, in the right setting, to say that acceptance of the theory is *justified;* and to say that acceptance of a statement is (completely) justified is to say that one ought to accept the statement or theory. If *action guiding* predicates are "ontologically queer," as John Mackie urged, they are nonetheless indispensable in epistemology. Moreover, every argument that has ever been offered for noncognitivism in ethics applies immediately and *without the slightest change* to these epistemological predicates: there are disagreements between cultures (and within one culture) over what is or is not coherent or simple (or "justified" or "plausible," and so forth). These controversies are no more settleable than are controversies over the nature of justice. Our views on the nature of coherence and simplicity are historically conditioned, just as our views on the nature of justice or goodness are. There is no neutral conception of rationality to which one can appeal when the nature of rationality is itself what is at issue.

Richard Rorty[3] might suggest that "justified relative to the standards of culture A" is one property and "justified relative to the standards of culture B" is a different property. But, if we say that it is a *fact* that acceptance of a given statement or theory is "justified relative to the standards of culture A," then we are treating "being the standard of a culture" and "according with the standard of a culture" as something *objective,* something itself *not* relative to the standards of this-or-that culture. Or we had better be: for otherwise, we fall at once into the self-refuting relativism of Protagoras. Like Protagoras, we abandon all distinction between *being right* and *thinking one is right.* Even the notion of a culture crumbles (does every person have his or her own "idioculture," just as every person has his or her own idiolect? How many "cultures" are there in any one country in the world today?).

The fact is that the notions of "being a standard of a culture" and "being in accord with the standards of a culture" are as difficult notions (epistemically speaking) as we possess. To treat these sorts of facts as the ground floor to which all talk of objectivity and relativity is to be reduced is a strange disease (a sort of scientism which comes from the social sciences as opposed to the sort of scientism which comes from physics). As I put it in *Reason, Truth, and History,* without the cognitive values of coherence, simplicity, and instrumental efficacy we have no world and no facts, not even facts about what is so *relative to* what. And these cognitive values, I claim, are simply a part of our holistic conception of human flourishing. Bereft of the old realist idea of truth as "correspondence" and of the positivist idea of justification as fixed by public "criteria," we are left with the necessity of seeing our search for better conceptions of rationality as an intentional activity which, like every activity that rises above the mere following of inclination or obsession, is guided by our idea of the good.

Can coherence and simplicity be restricted to contexts in which we are choosing between *predictive* theories, however? Logical positivism maintained that nothing can have cognitive significance unless it contributes, however indirectly, to predicting the sensory stimulations that are our ultimate epistemological starting point (in empiricist philosophy). I say that *that* statement itself does not contribute, even indirectly, to improving our capacity to predict anything. Not even when conjoined to boundary conditions, or to scientific laws, or to appropriate mathematics, or to all of these at once, does positivist philosophy or any other philosophy imply an observation sentence. In short, positivism is self-refuting. Moreover, I see the idea that the only purpose or function of reason itself is prediction (or prediction plus "simplicity") as a prejudice—a prejudice whose unreasonableness is exposed by the very fact that *arguing for it* presupposes intellectual interests unrelated to prediction as such. (That relativism and positivism—the two most influential philosophies of science of our generation—are *both* self-refuting is argued in one of the chapters of my book, the one titled "Two Conceptions of Rationality," by the way.)

If coherence and simplicity are values, and if we cannot deny without falling into total self-refuting subjectivism that *they* are objective (notwithstanding their "softness," the lack of well-defined "criteria," and so forth), then the classic argument against the objectivity of ethical values is *totally* undercut. For that argument turned on precisely the "softness" of ethical values—the lack of a noncontroversial "method," and so on—and on the alleged "queerness" of the very notion of an *action guiding fact*. But *all* values are in this boat; if *those* arguments show that ethical values are totally subjective, then cognitive values are totally subjective as well.

Where are we then? On the one hand, the idea that science (in the sense of exact science) exhausts rationality is seen to be a self-stultifying error. The very activity of arguing about the nature of rationality presupposes a conception of rationality wider than that of laboratory testability. If there is no fact of the matter about what cannot be tested by deriving *predictions,* then there is no fact of the matter about any philosophical statement, including *that* one. On the other hand, any conception of rationality broad enough to embrace philosophy—not to mention linguistics, mentalistic psychology, history, clinical psychology, and so on—must embrace much that is vague, ill-defined, no more capable of being "scientized" than was the knowledge of our forefathers. The horror of what cannot be "methodized" is nothing but method fetishism; it is time we got over it. Getting over it would reduce the intellectual *hubris* that I talked about at the beginning of this essay. We might even recover our sense of *mystery;* who knows?

I am fond of arguing that popular philosophical views are incoherent or worse. In *Reason, Truth, and History* I also try to show that the two most influential theories of truth—the empiricist theory (it's all a matter of getting the "sense data" right—note that Ramsey endorsed that one in the quote I gave earlier) and the correspondence theory (there is some special "correspondence" between words and objects, and *that* is what explains the existence of reference and truth)—are either unexplanatory or unintelligible.

So far, what I have said could be summarized by saying that if "values" seem a bit suspect from a narrowly scientific point of view, they have, at the very least, a lot of "companions in the guilt": justification, coherence, simplicity, reference, truth, and so on, all exhibit the *same* problems that goodness and kindness do, from an epistemological point of view. None of them is reducible to physical notions; none of them is governed by syntactically precise rules. Rather than give up all of them (which would be to abandon the ideas of thinking and talking), and rather than do what we are doing, which is to reject some—the ones which do not fit in with a narrow instrumentalist conception of rationality which itself lacks all intellectual justification—we should recognize that *all* values, including the cognitive ones, derive their authority from our idea of human flourishing and our idea of reason. These two ideas are interconnected: our image of an ideal theoretical intelligence is simply a *part* of our ideal of total human flourishing, and makes no sense wrenched out of the total ideal, as Plato and Aristotle saw.

In sum, I don't doubt that the universe of *physics* is, in some respects, a "machine," and that it is not "caring" (although describing it as "uncaring" is more than a little misleading). But—as Kant saw— what the universe of physics leaves out is the very thing that makes that universe possible for us, or that makes it possible for us to construct that universe from our "sensory stimulations"—the intentional, valuational, referential work of "synthesis." I claim, in short, that without *values* we would not have a *world*. Instrumentalism, although it denies it, is itself a value system, albeit a sick one.

10. The Place of Facts in a World of Values

Science tells us—or at least we are *told* that "science tells us"—that we live in a world of swarming particles, spiraling DNA molecules, machines that compute, and such esoteric objects as black holes and neutron stars. In such a world, where can we hope for meaning or for a foundation for our values? Jacques Ellul tells us—and I think he is right—that the themes of the present day are science and sexuality.[1] He also tells us that in modern secular society most people—the people who think of themselves as "enlightened," in fact—are caught in a peculiar contradiction. On the one hand, nothing is regarded as more *irrational* than Christianity (or Judaism). On the other hand, Europeans and Americans are going in droves for every kind of pseudoreligion one can think of. And the *verboten* desire for religion (*verboten* as "irrational," "unscientific"—the two words are treated as synonyms) does not only break out in the form of a million and one new and revived cults; it breaks out even more alarmingly in the form of a certain religionizing of the political—even "middle of the roaders" rarely discuss political questions any more without a special kind of commitment, more appropriate to the defense of a faith than to the discussion of public policy. At the same time, Leszek Kolakowski writes despairingly (only he would not agree that this is despairing) that "the gulf between normative and empirical knowledge" cannot be bridged, and "the former can be justified only by the force of tradition and myth."[2] But if Kolakowski is right, and at the same time "tradition and myth" are in vast disrepute, what then? Dostoevsky's "if God is dead then everything is permitted" may have been invalid logic, but accurate sociology. Indeed, looking at the world in which we live—this Babylon!—who can doubt it?

But a word of caution is perhaps not out of place. *Many* world-views—even if some of them denied that they *were* world-views—have been advanced in the name of science in the past two centuries.

At one time Evolutionism, by which I mean not the theory of evolution but the doctrine that the fate of Man is to evolve and evolve until Man is virtually God—a doctrine which appeared on the scene at least fifty years *before* the theory of evolution, and which permeates the thought of Marx and Spencer (and perhaps even so moderate a liberal as John Dewey?)—was supposed to be *the* scientific view of things. More recently, I have heard extreme pessimism advanced for the same role: John von Neumann told me before he died that it was absolutely certain that (1) there would be a nuclear war; and (2) everyone would perish in it (let us hope that he was not right in these predictions). To move from such moral and human questions to more abstract metaphysical questions, both idealism (rebaptized "phenomenalism" or "positivism"), that is, the view that all there really is (or all that can be spoken of, anyway) is *sensations* and similar mental phenomena, and materialism (rebaptized "scientific realism") have been enthusiastically espoused as *the* philosophy of science. And both the view that there is an unchanging *scientific method,* and the view that what science *is* is itself all historical and relative, have been held with the same enthusiasm.

Moreover, the metaphysical view that laymen widely assume to be the view dictated by modern science—the view that it is all atoms swarming in the void, and that there are no objective values, only swarming instincts and desires and the interests of various groups—does not even have the virtue of novelty. Lucretius already thought it was all atoms swarming in the void, and ethical relativism and skepticism were well known to the Greeks of Plato's day. If science really does reveal to us what our metaphysics and moral outlook should be, its revelation is neither monolithic nor new. Some revelations in history have had undeniable dignity and beauty, even for those of us who disbelieve in them; is it not rather sad, even a bit Prufrockian, if the *final* revelation turns out to consist of a half-dozen ideas which are not mutually consistent (you have to take your pick), and each of which looks, well, just a little bit *half-baked?*

In this essay I want to defend the view that "scientific" is *not* coextensive with "rational." There are many perfectly rational beliefs that cannot be tested "scientifically." But more than that, I want to defend the view that there are whole domains of fact with respect to which *present-day* science tells us nothing at all, not even that the facts in question exist. These domains are not new or strange. Three of them are: (1) the domain of objective values; (2) the domain of freedom;

(3) the domain of rationality itself. I shall discuss each of these domains in turn.

Objective Values

Let me begin on a personal note. My training as a philosopher of science came from logical positivists (or "Logical Empiricists," with a capital "L" and a capital "E," as they preferred to style themselves). These philosophers firmly believed in the "emotive theory of ethical discourse"—that is, they firmly believed that the sole function of ethical discourse is to express feelings or acts of will or, more vaguely, "attitudes."

Although it is not *quite* right to say that they thought values were matters of "subjective taste," which is how any layman would describe this view to any other layman—and, indeed, how else *can* it be described in language that *tout le monde* can understand?—it is essentially right. Choosing a morality is choosing a way of life, Professor Hare of Oxford tells us. Although I rather think he uses "choice of a way of life" as a mystifying phrase, his too is a correct expression of this view, provided we think of choosing a way of life as something like choosing, say, an outdoor life as opposed to a life of listening to classical music and engaging only in sedentary pursuits (note that a "way of life" in the *literal* sense is something that can be unalterable for a person, something he can be passionate about, and something he can be—though he need not be—intolerant about).

For several years after I got my doctorate I firmly believed this view, or a sophisticated variant (at least I thought it was sophisticated) of my own devising. I thought that something was good in the specifically moral sense if it "answers to the interests associated with the institution of morality"—a view suggested by the analysis of the meaning of the word *good* in Paul Ziff's book *Semantic Analysis,* though not specifically contained in that book. The advantage of this view over the older emotivism was that it allowed me to say that value judgments were *true* or *false:* to find out if a judgment of the form X *is good* is true one just has to discover if X answers to "the interests associated with the institution of morality." *How* one discovers what those interests are, I was never able to answer to my own satisfaction. But, this difficulty aside, I never doubted Professor Hare's view— although I disagreed with his semantic analysis of *good*—the view that the decision to try to be or do good is just a "choice of a way of life," namely, to subscribe or not to subscribe to an "institution."

Anyway, in the middle of this period I found myself with a severe moral problem in my own life (what it was I am not going to discuss, nor would it be particularly relevant as far as I can see). And the interesting thing is that I found myself agonizing over whether what I was doing, or contemplating doing, or had done, was *right—really* right. And I did not just mean whether it was in accord with the Utilitarian maxim to do what will lead to the greatest happiness of the greatest number (although I thought about that), but whether, if it was, then was that the *right* maxim for such a case? And I do not think I meant would some semantic analysis of the word "good," or some analysis of "the institution of morality," support what I was doing. But the *most* interesting thing is that it never occurred to me that there was any inconsistency between my meta-ethical view that it was all just a choice of a "way of life" and my agonized belief that what I was doing had to be either *right* or *wrong*. (I do not mean that there are no borderline cases; I felt that in *this* case what I was doing was either right or wrong.)

I would not want to give the impression that this inconsistency was peculiar to me, however. My emotivist teachers and colleagues—in particular Hans Reichenbach and Rudolf Carnap—were fine and principled human beings. Both had been anti-Nazi when, to the shame of the philosophical profession, some world-famous German philosophers succumbed to Nazi ideology, and both were generous and idealistic men, wonderful to their students. I am sure that both had deep convictions about right and wrong—convictions that they would have laid down their lives rather than betray.

But the most charming example of this sort of inconsistency occurs in a famous lecture by Frank Ramsey, the British philosopher of the 1930s who was regarded as so brilliant by such men as Russell and Wittgenstein, and who died while still not 30 years old. The lecture[3] wittily defends the thesis that "there is nothing to discuss"—that is, there is nothing that can sensibly be discussed any more *by laymen*. As Ramsey put it:

> Let us review the possible subjects of discussion. They fall, as far as I can see, under the heads of science, philosophy, history and politics, psychology, and aesthetics; where, not to beg any question, I am separating psychology from other sciences.
>
> Science, history, and politics are not suited for discussion except by experts. Others are simply in the position of requiring more information; and, till they have acquired all available information, cannot do anything but accept on authority the opinions of those

better qualified. Then there is philosophy; this, too, has become too technical for the layman. Besides this disadvantage, the conclusion of the greatest modern philosopher [Wittgenstein] is that there is no such subject as philosophy; that it is an activity, not a doctrine; and that, instead of answering questions, it aims merely at curing headaches. It might be thought that, apart from this technical philosophy whose centre is logic, there was a sort of popular philosophy which dealt with such subjects as the relation of man to nature, and the meaning of morality. But any attempt to treat such topics seriously reduces them to questions either of science or of technical philosophy, or results more immediately in perceiving them to be nonsensical.

Ramsey takes as an example a lecture of Russell's. He remarks that Russell's philosophy of nature "consisted mainly of the conclusions of modern physics, physiology, and astronomy, with a slight admixture of his own theory of material objects as a particular kind of logical construction." This, he points out, is something that can only be discussed "by someone with adequate knowledge of relativity, atomic theory, physiology, and mathematical logic." Then he adds,

> His philosophy of value consisted in saying that the only questions about value were what men desired and how their desires might be satisfied, and then he went on to answer these questions. Thus the whole subject became part of psychology, and its discussion would be a psychological one.
>
> Of course his main statement about value might be disputed, but most of us would agree that the objectivity of ethics was a thing we had settled and dismissed with the existence of God. *Theology and Absolute Ethics are two famous subjects which we have realized to have no real objects.* (italics mine)

This is, for once, an unvarnished and unsoftened statement of the view that there are *no* objective ethical judgments. But let me recall for you the concluding words of Ramsey's charming lecture that I quoted in the previous essay.

> I find, just now at least, the world a pleasant and exciting place. You may find it depressing; I am sorry for you, and you despise me. But I have reason and you have none; you would only have a reason for despising me if your feeling corresponded to the fact in a way mine didn't. But neither can correspond to the fact. The fact is not in itself good or bad; it is just that it thrills me but depresses you. On the other hand, I pity you with reason, because it is pleasanter to be

thrilled than to be depressed, and *not merely pleasanter but better for all one's activities*. (italics mine)

So even Ramsey finds *one* judgment of value to be a judgment of *reason*!

But is the emotivist really inconsistent? True, the man on the street naturally assumes that, if someone really thinks all moralities are just expressions of subjective preference, choices of a "way of life," then that person must agree that no morality is better or worse than any other, that all moralities are equally legitimate. But that does not strictly follow. The emotivist can reply that words like "legitimate" are emotive words too! The emotivist can say that torture is wrong (or, on the contrary, that it is right when the nation needs to find out the military secrets of an enemy, or whatever) and *also* say that any other point of view about the matter is *bad, evil, monstrous, not legitimate*—anything except that the point of view he opposes is *false*. (Why he does not say that *true* and *false* are emotive too is not quite clear.)

Yehuda Elkana has spoken of "two-level thinking" on the part of some scientists, philosophers, and so on.[4] The "two-level thinker" speaks like a realist on the "first-order" level (when he is talking about things other than his own talk). For example, he says "electrons are flowing through this wire," or "there is an inkwell on the table," or "torture is wrong." But he denies the objectivity of his own first-level talk (that is, that it possesses truth or falsity, except relative to a culture, or whatever) when he comes to comment philosophically on this level of talk. On the "meta" level he says things like "electrons are just permanent possibilities of sensation," or "*right* and *wrong* are just performatory locutions for performing the speech acts of prescribing and proscribing." In Elkana's terminology, the emotivist can avoid the charge of inconsistency by saying that he is engaging in two-level thinking in ethics.

Although it is true that the emotivist can avoid the charge of strict formal inconsistency in this way, it seems to me that the layman's feelings that something "inconsistent" is going on possesses a deep basis. For one thing, on such a conception, what sense does it make to *worry* if something is right or wrong, as I did? Of course, one can worry about the facts (whether something really conduces to the greatest happiness of the greatest number, or whatever). One can worry about whether an action really agrees with a maxim; but how can one worry about whether or not one has the right maxim? It would seem that one should say to oneself in such a case, "you must simply *choose* a morality." The idea that there is such a thing as being right or wrong about which morality one chooses must just be a hangover from absolute ethics—that "subject which we have realized to have no real object."

And what could our *motive* for being ethical possibly be? The favorite categories of motivation employed by *scientistic* thought are *instinct* and *conditioning*. I see no evidence whatsoever that being ethical is an instinct. E. O. Wilson suggested recently that ethics may be based on altruistic and gregarious instincts which are themselves the product of natural selection. (He is very careful not to derive a theory of what we should do from this.) However, whatever may be the *origin* of our altruistic and gregarious impulses, our loyalty, and so on, it is not the case that following these impulses is the way to be ethical. There is no instinct or instinctual impulse which may not lead to great evil if followed to extremes, as moralists have long known. Altruism, insofar as it is just an instinct or instinctual impulse, may lead one to kill the old people in the tribe for the sake of posterity (more food for the young); or to torture someone to discover the military secrets of an enemy state; and so forth. Even feelings of kindness may lead one to do wrong, for example, if one's sympathy for a hunted person leads one to allow a Martin Bormann to escape deserved punishment, or one's sympathy for the workers leads one to set wages so high that disastrous inflation results. And there is no instinct which it may not be one's duty to follow in some situations. The whole idea that our natural instincts can be classified into good and evil instincts or our natural emotions into good and evil emotions is an error, as moral writers have often pointed out.

But suppose that the motivation for ethical behavior *is* an instinct. (Imagine that sociobiology discovers the instinct.) Why should we not *suppress* it? We suppress all of our other instincts sometimes; indeed, we have to in order to avoid disaster. Why should we not suppress our instinct to be ethical, whenever following it will lead to loss of our life, or loss of a loved one, or other hardship to ourselves? Why should we not be moral only when it does not cost too much, or when it does not pay too well to be immoral?

Nor does appeal to "conditioning" help matters any. What this comes to is either (1) the claim that we act ethically because we cannot help it (our toilet training, and so on, just left us with this "super-

ego structure," according to the Freudian version—Freud, in particular, is often credited with a "Copernican Revolution" in psychology
for giving just this explanation of our conscience), or (2) the claim
that we act ethically because we want our neighbors to approve of us.
(Of course, (1) and (2) are not incompatible, and both (1) and (2)
assume instincts as well as conditioning.) But it is just false that we
cannot help acting ethically! We do have a choice—and it is often
terribly hard to act ethically. The fact of both personal life and human
history is that people do not act ethically, not that they do. And the
desire for the approval of our neighbors can be worthy or unworthy.
Many people do wrong things because they want the approval of their
neighbors. If wanting to be ethical is like wanting an expensive and
vulgar house because the neighbors will be impressed, why should
anyone bother?

Let me try to make the problem vivid by means of an example. (I
lack the literary skill required to do it properly; the reader who wants
to see this sort of example really developed in full human richness
should read Kamala Markandaya's moving novel *A Handful of Rice*.)
Imagine a poor peasant boy growing up in poverty-stricken Sicily
(Markandaya's novel is set in even more poverty-stricken Calcutta).
Let us suppose he is offered the opportunity to become a member of
the Mafia. If he accepts, he will do evil things—sell terrible drugs, run
prostitution and gambling rackets, and even commit murders; but he
will also live comfortably, have friends and women, and, perhaps,
even enjoy a kind of respect and admiration. If he refuses, he will live
a life of almost unimaginable poverty, will probably see some of the
children he will have die for lack of food and medicine, and so on.

I am not supposing that the boy will be perfectly happy as a *mafio-
so*. Perfect happiness is not one of the options here. Notice that this
kind of sacrifice—and it is just as real as and even more bitter than
the sacrifice on the battlefield, or the public execution for one's convictions—is one that millions of people, millions of the poor, make
and always have made. And unlike the sacrifice on the battlefield or
the public execution, there are no posthumous medals, no stories told
to the children and grandchildren—some of the bitterest sacrifices
that people make for what is right are (and, indeed, must be) taken
as simply a matter of course by their neighbors and friends.

Now I ask, would anyone make such a sacrifice if he believed that
the thing that was impelling him to make it was, at bottom, just a
desire to impress (some of) his neighbors, or even in the same ballpark

as a desire to impress the neighbors? Or his toilet training? It is all very fine for comfortable Oxford professors and comfortable French existentialists to wax rhetorical about how one has to "choose a way of life" and commit oneself to it (even if the commitment is "absurd," the existentialists will add). And this rhetoric really impresses people like ourselves, who are reasonably prosperous. But the poor person who makes such a sacrifice makes it precisely because he does not see it that way. Would anyone *really* choose such a life if he thought that *all* it was was "a choice of a way of life"? Of course, he makes the choice he does because he knows that that choice is his *duty*. And he knows that he cannot choose his duties, at least not in this respect.[5]

The situation is this: the popular line of thought today has no room for the traditional notion of reason as a faculty that dictates *ends* to us and not only means to ends dictated by instinct and modified by conditioning. Hume's dictum that "reason is and ought to be the slave of the passions" expresses the modern idea exactly—reason *equals* instrumental reason. But if reason *cannot* dictate ends, then there cannot be a reason why I should go *against* my "passions," except the inadequate reason of another "passion." There cannot be such a thing as a *rational* answer to "Why should I do my duty?" And an irrational answer which is admitted and recognized to be irrational or arational is no good.

The fact is that the knowledge that there are objective values involves not merely the knowledge that moral judgments are true or false, but just as importantly the knowledge that what regulates the behavior of the person who acts from the motive of duty, what directs him to suppress this instinct now and gratify it then, to withstand and resist this kind of conditioning when his neighbors attempt it, but not to object to this other kind, is neither mere "instinct" nor mere "conditioning."

Recently Iris Murdoch has put forward the view that the whole "fact/value" dichotomy stems from a faulty moral psychology: from the metaphysical picture of "the neutral facts" (apprehended by a totally *uncaring* faculty of reason) and the will which, having learned the neutral facts, must "choose values" either *arbitrarily* (the existentialist picture) or on the basis of "instinct."[6] I think she is right; but setting this faulty moral psychology right will involve deep philosophical work involving the notions of "reason" and "fact" (as she, of course, recognizes).

Freedom

The problem of the freedom of the will has many aspects. Here I am going to discuss only one: our belief that we could have done otherwise in certain situations, for example:

> *I could have refrained from boasting on that occasion,*
> *I could have taken a different job,*
> *I could have spent my vacation in a different place.*

One of the first English-speaking philosophers to try to reconcile freedom and determinism was David Hume. Although in the *Treatise* Hume denies the freedom of the will, in the *Inquiry* he puts forward the theory that the incompatibility is only apparent. One of the simplest statements of this sort of view (like all philosophical positions, it has versions which are almost infinitely complicated) is the following: "we could have acted otherwise" is false when the causal chain that ended with our action (or with the trajectory of our body that was the "physical realization" of our action) was of one kind—when it did not "pass through our will," in the simplest version of the theory—and is true when the causal chain was of another kind—when it did "pass through the will." If someone ties me up and carries me to Vienna, then it is false that I could have done otherwise than go to Vienna; but if I decide to go to Vienna, then buy the ticket, then take the plane, and so on, and the causal chain is of the usual type for a "voluntary" action, then I could have done otherwise. (The Hegel-Marx dictum that "Freedom is obedience to Law" is a variant of the same idea, I believe.)

There is one obvious difficulty: asking whether it is true that an event could possibly have failed to happen is just not the same question as whether its cause was of kind X or kind Y! Hume is just substituting a different question for the question that was asked. It is true that in ordinary language we often use "can" and "could" in senses that do not imply full possibility. Sometimes "John can do X" just means that John has the ability (nothing said about opportunity); sometimes it means that John has the opportunity (nothing said about ability). But that is not at issue. What we are concerned with is whether we "really actually fully could" have done otherwise, in John Austin's phrase.

Consider the case of a man, call him McX, who suffers from a debilitating compulsion neurosis. McX cannot bear not to be in contact with a wall; walking across an open courtyard without touching any wall is not possible for him (a famous English philosopher had such a compulsion). Is it true that McX "has the ability" to walk across the courtyard without touching any wall?

In one sense it is: McX is not paralyzed and has learned to walk. In another sense it is not: McX breaks into a cold sweat at the mere thought; no matter how hard he tries he "just cannot do it"; and so on. "Ability" talk is not helpful here; what is clear is that McX *cannot* walk across the courtyard without touching a wall.

Similarly, if *events out of my control* determine with physical necessity that I will pick up a newspaper at time *t*, then it is false that I could have refrained from picking up the newspaper at time *t*. "I could have done something else" in the sense of having the ability, in one sense of "having the ability," just as McX was "able" to cross in the sense of having learned to walk; "I could have done something else" in the sense of having had the opportunity, just as McX "could have crossed" in the sense of having had the opportunity; but in the sense of "really actually fully could have," it is just *false* that I could have done something else, on the supposition that determinism is true.

This simple and correct argument has been challenged, however. Some say that the argument is fallacious; that it exhibits the invalid form:

Necessarily (if p *then* q)

p
_____

(Therefore) Necessarily q.

Is this the case?

It is not. The argument form shown above is clearly fallacious when "necessarily" is taken in the sense of "it is a necessary truth that" (either in the sense of logically necessary or in the sense of physically necessary). Thus it would be fallacious to argue:

It is a necessary truth that all triangles are three-sided
This table is a triangle (in shape)
_____

(Therefore) It is a necessary truth that this table is three-sided.

But the argument that:

> *Necessarily (If the state of the world at time* t *was S, then I will pick up the newspaper)*
> *The state of the world at time* t *was S*
> _____
> *(Therefore) It is* impossible *that I will not pick up the newspaper*

is not of this form. Saul Kripke has given an elegant rejoinder to the claim that the arguments are of the same form (and therefore that the second argument, like the first, is fallacious).[7] Kripke simply pointed out that if that is all there is to the second argument, then the following everyday argument must *also* be fallacious:

> *Necessarily (If I miss all the trains to London then I cannot get to London today)*
> *I have missed all the trains to London*
> _____
> *(Therefore) It is impossible for me to get to London today*

—but this argument is clearly correct!

Moreover, Kripke points out, it is easy to give a modal semantics that justifies this pattern of argument (Kripke is the greatest modern authority on modal logic). Consider a world in which there are branching futures. Call the tensed statement "It is possible that X will occur" true as long as there is a branch in the future that leads to the occurrence of X, and false as soon as the last branch leading to the occurrence of X has been passed. It is easy to check that with this semantics—which is just the intuitive semantics for tensed possibility statements—both the "last train to London" argument and the argument that determinism is incompatible with freedom are perfectly correct.

However bad this incompatibility might have been in the heyday of Newtonian physics, the important fact is that here it was the science that turned out to be wrong and not the belief that we are free in the sense that we could have done otherwise. Present-day physics is indeterministic, not deterministic, and there is absolutely no incompatibility between indeterministic physics and tensed possibility statements. I am not claiming that "could" applied to a human action *just* means "compatible with physical law and antecedent conditions";

indeed, I am not proposing an analysis of "could" at all. I am saying that the *case* for incompatibility has dissolved; further problems of philosophical analysis will, of course, continue to be with us.

Now, one might expect that philosophers would have hailed this result. Should we not be glad if something we seem to know so clearly as the fact that we could have spent our vacation at a different place from where we did has turned out not to be incompatible with well-confirmed scientific theory? But, in fact, with very few exceptions, philosophers have scoffed at the significance of quantum mechanical indeterminacy for the free will problem. The reason, I think, is that the philosophers find anything but mechanism an embarrassment; they are in the grip of a fashion, and the only thing more powerful than reason in the history of philosophy is intellectual fashion. One exception to this regrettable tendency is Elizabeth Anscombe: in her powerful inaugural address[8] she recognizes both the importance of the determinism issue and the importance of the fact that the scientific evidence no longer supports determinism, if it ever did.

One way of scoffing at the significance of indeterminism is to pretend that it makes no difference to "ordinary macroscopic events" such as the motions of human bodies. This is an outright mistake, and Anscombe disposes of it with great elegance. Another way is to say that we are "no better off" (in terms of moral responsibility for our actions) if our actions are "the product of chance" than if they are determined.

This claim changes the question, of course. We were not talking about moral responsibility but about freedom; and although these are related (no freedom, no moral responsibility, at least in Kant's view), they are not the same. The original problem was an incompatibility between deterministic physics and freedom; and we have seen that that does not exist any longer. I know of no argument whatsoever that there is an incompatibility between *indeterministic* physics and freedom. But responsibility is important too. What reason is there to think that there is an incompatibility between indeterministic physics and responsibility?

The argument is that indeterministic physics says that our actions (or at least their component bodily motions) are produced by chance. And how can we think of ourselves as a kind of roulette wheel and still ascribe moral predicates? But it is just false that indeterministic physics says that our actions are "produced by chance"—that is, *caused* by Chance (with a capital "C").

Let us be clear on this. Indeterministic physics uses the notion of *probability*. And while the analysis of the notion is still in dispute, there is no reason to interpret probability as Aristotelian Chance (which *was* a cause—a cause of whatever is unexplainable). If we stick to what is generally agreed upon among scientists, all we can say that "probability" means is *the presence of statistical regularities*. Now, no philosopher ever doubted that there are statistical regularities in human behavior, even if the terminology "statistical regularity" was not always available. No one ever doubted that, for example, there are true statements of the form *90 percent of people with such-and-such a temperament and upbringing tend to succumb to such-and-such a temptation*. This statement does *not* say that each individual succumbing is "produced" by something called "chance." It does not say anything about the individual event *at all*.

Nor does it help to say that our actions are "random" rather than "chance." There are many concepts of randomness used in statistics; they all have to do with the distribution of frequencies in subsequences of the main sequence. None of them means "produced by chance." The incompatibility is *not* between indeterministic physics and moral responsibility; it is between moral responsibility and a metaphysics—the metaphysics of Chance.

The suggestion that quantum mechanical indeterminacy may, after all, bear on questions of responsibility is supported by the following reflection. Assume that determinism is true, and assume—what is extremely plausible—that very few people who commit evil deeds are determined to commit them by their genes *alone*. (Indeed, if someone had *such* bad heredity that he was bound to commit crimes no matter how he was brought up or in what circumstances he found himself, we would be inclined to *excuse* him on just that account.) It is part of our contemporary moral sensibility that certain environmental conditions are (at least partly) *excusing*. For example, someone raised in poverty, especially if raised by cruel and unloving parents, deprived of proper moral guidance, and so on, seems to us less blameworthy than a rich, "advantaged" person who does wrong. Yet, if our supposition is correct, the rich, "advantaged" person is also the victim of a pattern of environmental circumstances—one that we do not have a name for (like "poverty"), and, indeed, one we do not recognize. It is also true of the rich, "advantaged" person that if he or she had had a different upbringing and environment, he or she would not have become evil. So, in this sense, determinism does threaten our entire way of thinking about moral responsibility and excusability.

On the indeterminist picture, the situation is different. What similarity is there between the "advantaged" person who does something he might well not have done and the disadvantaged person who does something he had virtually no chance of not doing (or performs an act such that he was virtually bound to perform some act of that *type*, if not that token action itself)? The answer "they were both caused to do what they did by Chance" is a kind of metaphysical joke. There is a difference between real environmental conditions and metaphysical bogeys.

Reason

I want to say something now about a very old problem in philosophy—Hume's problem of induction. One way of stating the problem is this: we believe that the future will resemble the past—not, of course, in every respect, but in the respect that the statements we call "laws of nature" will continue to be true in the future (or *as* true as they have been in the past). Some scientists think that even this may not be true; that in billions of years the "laws of nature" may change, or at least the values of the basic physical constants they contain may change; but I shall not be concerned with such a vast time scale as billions of years. If we confine ourselves to the next hundred, or thousand, or even million years, then we do believe that the laws of nature will be the same—at least the basic laws of physics and chemistry (and it is not clear that the other sciences, such as sociology, *have* "laws" in the same sense as physics and chemistry do). Also, we believe that the universe will continue to consist of electrons, neutrons, protons, and so on. There are other very general respects in which we assume that the future will resemble the past; but for our purposes these two will suffice. If this is false, if at some future time *t* the universe stops obeying the laws it has always obeyed, stops even consisting of the same elementary constituents it has always consisted of, we may speak of a global catastrophe. The assumption that the future will resemble the past means that there will not be a global catastrophe (in the next thousand, or whatever, years). How do we know that this is true or even probably true?

Some people say that if there is going to be such a global catastrophe, we cannot do anything about it anyway, so we are justified in ignoring the possibility; but it is not true that "we cannot do anything about it anyway" (unless we assume the global catastrophe would wipe out life, which is not necessarily the case—remember, the *laws* are going to be different!). Suppose that in California there is an occultist sect which in fact predicts a global catastrophe for next year, and which pretends to tell us exactly what we must do to survive it. Then there is something we can "do about it," if that sect is right—we can all join that sect and follow its instructions. It is not as if the human race could not help being scientific—that is hardly the case!—or was incapable of joining and following cults. What is really meant by the statement that "we cannot do anything about it" if there is going to be a global catastrophe is that we cannot have *good reason* to believe such a cult rather than any other cult or fad or school of thought. But do we have *good reason* to believe what we do believe? Is there such a thing as good reason?

Some philosophers nowadays say that reasonableness is just "coherence"; our beliefs are reasonable just in the case that our experiences, methods, and beliefs all mutually "cohere" or support and accord with one another. I do not know just what "coherence" is (nor do I know where the *criteria* of "coherence" are supposed to come from—do they too only have to "cohere"? If so, anyone can reasonably believe *anything,* provided he just has the right notion of "coherence"). But, assuming that we are allowed to use our natural judgments of what is plausible and implausible in judging "coherence" (and one cannot reason at all if one tries to stand outside of every tradition of reasoning), let us ask whether our beliefs *are* all that "coherent" with respect to the future resembling the past.

In one sense they are. We believe that a great many *specific* laws will continue to be true (or as true as they are now) in the future; and each of these beliefs supports the general belief that there will not be a global catastrophe. But each of these specific beliefs was confirmed *assuming* there would not be a global catastrophe. This only shows that our belief that the future will resemble the past is a very fundamental belief—so fundamental that all specific beliefs are adjusted to it. In itself this is good, not bad—we would expect a coherent system to have some fundamental assumptions, and some kind of logical structure. But one more question: what is the *cause* of our belief that the future will resemble the past? Knowledge is part of the subject matter of our knowledge; we should expect a really coherent system to include some plausible account of how we know that system itself to be true, or approximately true.

The question is, of course, very strange. Traditionally, philosophers thought beliefs had *reasons,* not *causes.* But it is an essential part of the story that belief is itself a formation of brain traces, or something of that kind, and that it is *caused*—caused by natural selection plus cultural conditioning. We are caused to believe that the future will resemble the past—caused, no doubt, by the fact that that belief has had survival value *in the past*.

But that means our belief that the future will resemble the past is exactly like the belief (or rather the expectation) that dinosaurs doubtless had that conditions would continue to be excellent for dinosaurs! There is *no* general law that what had survival value in the past will continue to have survival value in the future. In the words of the philosopher George Santayana, our belief that the future will resemble the past, and indeed all of our "inductive" beliefs, are based on *animal faith*.

But belief that the future will resemble the past is at least *reasonable* (even if we seem to have trouble in saying why). I want to talk now about some other things that we believe that are not even reasonable. By all the evidence, *Homo sapiens,* especially as we know him today, was already on the planet thirty thousand years ago. At that time there was no civilization, no mathematics beyond, perhaps, a little counting, and no technology beyond stone axes and fires. Yet our intellectual abilities were, according to evolutionists, essentially as they are today—a Cro-Magnon or *Homo sapiens* boy or girl of that period, if transported to the present day, could learn calculus or physics, perhaps even become a scientist or inventor. According to the current scientific view, all this latent intelligence was the result of natural selection.

Think about what this means. We are, on this view, computing machines programmed by blind evolution—computing machines programmed by a fool! For evolution *is* a fool as far as knowing about calculus, or proving theorems, or making up physical theories, or inventing telephones is concerned. A fool, but not a moron—evolution is very smart as far as the behavior of deer or manipulating stone axes is concerned. What I mean is this: selection pressure would naturally weed out members of the different humanoid species who could not learn to hunt deer, use stone axes and spears, make fires, or cooperate in a hunt. In that sense, being programmed by blind evolution (selection pressure) is like being programmed by someone who has a good idea of what it takes to make a fire, hunt deer, and so forth. It is as if we had a maker who knew a lot about deer, fires, hunts, and so on. But there was no selection pressure for being able to make up scientific theories—that was not something *any* member of the several humanoid species did *then*. So that a device molded by selection pressure to do the one thing should be able to do the other is quite a miracle—exactly as if we set a fool (who knew about hunting with stone axes and spears) to program a computer and he programmed it so that it could *also* discover the theory of relativity.

Sometimes the suggestion is advanced that our abilities to do mathematics, discover physical laws of an abstract kind, and so forth are the result of concomitant variation and not selection pressure. (What this means is that sometimes an organ appears because the DNA instructions for manufacturing that organ happened to be carried on a gene that also carried something else that did have survival value. So the species acquired the organ; but the survival value of the organ was quite irrelevant.) After all, it is pointed out, we do not know what constraints nature operated under in packing billions of neural connections into a small brain pan.

Again, think about what this means. Nature—which imposed the constraints on how neural connections could be manufactured and installed—does not even have the pseudo-"intelligence" that selection pressure does; that is, nature has no *ends,* and does not simulate having any. (Selection pressure at least *simulates* having ends.) So it is as if selection pressure—the fool that programmed us—had to operate subject to constraints imposed by a *moron.* And it just happened that the moron imposed such lucky constraints that the only way the fool could program us involved making us intelligent enough to do mathematics, discover general relativity, and so on! The theory that we are computers programmed by a fool operating subject to the constraints imposed by a moron is worse, not better, than the "selection pressure" theory. And "concomitant variation" is just a fancy name for *coincidence.*

At this point I imagine that an objection will occur to you. Is it not our *intelligence* that accounts for the ability of our species to do natural philosophy, mathematics, and so on? And does not intelligence have survival value if anything does? The answer is that intelligence, in the sense of the ability to use language, manipulate tools, and so on, is not enough to enable a species to do science. It also has to have the right set of *prejudices.* But let me explain.

Suppose we have evolved with all the intelligence that we have (whatever "intelligence" is), but with a firm prejudice against the unobservable. Suppose we only believed in things we could see, hear, feel, touch, and so forth. (We would make an excellent race of logical positivists.) We would not believe in gods, spirits in the trees and in the rivers, substance and accidents, forces and "natural motions," and so on. We would never develop a religion or a metaphysics. But as far as observable things are concerned, we could be as "scientific" as you please. We might even be more "rational" than humans are, because we would not be led astray by "metaphysical prejudices." Then we—or such a race of beings—could hunt deer, use stone axes and spears, make fires, and so forth, just as well as we actually can. Such a race might even develop a civilization to the level of ancient Egypt. It would not develop geometry, beyond the Egyptian level of practical land measurement, because the notion of a straight line with no thickness at all, or the notion of a point with no dimensions at all, would make no sense to it. It would never speculate about atoms swarming in the void, or about *vis viva*. And, interestingly enough, it would never develop physics or mathematics!

There are only two possibilities here. Either we postulate unobservable causes for observable events, and speculate about what these might be because it is *reasonable* to do so (but then what is reason?); or this is just a habit that we evolved with by *luck*. If, as positivists claim, *all* of our speculations about unobservables prior to modern science were *wrong*, as belief in objective values, God, and essences are supposed to be—or at best totally untestable prior to the nineteenth century, as belief in atoms swarming in the void was—then our incurable habit of speculating about unobservable causes for observable phenomena either had no survival value, or only had psychological value (it gave us comfort, and so on), which is irrelevant to and has no bearing upon truth and falsity. So then it is sheer *luck* that this metaphysical prejudice of ours, which we need to have to do science, evolved at all, or that we did not evolve with metaphysical prejudices which would prevent us from ever thinking of good scientific theories!

Although the point of view I am advancing here—that one cannot discover laws of nature unless one brings to nature a set of *a priori* prejudices which is not hopelessly wrong (one mathematical model for this idea is the idea of the scientist as "internalizing" a so-called "subjective probability metric" which assigns an antecedent probability—a probability *prior to experiment*—to hypotheses)—is becoming commonplace among inductive logicians, it is obvious why it should make some people feel uncomfortable. So an alternative account of the success of science is often proposed. This alternative account uses the notions of *trial and error* and *simplicity*.

After all, it is said, it took thousands of years before the theory of relativity was thought of. Maybe what happens is that we just test one scientific hypothesis after another until by trial and error we come to the right one. (Often it is added that we *must* eventually come to the true laws of nature, provided only that they are sufficiently "simple." This is where "simplicity" comes in.)

Now, the notion of simplicity is not really a very clear one. Almost *any* theory can be made to *look* "simple" if we are allowed to invent a notation specially for the purpose. And this is exactly what we do in science—we make up our notations so that our theories will look simple and elegant. It is not as if we were given a notation in advance and told "the laws of nature are expressible by simple and elegant formulas in *this* notation."

And, indeed, the history of science does not support the view that it was all trial and error, either in the sense of random trial and error or systematic search through all possibilities. Galileo discovered the Law of Inertia by thinking about and modifying fourteenth-century ideas, which themselves were a modification of Aristotle's ideas. It was a metaphysical line of thought that provided the general ballpark in which to look for a law of inertia. Einstein was working in the general ballpark provided by philosophical speculations about the relativity of motion, themselves centuries older than the evidence, when he produced the special theory of relativity. The general theory of relativity was suggested by geometrical analogies. And so on. There does not seem to be anything common to all the good theories that scientists succeeded in producing except this: each was suggested by some line of thinking that seemed *reasonable,* at least to the scientist who came up with the theory. (Of course, there is a great deal of disagreement about what seems reasonable, especially where "far-out" ideas are concerned.)

I am suggesting that the old term "natural philosophy" *was* a good name for what we now call "science." Science is arrived at by reason—not infallible, *a priori* reason that makes no mistakes, to be sure, but plausible reasoning that is often subjective, often controversial, but that, nevertheless, comes up with truths and approximate truths far more often than any trial-and-error procedure could be expected to do.

My purpose is not to argue that the theory of evolution is wrong.

Nor am I covertly arguing for the doctrine of special creation. My own view is that the success of science cannot be anything but a puzzle as long as we view concepts and objects as radically independent; that is, as long as we think of "the world" as an entity that has a fixed nature, determined once and for all, independently of our framework of concepts.[9] Discussing this idea goes far beyond the bounds of this essay. But if we do shift our way of thinking to the extent of regarding "the world" as partly constituted by the representing mind, then many things in our popular philosophy (and even in technical philosophy) must be reexamined. To mention just two of them: (1) Locke held that the great metaphysical problem of realism, the problem of the relation of our concepts to their objects, would be solved just by natural scientific investigation, indefinitely continued. Kant held that Locke was wrong, and that this *philosophical* question was never going to be solved by empirical science. I am suggesting that on this subject Kant was right and Locke was wrong (which does not mean that science is unimportant in philosophy). (2) Since the birth of science thousands of years ago we have bifurcated the world into "reality"—what physical science describes—and appearance. And we have relegated aesthetic qualities, ethical qualities, psychological traits ("stubbornness," "patience," "rudeness"), and sometimes even dispositions and modalities, to the junk heap of "appearance." I am suggesting that this is an error, and a subtle version of Locke's error. The "primary/secondary" or "reality/appearance" dichotomy is founded on and presupposes what Kant called "the transcendental illusion"— that empirical science describes (and *exhaustively* describes) a concept-independent, perspective-independent "reality."

This essay has neither explained nor defended these views of mine. Its purpose has been more modest: to encourage those who read it *not* to confuse science as it actually is—an ongoing activity whose results, spectacular as they are, are ever subject to modification, revision, and incorporation in a different theory or a different perspective—with any metaphysical picture that tries to wrap itself in the mantle of science; and to remind the reader that common sense and critical intelligence still have to be brought *to* scientific (as to all other) ideas; they are not a commodity to be purchased *from* "science." And, last but not least, I have tried to suggest that an adequate *philosophical* account of reason must not *explain away* ethical facts, but enable us to understand how they can be facts, and how we can know them.

11. Objectivity and the Science/Ethics Distinction

The logical positivists argued for a sharp fact/value dichotomy in a very simple way: scientific statements (outside of logic and pure mathematics), they said, are "empirically verifiable" and value judgments are "unverifiable." This argument continues to have wide appeal to economists (not to say laymen), even though it has for some years been looked upon as naive by philosophers. One reason the argument is naive is that it assumes that there is such a thing as "the method of verification" of each isolated *scientifically meaningful* sentence. But this is very far from being the case. Newton's entire theory of gravity, for example, does not *in and of itself* (that is, in the absence of suitable "auxiliary hypotheses") imply any testable predictions whatsoever.[1] As Quine has emphasized,[2] reviving arguments earlier used by Duhem, scientific statements "meet the test of experience as a corporate body"; the idea that each scientific sentence has its own range of confirming observations and its own range of disconfirming observations, independent of what other sentences it is conjoined to, is wrong. If a sentence that does not, in and of itself, by its very meaning, have a "method of verification" is meaningless, then most of theoretical science turns out to be meaningless!

A second feature of the view that "ethical sentences are cognitively meaningless because they have no method of verification" is that even if it had been correct, what it would have drawn would not have been a *fact/value* dichotomy. For, according to the positivists themselves, metaphysical sentences are cognitively meaningless for the same reason as are ethical sentences: they are "unverifiable in principle." (So are poetic sentences, among others.) The positivist position is well summarized by Vivian Walsh:[3]

> Consider the 'putative' proposition 'murder is wrong'. What empirical findings, the positivists would ask, tend to confirm or discon-

firm this? If saying that murder is wrong is merely a misleading way of reporting what a given society believes, this is a perfectly good sociological fact, and the proposition is a respectable empirical one. But the person making a moral judgement will not accept this analysis. Positivists then wielded their absolute analytic/synthetic distinction: if 'murder is wrong' is not a synthetic (empirically testable) proposition it must be an analytic proposition, like (they believed) those of logic and mathematics—in effect, a tautology. The person who wished to make the moral judgement would not accept this, and was told that the disputed utterance was a 'pseudo-proposition' like those of poets, theologians and metaphysicians.

As Walsh goes on to explain, by the end of the 1950s "most of the theses necessary for this remarkable claim" had been abandoned; the positivist theory of "cognitive significance" had fallen. The absolute analytic/synthetic distinction was seen to fail as an account of how scientific theories are actually put together. Writing in a volume honoring Carnap,[4] Quine summed up its demise, writing that "the lore of our fathers is black with fact and white with convention, but there are no *completely* white threads and no quite black ones." Explaining the impact of all this, Walsh wrote:

> Another retreat, forced upon logical empiricism by the *needs* of pure science, opened the way for a further rehabilitation of moral philosophy. The old positivist attack on the status of moral judgements had required the claim that each *single* proposition must, at least in principle, be open to test. It became evident that many of the propositions of which the higher theory of pure science are composed could not survive this demand. Theoretical propositions, the logical empiricists decided, became 'indirectly' meaningful if part of a theory which possessed (supposed) observation statements which had empirical confirmation to some degree (never mind that the theoretical statement/observation statement dichotomy itself broke down!); but the clear fact/value distinction of the early positivists depended upon being able to see if *each single* proposition passed muster. To borrow and adapt Quine's vivid image, if a theory may be black with fact and white with convention, it might well (as far as logical empiricism could tell) be red with values. Since for them confirmation *or* falsification had to be a property of a theory *as a whole,* they had no way of unraveling this whole cloth. Yet even today economists whose philosophical ancestry is logical empiricism still write as if the old positivist fact/value dichotomy were beyond challenge.

The collapse of the grounds on which the dichotomy was defended during the period Walsh is describing has not, however, led to a demise of the dichotomy, even among professional philosophers. What it has led to is a change in the nature of the *arguments* offered for the dichotomy. Today, it is defended more and more on metaphysical grounds. At the same time, even the defenders of the dichotomy concede that the old arguments for the dichotomy were bad ones. For example, when I was a graduate student, a paradigmatic explanation and defense of the dichotomy would have been Charles Stevenson's. I attacked Stevenson's position at length in a book published some years ago.[5] When Bernard Williams's last book appeared,[6] I found that Williams gave virtually the same arguments against this position. Yet Williams still defends a sharp "science/ethics" dichotomy; and he regards his science/ethics dichotomy as capturing something that was essentially right about the old "fact/value" dichotomy.

Something else has accompanied this change in the way the dichotomy is defended. The old position, in its several versions—emotivism, voluntarism, prescriptivism—was usually referred to as "non-cognitivism." Non-cognitivism was, so to speak, the generic name of the position, and the more specific labels were the proprietary names given the position by the various distributors. And the generic name was appropriate, because all the various slightly different formulations of the generic product had this essential ingredient in common: ethical sentences were "non-cognitive," that is to say, they were neither true nor false. Today, philosophers like Williams[7] do not deny that ethical sentences can be true or false; what they deny is that they can be true or false *non-perspectivally*. Thus, the position has been (appropriately) renamed: while the proprietary versions of the new improved drug still have various differences one from the other, they all accept the name relativism. *Non-cognitivism has been rebaptized as relativism.*

The Entanglement of Fact and Value

Just why and how non-cognitivism has given way to relativism is a complicated question, and it is not the purpose of this essay to explore it in detail. But one reason is surely an increased appreciation of what might be called the *entanglement* of fact and value. That entanglement was a constant theme in John Dewey's writing. But this aspect of pragmatism was neglected in Anglo-American philosophy after

Dewey's death, in spite of Morton White's valiant effort to keep it alive,[8] and it was, perhaps, Iris Murdoch who reopened the theme in a very different way.

Murdoch's three essays[9] contain a large number of valuable insights and remarks; two have proved especially influential. Murdoch was the first to emphasize that languages have two very different sorts of ethical concepts: abstract ethical concepts (Williams calls them "thin" ethical concepts), such as "good" and "right," and more descriptive, less abstract concepts (Williams calls them "thick" ethical concepts) such as, for example, *cruel, pert, inconsiderate, chaste*. Murdoch (and later, and in a more spelled-out way, McDowell)[10] argued that there is no way of saying what the "descriptive component" of the meaning of a word like *cruel* or *inconsiderate* is without using a word of the same kind; as McDowell put the argument, a word has to be connected to a certain set of "evaluative interests" in order to function in the way such a thick ethical word functions; and the speaker has to be aware of those interests and be able to identify imaginatively with them if he is to apply the word to novel cases or circumstances in the way a sophisticated speaker of the language would. The attempt of non-cognitivists to split such words into a "descriptive meaning component" and a "prescriptive meaning component" founders on the impossibility of saying what the "descriptive meaning" of, say, *cruel* is without using the word *cruel* itself, or a synonym. Second, Murdoch emphasized that when we are actually confronted with situations requiring ethical evaluation, whether or not they also require some action on our part, the sorts of descriptions that we need—descriptions of the motives and character of human beings, above all—are descriptions in the language of a "sensitive novelist," not in scientistic or bureaucratic jargon. When a situation or a person or a motive is appropriately described, the decision as to whether something is "good" or "bad" or "right" or "wrong" frequently follows automatically. For example, our evaluation of a person's moral stature may critically depend on whether we describe her as "impertinent" or "unstuffy." Our life-world, Murdoch is telling us, does not factor neatly into "facts" and "values"; we live in a messy human world in which seeing reality with all its nuances, seeing it as George Eliot, or Flaubert, or Henry James, or Murdoch herself can, to some extent, teach us to see it, and making appropriate "value judgments" are simply not separable abilities.

When I first read *The Sovereignty of Good* I thought that Murdoch gave a perceptive description of the sphere of private morality (which is, of course, the sphere with which a novelist has to deal), but that she too much ignored the public sphere, the sphere in which issues of social justice arise and must be worked out. But more recently I have come to think that a similar entanglement of the factual and the ethical applies to this sphere as well. It is all well and good to describe hypothetical cases in which two people "agree on the facts and disagree about values," but in the world in which I grew up such cases are unreal. When and where did a Nazi and an anti-Nazi, a communist and a social democrat, a fundamentalist and a liberal, or even a Republican and a Democrat, agree on the facts? Even when it comes to one specific policy question, say, what to do about the decline of American education, or about unemployment, or about drugs, every argument I have ever heard has exemplified the entanglement of the ethical and the factual. There is a weird discrepancy between the way philosophers who subscribe to a sharp fact/value distinction *make* ethical arguments sound and the way ethical arguments *actually* sound. (Stanley Cavell once remarked that Stevenson writes like someone who has *forgotten* what ethical discussion is like.)[11]

Relativism and the Fact/Value Dichotomy

According to Bernard Williams, a properly worked out relativism can do justice to the way in which fact and value can be inseparable—do justice to the way in which some statements which are both descriptive and true ("Caligula was a mad tyrant") can also be value judgments. The idea is to replace the fact/value distinction by a very different distinction, the distinction between *truth* and *absoluteness*. Although Williams does not explain very clearly what he understands truth to be, he seems to think truth is something like right assertibility in the local language game; that is, if the practices and shared values of a culture determine an established use for a word like "chaste," a use which is sufficiently definite to permit speakers to come to agreement on someone's chastity or lack of chastity (or whatever the example of a "thick ethical concept" may be), then it can be simply true that a person in the culture is "chaste" (or "cruel," or "pious," or whatever). Of course, if I do not belong to the culture in question and do not share the relevant evaluative interests, then I will not describe the person in question as "chaste," even if I know that that is a correct thing to say in that culture; I will be "disbarred" from using the word, as Williams puts it. As he also puts it (with deliberate paradox), that so-and-so is chaste is possible knowledge for someone in the culture, but not possible knowledge for *me*.

If truth were the only dimension with respect to which we could evaluate the cognitive credentials of statements, then Williams would be committed to ethical realism, or at least to the rejection of ethical *anti*-realism. For, on his view, "Mary is chaste," "Peter is cruel," "George is a perfect knight" can be true in the very same sense in which "snow is white" is true, while still being ethical utterances. But there *is* an insight in non-cognitivism, these philosophers claim, even if non-cognitivism was mistaken in what it took to be its most essential thesis, the thesis that ethical sentences are not capable of truth (or, alternatively, the thesis that an ethical sentence has a distinct "value component," and this "value component" is not capable of truth). That thesis (or those theses) are rejected by Williams. As I said, he accepts the arguments of Murdoch and McDowell against the "two components" theory; he recognizes the way in which fact and value are entangled in our concepts; and he agrees that ethical sentences can be true. How, then, can he maintain that there was an insight contained in non-cognitivism? What *was* the insight that the fact/value distinction tried to capture?

According to Williams, there are truths and truths. If I say that grass is green, for example, I certainly speak the truth; but I do not speak what he calls the *absolute* truth. I do not describe the world as it is "anyway," independently of any and every "perspective." The concept "green," and possibly the concept "grass" as well, are not concepts that finished science would use to describe the properties that things have apart from any "local perspective." Martians or Alpha Centaurians, for example, might not have the sorts of eyes we have. They would not recognize any such property as "green" (except as a "secondary quality" of interest to human beings, a disposition to affect the sense organs of *Homo sapiens* in a certain way), and "grass" may be too unscientific a classification to appear in their finished science. Only concepts that would appear in the (final) description of the world that any species of determined natural researchers is destined to converge to can be regarded as telling us how the world is "anyway" ("to the maximum degree independent of perspective"). Only such concepts can appear in statements which are "absolute." And the philosophically important point—or one of them, for there is something to be added—is that although value judgments containing thick ethical concepts can be true, they cannot be absolute. The world, as it is in itself, is *cold*. Values (like colors) are *projected* onto the world, not discovered in it.

What has to be added is that, on Williams's view, values are even *worse off* than colors in this respect. For the discovery that green is a secondary quality has not undermined our ability to use the word. We no longer think that colors are nondispositional properties of external things, but this in no way affects the utility of color classification. But the realization that value attributes, even "thick" ones ("chaste," "cruel," "holy"), are projections has a tendency to cause us to lose our ability to use those terms. If we become reflective to too great a degree, if we identify ourselves too much with the point of view of the Universe, we will no longer be able to employ our ethical concepts. The realization that ethical concepts are projections places us in a ticklish position: we cannot stop being reflective, but we cannot afford to be (very much of the time) *too* reflective. We are in an unstable equilibrium.

The reason for this difference between ordinary secondary qualities like green and thick ethical attributes like chastity, according to Williams, is that the interests which color classification subserves are universal among human beings, whereas the interests that thick ethical concepts subserve are the interests of one human community (one "social world") or another. Even if different cultures have somewhat different color classifications, there is no *opposition* between one culture's color classifications and those of another culture. But the interests which define one social world may be in conflict with the interests which define a different social world. And realizing that my ethical descriptions are in this way parochial (however "true" they may also be) is decentering.

Williams believes that coming to realize just how far ethical description misses describing the world as it is "absolutely" not only does but *should* affect our first-order ethical judgments. There are *moral* consequences to the "truth in relativism" (speaking, of course, from within *our* social world). The moral consequence (and perhaps also the metaphysical consequence), according to Williams, is that moral praise or condemnation of another way of life loses all point when that other way of life is too distant from ours (too distant in the sense that neither way of life is a live option for the other). It makes no sense to try to evaluate the way of life of the ancient Aztecs, for example, or of the Samurai, or of a Bronze Age society. To ask whether their ways of life were *right,* or their judgments *true,* is (or should be) impossible for us; the question should lapse, once we understand the nonabsoluteness of ethical discourse. And the fact that the question lapses *constitutes* "the truth in relativism."

Absoluteness

This dichotomy between what the world is like independent of any local perspective and what is projected by us seems to me utterly indefensible. I shall begin by examining the picture of science which guides Williams: that science converges to a single true theory, a single explanatory picture of the universe. But one is hard put to know why one should believe this.

If we start at the level of commonsense objects, say stones, it suffices to note that, in rational reconstruction, we can take a stone to be an aggregation, or as logicians say a "mereological sum," of time-slices of particles (or, alternatively, of field-points—notice that these are incompatible but equally good choices!), or we can take a stone to be an individual which consists of *different* particles in different possible worlds (and also occupies different locations in space in different possible worlds) while remaining self-identical. If a stone consists of *different* time-slices of particles in different possible worlds, then it cannot (as a matter of modal logic) be *identical* with an aggregation (mereological sum) of time-slices of particles,[12] and obviously it makes no sense to say that a collection of space-time points could have occupied a different location than it did. So, if it is simply a matter of how we formalize our language whether we say (with Saul Kripke) that stones, animals, persons, and so on are *not* identical with mereological sums at all, or say (as suggested by Lewis)[13] that they *are* mereological sums (and take care of Kripke's difficulty by claiming that when we say that "the" stone consists of different particle-slices in different possible worlds, then what that means is that the various modal "counterparts" of the stone in different possible worlds consist of different particle-slices, and not that the self-identical stone consists of different particle-slices in different possible worlds)—and to me this certainly looks like a mere choice of a formalism, and not a question of fact—we will be forced to admit that it is partly a matter of our conceptual choice which scientific object a given commonsense object—a stone or a person—is identified with.

Nor is the situation any better in theoretical physics. At the level of space-time geometry, there is the well-known fact that we can take points to be individuals *or* we can take them to be mere limits. States of a system can be taken to be quantum mechanical superpositions of particle interactions (à la Feynman) or quantum mechanical superpositions of field states. (This is the contemporary form of the wave-particle duality.) And there are many other examples.

Not only do single theories have a bewildering variety of alternative rational reconstructions (with quite different ontologies), but there is no evidence at all for the claim (which is essential to Williams's belief in an "absolute conception of the world") that science converges to a *single* theory. I do not doubt that there is some convergence in scientific knowledge, and not just at the observational level. We know, for example, that certain *equations* are approximately correct descriptions of certain phenomena. Under certain conditions, the Poisson equation of Newtonian gravitational theory gives an approximately correct description of the gravitational field of a body. But the theoretical picture of Newtonian mechanics has been utterly changed by general relativity; and the theoretical picture of general relativity may in turn be utterly replaced by supergravitation theory, or by some theory not yet imagined. We simply do not have the evidence to justify speculation as to whether or not science is "destined" to converge to some one definite theoretical picture. It could be, for example, that although we will discover more and more approximately correct and increasingly accurate equations, the *theoretical picture* which we use to explain those equations will continue to be upset by scientific revolutions. As long as our ability to predict, and to mathematicize our predictions in attractive ways, continues to advance, science will "progress" quite satisfactorily; to say, as Williams sometimes does, that convergence to one big picture is required by the very concept of knowledge is sheer dogmatism.

Yet, without the postulate that science converges to a single definite theoretical picture with a unique ontology and a unique set of theoretical predicates, the whole notion of "absoluteness" collapses. It is, indeed, the case that ethical knowledge cannot claim absoluteness; but that is because the notion of absoluteness is incoherent. Mathematics and physics, as well as ethics and history and politics, show our conceptual choices; the world is not going to impose a single language upon us, no matter what we choose to talk about.

According to Williams, what makes the truth of a statement "absolute" is not the fact that scientists are destined to converge on the truth of that statement, that is to say, admit it to the corpus of accepted scientific belief in the long run, but rather the *explanation* of the fact of convergence. We converge upon the statement that *S* is true, where *S* is a statement which figures in "the absolute conception of the world," because "that is the way things are" (independently of perspective). But what sort of an explanation is *this?* The idea that some statements force themselves upon us because "that is how things are" is taken with immense seriousness by Williams; indeed, it is the center of his entire metaphysical picture. Sometimes when I don't want to give a reason for something I may shrug my shoulders and say, "Well, that's just how things are"; but that is not what Williams is doing here. "That is how things are" (independently of perspective) is supposed to be a *reason* (Williams calls it an "explanation"), not a refusal to give a reason.

The idea that some statements get recognized as true (if we investigate long enough and carefully enough) because they simply describe the world in a way which is independent of perspective is just a new version of the old "correspondence theory of truth." As we have already seen, Williams does not claim that truth is correspondence; for him, truth is rather right assertibility in the language game. But *some* truths—the "absolute" ones—are rightly assertible in the language game *because* they correspond to the way things (mind-independently) are. Even if correspondence is not the definition of truth, it is the *explanation* of absolute truth. And I repeat my question: What sort of an explanation is *this?*

The idea of a statement's corresponding to the way things are, the idea of a term's having a correspondence to a language-independent class of things, and the idea of a predicate's having a correspondence to a language-independent attribute are ideas which have no metaphysical force at all unless the correspondence in question is thought of as a genuine relation between items independent of us and items in language, a correspondence which is imposed by the world, as it were, and not just a tautological feature of the way we talk about talk. What I have in mind by this remark, which may sound puzzling, is this: if you think it is just a *tautology* that *snow* corresponds to snow, or that "Snow is white" is true if and only if snow is white, then you regard the "correspondence" between the word *snow* and snow as a correspondence *within* language. Within our language we can talk about snow and we can talk about the word *snow* and we can *say* they correspond. To this even a philosopher who rejects the very idea of a substantive notion of truth or a substantive notion of reference can agree. But if, as Williams believes, the fact that we are "fated" to accept the sentence "Snow is white" is *explained* by something "out there" and by the fact that the sentence corresponds to that something "out there," then the correspondence too must be "out there." A *verbal* correspondence cannot play this kind of explanatory role. Williams's picture is that there is a *fixed* set of objects "out there," the "mind-independent objects," and a fixed relation—a relation between words and sentences in *any* language in which "absolute" truths can be expressed and those fixed mind-independent Reals—and that this relation *explains* the (alleged) fact that science converges. If this picture is unintelligible, then the notion of an "absolute conception of the world" must also be rejected as unintelligible.

Now, I have argued for a number of years that this picture *is* unintelligible. First, I contend that there is not *one* notion of an "object" but an open class of possible uses of the word *object*—even of the technical logical notion of an object (value of a variable of quantification). The idea that reality itself fixes the use of the word *object* (or the use of the word *correspondence*) is a hangover from prescientific metaphysics.[14] Second, the idea of the world "singling out" a correspondence between objects and our words is incoherent. As a matter of model-theoretic fact, we know that even if we somehow fix the intended truth-values of our sentences, not just in the actual world but in all possible worlds, this does *not* determine a unique correspondence between words and items in the universe of discourse.[15] Third, even if we require that words not merely "correspond" to items in the universe of discourse but be causally connected to them in some way, the required notion of "causal connection" is deeply *intentional*. When we say that a word and its referent must stand in a "causal connection of the appropriate kind," then, even in cases where this is true, the notion of "causal connection" being appealed to is fundamentally the notion of *explanation*. And explanation is a notion which lies in the same circle as reference and truth.[16]

But why should this be a problem? Why shouldn't Williams and other metaphysical realists just say, "Very well, then. The ultimate description of the world—the world as it is in itself—requires intentional notions"? (In fact, Williams does not say this; Williams ends his book on Descartes[17] with an endorsement of Quine's criticism of intentional notions!) The answer, of course, is that a science of the intentional is a we-know-not-what. According to Williams, what gives the notion of an absolute conception of the world clout, what saves this notion from being a we-know-not-what, is that we have a good idea of what an absolute conception of the world would look like in *present-day physics*. But Williams does not expect present-day physics, or anything that looks like present-day physics, to yield an account of the intentional. He is thus caught in the following predicament: a correspondence theory of truth requires a substantive theory of reference. (And, I have argued, a belief in such a theory is hidden in Williams's talk of "the way things are" *explaining* why we will come to believe "the absolute conception of the world.") If we say, "Well, who knows, perhaps future science—we know not how—will come up with such a theory," then we abandon the claim that we know the *form* of the "absolute conception of the world" *now*. The absolute conception of the world becomes a "we know not what." If we say, on the other hand, "Reference can be reduced to physical parameters," then we commit ourselves to refuting the arguments[18] against the possibility of a physicalist reduction of semantic notions. But Williams clearly does not wish to undertake any such commitment.

Instead, Williams's suggestion is that the intentional (or the "semantic") is itself perspectival, and the absolute conception will someday explain why this kind of talk is useful (as it explains why talk of "grass" and "green" is useful, even though "grass" and "green" are not notions that figure in the absolute conception of the world). But here Williams shows a wobbly grasp of the logical structure of his own position. For the absolute conception of the world was *defined* in terms of the idea that some statements describe the world with a minimum of "distortion," that they describe it "as it is," that they describe it "independently of perspective"—and what does any of this talk mean, unless something like a correspondence theory of truth is in place? Williams tacitly assumes a correspondence theory of truth when he *defines* the absolute conception, and then forgets that he did this when he suggests that we do not need to assume that such semantic notions as the "content" of a sentence will turn out to figure in the absolute conception itself.

Metaphysics and Entanglement

What led Williams to defend this complicated metaphysical theory was the desire to assert a "truth in relativism" while resisting relativism in science. But in the process of building up this intricate construction with its two kinds of truth (ordinary and "absolute"), its perspectivalism about secondary qualities, ethics, and, oddly, also about the intentional, and its antiperspectivalism about physics, he often ignores the entanglement of the factual and the ethical—although he himself stresses that entanglement at other points in his discussion. Consider, for example, the question as to whether we can condemn the Aztec way of life, or, more specifically, the human sacrifice that the Aztecs engaged in. On Williams's view, the Aztec belief that there were supernatural beings who would be angry with the Aztecs if they did not perform the sacrifices was, as a matter of scientific fact, wrong. This belief we *can* evaluate. It is simply false; and the absolute conception of the world, to the extent that we can now approximate it, tells us that it is false. But we cannot say that "the Aztec way of life" was wrong. Yet, the feature of the Aztec way of life that troubles us (the massive human sacrifice) and the belief about the world that conflicts with science were interdependent. If we can say that the Aztec belief about the gods was false, why can we not say that the practice to which it led was wrong (although, to be sure, understandable given the false factual belief)? If we are not allowed to call the practice wrong, why are we allowed to call the belief false? The so-called absolute and the ethical are just as entangled as the "factual" and the ethical.

For a very different sort of example, consider the admiration we sometimes feel for the Amish (traditional Mennonite) way of life. Even atheists sometimes admire the community solidarity, the helpfulness, and the simplicity of the Amish way. If a sophisticated atheist who felt this way were asked why she admires the Amish, she might say something like this: "I am not necessarily saying that we should give up our individualism altogether. But the kind of individualism and competitiveness which has brought so much scientific and economic progress also brings with it egotism, arrogance, selfishness, and downright cruelty. Even if the Amish way of life rests on what I regard as false beliefs, it does show some of the possibilities of a less competitive, less individualistic form of life; and perhaps we can learn about these possibilities from the Amish without adopting their religion." Now, Williams does not deny that we can say things like this; that we can learn from cultures to which we stand in the relation he calls "the relativity of distance," cultures which are not "real options" for us. But how does this differ from saying, "Some of the Amish beliefs are false, but other of their beliefs may be true"? Many of Williams's examples load the dice in favor of relativism by taking science to consist of individual judgments which may be called true or false, while taking cultures to offer only "take it as a whole or reject it as a whole" options.

The problem with the whole enterprise lies right here: Williams wants to acknowledge the entanglement of fact and value and hold on to the "absolute" character of (ideal) scientific knowledge at the same time. But there is no way to do this. It cannot be the case that scientific knowledge (future fundamental physics) is absolute and nothing else is; for fundamental physics cannot explain the possibility of *referring to* or *stating* anything, including fundamental physics itself. So, if everything that is *not* physics is "perspectival," then the notion of the "absolute" is itself hopelessly perspectival! For that notion, as I have already pointed out, is explained (albeit in a disguised way) in terms of notions which belong to the theory of reference and truth, and not to physics. And the idea of a "relativism of distance" which applies to ethics but not to science also fails, because ethics and science are as entangled as ethics and "fact." What we have in *Ethics and the Limits of Philosophy* is, in fact, *not* a serious argument for ethical relativism, but rather an expression of a mood. Reading Williams's book, one gets the feeling that one is being told that ethical relativism is the "sophisticated" point of view, the "modern" point of view, and that what is being offered is a *sophisticated reflection on the consequences of this presupposition*. But the presupposition itself does not stand up to any kind of examination—or at least, the way Williams defends the presupposition crumbles the moment one tries to subject it to any sort of careful examination.

Entanglement and Positivism

Relativism appeals to sophisticated people for different reasons. It appeals to Williams because the idea of ethical objectivity is metaphysically unacceptable; he does not see how we could *know* objective ethical truths if there were any. This metaphysical (or is it epistemological?) appeal is one I do not myself feel. It is not that I *do* know how I know that, for example, human dignity and freedom of speech are better than the alternatives, except in the sense of being able to offer the sorts of arguments that ordinary nonmetaphysical people with liberal convictions can and do offer. If I am asked to explain how ethical knowledge is possible at all in "absolute" terms, I have no answer. But there are all sorts of cases in which I have to say, "I know this, but I don't know how I know it." Certainly *physics* doesn't tell me how I know anything.

Another, very different, appeal is to those who fear that the alternative to cultural relativism is cultural imperialism. But recognizing that my judgments claim objective validity and recognizing that I am shaped by a particular culture and that I speak in a particular historical context are not incompatible. I agree with Williams that it would be silly to ask if the way of life of an eighteenth-century Samurai is "right" or "wrong"; but the reason this is a silly question isn't that we are too "distant," or that becoming an eighteenth-century Samurai isn't a "real option" for us. In my view, it would be a silly question if we *were* eighteenth-century Samurai. Indeed, "Is our own way of life right or wrong?" is a silly question, although it isn't silly to ask if this or that particular feature of our way of life is right or wrong, and "Is our view of the world right or wrong?" is a silly question, although it isn't silly to ask if this or that particular belief is right or wrong. As Dewey and Peirce taught us, real questions require a context and a point. But this is as true of scientific questions as it is of ethical ones. Instead of trying once again to discover some deep truth contained in positivism—in the fact/value dichotomy, or in "non-cognitivism," or in the verifiability theory of meaning—we should break the grip of positivism on our thinking once and for all.

The failure of the latest attempt to find some deep truths in positivism is no accident. Although Williams tries to do justice to the entanglement of fact and value, he fails to do so, because positivism was fundamentally a denial of entanglement, an insistence on sharp dichotomies: science/ethics, science/metaphysics, analytic/synthetic. The science/ethics dichotomy that Williams wants to preserve presupposed the science/metaphysics and analytic/synthetic distinctions that he rejects. This is why Williams's book-length attempt to spell out his position is either self-contradictory or hopelessly ambiguous at every crucial point.

Recognizing that the entanglement of fact and value, as well as of science and ethics, science and metaphysics, analytic and synthetic, is here to stay may also help us to see our way past another contemporary shibboleth: the supposed incompatibility of universalist (or "enlightenment") and parochial values. Recently I was struck by something Israel Scheffler has written: "I have always supposed that the universal and the particular are compatible, that grounding in a particular historical and cultural matrix is inevitable and could not conceivably be in conflict with universal principles. I have thus belonged to both sides of a divide which separated most Jewish academics and intellectuals of my generation."[19] When we argue about the universal applicability of principles like freedom of speech or distributive justice we are not claiming to stand outside of our own tradition, let alone outside of space and time, as some fear; we are standing within a tradition, and trying simultaneously to learn what in that tradition we are prepared to recommend to other traditions *and* to see what in that tradition may be inferior—inferior either to what other traditions have to offer, or to the best we may be capable of. Williams is right when he says that this kind of reflection may destroy what we have taken to be ethical knowledge: it may certainly lead us to reevaluate our beliefs, and to abandon *some* of them; but he is wrong when he fears that the most ultimate kind of reflective distance, the kind which is associated with the "absolute conception of the world," will destroy *all* ethical knowledge. Here he is worrying about a distance which is wholly illusory. No conception of the world is "absolute."

Williams describes the "absolute conception of the world" as something required by the very concept of knowledge. What this transcendental moment in Williams's argument shows is that, for him, there is no conceivable alternative to the idea of an absolute conception of the world—or no alternative save, perhaps, a skepticism as total as that of the ancient Greeks. But we are not forced to choose between scientism and skepticism in the way Williams thinks. The third possibility is to accept the position we are fated to occupy in any case, the position of beings who cannot have a view of the world that does not reflect our interests and values, but who are, for all that, committed to regarding some views of the world—and, for that matter, some interests and values—as better than others. This may mean giving up a certain metaphysical picture of objectivity, but it does not mean giving up the idea that there are what Dewey called "objective resolutions of problematical situations"—objective resolutions to problems which are *situated* in a place, at a time, as opposed to an "absolute" answer to "perspective-independent" questions. And that is objectivity enough.

12. How Not to Solve Ethical Problems

Philosophers today are as fond as ever of *a priori* arguments with ethical conclusions. One reason such arguments are always unsatisfying is that they always prove too much; when a philosopher "solves" an ethical problem for one, one feels as if one had asked for a subway token and been given a passenger ticket valid for the first interplanetary passenger-carrying spaceship instead. Conservatives, for example, often temper their praise for Robert Nozick's *Anarchy, State, and Utopia* a tiny bit. Nozick, they say, should not have come out against absolutely *all* welfare spending. But either Nozick's book proves that orphanges and public hospitals are not legitimately to be supported by public revenue, or it proves nothing at all. It is characteristic of a great deal that is published under the name of moral philosophy that even the reader who thinks that part of what is proved is reasonable is put off by the fact that the philosopher "proves too much."

Nozick's libertarianism is by no means the only, or even an unusual, example of this kind of philosophical extremism. Bernard Williams has pointed out that a particular moralistic argument against nuclear deterrence—the argument that depends upon the two premises that (1) effective deterrence depends upon a genuine intention to use nuclear weapons under certain conditions, and (2) it is immoral to intend to use a weapon that it would be immoral to actually employ—has the property that, if the argument is correct, then it makes no difference what the *facts* are.[1] It makes no difference, according to this reasoning, whether we do or do not have good reason to think that the threat posed by the deterrent will save millions of lives, or even whether it will or will not save millions of lives. Moreover, according to the argument, it is as much an instance of absolute immorality to possess a credible nuclear deterrent as to actually use atomic missiles to incinerate the entire population of North America.

Anyone familiar with the literature of moral philosophy can supply further examples of arguments that "prove too much."

To remind ourselves just how much Nozick's claim, that taxation for *any* purpose beyond the "minimal" purpose of protection of the property right amounts to state theft, contradicts the moral outlook of the whole Western tradition, let us recall that public orphanages are at least as old as the Eastern Roman Empire, while community charity is enjoined in the Old Testament (leaving grain for widows and orphans), as are many other violations of the Nozickian "right to property" (return of alienated land every fifty years, for example). The idea that there are trade-offs between rights to property, protection of the poor and helpless, and other interests of the community has long been central to our moral practice. Against both our practice and our intuitions, what Nozick has to offer is a brilliant series of analogies. If the analogies constrained our thought and transformed our lives, Nozick would be a great political leader (for better or for worse); as it is, he is only a tremendously ingenious philosopher.

Part of what makes moral philosophy an anachronistic field is that its practitioners continue to argue in this very traditional and aprioristic way even though they themselves do not claim that one can provide a systematic and indubitable "foundation" for the subject. Most of them rely on what are supposed to be "intuitions" without claiming that those intuitions deliver uncontroversial ethical premises, on the one hand, or that they have an ontological or epistemological explanation of the reliability of those intuitions, on the other. (Nozick's later book, *Philosophical Explanation,* provides an epistemology for ethics that is so abstract as to provide no reason for accepting the particular ethical intuitions underlying *Anarchy, State, and Utopia* as opposed to any other.) With only a few exceptions, they are proud of giving ingenious arguments—that is what makes them "analytic" philosophers—and curiously evasive or superficial about the relation of the premises of these arguments to the ideals and practices of any actual moral community. (One conspicuous exception to this is John Rawls, whose Dewey Lectures discuss exactly this question; another is Bernard Williams.)

Still, it may be said, and with justice, that we do have to use our heads as best we can with our ethical problems. Those who conclude, on whatever grounds, that we should stop reasoning in ethics throw us back on unexamined prejudices and selfish interests as often as on fairness and community. Must we not, then, go on trying to find solutions using whatever principles seem best to us, and arguing carefully from those principles, just as the moral philosophers urge us to do?

Yes and no. We should reflect on principles—not only our own, but those of the persons with whom we disagree. But the way *not* to solve an ethical problem is to find a nice sweeping principle that "proves too much," and to accuse those who refuse to "buy" one's absolute principle of immorality. The very words *solution* and *problem* may be leading us astray—ethical "problems" are not like scientific problems, and they do not often have "solutions" in the sense that scientific problems do. The extreme deductivism of much contemporary analytic philosophy may reflect the grip of the problem/solution metaphor. I suggest that our thought might be better guided by a different metaphor—a metaphor from the law, instead of a metaphor from science—the metaphor of *adjudication*.

I shall give an example—one that is bound to be controversial. (But it is part of the metaphor of adjudication that a good example must be controversial.) My favorite example of a wise adjudication of a difficult dispute is the Supreme Court's decision on abortion. Since I regard it as wise, I am obviously not a partisan of one of the strong views we have all heard in the dispute—we may have souls, but they are not invisible objects which join our cells at the moment of conception (we become *ensouled*, rather than being souls-plus-bodies); and we may have rights over our own bodies, but they do not extend to an absolute privilege. In calling the Supreme Court decision "wise," I am *not* saying that it is the "last word" on the abortion issue. If it were the last word, it would be a solution and not an adjudication. What I say is that reasonable men and women should agree that it would have been decidedly *un*wise for the Court either to (1) read Roman Catholic theology into the Constitution; *or* (2) grant that persons have the right to receive and perform abortions even in the ninth month of pregnancy.

That we cannot "solve" the abortion problem should not be surprising. The issues most discussed in connection with the problem, the issue of when personhood begins and the issue of the extent of rights to privacy as they affect the termination of one's own pregnancy, are ones we cannot see to the bottom of. We do not have clear criteria of personhood; and this is connected with our lack of even the faintest shadow of a genuine theory of such things as intentionality and value. (I have argued in a recent series of books and lectures that current "physicalist" speculations about intentionality and value are wholly incoherent.) The Supreme Court decision—that a first-trimester fetus does not have legal protection; that abortion of a second-trimester fetus is something to be regulated, primarily in the interest of the mother's health, though not forbidden; and that a third-trimester fetus must be amply legally protected—is not a "theory," but a reasonable stance in the absence of a theory. Even if we could settle the issue of "when one becomes a person," there are other issues connected with when a person's life may be taken (or allowed to be lost) which are also controversial. The expectant woman's right to privacy figured in the Supreme Court decision. There is a well-known argument for an absolute right to abortion in *any* trimester, due to Judith Thomson, which turns on rights with respect to one's own body, and not at *all* on the issue of the personhood or non-personhood of the fetus. Even if reasonable persons can be sure that Judith Thomson's argument "proves too much," we do not have a set of principles with which to "solve" all the problems in this area either. We need adjudications precisely in cases such as this—cases in which we cannot find a noncontroversial principle or application of a principle which settles what we should do.

A very different metaphor may be of help here—the metaphor of *reading*. Consider the following two interpretations of *Hamlet* (they are not meant to be exhaustive): (1) an interpretation—an unsophisticated reader might give this—in which Hamlet's "uncertainty" is *merely* epistemic, merely a belief that there is not enough evidence on which to act against the King, and on which Hamlet feigns madness *merely* to buy time to find out what the facts are; (2) an interpretation in which Hamlet's hesitation reveals a "conflict." One need not go as far in this direction as to "buy" a psychoanalytic interpretation of the play to contrast Hamlet's ability to act decisively when he brings about the deaths of Rosenkrantz and Guildenstern, or when he struggles with pirates, with his inability to act in the case of greatest concern to him; nor is it implausible that the phenomenon of finding oneself to be unable to act (for reasons one cannot understand) would be one with which a dramatic genius would be acquainted, without having read Freud, and would find rending, and thus of great potential interest. A sensitive reader will see that the second interpretation is better than the first. (A still better reading might include both perspectives.) Yet very few readers today think there is such a thing as the "final" interpretation of *Hamlet,* the one that contains all the perspectives on the play in all its dimensions. We do think that there are such things as better and worse interpretations—otherwise what is the point of discussing at all? What we have given up is the belief that the existence of better and worse interpretations commits us to the existence of an "absolute perspective" on the work of art.

Seeing that an adjudication of an ethical dispute is reasonable (at a given time, for a given purpose, for a given group of people) and that another is unreasonable is like seeing that one reading is better than another. We are not committed to the existence of an unimaginable "absolute perspective" in ethics, an ethical theory that contains and reconciles *all* the possible perspectives on ethical problems in all their dimensions; we *are* committed to the idea of "better and worse opinions." Reading great works of art and reading life are different but not unrelated activities.

A common feature of both metaphors—the metaphor of adjudication and the metaphor of reading—is openness or nonfinality. Accepting the Supreme Court's adjudication of the abortion issue, its "reading" of the situation, is accepting something that is by its very nature provisional—not in the sense that there must be a better perspective, a "true" reading (or a *truer* reading) which we will someday get to if we are lucky, but in the sense that (for all we know) there may be. Some things which were once problematic are now issues for condemnation or approbation and not adjudication. Human slavery is no longer problematic; it is just plain wrong. Racism and male chauvinism are simply wrong. Someday there may be a better perspective on the abortion issue—things may come into better focus. Both metaphors leave this open.

The second metaphor—the metaphor of reading—also has a place for the special role of philosophical imagination. New perspectives on moral issues, new readings of moral situations, have often come from philosophy. One thinks of the role that Locke's combination of moral vision and argument played in defeating the doctrine of the Divine Right of Kings, or of the origin of the great idea of the French revolution—the Rights of Man—in the writing of the *philosophes*. Like the readings of a literary text, philosophical perspectives may be rich or impoverished, sophisticated or naive, broad or one-sided, inspired or pedestrian, reasonable or perverse (and if the latter, brilliantly perverse or merely perverse). Like the readings of a great novel, philosophical perspectives never succeed in capturing their "text" in all its dimensions; and (as the deconstructionists claim is the case with literary works) they are always to some extent "subverted" by the very "text" they are reading, defeated by the complexity of life itself.

If the essay thus far were to be reviewed in a professional journal,

I can predict exactly what the reviewer would say. He would mention my metaphors, and then say, "But the author himself admits that all this is just metaphor. Does he believe that there are objective ethical facts or doesn't he? And if he does, what account does he have of their nature?"

The question assumes what is not the case—that there *is* a workable philosophical notion of an "objective fact." In my recent series of books, I argue that the *philosophical subjective/objective* distinction is today in total collapse. Philosophy has tried to draw this distinction in two quite different ways: *ontologically*, by making an inventory of the Furniture of the Universe, and banishing from the realm of the "objective" whatever cannot be reduced to what the philosopher takes to be the basic building blocks of Reality (material objects and sense data being the two favorite candidates in recent philosophy); *epistemologically*, by making an inventory of the possible modes of verification, and banishing from the realm of the "objective" whatever cannot be "verified" by what the philosopher takes to be the "scientific" means of verification. The ontological approach has ended up in a precritical materialism which has no account of such epistemological properties as *confirmation*, of such semantic relations as *synonymy* and *paraphrase*, of such intentional relations as *reference*, or even of its own favorite notions of *explanation* and *causation*, while the epistemological approach is immediately self-refuting: the criteria of "objectivity" proposed by the epistemologists are self-violating. It is not that I have *better* criteria of objectivity and subjectivity to offer, let me add: it is the whole conception of philosophy as a Master Science, a discipline which surveys the special activities of natural science, law, literature, morality, and so forth, and *explains* them all in terms of a privileged ontology or epistemology, that has proved to be an empty dream. The "scientific realists" are right about this much: if there *were* such a discipline, it would be natural science itself and not philosophy. The days when philosophy had a right to such grand pretensions are long past. But they are wrong in thinking that natural science can play this role. In this epoch, at least, we are left without a Master Science.

In addition to the philosophical distinction, there is an "ordinary" or vernacular distinction between objective and subjective. In the vernacular, to call something "objective" is to say that it is uncontroversial, or to suggest that it would be if folks weren't so *dumb;* while to call something "subjective" is to dismiss it as mere *affect.* In these terms, as they stand when they are not infected (as they often are) by the projects of the ontologists and the epistemologists, most of the facts that are important for our lives, including most of the important ethical facts, are *neither* "objective" nor "subjective." They are facts concerning which there are relative truths even if we don't know what an "absolute" truth would be; and among these relative truths there are, as has been said, better and worse.

II

To adjudicate ethical problems successfully, as opposed to "solving" them, it is necessary that the members of the society have a sense of community. A compromise that cannot pretend to be the last word on an ethical question, that cannot pretend to derive from binding principles in an unmistakably constraining way, can only derive its force from a shared sense of what is and is not reasonable, from people's loyalties to one another, and a commitment to "muddling through" together. When the sense of community is absent or weak, when individuals feel contempt or resentment for one another, when the attitude becomes that any consensus that isn't the one an individual would have chosen himself isn't binding on him, then fantasy and desperation have free reign.

Concern with a "moral crisis" is not new. Writing in his great work, *De la division du travail social*, Emile Durkheim succinctly described the crisis as it appeared in the nineteenth century:

> It has been said with justice that morality—and by that must be understood, not only moral doctrines, but customs—is going through a real crisis ... Profound changes have occurred in the structure of our societies in a very short time; they have been freed from the traditional type with a speed and on a scale that has never before been seen in history. As a result, the morality that corresponds to [traditional society] has regressed, but without another developing rapidly enough to take the place that the former left empty in our consciences. Our faith has been troubled; tradition has lost its sway; individual judgment has been freed from collective judgment.[2]

Every word in this description will be recognized as applying perfectly to present conditions.

Durkheim thought that part but not all of the malady could be ascribed to the fact that there had not been sufficient time for a new moral code to take shape: one adapted to the division of labor, the fact that many persons do work that most people can never understand in detail and are confronted with moral issues of unprecedented sorts, and to the fact that "the collective consciousness is more and more becoming a cult of the individual"—something that Durkheim regarded as a *humanization* of society and not something to be deplored. He rejected the idea, which is still put forward ninety years later, that we can or should go back to a morality justified by the forces of tradition and myth. But he did not think that giving ourselves more time would rectify matters by itself. Quite simply and quite strikingly, Durkheim found the root cause of our "crisis" to be—*injustice.*

Let us look at this idea with present-day conditions in mind—at Durkheim's remark that "the remedy for the evil is not to seek to resuscitate traditions and practices which, no longer corresponding to present conditions of society, can only live an artificial, false existence. What we must do to relieve this *anomie* is to discover means for making the organs which are still wasting themselves in discordant movement harmoniously concur by introducing into their relations more justice by more and more extenuating the external inequalities which are the source of the evil" (p. 409).

A few years ago I visited Peru and got to know a fine philosopher there, Francisco Miro Casada. Miro Casada has been an idealist all his life, while being, at the same time, a man of great experience (a former member of several governments and a former ambassador to France). I found him a man who represents the social democratic vision in its purest form. Talking to him, and to my other friends in Peru (who represented quite a spectrum of political opinion), I heard something that was summed up in a remark that Miro Casada made to me, "Whenever you have a Republican president, we get a wave of military dictatorships in Latin America." Out of context, this remark might suggest that the Republican Party is the cause of all the evils in Latin America; but that was not the tenor of the conversation. The willingness of Republican administrations to impose what they are pleased to describe as "authoritarian" (as opposed to "totalitarian") regimes is only the most extreme manifestation of the evil, not the evil itself.

If Jesse James had had the effrontery to tell the victims of one of his train robberies that he was holding them up for "their own good," the rage and frustration he would have produced could hardly have been greater than the sense of outrage and frustration produced when our administrations, both Democratic and Republican, and our great corporations as well, dictate economic policy, foreign policy, and internal "security" arrangements to Latin American governments with precisely this unctuous excuse—"it's for your own good"—and any knowledgeable Latin American can cite horrifying examples of such dictation. Nor is this combination of selfishness and hypocrisy confined to Latin America; Oriana Fallaci's autobiographical novel, *A Man,* gives a "thicker" description of the horrors of life under an "authoritarian" regime, including the complicity of our CIA in the maintenance of the regime, than any journalistic report could possibly do, and the regime she describes—the regime that ultimately killed her husband—was that of *Greece* (under the colonels). I am not talking of the rage produced in leftist students or in Marxist guerrillas, which can be taken for granted. I am talking of the sense of outrage that fills democratically minded people all over the Third World.

A democratic world society, a "Parliament of Man," is a long way off, and there is no guarantee that it will ever be realized. But the divisions which make it so far from realization are not just the divisions between the superpowers. We cannot do anything about the division between us and the Soviet Union except try to keep those divisions from destroying the world. But the divisions between us and the Third World are divisions produced, in significant measure, by injustices for which we are responsible and which we *are* in a position to do something about, if we will.

But injustice, like charity, begins at home. The same hypocrisy and greed that characterize so many of our actions in Latin America appear more and more in our relations to poor people, our relations to women asking for equal pay and professional recognition, our relations to those concerned about saving our atmosphere, lakes, and national forests, and, for that matter, in our relations to our middle-western blue-collar workers in steel and the auto industry. Every issue of *Common Cause* reports a disgusting flood of special interest legislation, while the news reports on the radio and television include stories of hunger and malnutrition, for the first time in years, stories of unemployment rates in excess of 10 percent, stories of over a million "discouraged workers," stories of a teenage unemployment rate in excess of 50 percent and a black teenage unemployment rate described as "off the chart," stories of black gains in the 1960s and

1970s which are now being eroded, and much more. Granted that often the justice or injustice of specific policies and programs is controversial, there are two values to which Americans of almost every political persuasion have long paid lip service: that every person who is able to work and wants to work has a "right to a job"; and the value of "equality of opportunity" (as opposed to equality of *result*, which is highly controversial). Yet both of these "lip service" values are openly flouted.

When we take the stand that nothing can be done about high unemployment rates, and that a whole generation of young people in their teens and twenties will simply have to wait for better times before they can hope to have better than a dead-end job (or, in many cases, any job at all), we are flouting our professed commitment to a "right to a job." Unemployment did not come about by accident, after all: government decisions to raise interest rates and "wring out" the economy in order to bring down the rate of inflation *predictably* had the effect of throwing millions out of work and causing the disappearance of entry-level jobs. If it is right for government to regulate the rate of employment at all (and "wringing out" the economy *is* regulating it— regulating it *downwards*), then the government, which is supposedly acting in the interest of the majority who still have jobs, has a moral obligation to protect and help the minority which is asked to suffer for the sake of the community. To ask young people who are unemployed to give up their life chances by deferring entry into real jobs for five, or ten, or however many years so that the middle class won't have to worry about inflation is to ask too much.

Viewed in these terms, it is not to be wondered at that a young black, or a working-class white teenager, who is unemployed or washing dishes or employed in a car-wash place (if there are any car-wash places that have not replaced their employees by machines) should experience the combination of total loss of social solidarity and loss of a sense of moral purpose in life that Durkheim called *anomie*. As Durkheim put it, our society "has not been organized in a way to satisfy the need for justice which has grown more ardent in our hearts." And to seriously ask the question, what has happened to our professed commitment to equality of opportunity? is already to answer it. Today the question can, sadly, only be a rhetorical one.

It is not by chance that Durkheim came to view our "illness" as "not of an intellectual sort." Durkheim worked from the very interesting hypothesis that the human need from which the moral codes spring is the need for social solidarity. Even if this is not the only need from which morality springs (and Durkheim himself mentions an increasing need for "development of the personality"), it cannot be doubted that it is a need, and a central one. Viewing morality as the expression of a deep-seated human need, one which was fulfilled in one way by traditional societies and which must now, because of the change in the conditions of our common life, be fulfilled in a different way, at once pushes the issue of social solidarity, or, as we would say today, the issue of *community,* into the center of attention. It shifts the focus from the question of helping "others" and bettering individual life chances—the focus of traditional New Deal liberalism—to a focus in which we see the quality of our *common* life as the subject of concern. As Michael Walzer has emphasized, it requires a change in our model of politics from one in which interest groups form coalitions and fight over the division of the pie to a model in which we think of ourselves—of all of us—as a community and of our social and cultural life as public business.

There are many different responses that such a perspective of community must confront, ranging from Nozickian (or, more moderately, Friedmanian) libertarianism and "unfettered capitalism" perspectives through New Deal liberalism to Marxism-Leninism. I shall comment very briefly about just two: the perspectives of Marxism-Leninism and of "neoconservatism."

I have to say something about Marxism-Leninism for an autobiographical reason, for which I hope I will be forgiven. I was twice in my life—in my high school days and again for several years during the Vietnam war—a Marxist. The Marxism of my high school days was largely a reflection of my father's views at that time, but the Marxism-Leninism of my mature years was a reaction to the very injustices I have been citing. It seemed to me, at that time, in my despair over the behavior of this country both in Latin America and in Vietnam, that only a revolution could put an end to injustice. I finally abandoned my Marxist-Leninist views when I realized—this was in 1972—that I would rather be governed by Nixon than by my own "comrades."

What is wrong with the argument that "it will take a revolution" to end injustice is that revolutions *don't* mean an end to injustice. A Marxist-Leninist revolution—here I follow the advice of Raymond Aron and look at actual history and actual regimes, and not just at ideals—replaces one ruling party by a different ruling party—one with terrible powers, and one which brooks no elections and no opposition political party. As Djilas told us, such a party becomes in its turn a new ruling class. The idea that all this will "wither away" is an empty promise. The Gulags, the political prisoners in Cuba, the boat people, and the Reform through Labor camps in China are the reality.

"Why didn't you know all this in 1968?" I will be asked, especially by my social democratic friends who were never tempted by the vision of Marxism-Leninism. Well, I did know about the Gulags. That is why I joined a group that supported no existing state. But I found within the group itself the same contempt for genuine discussion, the same manipulation, the same hysterical denunciation of anything that attempted to be principled opposition, that my father had found in the American communist party back in the forties. Perhaps I was just dumb. Certainly I was depressed and desperate.

There is something to be learned from such experiences. Certainly there is much greed and hypocrisy in our public life. But, when I look today, I do not find that the blame lies with any one group of people. I do not find that, individually, the economically and politically powerful are much worse, morally, than most people are in their private lives (of course the *actions* of a powerful person who also happens to be immoral can hurt a lot more people than the actions of a bad person who is only a father, or a teacher, or a husband or wife). I do not find that there is some blueprint, or some sketch of a blueprint, which we only have to impose on society to put an end to injustice, or that the supreme proof of the greed and hypocrisy of the "ruling class" is their unwillingness to implement any such blueprint. The millennial optimism of the Marxist—his belief in the inevitability of progress—coupled with his belief that the solution is at hand—the truth is transparent, and only "false consciousness" keeps us from seeing it—together lead to a terrible religion, it seems to me, the religion of *hatred in the name of love.*

Neoconservativism is a much more civilized and much less extreme ideology than Marxism. Yet, as set forth in the pages of *Commentary,* it shares a certain number of premises with Marxism. I don't mean the antidemocratic premises, I hasten to explain; but a certain deference to economic theory, and to what economic theory is supposed to show (Friedman, rather than Marx, is the economist of choice, of course), and a certain doctrine of inevitability are as characteristic of neoconservativism as they are of Marxism. Neoconservativism, in its standard disenchanted we-have-to-live-without-our-old-liberal-illusions form, holds that unemployment and inequality of opportunity and racial discrimination *are* injustices, but not injustices we can do anything about. There is a cost side to every social program that might be conceived of to ameliorate them (this is, of course, true) and the costs *always* outweigh the benefits, as the argument goes. (Sometimes it is said that this was not true at the time of the New Deal; it is just that it is true in present conditions.)

Now, I don't claim to be an economist; I don't know how to secure full employment without inflation. But if economists tell us, "It's impossible. If you don't want inflation you will just have to put up with unemployment for a few years," then I think we should reply, "People wouldn't accept your pessimism during the Depression, and Keynes came along. Keynes may not be the answer today. But we *need* an answer—a way of avoiding both disastrous levels of inflation and disastrous levels of unemployment, and especially of avoiding youth unemployment. Human experience suggests that if we, the public, insist long enough that this is what we want and need, then, surprise! it will turn out that there is a way to do it after all." If sociologists, or economists, or whoever, tell us that there is no way to extend equal opportunity to blacks and Chicanos and other disadvantaged groups, or that any attempt would involve a politically unacceptable "reverse discrimination," then we should similarly insist that a way be found— not all at once, of course, but that progress, not regress, be what takes place. We are far too ready today to think that we have "discovered" that progress was an illusion, and that we have to simply give up. But as Kant wrote a long time ago, we must live with an "antinomy of practical reason." We cannot prove that progress is possible, but our action is "fantastic, directed to empty, imaginary ends" if we do not postulate the possibility of progress.

The similarity between Marxism and neoconservativism might be expressed in the following way: both perspectives say that certain injustices cannot be cured under our present system of political democracy and mixed economy. The Marxist concludes that we have to overthrow the present system, and the neoconservative concludes that we have to live with the injustices. But they are both wrong.

I have already said why the Marxist is wrong. The neoconservative is wrong because living with the injustices isn't a *real* option. Even if *we* can shut our eyes to the injustices, those who suffer from them cannot. Social solidarity is falling apart, and the effects—an exponentially increasing rate of youth suicide in the last fifteen years, to cite just one statistic—are everywhere apparent. The *fin de siècle* wisdom that says that progress is an illusion is the fad of the moment—even Rorty warns us against trying to be "constructive and progressive." But the fact is that we do not know that progress is impossible, any more than we know that progress is inevitable, and we never shall know either thing. A great Jewish sage once wrote that "It is not given to us to finish the task, but neither are we permitted not to take it up." Emerson or Thoreau might well have said the same. At our best we have always been a nation with an unfinished task and an unfashionable faith in progress. Let us return to our best. Then, perhaps, we may appreciate the wisdom of Durkheim's concluding words in the book I cited, his answer to the question of where a moral code is to come from: "Such a work cannot be improvised in the silence of the study; it can only arise by itself, little by little, under the pressure of internal causes which make it necessary. But the service that thought can render is fixing the goal we must attain. That is what we have tried to do."

13. Taking Rules Seriously

This essay was a contribution to a symposium sponsored by *New Literary History*. The papers were published together under the title "Literature and/ as Moral Philosophy," *New Literary History*, 15 (Autumn 1983). The following chapter is primarily a response to Martha Nussbaum's contribution to that volume, "Flawed Crystals: James's *The Golden Bowl* and Literature as Moral Philosophy" (pp. 25–50). Nussbaum replies to my remarks on pp. 203–207 of the same volume.

The papers in this symposium show remarkable sensitivity and knowledge when it comes to reading difficult works of fiction. Psychoanalysis is also treated with considerable respect. Only poor old morality comes off rather bruised and bloody. For Martha Nussbaum, Aristotle gets high marks; after that, it seems that novels are the works of choice in "moral philosophy." For Richard Wollheim, morality "may not be all of a piece or continuous." For Angel Medina, Thrasymachus turns out to have been right: it is all authority and selfish drives (French structuralists and deconstructionists get the credit, rather than Greek Sophists).

Martha Nussbaum is surely right in stressing that values can conflict (and rules can also conflict, and there can be conflicts between values and rules). I know that Nussbaum admires Iris Murdoch's *The Sovereignty of Good*, and so do I; and the emphasis on *seeing* as the metaphor of choice for moral cognition in that book is one that would have been congenial to Henry James. (We should learn to see moral situations as a "sensitive novelist" would see them, according to Murdoch.) What troubles me is Nussbaum's derogatory attitude toward rules and toward the "Kantian account."

What is wrong with a derogatory attitude toward rules was well expressed by Arthur Dyck in a recent conversation: "The problem is not to let the exceptions become the rule," as Dyck put it. If one is sensitive to the ever-present danger that "all rules have exceptions" will become a license for an absolutely empty "situation ethics" (itself a ratification of the idea that anything goes as long as one is "sensitive"), then one should be able to see that the very notion of an exception to a moral rule is meaningless *unless the exception is carefully "hedged."* Someone who thinks that torture is morally impermissible, and who is *serious* about this view, will not suggest torture (or go along when someone else makes the suggestion) even if it is a case of finding where a bomb is going to go off before many innocent lives are lost—not even a case of finding where a nuclear bomb is going to go off (imagine nuclear terrorists), Dyck pointed out. If the idea of tricking the terrorist rather than torturing him does not occur to one; if, at worst, one does not consider sodium pentothal rather than torture; if one is not too scrupulous about whether one is *sure* one has caught a terrorist and that the explosion is imminent—then one's "principle" of nontorture is just *talk.* Even if one regards the case I have just evoked as a hopeless moral dilemma rather than as an exception, the same point applies. Since "hopeless dilemmas" often turn into "exceptions," the decision that a situation is a dilemma for a rule had better be made only in situations that are strongly hedged. But to think in terms of hedging exceptions is thinking in terms of *rules.*

One reason that Kant comes in for a lot of abuse is that Kant took such an extreme position on certain ethical issues. In particular, Kant's refusal to allow one *ever* to tell a lie (even, so to speak, to the Gestapo) is always cited. But it is just wrong to conclude that Kant did not realize that moral rules can be complex, or that he thought that such rules can decide all one's life choices for one, or that he thought that philosophers can simply write down a final set of moral rules from an armchair. (Yirmiahu Yovel's fine book, *Kant and the Philosophy of History,* is an excellent corrective to such ideas about Kant.) Even the reason why Kant took an extreme—and, I agree, mistaken—view on the Principle of Truth-Telling is instructive.

Kant believed that in a just society (and Yovel's book stresses the extent to which Kant anticipates Hegel and Marx by thinking in *social* rather than individual terms), the fundamental principle is that the maxim of one's action should be one to which others can be imagined as *consenting.* (John Rawls's Dewey lectures brought out the connection between this and Rawls's own "Kantian conception of justice," as well as the connection between such a conception of justice and the democratic ideals of the French Revolution.) What is bad about lying is that it violates the fundamental premise of a society based on mutual consent; it treats others in a way in which they would not conceivably consent to be treated. Kant was wrong in thinking that the ethical rules of an ideal society can simply be transferred to a society in which some people violate the very fundamentals of such a society, and do so intentionally; but certainly the reasoning is morally serious, and the light it throws on our practice of telling "white lies," "harmless lies," "lies of convenience," "lies for security reasons," and so forth is intense. If stopping to think: "Is this lie *really* justified? How is the exception hedged? Is there really no alternative?" is "moralistic" thinking, then we would seem to need more and not fewer moralistic people around us.

The problem with thinking in terms of "values" and "conflicts" rather than in terms of "rules" and "exceptions" (and rules to prevent the exceptions from becoming rules) is that the metaphor of *balancing* quickly gets the upper hand. To think of all moral problems in terms of "trade-offs" is precisely not to think morally at all. Aristotle was right in thinking that it is difficult to discern where courage ends and recklessness begins; in this kind of case it is true to say, as Aristotle did, that "the judgment lies with perception." But Aristotle did not question the need for certain moral rules; for example, he did not think that it is sometimes right to disobey one's officers in battle and simply run away to save one's life. Not everything is a matter of trade-offs. And if not everything is to be thought of in terms of trade-offs, then the insights of Aristotelian ethics and the insights of Kantian ethics need not conflict.

Rules (from the Decalogue to the ERA) are important because they are the main mechanism we have for challenging (and, if we are successful, shaping) one another's consciences. Martha Nussbaum is right in thinking that works of fiction can also shape our conscience, but in a complementary way (much as Kantian ethics and Aristotelian ethics can be seen as complementary rather than as contradictory). The complementarity is nowhere better expressed than in a remark George Eliot makes about the miserable Bulstrode in *Middlemarch* (chap. 61): "There is no general doctrine which is not capable of eating out our morality if unchecked by the deep-seated habit of direct fellow-feeling with individual fellow-men." The implication is that we need "general doctrine" *checked* by "direct fellow-feeling with individual fellow-men," *not* that "general doctrine" is unnecessary or dumb.

It may be, however, that I have radically misunderstood Nussbaum's references to the "Kantian account." It may be that her target is not Kant himself but a certain contemporary phenomenon, namely, the rash of moral philosophers who are ready to solve contemporary problems for us—ready to resolve issues concerning vegetarianism, animal rights, nuclear deterrence, and our obligations to future generations, among others—by means of arguments that, so to speak, prove too much. These arguments are typically aprioristic in style, and yield conclusions far stronger than any consensus that reasonable men and women are able to arrive at today. I share a deep distrust of this style of moral philosophy, with its philosophical extremism and its remoteness from the kinds of individual and collective experiences that do shape and produce a consensus. As Durkheim told us a hundred years ago, a new consensus cannot be arrived at "in the quiet of the study"; moral philosophers would do better to reflect on the conditions that make it increasingly difficult for many people to feel any sense of social solidarity at all than to issue overly elaborate arguments from unconvincing premises. Framing rules to cover issues that we cannot see to the bottom of *can* be premature.

What is wrong is to think that the sort of unrealistic and aprioristic thinking just described is typical of Kantian procedure (which is not to say that Kant never fell into such thinking). When Kant writes about a World State in *Perpetual Peace,* for example, he does *not* simply reason *a priori.* He describes contemporary conditions with genuine moral outrage:

> If we compare the barbarian instances of inhospitality referred to with the inhuman behavior of the civilized, and especially the commercial, States of our continent, the injustice practiced by them even in their first contact with foreign lands and peoples fills us with horror, the mere visiting of such peoples being regarded by them as equivalent to a conquest. America, the Negro lands, the Spice Islands, the Cape of Good Hope, etc., on being discovered, were treated as countries that belonged to nobody; for the aboriginal inhabitants were reckoned as nothing. In the East Indies, under the pretext of intending merely to plant commercial settlements, the Europeans introduced foreign troops, and with them oppression of the natives, instigation of the different States to widespread wars, famine, sedition, perfidy and all the litany of evils that can oppress the human race . . . And all this has been done by nations who make a great ado about their piety, and who, while drinking up iniquity like water, would have themselves regarded as the very elect of the orthodox faith.

The central purpose of Kant's ethical writing, in fact, is not to issue detailed rules at all but to give us a normative picture of the activity of arriving at such rules. In Kant's picture there are two principles which guide us in arriving at moral rules: the formal (categorical) imperative, which directs us to act so that the maxim of our action might be one to which others could be imagined as consenting, and the principle of the highest good, identified first with my own private virtue and happiness and eventually with the happiness of all mankind in a world governed by just institutions. What is all-important, for Kant, is that pursuit of the *summum bonum* not be allowed to degenerate into a consequentialist ethics: "So much depends, when we wish to unite two good things, on the order in which they are united!" The formal imperative always takes precedence, for Kant, over the material imperative (to seek the highest good). Our duty is not to pursue a utopian vision by manipulative, dishonest, or cruel means, but to pursue an idealistic vision by moral means. While the *Idea for a Universal History* conceives irrational forces as the driving force of history (much like contemporary French structuralism!), Yovel calls our attention to the manner in which such later discussions as *Theory and Practice, What Is Enlightenment?* and *Religion* come to conceive the moral will as a force in history. And what is the point of acting in history at all if one does not think there is some truth to this idea?

To be sure, Kant was a man of his time, and also a depressed and neurotic man. When he came to spell out details he could be magnificently prescient or intolerably quirky. But let me say at once that I see nothing essentially "sick," repressive, or reactionary in Kant's normative picture. Quite the contrary. Kant's picture sheds a rich light on how morality works *at its best* and on the ways in which a fine morality can interconnect with both personal choice and social destiny.

Where Kant's picture is defective, the problem lies with his dualistic conception of happiness. Morality is governed by two principles, and corresponding to these two principles there are two sorts of gratification: the gratification of the "moral ego" and the gratification of the "sensuous ego." The goals of the latter are a part of the total personality and cannot be ignored (contrary to some readings of Kant's ethics); but the dualism of a transcendental and an empirical self results in a portmanteau conception of happiness, happiness as moral "gratification" *plus* satisfaction of the "inclinations." This obviously will not do.

In contrast, Aristotle's picture is strong precisely where Kant's picture is weak. For Aristotle an adequate conception of happiness (*eudaimonia*) involves an adequate conception of our biological and social nature, an adequate conception of reason (*nous*), and an adequate conception of virtue; and these are interdependent. Aristotle is centrally concerned with the connection between happiness and character and with the vicissitudes that can shape character. For this reason it is natural that his position would be congenial to a philosopher who is also a talented student of literature. But there are dangers in becoming wedded to just one picture of our moral life—and not least in the reading of literary works.

II

Martha Nussbaum is right in stressing the extent to which Henry James's novel *The Golden Bowl* describes the replacement of an infantile morality by a morality which requires "improvisation," a morality in which there is, as she writes, "no safety at all." Just as *The Ambassadors* shows a struggle between a repressive conception of morality (personified by Mrs. Newsome, whose presence is almost overpowering even though she never "appears" in the novel) and a conception which leaves one free to "see" how things actually are and free to accept actions which breach Mrs. Newsome's (and Lambert Strether's own) "rules," so *The Golden Bowl* shows the limits of being "right."

But I would not go so far (and I am not sure Nussbaum wants to go so far) as to identify improvisation with balancing, or to conclude that for Maggie at the end of *The Golden Bowl* (or for Lambert Strether—the protagonist who is so similar in age to Henry James at the time he was writing this novel—at the end of *The Ambassadors*) morality has simply become a matter of "conflicts between values" and "trade-offs." Let me suggest a way of reading *The Golden Bowl* which incorporates much of what Nussbaum, as well as Wollheim and Patrick Gardiner, say about this novel, but which moves *away* from the conception of morality as a balancing act.

In the first half ("The Prince"), the two "couples" that are *not* married—that is, the Ververs considered as one couple, and Charlotte Stant and the Prince considered as the other—are alike in important respects. Both couples are manipulative, and both couples believe they are behaving "beautifully." As critics have always noted, the "good" characters are far from perfect and the "bad" characters are not really evil (although their actions are described as "evil" by Fanny Assingham, who is considered to be James's spokeswoman). If we stop with these observations, however, we are in danger of missing everything. What the Ververs do is open and aboveboard: they make clear what their motives and intentions are, they broadcast them to all and sundry (including the parties involved), and they secure the consent of Charlotte and the Prince to what they do at each stage. In contrast, what Charlotte and the Prince do is done in secret, and it depends on a fundamental violation of the idea of a community in which one does not treat people in ways to which they would not consent. The behavior of the Ververs is in many ways wrong, as well as immature, and the magnitude of the temptation to which the Prince and Charlotte are subjected is great (although stressing this *too* much can lead one to miss the "tigerish" aspect of Charlotte, the sense that she is the sort of character James calls a "headlong fool," or better, a powerful animal—the metaphor used in connection with the crystal cage). But there remains, on my reading, a fundamental asymmetry between the two couples.

The same asymmetry continues into the second half of the novel ("The Princess"). Maggie does lie to Charlotte by denying that she suspects Charlotte of anything. She insists to Charlotte's face that she thinks Charlotte is "splendid." But consider the situation: Charlotte's love affair has been broken off by the Prince (who has learned from Maggie that she "knows"). Charlotte is miserable, and wishes to be accused by Maggie so that she, Charlotte, can create an accusatory scene—a scene which can only rupture *all* of the relationships (if Maggie is right; and Maggie's almost telepathic perception of what is going on inside Charlotte and the Prince is the central force in this novel). Maggie's lie is in no way a violation of the idea of community; it is a lie which saves what can be saved of a community, told to a person who, at that point, is out to rupture the community (like an animal that has broken out of a crystal cage). I have to agree with Patrick Gardiner that the reasons Maggie has to lie "are made very clear and compelling," and I share his doubt that it is appropriate to think of Maggie as "taking on conscious guilt" for the "badness" of her actions. That moral rules can *guide* us but not *decide* exactly how we are to act is certainly something that James saw as important to many of his artistic concerns; but I think it is just wrong to see Maggie as balancing two standards, loyalty to a friend and telling the truth, and regretfully having to violate one in the situation just described.

III

Are works of fiction also works of moral philosophy? Both Wollheim and Raphael give carefully guarded responses to this question.[1] (Kuhns's fine reading of *Michael Kohlhaas* is also relevant in reminding us that fiction can wear its moral significance very far from its sleeve.)[2] The disagreement between Nussbaum and myself, if it *is* a disagreement, suggests that Wollheim is probably right: the work of fiction must not be confused with our "commentary," and it is the commentary that is (or can be) a work of moral philosophy. I can think of an answer that Nussbaum could give to this, but it would require her to be more tolerant of moral philosophies other than the Aristotelian.

As long as moral philosophies are thought of as theories which tell us what the "foundation" of morality is, or else as "methodologies"— methods for deciding what to do in concrete cases—it seems quite clear that a work of moral philosophy is one thing and a work of fiction is quite a different thing, no matter how much moral insight went into the creation of the latter. I suspect that both the ontological pretensions and the epistemological pretensions of philosophy have failed, however—and not only in moral philosophy. I do not mean that it has become clear that it's all Marx-cum-Lacan, or all physicalism-cum-cultural-relativism (*pace* Richard Rorty). If the great pretensions of philosophy have collapsed, so have the equally great pretensions of those who would debunk the problems of philosophy. A great philosophical picture, one *might* argue, should be viewed as we view great artistic creations: as something which does not simply copy a ready-made world, but rather as something which creates a world—or even, as Nelson Goodman has put it, a "world of worlds."

If such a view of philosophy can be elaborated and defended, then it may be that we have to view all philosophy as having an expressive component: as being concerned to reveal (or conceal) an author as much as to "solve problems." The gap between works of fiction and works of philosophy might then appear considerably narrower. (The commentary on a work of fiction can require a commentary, too.) Martha Nussbaum may be right; but it would take an enormous amount of further work to show that she *is* right.

14. Scientific Liberty and Scientific License

There are old and convincing arguments for intellectual liberty in all of its forms—freedom to think, to speak, to publish. Part of the pull of these arguments is that they appeal to assumptions that we who have been brought up in Western democratic countries take for granted. But whether we do more than take them for granted—whether we have the commitment to make those assumptions operative, or whether they have become a kind of hypocrisy—is another question. In Doris Lessing's great novel *The Golden Notebook*,[1] the American, Saul Green, says to Anna, "That's why I love this country [England], it [McCarthyism] couldn't happen here." Anna's reaction is decidedly not agreement that McCarthyism couldn't happen in England:

> Because what he said was sentimental, stock from the liberal cupboard. I said, 'During the cold war, when communist hue and cry was at its height, the intellectuals here were the same. I know everyone's forgotten about it, now everyone's shocked at McCarthy, but at the same time our intellectuals were playing it down, saying things were not as bad as they seemed. Just as their opposite numbers were doing in the States. Our liberals were mostly defending, either openly or by implication, the anti-American activity committee. A leading editor could write a hysterical letter to the gutter press saying if only he'd known that X and Y, who were old friends of his, were spies, he'd have gone straight to M.I.5 with information about them. No one thought the worse of him. And all the literary societies and organizations were engaged in the most primitive form of anti-communism—what they said, or a great deal of it, was quite true of course, but the point is, they were simply saying what might have been found any day in the gutter press, no attempt to really understand anything, they were in full cry, a pack of barking dogs. And so I know quite well that if the heat had been turned on even a little harder, we'd have had our intellectuals packing anti-British activities committees, and meanwhile we, the reds, were lying black is white'.

'Well?'

'Well, judging from what we've seen happening in the last thirty years, in the democracies, let alone the dictatorships, the number of people in a country really prepared to stand against a current, really ready to fight for the truth at all costs is so small that . . .'

He suddenly said, 'Excuse me', and walked out with his stiff blind walk.

I sat in the kitchen and thought over what I'd just said. I and the people I knew well, some of them fine people, had been sunk inside the communist conformity and lied to themselves or to others. And the 'liberal' intellectuals could be and had been swung into witch-hunts of one kind or another very easily. Very few people really care about freedom, about liberty, about the truth, very few. Very few people have guts, the kind of guts on which a real democracy has to depend. Without people with that sort of guts a real democracy dies, or cannot be born. (p. 484)

And Anna sits there, "discouraged and depressed. Because in all of us brought up in a Western democracy there is this built-in belief that freedom and liberty will strengthen, will survive pressures, and the belief seems to survive any evidence against it. This belief is probably in itself a danger. Sitting there I had a vision of the world with nations, systems, economic blocs, hardening and consolidating; a world where it would become increasingly ludicrous even to talk about freedom, or the individual conscience. I know that this sort of vision has been written about, it's something one has read, but for a moment it wasn't words, ideas, but something I felt, in the substance of my flesh and nerves, as true."

I begin with this extended quotation because the tough-minded novelist has a kind of realism about the issue of intellectual freedom that is missing in academic discussions. But the philosophical questions are nonetheless worth pursuing. Belief in liberty may need "people with guts" to survive, as Doris Lessing says, but why are we so convinced that it should survive, that it would be a tragic loss if the world should "harden and consolidate" into "nations, systems, economic blocs" without intellectual liberty?

Two major arguments (or groups of arguments, for each has many forms) have been offered for intellectual liberty—and both are powerful. The first I shall call the Utilitarian argument, and the second the Kantian argument. The Utilitarian argument, in its simplest form, is that without intellectual liberty, freedom of thought and speech, any party and any government will harden into an exploiting class, a tyranny. That argument has been rehearsed so often that I do not need to spell it out in detail. I call it a "Utilitarian" argument because it appeals to a felt practical interest to avoid exploitation and tyranny; but it connects with broader epistemological concerns, above all with the need stressed by the great pragmatists to "keep the paths of inquiry open." A society that is not intellectually free "blocks the path of inquiry"; it substitutes "the method of authority" for the method of science, in Peircian terms. A commitment to the progressive rational resolution of human "problematic situations" absolutely requires intellectual freedom, as Dewey stressed again and again.

The Kantian argument is complementary to the Utilitarian one. The Kantian argument is that, quite apart from its value to society, intellectual liberty—Kant calls it autonomy—is absolutely indispensable to the integrity of the person. Why? If you are autonomous, if you think for yourself in moral and political matters, then that is not a real question for you. The autonomous person can no more imagine giving up his autonomy, his capacity to think for himself and his habit of exercising that capacity, than he can imagine submitting to a lobotomy. Autonomous persons respect not only themselves but also others for being what Kant called "self-legislating beings."

Let me say, without further ado, that here I am a Kantian (as well as a Deweyan). Asking me "But how do you *know* autonomy is a good thing?" in the familiar philosophical-epistemological fashion is inviting me to provide a "foundation" for my own integrity as a human being. Rather than do that, I have to say "I have reached bedrock, and my spade is turned."[2] Yet, without doubting for one moment the supreme value of autonomy, and the need to keep the paths of inquiry unblocked, the need for freedom of inquiry, of speech, of press, of assembly, and so on, I want to discuss troubling issues about the *use,* or rather the abuse, of that freedom. These issues have been discussed before, and I don't know that I or anyone else has anything really new to say about them. Perhaps all we can hope to do is bring a little more honesty, or rather a little more realism, to the discussion.

The first kind of issue has to do with the use of the principle of intellectual liberty, and particularly of scientific liberty, to gossip in a slanderous way about racial groups. This issue arises again because Herrnstein and Wilson have recently chosen to speculate in print about possible genetic causes of crime.[3] They do not say that the "constitutional factors" in which they believe are racial or racially linked—on the contrary, they conclude there is insufficient scientific evidence to support such a conclusion, in the case of blacks at least ("There is not enough evidence to evaluate their claims [the claims of people who believe black crime rates are explained by constitutional factors] carefully" [p. 485]). But they say this at the end of a chapter in which they report various scientific "studies," all of which they themselves finally decide are not probative, but many of which are attempts to show that blacks are in one or another way defective. They even cite a study purporting to show that black Ph.D.'s are more emotionally unstable than white Ph.D.'s!

I have discussed the substantive issues about I.Q. and heredity in the past,[4] and I shall not review that side of the discussion here. What horrifies me about this new discussion is its utter social and moral irresponsibility. Black people were brought to the United States as slaves. They were deprived of their African languages (although some conceptual forms are said to survive in Black English); their families were broken up; they were reduced to near slaves, at least in the South, and to lumpen proletariat in the North, after Reconstruction. The stereotype against them—the "nigger" stereotype—has been, at its worst, as vile as the Hitler stereotype against Jews that led to the Holocaust—and that stereotype is by no means completely dead today. To report scientifically unsubstantiated charges of instability, constitutional tendencies to criminality, genetic inferiority in intelligence, and so forth directed against blacks in a major work on crime and its causes is to lend the prestige of the authors (who are both Harvard professors) to the "nigger" stereotype itself. It is to pour gasoline on the fires of race prejudice.

I said earlier that Herrnstein and Wilson report that "there is not enough evidence" to evaluate any of the theories of black criminality that they consider (they say this not only about the "constitutional" theory, but also about "culture of poverty," "subculture of violence," and "inadequate socialization" theories). Yet it is revealing of their own mentalities that on the very same page, and only a few sentences later, they add: "It is tempting—and probably true—to say that each theory is partially correct" (p. 485). So Herrnstein and Wilson *do* think that the blatantly racist "constitutional tendency to crime" theory is "partially true"—or that this is "probably true"—notwithstanding the lack of "enough systematic evidence to evaluate it."

The way in which Herrnstein and Wilson deal with the moral issue is especially relevant to my topic. What they say is short, and worth our attention: "Honest, open scientific inquiry that rests on carefully stated findings cannot be ethically wrong unless one believes that truth itself is wrong" (p. 468).

Can Truth Be Wrong?

First, it may be well to note that even Western democracies do not accept the principle that "truth can't be wrong" if that principle is understood to say that the act of *publishing* truth (let alone "carefully stated findings") can't be wrong. A short handbook might give carefully stated findings about how to make an atom bomb, but there would be massive objections to publishing and advertising such a handbook. This raises another type of issue about intellectual liberty, in fact, which I shall discuss shortly. To dismiss moral issues about the responsibility of the scientist with the sentence I quoted is in itself an irresponsible act.

Another kind of case, one not involving the dissemination of dangerous information about "how to do it," is the following: when a juvenile commits a crime, many American states "seal the record." This means that, if the individual refrains from crime upon reaching 18, or whatever the age is in the individual state, his criminal record in his juvenile years will be concealed; the slate is, in effect, clean. Clearly the framers of these laws did not think that all truth should be published "unless truth itself is wrong." Their intention—and I think it is an excellent one—was to give individuals a chance to make a fresh start, and not to let a whole life be blighted by a juvenile criminal act.

Now, imagine that I suspect, perhaps from something he lets drop, that a respected and decent member of the community has, in fact, a juvenile "record." Suppose that by "open scientific inquiry" I succeed in proving that he *did* commit a crime in early adolescence, and I publish my "carefully stated finding." What would any of you think of me? What would any good person think of me? If the truth can hurt, and there is no overriding reason to make it public, can one really suppose that it isn't "ethically wrong" to publish it "unless truth itself is wrong"?

To come still closer to the case at hand, suppose a rumor reaches me that my colleague, Professor X, has engaged in sexual misconduct with his students (perhaps the rumor was started by enemies of Professor X). (I assume that no one has actually brought charges against Professor X, and that I am not, in any case, authorized to hear or investigate such charges.) Suppose out of sheer curiosity I investigate the rumor, find the evidence very insubstantial, and publish a "carefully stated finding" that (to use Herrnstein and Wilson's own words in connection with the theories of "constitutional" black predisposition to crime, "inadequate socialization," and so on), "there is not enough systematic evidence to evaluate their [the people who say Professor X has done these things] claims carefully." I may be wrong, but I suspect that under American law Professor X could successfully recover against me in an action for libel. (Especially if I added that "it is tempting—and probably true—to say that each of the theories about what Professor X did is partially correct".)

The point, quite simply, is that if you investigate slanderous charges, then merely concluding that "there is not enough systematic evidence to evaluate the claims carefully" does not let you off the moral hook. By giving the charges respectful attention, you take on a responsibility. The principle stated by Herrnstein and Wilson ("Honest, open scientific inquiry cannot be ethically wrong") is an all-purpose dismissal of responsibility.

Let me make it perfectly clear that I am not proposing to take away the *legal* right to publish books of this kind. I am not advocating a state which dictates answers to moral questions to individuals—especially not to authors. Indeed, the existence of laws against slandering racial groups in the Soviet Union has not prevented massive slander directed against Jews (thinly disguised as "anti-Zionist" material) from being published there and in other socialist countries. I *am* saying that the existence of a legal right to publish what one thinks goes with an obligation for "people with guts" to scream bloody murder when that right is abused. What I have just described seems to me, frankly, an abomination; but the chances that many people will scream bloody murder are not good.

Razor Blades and Four-Year-Olds

Some decades ago I was privileged to hear Norbert Wiener talk. Wiener had recently let it be known that he would not work any longer on defense contracts, and he stated his reasoning with his characteristic combination of simplicity and depth: "I don't give four-year-olds razor blades." I have been haunted by that remark ever since. It, and the action it accompanied and explained, have a Tolstoyan, or a Gandhian, simplicity that takes one's breath away. I am by no means sure Wiener's position is right; but neither am I sure it is wrong. Let me share my irresolution with you.

We all know, deep down, that the atomic bomb is not just another weapon. The possibility of an annihilating nuclear war haunts us, as does the possibility of the end of mankind. This really is different. And yet we seem—all of the governments of the earth seem—to be gripped in a collective madness.

Wiener's analogy is stunning. Imagine a group of four-year-olds fighting. Some of them really are bullies. Some of them really are engaged in "self-defense." Or not. Does it matter? Would you give any of the children a *razor blade*? Even if some other child had one?

Wiener's remark is not as simple as it first looks to be. Is it wrong to give four-year-olds razor blades because they aren't *rational*? So the point would be that we can no longer pretend that governments are rational? (Which is perfectly true.) Or is it wrong to give four-year-olds razor blades because *there is no such thing as the rational use of a razor blade* in a fight between children? Or both at once?

Given the power of Wiener's analogy, and the charismatic simplicity of his decision, why do I, as a philosopher, not conclude that I should advise *all* scientists, everywhere, to refuse to work on weapons of nuclear, or germ, or chemical warfare—indeed, to refuse to work on weapons, since in this age of technology all weapons are "razor blades"? (I do not mean to ask about limited questions, such as refusing to work on weapons while the Vietnam war was going on; I mean refusing to work on the means of "deterrence.")

The bind is this (it is very similar to the bind one feels with respect to all pacifist doctrines): one is troubled by *consequences*. But there is a difference in the nuclear case. In the ordinary pacifist case, non-pacifists, such as myself, feel that if the democracies refused to fight *ever*, under *any* conditions, there would simply stop being democracies (and pretty soon stop being pacifists, except in prison). And we just can't see what *good* that would do. Not that we are Utilitarians (I'm not, at any rate); consequences aren't everything. But they do matter.

In the nuclear case, it might also be true that if the democracies maintained *no* deterrent, there would pretty soon stop being democracies. And it wouldn't even stop war if one system "won," since socialist states can go to war with one another just as well as capitalist ones. So again, it doesn't look as if universalizing Wiener's decision would do any *good*.

The problem is, a deterrent is at best a *short-term* way of avoiding a world war (smaller wars it hasn't avoided). And there seems to be not the slightest indication of any progress toward or any thinking about long-term solutions on the part of the powers, the nations, blocs, systems. Even if arms control negotiations were not in their current dismal state, even if SALT treaties were still being negotiated every few years, the kind of semicosmetic arms control that was institutionalized for a while is no more a long-term solution than the cosmetic reforms in South Africa are a solution to the concrete and intolerable evil of apartheid. So we continue passing out razor blades to the children, and the children continue promising not to use them . . .

I said before that I didn't mean to talk about "limited questions," such as refusing to work on weapons as long as one's country is engaged in an unjust war. But perhaps that is just where my reasoning went wrong. The fact is that in the real world "limited solutions" are the only solutions we ever find, and only limited questions have limited solutions. As soon as we ask whether it is *ever*, under *any* conditions, right to work on nuclear weapons, we move to the level of abstract philosophy—and our bind is not an abstract philosophical bind. The fact is that I do not believe that it can possibly be right to help make weapons—*any sort of weapons*—under *present* conditions, when we live under a government that does not—I believe—have the slightest desire for arms control at all, a government that refuses to move in the direction of reducing the danger of nuclear war. That much seems clear to me. What the solution to the larger problem is—what sort of a compromise we should make between our desire for short-term survival as a nation and our desire for long-term survival as a biological species—I don't know. But no "philosophical question" is more important.

15. Is There a Fact of the Matter about Fiction?

What I wish to do in this essay is point out an interesting and apparently unnoticed convergence in the doctrines of America's most famous contemporary philosopher of language and those of deconstructionist literary critics, and to discuss the relevance that post-Quinian ways of looking at issues concerning "meaning" might have for critical theory.

In 1951 Quine published a devastating attack on philosophers' use of the notion *same meaning* as well as on the use of the notion *true by virtue of the meaning*. After the appearance of *Word and Object* in 1960, Quine's "pessimism" about meaning talk became a large topic of discussion. Quine argued that there are no general rules which determine what does and what does not count as a situation in which a particular sentence is *assertible*. Assertibility, to the extent that it is rational, is pragmatic and depends on the entire context. When beliefs clash we have trade-offs between different desiderata (for example, *simplifying the system* and *preserving core beliefs*), and there cannot be algorithms (much less rules associated with the individual sentences) which tell us how to make the best trade-off in each case. The "meaning" of a sentence cannot be identified with the rule or battery of rules which determine its assertibility conditions, for there are no such rules.

Quine proposed, in fact, that talk of "the meaning" of a sentence or text only makes sense when *relativized*—relativized to an interpretation, or, as he put it, to a "translation manual." He advanced the radical thesis that there is "no fact of the matter" as to which translation manual is the right one: all translation manuals satisfying certain extremely weak constraints are formally possible, and the choice of one of the manuals (satisfying the constraints) over the others is subjective.

In effect, Quine said that *we should talk about interpretation and not about meaning.* The similarity between Quine's views and those of a number of leading Continental *penseurs* went, however, totally unremarked. Quine's relentless scientism and his choice of examples (a typical text, in Quinian philosophy of language, is "Lo, a rabbit!") may have had something to do with this.

There is a difficulty, of course—one pointed out by many of Quine's critics. If all sentences and texts lack determinate meaning, then how can Quine view his *own* utterances as anything more than mere noise? (Quine's scientism does lead him to regard all discourse, including his own, as patterns of sound or inscription produced in accordance with Skinnerian schedules of conditioning.) Quine's answer, that his utterances have determinate meanings *relative to themselves* (if you ask me in my own language, "Under what conditions is 'snow is white' true?" I will answer that this sentence is true *if and only if snow is white*—using the very sentence you inquired about to state its own truth conditions), hardly seems to acknowledge, let alone respond to, the objection. The difficulty is, in fact, the familiar self-application problem encountered by all relativisms which become total. When one of the European *penseurs* I mentioned insists that truth and justification, to the extent that there are such things, are determined by criteria internal to a discourse, we naturally ask him whether there is a fact of the matter as to what the "criteria internal to a discourse" really are and as to what counts as fulfilling them. Can Michel Foucault's "archeology of knowledge" really be objective if all other discourse is subjective?

In *Meaning and the Moral Sciences* I argued that there is a way of preserving Quine's insights without being carried along into total relativism. One can agree with Quine that there are not such things as "meanings," "semantical rules," and so on, and that talk of meanings should give way to study of the activities of interpretation. But one need not agree that there are no better and worse interpretations (among those that satisfy the four constraints listed in *Word and Object*). What Quine called "the indeterminacy of translation" should rather be viewed as the *interest relativity* of interpretation.

As I use the term, "interest relativity" contrasts with *absoluteness*, not with objectivity. It can be objective that an interpretation or an explanation is the correct one, *given* the context and the interests which are relevant in the context. Something can be interest-relative *and* "objective humanly speaking," in David Wiggins's excellent phrase. Chomsky's contention (in *Rules and Representations*) that the doctrine of interest relativity commits me to total subjectivism assumes, what is not the case, that all interests must be taken to be on a par. There are silly interests, deluded interests, irrational interests, and so on, as well as reasonable and relevant ones (even if there is no general rule for determining which are which). A sane relativism can recognize that there is a fact of the matter in interpretation without making that fact of the matter unique or context-independent.

With these remarks as background information, I want to turn now to the subject of criticism. Everyone is familiar with the fact that Aristotle's *Metaphysics* has had many interpretations and with the fact that *King Lear* has had many interpretations. Not only do critics "read" the *Metaphysics* or *Lear* differently; there are recognizable differences in the assumptions of criticism and the styles of criticism in different centuries. If variant interpretations of the sentence "Lo, a rabbit!" exist only as a philosopher's example, the same cannot be said of variant interpretations of *Lear*. It is surely high time that we brought some of our theory to bear on genuine textual and critical problems.

I used to say—as a rueful joke—"as I get smarter, Aristotle gets smarter." The notion of an ideal "correct" interpretation seems problematic. Yet the radical view that interpretations are simply the inventions of the interpreter is just the old self-refuting relativism in its latest guise. What should we say?

If we follow what I have described as Quine's insight, and think of interpretation as correlation—correlation of Aristotle's words and sentences with words and sentences in our present-day language—then some of the mystery evaporates. Aristotle's words depended for their life on particular "contexts"—which is to say, particular institutions, particular assumptions, particular positions that real people once occupied and no longer occupy. Any "translation manual" interprets Aristotle using words which depend for *their* life on different institutions, assumptions, and positions. It is not surprising, from such a perspective, that each century should require new interpretations, nor that each interpretation should be capable of improvement in an infinity of directions. Once we give up the idea of the Platonic "meaning" that all interpreters are trying to snare and think of interpretation as human interaction—between two or more forms of life—then we will not be dismayed (or driven to an insane relativism) by the open-ended character of the activity.

In the case of Aristotle, the interest relativity of interpretation takes a particular form. Even if Aristotle had written present-day English, there would still be an interpretation problem. Even if he had written "Happiness is the activity of the psyche according to virtue in the complete life" and not the Greek sentence he actually wrote, we could not answer the exegetical question by saying "The sentence is true if and only if happiness is the activity of the psyche according to virtue in the complete life." For we are interested in the *implications* of what Aristotle wrote, and in cases where what Aristotle wrote was vague or ambiguous, we are interested in knowing what (more precise) senses it could be given and what it implies about our problems when given these various possible more precise readings.

There is, to be sure, a difference in this regard between a philosophical text and a literary one; but not a total difference. Whether or not we agree with Henry James in criticizing the explicit moralizing by the omniscient narrator in *Middlemarch,* we recognize that various meanings can be given to the remark that "Bulstrode was not a hypocrite—he was simply a man whose desires were stronger than his theoretic beliefs, and who always rationalized the latter into satisfactory agreement with the former." (Some of the meanings are indicated by the sentence which appears a little later in the same paragraph: "There is no general doctrine which is not capable of eating out our morality if not accompanied by the daily habit of direct fellow feeling with individual human beings.") George Eliot is trying to "tell us something"—and so is Henry James, even if he uses different devices. Nor is it only the "big" remarks or attitudes in a literary work that prompt the effort at interpretation. Today virtually any aspect may initiate a line of questioning: the kind of audience the writer seems to have in mind, the assumptions the writer seems to take for granted, the relation between narrative devices such as *suspense* and the deeper issues in the work, and so on. As in the history of philosophy, the questioning clearly can and does go far beyond the literal question: "What is the meaning (truth-conditions) associated with this line?"

But now it may look as if I have simply overlooked the difference between an exegesis and a commentary. A commentary, it might be said, must depend on what are important questions for us, on our interests, assumptions, even (regrettably) our intellectual fashions. There can never be a final commentary, one that is perfect from the standpoint of every cultural position, every set of interests and assumptions. But why should there not be a perfect exegesis?

Indeed, Donald Davidson would say that *in principle* there is.[1] If the work is in our language, then its homophonic or "face value" interpretation is the perfect one (ignoring the problem Borges more than once raises, that even the text of *Don Quixote* itself may no longer function as a "literal translation" of *Don Quixote* into Spanish—even if we are Spanish speakers—that what we mean by it may not be what Cervantes did!).

But the very fact that even in the ideal case, the case in which the work is written in, say, standard present-day English with no idiosyncrasies whatsoever (if there is such a language), the only "perfect exegesis" would, in general, be the work itself makes my point in another way: in a significant sense, the exegesis/commentary distinction cannot be drawn. Any exegesis that is *nontrivial* must, to that extent, be commentary-laden.

As I have already said, I see in this no cause for despair. If new exegeses and new critical interpretations are always necessary, if there is no convergence to One True Interpretation, then, by the same token, the fashion of seeing the interpretations of past centuries as *wholly* superseded by contemporary "insights" may be recognized as the naive progressivism that it is. Perhaps we can come to see criticism as a conversation with many voices rather than as a contest with winners and losers.

Part III

Studies in American Philosophy

16. William James's Ideas

with Ruth Anna Putnam

There are several ways of coping with the work of William James. In his recent *William James: His Life and Thought,* Gerald Myers seems to have understood James's *Principles of Psychology* and his pragmatism as leading ultimately to the philosophical theory that James advanced late in his career under the name "radical empiricism"; in Myers's book, the moral and religious views, though treated in detail, are not shown to be connected. Alternatively, James's conception of truth, that is to say, his pragmatism, might be taken as a key or unifying aspect of his work. (This part of James's philosophy has been the most deeply misunderstood.) Or one might recall James's own words: "You see that pragmatism can be called religious, if you allow that religion can be pluralistic or merely melioristic in type . . . If you are neither tough nor tender in an extreme and radical sense, but mixed as most of us are, it may seem to you that the pluralistic and melioristic religion that I have offered is as good a religious synthesis as you are likely to find." If, with James, pragmatism is regarded as a religion, then he is surely its foremost preacher, one whose ultimate motivation is ethical rather than consolatory. But even if pragmatism is not regarded as a religion, attention to James's ethical intentions is essential to an understanding of him. We shall proceed from the assumption that, early and late, James's motivation was ultimately ethical, and that his essays in, for example, *The Will to Believe and Other Essays,* and particularly "The Moral Philosopher and the Moral Life," can play a key role in understanding both his pragmatism and his radical empiricism.

James's moral philosophy has a fundamental principle that is quasi–*a priori* ("quasi" because, in our view, even what look like *a priori* elements in James's philosophy are subject to revision). At the same time, as in almost all moral philosophies, facts about what will and will not make human beings happy are important in determining what our detailed obligations are. (Even in Kant's ethics, such facts enter through the obligation to strive to bring about a world in which "happiness is proportional to virtue.") The quasi–*a priori* principle, as James states it in "The Moral Philosopher and the Moral Life," is that "without a claim actually made by some concrete person there can be no obligation, but there is some obligation wherever there is a claim." What those claims are is a contingent fact. The idea that nothing is desirable unless something is desired comes, of course, from utilitarianism (and James did dedicate *Pragmatism* to Mill); but, as we shall see, James gives a very different twist to even such utilitarian-sounding remarks as this from "The Moral Philosopher and the Moral Life": "Must not the guiding principle for ethical philosophy be simply to satisfy at all times as many demands as we can?"

If there is a strong utilitarian strain in James's ethics, there are also some striking similarities to Kantianism. Like Kant, James rejects the Humean idea that free will is compatible with determinism, and like Kant he came to see a belief in free will and a belief in what he called a theistic god (or, at other times, gods) as prerequisites for ethical action. This similarity to Kant is, perhaps, most striking in *Pragmatism*, where belief in free will and belief in God are defended as imperatives of practice:

> Free-will thus has no meaning unless it be a doctrine of *relief*. As such, it takes its place with other religious doctrines. Between them, they build up the old wastes and repair the former desolations. Our spirit, shut within this courtyard of sense-experience, is always saying to the intellect upon the tower: "Watchman, tell us of the night, if it ought of promise bear," and the intellect gives it then these terms of promise. *Other than this practical significance, the words God, free-will, design, etc., have none.*

Like Kant (who elevated "What may we hope?" to equal significance with the philosophical questions "What can we know?" and "What should we do?"), James believed that people cannot live and function in the world on a diet of mere pessimism; a world-view that can be a guide to action need not be full of rosy optimism, but it must not tell us that we are all the pawns of either blind chance or iron necessity. This, of course, raises the question: What entitled James to believe in "free will, etc."? Answering this question (and also the question: How do we know what is wrong with the world as it is, and hence what would be a better world?) will lead us deep into James's theory of truth.

Nothing is as responsible for the low esteem in which James has been held by philosophers as his so-called theory of truth, except perhaps the doctrine of "The Will to Believe." On August 26, 1898, in the lecture at the University of California titled "Philosophical Conceptions and Practical Results" announcing his pragmatism, James gave credit to Peirce for teaching him how to think about meaning and truth. Peirce, on the other hand, often referred to the James-Dewey view on truth, and by 1907 James was crediting that same theory to Dewey (whose *Studies in Logical Theory* had appeared in 1903) and to Schiller. What the great pragmatists have in common— and what creates a common difficulty in understanding them—is that they do not appear to have a clear "epistemology." Unlike Mill, Reichenbach, Carnap, or Frege, they do not see it as their task to reduce rationality to a set of canons. Of course, Peirce distinguished the invention of an explanatory scientific theory (which he called "abduction") from more elementary kinds of inductive inference; of course, he set the stage for the later pragmatists by stressing the doctrine that all our beliefs are subject to revision (which he called "fallibilism"); of course, he insisted that scientific theories must be tested. But he also insisted that scientists need good intuitions: intuition suggests theories; intuition suggests the order in which to test the theories that have come to mind. Dewey and James extended Peirce's observations by making explicit the idea that methodology itself is something that evolves in the course of inquiry. In our own day, Quine has emphasized that all inquiry involves "trade-offs" between simplicity, preservation of past doctrine, and successful prediction (all constraints which James had emphasized in *Pragmatism*). Such trade-offs, he says, are "where rational, pragmatic"; yet he doubts that the making of these trade-offs can be reduced to exact rules.

For James, pragmatism as "a method for settling metaphysical disputes" and pragmatism as "a certain theory of truth" were always closely linked. Pragmatism in the former sense meant for James an appeal to the following principle, which is his own, perhaps inaccurate, paraphrase of Peirce's famous "pragmatic maxim": "To attain perfect clearness in our thought of an object, then, we need only consider what conceivable effects of a practical kind the object may involve—what sensations we are to expect from it, and what reactions we must prepare. Our conception of these effects, whether immediate or remote, is then for us the whole of our conception of the object, so far as that conception has positive significance at all." Later it can be asked whether that is indeed all there is to the Jamesian method of settling metaphysical disputes; for now it is enough to see how this method is applied to the meaning of truth.

The dictionary says that truth means agreement with reality; but what does it mean for our beliefs or thoughts or ideas to agree with reality, and what does it matter anyway? That there is no single answer to this question has been a source of perplexity for readers of James. Peirce had said, quoting his contemporary Alexander Bain, that belief is "that upon which a man is prepared to act"; both James and Peirce hold that a true belief is one which, when acted upon, does not lead to unpleasant surprises. James emphasizes that truth serves practical interests. But, contrary to what many critics claim, James does not mean that anything that serves practical interests is true. Rather, the nature of a true belief's "agreement with reality," and which interests it is to serve, depend on the kind of belief it is.

Perceptual beliefs have to "lead us to the object itself." (James describes this as a realist strain in his thinking and chides his interpreters for ignoring it.) James says about scientific theories, with increasing frustration at being misunderstood, that all our knowledge of the world is a product of the world and our minds. Human beings develop the conceptual framework known as common sense, and human beings develop all other conceptual frameworks. But this is not done simply by "copying" facts that somehow dictate their own description: "The trail of the human serpent is over everything." He points out, additionally, that knowledge always grows. In that sense at least the universe is not complete and finished, and it is in our power to change it. But he points out also that "knowledge never grows all over: some old knowledge always remains what it was." That old knowledge, or "previous truths" as he calls them, combines with new experience to lead to new truths. Commonsense beliefs have withstood the test of experience particularly well; nevertheless, they are, in a way, merely very successful hypotheses. All our other modes of thinking, none of which succeeds in replacing all others, "are *instrumental,* are mental modes of *adaptation* to reality," not copies. Though James has no doubt that there is a world, though he himself in his radical empiricism proposes an account of the world's ultimate stuff, our commonsense and scientific and philosophical beliefs are only so many versions of the world, to use Nelson Goodman's term, each good for its purposes.

Commonsense beliefs are "in a way" merely successful hypotheses, even though *hypothesis* is not a term used in ordinary language to refer to the belief, say, that fire burns, or that water is wet. The term has a skeptical connotation for traditional philosophers that it does not have (or does not always have—James wobbles somewhat on this point) for pragmatists. For a traditional philosopher—for an empiricist like Hume, for instance—calling something a hypothesis suggests a certain degree of doubt. But one of the central contributions of pragmatism was to deny that doubt is always appropriate: the point of Peirce's celebrated charge that Descartes only *thought* he doubted the existence of the external world is that real doubt (and the pragmatists were the first to make the now widespread distinction between real doubt and "philosophic" doubt) requires a justification; it is not only beliefs that need to be justified, but also challenges to belief. Calling these commonsense beliefs "hypotheses" is a way of saying that they too are subject to revision, that no belief, however secure in the present context, is in principle exempt from challenge. To call them hypotheses is not to express some general skeptical doubt of their truth.

True beliefs are of vital importance; false beliefs may prove fatal. James's insistence that "true ideas . . . would never have acquired a class-name . . . suggesting value, unless they had been useful from the outset in this way" is perhaps responsible for the charge that he simply equates truth with utility. But the usefulness of true ideas is the result of their "agreement" with reality; their usefulness alone does not constitute that agreement. They are useful by "leading" us to act in such a way that our subsequent experiences do not come as unpleasant surprises.

What we have spoken of so far are what James called "half-truths," these being the best anyone can hope to achieve, but always subject to correction by subsequent experience. James also appears to accept the Peircean idea of truth (he calls it "absolute truth") as a coherent system of beliefs which will ultimately be accepted by the widest possible community of inquirers as the result of strenuous and attentive inquiry (what Peirce called the "final opinion"). However, James accepts this notion only as a regulative ideal; in *Pragmatism* he writes that this ideal "runs on all fours with the perfectly wise man, and with the absolutely complete experience; and, if these ideals are ever realized, they will all be realized together." Like the half-truth of everyday life, "it will have to be *made,* made as a relation incidental to the growth of a mass of verfication-experience, to which the half-true ideas all along are contributing their quota."

This bifurcation of the notion of truth into a notion of available truth (half-truth) and unavailable but regulative "absolute truth" is obviously problematic. Dewey proposes to remove the difficulty: he jettisons the notion of "absolute truth" and settles for half-truth (renamed "warranted assertibility"). But the price of this seems too high in another way; it loses a desirable distinction (and one that James recognizes) between saying of a statement that it is warrantedly assertible on the basis of all the evidence we have to date and saying that it is ("tenselessly") *true*. A majority of today's analytic philosophers would solve the problem in a way urged by Alfred Tarski and Rudolf Carnap: they would say that "half-truth" (or "warranted assertibility") is not truth at all but confirmation. James was, in this majority view, confused as to his subject matter: he thought that pragmatism was a theory of truth, when what he was offering was really a theory of confirmation. The notion of "absolute truth" is also a mistake, in the Tarski-Carnap view. "True" is not the name of a property at all, according to these thinkers; to say that a statement, like "Snow is white," is true, is just to affirm the statement. To say that "Snow is white" is true is not to say that "Snow is white" has a property of correspondence to something extralinguistic. Indeed, we do not ascribe a characteristic to the statement "Snow is white" at all; rather, we just indicate our willingness to affirm "Snow is white." This has sometimes been called a "disappearance" theory of truth— either because, on this theory, "the problem of the nature of truth" disappears, or because truth itself disappears as any kind of attribute.

Had we agreed that the very center of pragmatism involves a confusion which has been cleared up by modern "disappearance theories of truth," we would not have written this essay. Had we held the view just described, we would have said that it is empty to say that what we are trying to do in science or anywhere else is find the truth. One wants, of course, to affirm "Snow is white" only if snow indeed is white. But an understanding of the sentence "Snow is white" does not consist, in the "disappearance" view, of grasping conditions under which it is true; it consists, rather, in grasping conditions under which "Snow is white" is confirmed. The very criticism that the modern view makes of Dewey—that he loses the distinction between warranted assertibility and truth—is, in a way, valid against the modern view itself.

Is it incumbent, then, to go back to the Peirce-James view, that "truth" (as distinct from "warranted assertibility") is to be identified with the tremendously Utopian idea of "the final opinion," the theory to be reached (and to become coercive) at the end of *indefinitely continued investigation?* Not necessarily. James and Peirce want to deny that truth outruns what humans, or other sentient beings, could verify or find out. Very often, the problem in philosophy is that a philosopher who knows what he wants to deny feels that he cannot simply do so, but must make a "positive" statement; and the positive statement is frequently a disaster. Suppose, for the moment, that what is right in pragmatism is the leading idea that truth is an *idealization*— a useful and necessary idealization—of warranted assertibility. The idealization need not involve the Utopian fantasy of a theory satisfying all the requirements that absolute idealists placed on "the ultimate coherent account" (an account which, they argued, could only be known by the Absolute, that is, God). The idealists' ultimate coherent account had to contain the truth about every single question—it had to be what a contemporary logician would call a "complete and consistent" theory of everything. It is, perhaps, understandable that James and Peirce would accept the ideal of One Complete and Consistent Theory of Everything, since they were influenced by the very philosophy they were combating. Yet James's own pluralism eventually led him to reject the idea that all truth must cohere in one final system. If a statement can withstand all the criticism that is appropriate given its context, perhaps that is truth enough. This general sort of idea—the idea of truth as, in some way (not in Peirce's way, but in a more humanly accessible, modest way), an idealization of the notion of warranted assertibility—has recently been revived in writings by Michael Dummett, Nelson Goodman, and myself.[1]

James (as well as Dewey) takes the same approach to ethics as he does to common sense and science. Here too, he thinks, there are procedures which can be imperfectly characterized and which might be improved in the course of ethical inquiry itself. What is not available is a set of final ethical truths or a method by which they can be discovered. He tries to change our philosophical sensibility, rather than to replace one foundationalist ethical project with another, on the one hand, or to convince us that ethics is "noncognitive," on the other.

It is possible to extract from James's writings a description of how best to proceed in ethical inquiry. First, in ethics as in science, "experimentation" is necessary, not in the sense of random trials (which are not done in science either), but in the sense of hypotheses to be tested in practice. In ethics the hypotheses can include our ideals, our social philosophies, our plans for a better world; and the tests in practice consist in the struggle to implement these plans in the context of a democratic polity. In James's day it was not as well understood as it is now that scientists who propose theories often do so before any real experimental evidence is available, and often defend their untested theories with a passion—without which the evidence would probably never be collected or the experiments performed. (The life of Albert Einstein affords more than one illustration of this.) James's insistence in "The Will to Believe" that "science would be far less advanced than she is if the passionate desires of individuals to get their own faiths confirmed had been kept out of the game" shocked and bewildered many, including his graduate students at Harvard. E. A. Singer, Jr., recalled that his reaction on first hearing that essay as a lecture was like a "feeling of the absurd." One of his fellow students dubbed the essay "The Will to Make Believe." That the passionate advocacy of new ideas and ideals in the face of skepticism is the prerequisite for all social change is perhaps less controversial today than it was in James's day.

Our values—our "demands," as James calls them—cannot, however, be tested one by one, nor is there an algorithm for comparing and rank-ordering them. (That is why James is not a conventional utilitarian, whatever his debt to Mill.) The most important struggle is not between atomistic or isolated values, but between what James calls "ideals," visions which inform and unite large systems of demands. Individual demands may be unreconcilable, as may ideals. But with ideals there is at least the hope of incorporation in some more inclusive vision. That we should seek to work out the conflicts between our ideals in this way—by seeking more inclusive ones which bring out and preserve what was valuable in the ideals they replace— is a central part of the methodology James recommends to us. Peirce was confident that science would go on progressing if only we remain faithful to the spirit of fallibilism and continue to engage in abduction—theory construction, as opposed to mere induction from cases—and in ethics James is no less confident that social progress will result from this same spirit of fallibilism and a continued engagement in the construction and passionate advocacy of "ideals." In ethical cases, compassion corresponds to the corrective force of experiment in science. Just as no sequence of experiments will do any good, no matter how wonderful some of the theories under test, unless we pay attention to the outcomes, so no sequence of social experiments will do any good, no matter how wonderful some of the ideals involved in the struggle, if attention is not paid to "the cries of the wounded." Our moral image of the world must include values of procedural rationality which are closely connected with the values of intellectual freedom and mutuality.

In *A Theory of Justice* John Rawls introduced the notion of imperfect procedural justice. Trial by jury is an example of this kind of justice: the ideal—that all and only the guilty be convicted—is defined without reference to the procedure, and the procedure sometimes fails to produce the ideal result. (An example of perfect procedural justice is the well-known method of dividing a cake justly, that is evenly, by letting one person cut and the other choose.) A conception of, say, justice which defines it by reference to a procedure is called a "pure procedural conception" by Rawls. Trial by jury does not yield a pure procedural conception of what justice is. Nevertheless trial by jury, though imperfect, is a just procedure; it is, in practice, the best method we know to minimize false guilty verdicts. The pragmatists' conception of rationality, and James's (and Dewey's) conception of morality, is an imperfect procedural conception in a different sense. (Habermas has recently employed the notion in this new sense.) It is procedural because there is no other way to find truth or goodness; it is imperfect because there is no external point of view from which one can judge whether the method has been followed correctly. This differs from the case of trial by jury; here an outsider can judge whether the procedures have been followed.

On the other hand, the pragmatist does not believe that correctness of the outcome of the procedures—rational belief or just resolution of some conflict between demands—can be defined other than in terms of the outcome of the (endlessly self-improving) procedure. For pragmatists, our conceptions of rationality and justice are almost "pure procedural conceptions" even though the procedures are imperfect. (The guilt or innocence of the accused is not a fact quite independent of the procedure by which it becomes known; truth and goodness independent of the procedures are at best "regulative ideals.")

If the Jamesian conception is procedural, it is also a vision of personal responsibility, personal feeling and commitment, bounded by respect for the moral visions and commitments of others. The question is whether we can, whether we will, arrive at better shared conceptions of the good by struggling for our own deeply held personal conceptions within a framework of a commitment to democracy, struggling in a way which combines deep commitment with hatred for dogmatism. James raised and answered this question in "The Moral Philosopher and the Moral Life." And his answer is that we will succeed on one condition, that we must not be "deaf to the cries of the wounded."

Here again there is a link with utilitarianism. In a passage in *Utilitarianism*, Mill argues that anything is desirable—in analogy with the claim that anything is visible or audible—only if people do, or under specifiable circumstances will, desire it. On the basis of that passage, philosophers never used to tire of accusing Mill of committing the fallacy of passing from the premise that each (or a large majority) desires something to its being (objectively) desirable in the normative sense. If the something desired is a system of moral desires (an ideal, in a large sense) which would be the outcome of strenuous moral inquiry—inquiry conducted through democratic debate and practical testing in the social arena, not through appeals to the method of authority or the method of what is agreeable to reason—then the missing premise in the utilitarian argument is filled in by the pragmatist theory of truth! This is how K. O. Apel reads and applies Peirce today; in this respect, Apel follows in James's footsteps. Whereas Bernard Williams and David Wiggins claim that truth in morality is one thing (truth "humanly speaking") and something else ("absolute truth") in science, pragmatism urges that truth humanly speaking is all we've got. And the best idea we have of it is the "imperfect procedural conception" of how to get to it. From this flows the insistence on avoiding authoritarianism and not being deaf to the voices of complaint (the grandfather of the "ideal dialogic situation," in which every participant has a chance both to advance and to challenge claims, that Habermas writes about today) and the simultaneous insistence on being passionate—passionate but not fanatical—about putting forward moral, religious, and political views.

Although James is, then, a modified utilitarian in this sense, he is emphatically not a utilitarian in a certain classical sense. He denies that all our desires are reducible to a desire for pleasure and/or the absence of pain; indeed, he affirms emphatically that we have immediate moral emotions. We would recoil, James asserts in "The Moral Philosopher and the Moral Life," from the idea of securing the happiness of the whole world "on the one simple condition that a certain

lost soul on the far-off edge of things should lead a life of lonely torture." Indeed, it is because we have immediate moral emotions that
hearing the cry of the wounded makes a difference in our search for
the good.

That search would be futile, in James's view, a sentimental self-
indulgence, if the world were closed, if there were no real possibilities,
if individuals could not make a difference. Thus James was driven
early and late to confront what he called "The Dilemma of Determinism." He himself was pulled back—pulled himself back—from the
brink of a nervous breakdown by reading Renouvier's defense of free
will. There are certain questions—metaphysical questions—which are
of great importance in our lives but which cannot be settled by the
rational procedures discussed so far. Moreover, to suspend judgment
may have the practical effect of deciding one way rather than the
other. Belief in his or her own ultimate success has enabled many a
person to prevail where fainter hearts have failed. It is in these situations, and these situations only, that James exhorts us to "will to
believe." ("Our passional nature not only lawfully may, but must,
decide an option between propositions, whenever it is a genuine
option *that cannot by its nature be decided on intellectual grounds;*
for to say under such circumstances, 'Do not decide, but leave the
question open,' is itself a passional decision,—just like deciding yes
or no—and is attended with the same risk of losing the truth.")
According to James, the question of free will or determinism is one
of those questions. To be sure, determinism was a regulative ideal in
the Newtonian physics of James's day; but free will is also a regulative
ideal for James, and when regulative ideals conflict, it is philosophy
and not physics that must decide how much to give to each. James
believed that moral condemnations and moral regrets are senseless
"unless the right way was open to us as well." (The quote is from
"The Dilemma of Determinism," but the sound is unmistakably Kantian.) Finally, and most important, he could not "understand the willingness to act, no matter how we feel, without the belief that acts are
really good or bad."

Perhaps the most shocking claim that James makes—the claim that
is the centerpiece of the very first of the *Lectures on Pragmatism*—is
that the decision we make on any metaphysical question, like the
question of free will or the question of the existence of objective values, is and ought to be a matter of "temperament." Almost at the very
beginning of the lecture, James announces that "the history of philos-

ophy is to a great extent that of a certain clash of human temperaments." Of course, even if this statement is true, philosophers (as
James of course realized) are bound to regard it as irrelevant psy-
chologizing: "Temperament is no conventionally recognized reason,
so he urges impersonal reasons only for his conclusions. Yet his temperament really gives him a stronger bias than any of his more strictly
objective premises."

Here "temperament" does not have the connotations of arbitrariness, inexplicability, or irrationality that it most often has today. Temperaments, in James's sense, can put one in better or worse touch with
the universe (as James argues in the same lecture, and, indeed, in the
whole series of lectures). He claims that the extreme temperaments he
calls "tough minded" and "tender minded" both make one misper-
ceive (or worse, fail to perceive) important parts of reality. "You find
empiricism with inhumanism and irreligion; or else you find a rationalistic philosophy that indeed may call itself religious, but that keeps
out of all definite touch with concrete facts and joys and sorrows."
(James goes on to speak of Leibniz's "feeble grasp of reality.") The
pluralist temperament, James is convinced, is the best temperament
for this world.

Temperament, then, is subject to criticism. Part of what philosophical conflict is about is determining what sort of temperament is best
suited to the universe we live in. At the same time, the universe we
live in is not a "ready made world." It is open in many respects, and,
more important, it is up to us what it shall be like. Thus, we are
engaged in a struggle (a "real fight") to adapt the universe and our
temperaments to each other. "I find myself willing to take the universe
to be really dangerous and adventurous," James writes, "without
backing out and crying 'no play.'" And a few paragraphs later in the
same lecture ("Pragmatism and Religion"), James says that a genuine
pragmatist "is willing to live on a scheme of uncertified possibilities,
which he trusts; willing to pay with his own person, if need be, for
the realization of the ideals which he frames."

If we are careful to limit the "right to believe" to those options
which "cannot by their nature be decided on intellectual grounds,"
then we may add this "method"—this existential leap—to our list of
"acceptable" procedures. The resulting final procedural conception of
truth and goodness is troublesome. One seems to be asserting that
something is true (and/or warranted) and simultaneously admitting
that one cannot "prove" it to be true by already accepted public stan-

dards ("intellectual grounds"). Either one must give up the notion of truth in such a case, people suppose, or give up the notion of warrant (rational acceptability), or add a relativizer like the phrase "for me" or "for my culture" to one's talk of truth or one's talk of warrant. James's pragmatism—like existentialism, to which it has a definite relation—insists that the "publicity" of truth and warrant is something *de faciendo* and not de facto, that we are subject to both the imperative to take a stand, to be a person who stands for something, and the imperative to try to make our stand a shared one. (This was well understood by whoever selected the quotation which decorates the lobby of William James Hall at Harvard: "The community stagnates without the impulse of the individual; the impulse dies away without the sympathy of the community.") Believing that one's fundamental beliefs are true (or at least on the right track) even if they cannot be proved beyond controversy by appeal to already-shared standards is part of one's acceptance of the regulative ideal of absolute truth, as James describes that ideal.

At the same time, James's pragmatism is significantly different from existentialism—especially from Kierkegaard's. While defending the right of the existentialist to believe ahead of the evidence (James cites the "Danish thinker" who has taught us that "we live forwards but we understand backwards"), James equally and correlatively emphasizes fallibilism. Now, it is no part of Kierkegaard's conception of what it is to be a Christian that one is to regard one's own Christianity as subject to revision in the light of future experience: in this respect James's existentialism, if it is an existentialism, is sui generis. Staking one's life on one's ideals while recognizing that they are, in the nature of things, not final and may (we hope, will) be improved on in the progress of the species—this is a twist on existentialism that is deeply American.

To complete this account of James's ideas, we shall end with some remarks concerning his radical empiricism. As mentioned at the outset, Gerald Myers makes this the focal point of his recent lengthy study of James's philosophy. Myers's judgment concerning the centrality of James's radical empiricism is shared by other philosophers. Bertrand Russell, for example, in spite of his hostility to pragmatism (meaning James's theory of truth as Russell misunderstood it), was deeply impressed by radical empiricism, which he credited with inspiring his own "neutral monism" (the philosophy which is both defended and criticized in Wittgenstein's celebrated early work, the

Tractatus Logico-Philosophicus).[2] In a different way, Husserl, the father of phenomenology, was equally impressed, and to the present day phenomenologists are among the best students and expositors of James's thought. We cannot even attempt an account of this immense topic here; but a few words about it are necessary to round out our account of James as the preacher to the unchurched.

Since the seventeenth century the question of the existence of the "external" world—the world inhabited in common, of stars and mountains, chairs and tables, animals and humans—has been a central issue in epistemology. According to the traditional view, each of us is directly acquainted only with his or her own "sense data" from which he or she "infers" (Descartes) or "constructs" (Berkeley) the commonsense world of sticks and stones. Neither Hume nor Kant, both of whom recognized the difficulties of the standard view, managed to overcome the source of the problem: the central assumption is that the knower and the "given" are separate from the world that is known by means of the given.

One of James's central purposes in developing the complicated metaphysics-cum-epistemology he called radical empiricism was to combat that central assumption. Like John Austin many years later, but in a different way, James contended that there is nothing at all wrong with the commonsense idea that (apart from such special cases as illusion and hallucination) we directly perceive external things—people, trees, buildings, and the rest. James's radically nontraditional theory of perception provides a logically coherent and empirically adequate account of perception which does away with the baffling idea that one cannot really perceive external things (except in the Pickwickian sense of directly perceiving "sense data" which are caused by the external things). By putting an alternative in the field, James has shown that the sense-datum theory (which continues to influence philosophers more than they are likely to admit) is at best a hypothesis; it is to be accepted, or rejected, on grounds of likelihood or plausibility or simplicity or compatibility with other beliefs. Since the sense-datum theory can no longer claim to be the only possible account of what we are "given" in perception, of what we know for sure, regardless of how skeptical we may be, James, by simply putting an alternative in the field, succeeded in calling into question "foundationalist" epistemology, epistemology based on the idea that we have indubitable knowledge of our own private sense data.

This would be fascinating to investigate further,[3] but more relevant to our account of James as, first and foremost, a *moral* philosopher is his motivation for rejecting traditional sense-datum epistemology. James explains his motivation in a simple but shattering remark: "I simply cannot see," he says, "how from a large number of private worlds (the private worlds constituted by my sense data, your sense data, Dick's sense data, Jane's sense data . . .) we could ever arrive at knowledge of a common world." Even in pure epistemology and metaphysics, the concern with human beings as interdependent members of a community guides James's every move.

Recognizing the centrality of this concern helps one to perceive the connections between James's many ideas. In his radical empiricism, the distinction between the illusory or hallucinatory and the real is not that the illusory or hallucinatory has no experiential presence— to the victim, a hallucination is terrifyingly present—but that the illusory and the hallucinatory lack, James says, "general validity." The connection James insists upon here between reality and community echoes the connection between truth and community drawn in his earlier writings. For example, in "The Moral Philosopher and the Moral Life," James anticipated Wittgenstein's celebrated Private Language Argument. James imagined a world in which there is only one sentient being, and wrote that none of the being's beliefs could be called "true." Why not? Because "truth presupposes a standard external to the thinker." Such a world, a world with a single sentient being, James calls "a moral solitude."

In the same essay James imagines a world in which there are a number of thinkers who do *not* care about one another; he denies that the notion of truth would have application to the thought of such beings. They are, James says, in the same position as the solitary thinker in the first thought experiment; their world is a plurality of moral solitudes. Truth, then, presupposes community. But community is not enough. The "truth" of a Khomeiniist sect is not worthy of the name, according to the great pragmatists, because it is not responsive to anything except the will of the leader. (For the leader, there is no distinction at all between thinking he is right and being right, for there are no checks.) A community that subjects its beliefs to test is the minimum requirement for the existence of truth. This remarkable vision of a deep connection between truth, reality, and community drives James in propounding his "melioristic religion."

17. James's Theory of Perception

Although William James is usually thought of as a "literary" philosopher, in the *Essays in Radical Empiricism* he wrote what even Bertrand Russell recognized to be serious technical philosophy.[1] And indeed, these essays have the mysterious sort of depth that the most puzzling passages of the great philosophers seem to have: say, the Transcendental Deduction in the case of Kant, and the Private Language Argument in the case of Wittgenstein. These essays—especially the fourth essay, "How Two Minds Can Know One Thing"—are difficult writings, whose importance in understanding James's views cannot be overestimated.

James himself would have said, "These views presuppose pragmatism, but not vice versa." Bertrand Russell would have said that James was wrong about the presupposing of pragmatism—that pragmatism and radical empiricism (or at least what was correct about radical empiricism) were totally independent—and, indeed, Russell rejected James's pragmatism and accepted a significant aspect of his radical empiricism. In fact, what James actually says isn't quite that radical empiricism presupposes pragmatism; what he claims is that his pragmatism is a "propaedeutic" to radical empiricism. The idea must be that pragmatism is not strictly presupposed by radical empiricism, but nevertheless it is a good idea to have read—and, James would hope, to have accepted—pragmatism as what James called a "genetic theory of truth" before tackling these essays.

But the term "theory of truth" is one of the problems in understanding James's philosophy. In what sense is it a *theory* of truth? (The qualifier "genetic theory" indicates that it isn't a straightforward theory of the "essence" of truth.) And how are the vague terms that James employs in connection with his theory of truth—terms like "function" and "satisfaction"—supposed to clarify the notion of truth?[2] In any case, James thinks that accepting the thing he calls a "theory of truth" is a propaedeutic toward understanding radical empiricism. It would be wrong, however, to think of James as a philosopher whose primary interest is in the theory of perception, or even in resolving the subject-object dichotomy. We cannot suppose that all of James's grand remarks about life, morality, and religious belief are a mere propaedeutic to a discussion of the really interesting question of whether two different people see the same Memorial Hall. Obviously, it is the other way around. James does not think that radical empiricism is irrelevant to the rest of his philosophy. It may be that, if anything, the *Essays in Radical Empiricism* are best thought of as a propaedeutic to James's pragmatism.

If we regard James's radical empiricism as being a propaedeutic to his pragmatism, rather than the other way around, we can see that the rather cold metaphysical picture James presents in these essays is meant to turn hot. In this essay I shall not, however, attempt to read *Pragmatism* in the light of radical empiricism. For now, let me remark that when I do teach James's *Pragmatism,* my custom is to go through the lectures almost line by line. I think this is valuable in the case of *Pragmatism* because one's first impression is that the lectures are easy, and because James seems to write so clearly and so well; but if one is receptive to James's message at all, one soon realizes that something is happening which is very nuanced, and the problem is getting the nuance. In the *Essays in Radical Empiricism,* by contrast, we are dealing with a mass of technical detail, and therefore I am going to adopt the opposite strategy here of standing back from the technical detail and trying to summarize the picture.

It is a very unconventional picture. I had an idea as to what the picture might be some years ago, when Dieter Henrich gave a seminar on Kant's Transcendental Deduction at Harvard. Henrich was lecturing on the unity of the self, and making the point that, in spite of all the phenomenal disunity of the self, which Kant was well aware of, Kant thought that in some transcendental sense the "I," the "I" in "I think," the "I" to which I am prepared to relate all my representations, is metaphysically a unity. And the world is metaphysically a unity. Henrich described Kant's problem as the problem of establishing the connection between the unity of the world and the unity of the self; in some way these are transcendentally interdependent. As he was saying this, it occurred to me that James's view might be summarized in the following way: the self isn't a unity and the world isn't a unity, and so Kant had the wrong problem. The problem shouldn't be to show that the unity of the world is correlative with the unity of the self, but to show that the disunity of the world is correlative with the disunity of the self.

James and Darwin

In one of his lectures in *Pragmatism*—the lecture entitled "The One and the Many"—James says that there are ways of looking at the world in which it is a unity and ways of looking at it in which it is a disunity; but, he says, the pragmatist temperament favors, stresses, sees as of primary importance the disunities, the pluralities. And this is not a mere "psychological" observation, for the whole message of the book is that temperament is all-important, and pragmatism itself, after all, is an attempt to change one's temperament, to make one into a different sort of person. James is out of sympathy with what he calls the "rationalist" temperament, the temperament that sees unity as the most important thing. Of course, that temperament has had its victories, most notably in mathematics. However, a good example of the temperament James prefers would be Charles Darwin. In fact, James was an enthusiastic supporter of Darwin at a time when there was hardly an experimental biologist who believed in natural selection.

Many things make Darwin an appropriate representative of the pragmatist temperament. For one thing, he was a writer who consciously used literary devices in presenting his scientific theories. (In the last few years there have been several articles in the *New York Times Book Review* about the influence of Darwin's use of narrative devices on the modern novel.) And I believe that this crossing of the lines between literature and science would have delighted James. (Certainly his *Principles of Psychology* crosses them.) But this is not what I have in mind at the moment. Let us recall Darwin's theory. As Ernst Mayr has repeatedly pointed out,[3] it is a mistake to think that Darwin's theory had a single postulate, the postulate of natural selection; Darwin's theory had many parts. The first was evolution. At the end of the nineteenth century almost everybody believed in evolution, but very few people believed in natural selection. (Think of Lamarck, not to speak of Hegel, or of Herbert Spencer.) Second, Darwin believed in common descent, for example, we and the other simians have a common descent. That suggestion of Darwin's was widely accepted by biologists, who did not regard it as a speculation outside the bounds of experimental biology. This Darwinian idea was accepted because it at once made sense of taxonomy. Although today's "creationist" debates sometimes convey the impression that scientists accepted evolution and common descent *because* they accepted natural selection, this is not the case. Natural selection was the controversial element in Darwin's story. And one of the most important aspects of Darwin's new way of thinking about the world, the way based on the idea of natural selection, is what Mayr calls Darwin's "anti-essentialism."

It is an interesting fact that the people who produced the theory of natural selection, Darwin and his co-discoverer Wallace, and the people who early became converts to it were naturalists, not experimentalists; they were people who had been to odd places and seen a lot of flora and fauna. These people did not perform experiments, but they did an enormous amount of observing and comparing, and what they were interested in was variation. The traditional view in biology, the view associated with Aristotle (and, perhaps more fairly, with Plato) is that the real reality, the essence, is the *type*. In this view there is such a thing as the essence of a cat, that is, of the type Cat, and there is such a thing as the essence of a dog, that is, of the type Dog, and this essence is what is of scientific importance and interest. (As Mayr has remarked, racism can be viewed as an expression of this kind of essentialistic thinking; the racist thinks of blacks and whites and Jews and Caucasians and Asiatics as types with essential characteristics, rather than as huge populations which exhibit immense variation and which have enormous amounts of genetic overlap.) But for Darwin there was a flip: the reality is the variation. In a Darwinian view, no two humans are identical, not even identical twins. Even if the genotypes are identical, how they are expressed is not quite identical. No two human beings, no two rabbits, no two mice, no two cockroaches, no two amoebas, are identical. Although there is a "central tendency," this tendency is simply an average; Darwin would say that it is a mere abstraction. Thus the very thing that is the true reality to the rationalist temperament becomes a mere mathematical abstraction to the Darwinian. "See, you can add up a lot of numbers and divide by N, the number of things in the population, and you think you have some kind of transcendental reality," a Darwinian might scoff. Even averages change, the Darwinian points out: the average height we have seen in country after country has changed as food habits have changed; there have been enormous jumps without any corresponding jumps in the gene pool.

Now, this Darwinian attitude, the attitude that says that the reality is the individual with all his uniqueness, his variation, opens the way for the idea that species slide into one another—exactly what "Aristotelians" thought was prohibited. If there is an eternal essence of Ape and an eternal essence of Human, how can one of those slide into the other? But once you say "All there is is variation," all there is is individuals in their variety, you have totally changed the picture. We might say that, in this respect, Darwin was the most "pragmatist" of scientists.

I don't want to give the impression that we should (or that James thinks we should) *never* think in the "essentialist" or "rationalist" way. I have already mentioned the success of rationalistic ways of thinking in pure mathematics. And one could also cite aspects of contemporary physics as representing a limited but important success of "rationalism," in James's sense of the term. In fundamental physics, it is important that one electron be absolutely the same as every other electron. But James wants to remind us that even though the rationalistic type of thinking has its place—it is sometimes pragmatically effective—once it becomes one's only way of thinking, one is bound to lose the world for a beautiful model. I believe that this is a central part of the message of the *Essays in Radical Empiricism*.

Reality and Unrealities: From Universe to Pluriverse

I say all this because, although in one way James is taking on a classical problem, the so-called "problem of perception," and speaking to classical issues—*What about illusion, What about hallucination,* and so on—James does not believe that he can convince us that direct realism can be right, and all the sophisticated philosophical objections to it that have become familiar since Descartes can be wrong, without providing a "metaphysics," in a certain sense. To redescribe perception, James has to redescribe reality—but "reality" is a funny term here. For there is a sense in which James is describing *more* than just reality.

Now, how can one provide a description of *more* than reality? One can describe more than reality if reality isn't all there is. There is also unreality. And part of the extreme pluralist view that lies behind James's metaphysics is just that: that reality isn't all there is, that there is also unreality, or rather that there are, "intentionally, at any rate," unreal entities.[4]

James is not, of course, the only philosopher to think something like this: the name of Meinong springs to mind. And there are even logically minded philosophers who have tried to show that quantification over "Meinongian objects" can be made consistent, by formalizing Meinong's ideas. I have no doubt that one could formalize James as well (in fact, I have seen at least one paper that attempts to do this). But part of the reason James is not read all that much by analytic philosophers is that he does not consider issues of formalization—not because he is unwilling to argue, for in these essays he is arguing, and very technically, but because his stream in philosophy does not come from Frege and Russell, does not come from an interest in mathematical logic. Peirce is much easier for an analytic philosopher to relate to, because Peirce was a logician. The thing that James was trained in was psychology, or what *he* called psychology, which is not exactly what we call psychology today—which adds to the difficulty.

Nevertheless, James is not really inconsistent. The qualifier, "intentionally, at any rate," which James places before his claim that mental knives and real knives have the same "natures," is a way of restoring consistency, as is the distinction between an attribute's being part of the "nature" of an "experience" *adjectively* and its being part of the nature of the experience *intentionally*. But I shall not ask us to be *too* charitable. James's thought is certainly vague in part, which is why different people who were sympathetic to (some of) James's ideas could take quite different morals from them. (Russell and Husserl are good examples.) James is starting something in these essays, but what he is starting can be continued in different ways. So something that is still an interesting project would be to study James's radical empiricism and then look at how Russell reads it, leaving out the Meinongian objects (say, in *The Analysis of Mind,* when we see James's *Essays in Radical Empiricism* as a forerunner of Russell's neutral monism), on the one hand, and, on the other hand, how Husserl reads it (when we see the same essays as a forerunner of phenomenology). Phenomenologists themselves have written about the latter, but it would also be of interest for someone who is not in that movement to take a look at this question.

It is not hard to see why Russell leaves out the "Meinongian" objects when he takes over as much as he can accept of James's theory. What does it *mean* to say *there are* objects which aren't real? The very words explode from the page, from a logician's point of view. There ought to be subscripts on "are" and "real": one should write, "There are₁ objects that don't exist₂," or something like that. James tries to help us out with his term "pure experience," but that is somewhat of a trap, partly because James is ambivalent. Sometimes he does have a metaphysics of pure experience, and at other times he seems to draw back from this melting of pure experience into a substance, and so on. But also, quite apart from the issues about whether "pure experience" is some sort of metaphysical substance, it is hard for present-day Anglo-Saxon philosophers to understand the ways in which James and his contemporaries, who were much more familiar with German philosophy than we are today, used the word "experience." In the English-speaking as opposed to the German-speaking philosophical world, "experience" has tended to mean "sensation"; thus there is a tendency today to read "world of pure experience" as "world of pure sensation," which totally misses what James is talking about. So here, at least at the outset, I shall try to present James's view using this word "experience" as little as possible.

One reason to avoid the word "experience," at least until one has gotten some way into James's philosophy, is that if we use that word too early we may fail to realize that one of the things James wants to do is change our idea of what "experience" *is*. Of course, James also tries to change our view of what experience is in the *Principles of Psychology;* there we learn that experience is "thought and sensation fused." But there are interpretative problems with the *Principles of Psychology* too. So what term shall I use? I have said that James's theory isn't a "theory of reality," because reality is only a part of what it is a theory of, and I don't want to use the term "pure experience" (at least not yet). I don't want to say that it is a theory of the universe *tout court,* because we might think of the universe as a unity. So let me say that James's theory is a theory of the *pluriverse,* a term that I think does justice to his view. (Recall that perhaps the most quoted remark by James, after "it's true if it works," is that reality is a blooming buzzing confusion.) After all, James called the last book he wrote *A Pluralistic Universe,* and that title clearly suggests talking of a "pluriverse."

So out there is the pluriverse, and that contains everything. But we have to ask, "What is everything?" because, as already indicated, there is going to be a lot more in the pluriverse ("intentionally, at any rate") than in any standard rationalist or empiricist universe. James might well have said to all other philosophers, "There are more things between heaven and earth than dreamed of in your philosophy, Horatio."

The Pluriverse, Reality, and the Ongoing Community

For the moment the pluriverse is just a placeholder, about which all I have said is that there is going to be a lot there. Within the pluriverse there is a part—if I were to sketch it on the blackboard, I should draw it with fuzzy edges—which James will call "reality." That sounds as if reality is properly contained in the pluriverse; and that is the way James sometimes writes, when he "lets himself go," for example in "Does 'Consciousness' Exist?": "Mental knives may be sharp, but they won't cut real wood . . . With 'real' objects on the contrary [note the shudder quotes!], consequences always accrue; and thus the real objects get sifted from the mental ones, the things from our thoughts of them, fanciful or true, and precipitated together as the stable part of the whole-experience-chaos, under the name of the physical world. Of this our perceptual experiences are the nucleus, they being the originally *strong* experiences. We add a lot of conceptual experiences to them, making these strong also in imagination, and building out the remoter parts of the physical world by their means; and around this core of reality the world of laxly connected fancies and mere rhapsodical objects floats like a bank of clouds" (*Essays in Radical Empiricism*, pp. 17–18). Taken according to the letter, this means that there are a lot of things in the pluriverse which aren't "real" but which are still in some sense *there*. As I already explained, James does not worry about how one would say that *nicely* (that is, how one would "formalize such an ontology").

Let us take an example which is close to but not quite the one James uses. Suppose that someone hallucinates a fire. (James considers someone *imagining* a fire.) The fire, considered as a fire, is not part of what we call "reality." James, quoting Münsterberg, speaks of unreal things such as this fire as not having "general validity" (*Essays in Radical Empiricism*, p. 11), a term that indicates that what we call reality is in some way *shared*. But "shared" does not mean shared by just one particular culture. There is not one single line in James's writing that takes "general validity" to mean general validity *in a particular culture*.[5]

The problem of what constitutes "general validity" is not very often a *real* problem when we are talking about tables and chairs. It is when one gets to the areas that most interest James, the areas of ethics and religion, that the meaning of "general validity" becomes problematic. In the previous chapter Ruth Anna Putnam and I argued that James should be thought of as having what we called an "imperfect procedural conception" of validity in such areas; but a discussion of this would take us beyond the bounds of the present essay. What is important, if we are right, is that the effort to get general agreement, the effort to find "inclusive ideals" which can be shared, is an essential aspect of the procedure to be used in such areas. What has general validity is not always what satisfies standards that are already shared in a community; sometimes the problem is to *come to agreement on the standards* and not just to find what conforms to standards that we have already agreed upon; but the theme of sharing, of "general" validity, is still present in James's thought, even here.

Let us return to the example of the "unreal" fire, the fire that someone hallucinates. Well, is it really a fire? It isn't real, so can it be a fire? Does it have flames? Is it *hot?* As I said earlier, James is not a logician, and here he has to struggle for a terminology. What he says is that such an entity is connected with the property of being hot (being a fire, having flames, and so forth) "intentionally" but not "adjectively" (*Essays in Radical Empiricism,* p. 17). It possesses being hot—being hot is part of its "nature"—but not as an attribute. You cannot simply say—let me now use James's expression "pure experience," with all its dangers, just to have *some* term for this funny object—you cannot simply say that this "pure experience" *has* the attribute "hot"; you cannot simply say it *has* flames. We can only say that "is hot" is an attribute of a "pure experience" if the statement that that "pure experience" is hot is a statement about a reality.

But even that is too simple; James is more nuanced than that. In James's view the *same* pure experience may be *in here* under one description and *out there* under another description. More precisely, since James thinks of "location" as an *external relation,* the same "pure experience" may have one location ("in my mind") when "taken with one system of associations" and a different location (in physical space) when taken as belonging with a different system of associations (*Essays in Radical Empiricism,* p. 8). If I am the person having the hallucination, and I say that it is a real fire, I am making a mistake. Under the description "real fire" that "pure experience" belongs outside of reality; it doesn't have general validity. But if you describe what is in a sense the same "pure experience" as a psychiatrist would describe it, as John Smith's hallucination, then under that description the same pure experience is a piece of reality—albeit a member of the class "hallucinatory experience" and not a member of the class "fire." So basically the word "reality" is correlative to the word "truth." If the description is "true," then under that description the "pure experience" is a reality; if the description is false, then under that description it isn't a reality. And the same "pure experience" may possess both true descriptions and false ones.

Moreover, the "external relations" James speaks of (*Essays in Radical Empiricism*, p. 10) are not merely arbitrary associations; they are *experienced* relations, leadings-to and terminatings-in and representings; and James is a realist about experienced relations. An aspect of this realism which I plan to discuss in a future publication is his realism about *intentional relations* (as when he writes that one pure experience may be *about* another, or *represent* another, or *refer* to another). In my opinion, failure to see that, whatever James's "theory of truth" may be, it is *not* an attempt to reduce intentional to nonintentional notions is one of the fundamental sources of the many misunderstandings that have arisen in connection with it.

It follows that, in James's system, every pure experience is a part of reality under *some* description. (I cannot go into the details here; but the example of the way the mental fire is a part of reality under the description "John's image of a fire"—or better, "the inner content" of John's imagining a fire: respectively, thinking of a fire, having the illusion of a fire, hallucinating a fire, as the case may be [*Essays in Radical Empiricism*, p. 9] may serve to give the idea.) Consequently, James does not, at the end of the day, have as severe problems as the Meinongians do: everything in James's "ontology," everything James quantifies over, is a perfectly kosher object, a perfectly real thing, under an appropriate external relation. What looked initially like "Meinongian objects" turn out to be real (albeit "subjective") objects that possess properties "intentionally" which they do not possess adjectively.

The Purpose of James's Ontology

If I haven't got James all wrong, the machinery he develops in the *Essays in Radical Empiricism* has to connect with his wider moral-religious-ideological concerns. It cannot be that he is doing all this just for the sake of a theory of perception. But in this essay I am putting all that aside, and looking at James as a theorist of perception. In that narrow context, saying that there are bits of pure experience which are not part of "this core of reality" (*Essays in Radical Empiricism*, p. 18)—at least, not according to the description which is suggested by their "natures"—is going to be important in providing an alternative account of what may be called the subject/object distinction, or in overcoming the subject/object dichotomy.

Remember that there are certain very simple arguments, arguments with which we have been familiar since Descartes's *Meditations*, which philosophers have believed to show that what we directly and immediately perceive is subjective. Now, that view is not always *wholly* wrong, in James's view. If John Smith hallucinates a fire in the wastebasket, then under the description "fire burning in the wastebasket" what John Smith perceives is subjective. Obviously one cannot say that we immediately perceive the external world and only the external world, and everything we think we immediately perceive is really "out there." Like Peter Strawson,[6] James wants to separate the questions *Do we immediately perceive external things?* and *Do we perceive external things incorrigibly?* If we stated the traditional argument in a nutshell, stated it in a very unsophisticated way, it might be: *If we immediately perceived the external world, we would perceive it incorrigibly. But we don't perceive it incorrigibly, therefore we don't perceive it immediately.* But James wants to say that we can perceive external things immediately, and we don't perceive them incorrigibly. Immediacy is not the same as incorrigibility.

Now, there are post–World War II Anglo-Saxon philosophers who followed this line without being aware that in any respect they were following the path that James blazed many decades before. For example, although there are obvious and major differences between Austin's *Sense and Sensibilia* and James's *Essays in Radical Empiricism*, in one respect Austin follows James's line exactly: Austin too thinks the right strategy is to challenge the supposedly obvious link between "directness" and "incorrigibility."

The Seventeenth-Century Picture Criticized

Let us recall Berkeley's notorious slogan *esse est percipi*, to be is to be perceived. Philosophers rejected Berkeley's claim that *everything there is* is perceived; but almost all philosophers agreed with him about what is immediately perceived. If there is something you immediately perceive, the view runs, it must have all and only the properties it seems to have. Later on, after the term "sense datum" was invented, they would argue, "A physical thing might have one property and seem to have another; but how could the sense data that are produced in me by that physical thing seem to have one property and really have another? The sense datum *is* the appearance." That makes it sound like—a definition, right? Appearances are one set of objects and external things are another set of objects, and how can the appearances have properties other than the ones they *appear* to have? Appearances are a set of objects for which the principle *esse est percipi* is true.

A further feature of the traditional picture is that the physical thing does not have the property of color. As Strawson points out, on a commonsense view physical objects are recognized by us through the colored surfaces that they present; we see colors distributed on (objective) surfaces in an objective space. The things we say about these objects and their colors and movements are taken as *data* in scientific theory construction. So the view that science has shown that there aren't *really* any colors "out there" has the peculiar consequence that science has demolished its own data! On the traditional view the "subjective" table, the phenomenal table, has color properties, while the "objective" table has only dispositions to produce color sensations. One might say that the physical table is rather "ghostly" on the traditional view; and indeed, it was often claimed by epistemologists that the man on the street is a "naive realist" who has an incorrigible tendency to *identify* phenomenal tables with physical ones.

Note also that something analogous to hallucination happens even in veridical perception, on the traditional view. I immediately perceive something subjective—the sense data—even when I see a real fire; and I might perceive qualitatively identical subjective objects if I were to hallucinate a fire. This is why the traditional view is correctly described as a mind-body dualism. The sense data I have in the case of veridical perception as well as in the case of hallucination are mental, and the physical chair is material. So the traditional cut is not between real objects and unreal objects that have *some* kind of existence—what phenomenologists call "intentional inexistence"—rather, the cut is between mind and matter. In sharp contrast to all this, James's picture is that when I have a veridical perception of a fire I don't see a private sense datum of a fire and infer the fire; I just see the fire. When I have a hallucination, in James's picture, what I see is a fire that isn't really there.

The traditional move—the move which was thought to preclude

the very possibility of such a move as this (although some interpreters think Thomas Reid may have anticipated it, nonetheless)—was to ask the "stumper," "If you directly see a totally different thing when you see a fire and when you see a hallucination, then why do you (as it might be) think you see a fire when you see a hallucination?" This question was thought to have one (and only one) possible answer.[7] In fact, different theories of perception give it quite different answers. The sense-datum theory says that the sense data of the person who hallucinates a fire are similar to the sense data the person would perceive if he saw a real fire. So the hallucinatory fire is not similar to a real fire (in the traditional picture there is at most a problematic "correspondence" between the real fire and any sense data at all), but it is similar to the sense data produced by the presence of a real fire. James proposes the stunningly simple (it may be that it is preposterous, but it is stunningly simple) alternative that the hallucinatory object is similar in a certain way to the real object; you mistake the hallucination for a real chair because it *looks* like a real chair.

Notice that James is blocking one of the standard arguments for sense data, the argument that goes like this: "You are going to have to admit that all we perceive are sense data in at least one case, the case of hallucinations. When I hallucinate a chair (that isn't there), you can't say I see an external object, because there is no external chair for me to be seeing. It could even be that I'm in a totally dark room, and there is nothing before my eyes except blackness. Yet if I hallucinate a chair, I am directly presented with something. [J. L. Austin would challenge even that statement.] What I'm presented with, then, by universal agreement, is not a real external thing. What is it? It is something mental. So let us call it a sense datum. So we've agreed that in at least one case, when someone thinks he is perceiving a physical object, what he is really perceiving is something mental (is a sense datum). So it is plausible to suppose that even when it is a veridical perception, what you are directly perceiving is a sense datum."

Boom. Suddenly the external world has been taken away from you, and you never perceive anything directly except your own sense data. And James is perhaps the first philosopher—certainly the first twentieth-century philosopher—to cry, "Stop!"

The whole point of sense-datum theory in epistemology was to provide a *foundation* for knowledge. I contend that—whether or not it is the alternative we would accept today—James succeeded in showing that there is a consistent alternative to sense-datum theory. And if James succeeded in even that much, then he performed something stunning, because then sense-datum theory cannot be the basis or foundation of our knowledge; at best it is just one more theory. And in fact, James did succeed in worrying philosophers. Russell credits James with moving him from the sense-datum theory to the theory of the *Analysis of Mind*,[8] and (perhaps as a result of Russell's shift), Moore began worrying about many of the possibilities raised by James's theory (for example, could two sense data be perceived by one mind, could there be "ownerless" sense data, could a sense datum actually be *part of the surface* of a physical object—worries which were quite unprecedented at that time). The possibilities raised by James's theory had a corrosive effect, because once Moore realized that it was just an assumption that sense data had this property, just an assumption that they had this other property, the whole thing began to unravel.

So James was saying, "Here is an alternative hypothesis: sometimes we see real chairs and real fires, and I don't mean that we directly see something mental and do some inferring. Sometimes we see objects which are—under some description—private. And a private object can *resemble* a public object."

Now, this is not quite right as an account of James's view. The following qualification has to be introduced. A hallucinatory fire isn't hot in quite the way that a real fire is hot—a real fire is hot because the real fire has the properties of being a fire and being hot *adjectively*. The hallucinatory fire is connected to the properties "is a fire" and "is hot," but not adjectively. Nevertheless, at a certain level of abstraction, there is a similarity between the real fire and the hallucinatory fire. Some of the same properties belong to the "nature" of the "pure experience" that constitutes the hallucination and to the "nature" of a real fire. That is why the person who is subject to the hallucination (or to the illusion, in the case of a more mundane sort of perceptual error) mistakes the private fire for a real fire. He thinks that "the fire" has the properties he is aware of adjectively; he thinks his "pure experience" has general validity.

In sum, James argues that all the traditional epistemologist has shown by appealing to hallucinations (and other illusions) is that we *sometimes* experience things that are, in the traditional terminology, "mental." He has not shown that we *never* directly perceive parts of reality as they are. The essay "How Two Minds Can Know One Thing" plays an extremely important role in the presentation of this argument. On the traditional theory, if you and I stand, say, in front of Gund Hall on the Harvard campus and look at Memorial Hall, then even if we stand side by side, and even if the difference in parallax is too slight to make a difference to our visual experiences, even if our perceptual apparatus is in the same condition, even if we are identical twins, we don't directly perceive numerically the same object. You perceive your sense data of Memorial Hall, and I perceive my sense data of Memorial Hall. But James wants to say that it is possible that you and I could both directly perceive the identical external Memorial Hall, and the identical external aspect of Memorial Hall. As he himself puts it, "Our minds meet in a world of objects which would still be there if one or several of the minds were destroyed" (*Essays in Radical Empiricism*, p. 39). So, James is saying, "naive realism" is right in its most important claim, that immediate perception of external things is possible.

Two Objections to James's Theory

Let us stop for a moment and consider a couple of possible objections to James's theory. First of all, there is the obvious objection that the skeptical epistemological problem has not been met. Even if we accept everything James says, a traditional epistemologist would say, there is still no way to *know* when we are hallucinating and when we are not. To this objection James would reply that the problem is worse for the traditional theory. James begins his presentation of his own theory by explaining that the traditional theory puts each mind in a private world. Or, as James himself puts it: "[For the Berkeleyan school] . . . Our lives are a congeries of solipsisms out of which in strict logic only a God could compose a universe even of discourse . . . If the body that you actuate is not the very body that I see there, but some duplicate body of your own with which that has nothing to do, we belong to different universes, you and I, and for me to speak of you is folly" (*Essays in Radical Empiricism*, p. 37). In short, James does not see how several minds, each acquainted *only* with its own private objects, could arrive by any process of inference at knowledge or even thought of one another.

James is not, of course, going to give an "answer" to skepticism in the sense of a rationalist answer. Indeed, he may have been the first to use the metaphor of a "foundationless" philosophy—I am thinking of the letter to François Pillon in which James writes, "I fear you may find my philosophy too *bottomless* and romantic."[9] James is not going to give an answer to skepticism that is deeper than the perspective of shared human experience (to this extent, Rorty is right). But even the notion of *sharing* experience makes no sense on the traditional theory, James is claiming. Here am I, in my private world, having experiences which are qualitatively like experiences you are having in your private world, but what is the connection? If you say "simultaneity" (for example), what does *that* come to?

The advantage of pragmatism over foundationalist epistemology, in James's view, is that—as he argues in the *Lectures on Pragmatism*—the way in which pragmatist philosophers answer skeptical doubts is the way in which skeptical doubts are answered in practice, by appealing to tests that in fact work in our lives. If I think that what I see may be an illusion, I try looking at it from a different position, or I ask other people to take a look. If no one is with me, I take a photograph of it (if I have a camera with me). If that is not possible, we may examine the situation at a later time, and make inferences.

If we take seriously the idea that there are not *two* criteria or sets of criteria for "reality"—commonsense criteria and philosophical criteria—but only one,[10] then we are led naturally to the view that what demarcates "reality" is something human, not something abstract called "being real." To use the analogy with Darwinism that I suggested earlier, there is not one abstract property of being real, there is only variation. When one understands Darwinism, one's first reaction may be, "If Darwin is right, we can't speak of species any more." And the answer is, "You can, but you have to think of species in a new way. You have to learn what Mayr calls 'population thinking.' One *can* group cats together, even though they don't possess a common 'essence.' One has to look for groups which it is *functional* to group together for certain purposes, for instance understanding the history of the various phenotypes and genotypes that we see around us." I stress the analogy to Darwinism because the adjective that qualifies "theory of truth" in James's *Pragmatism* is "genetic." I think that we would be right to say that what James is describing when he writes about truth is a historical process, just as Darwin is describing a historical process. When James writes about truth, what he does is describe the process by which we come to call things true; and when James writes about "reality" he describes the process by which we come to call things "real."

Up to a point, this can sound like what a sense-datum theorist (say,

C. I. Lewis—the only philosopher to call himself a "pragmatist" who believed in sense data) would say. For James, Memorial Hall is the sum of its various aspects—its spatial extension, its color properties, its solidity, its massiveness, and so on. And if enough of those aspects are shared, it is what we call a real building. Now, many phenomenalists would talk the same way. But there is a difference. For a phenomenalist, "shared" does not mean literally shared because two people can't literally share a percept, they can only have similar percepts. And the phenomenalist has an obvious problem, since one person might be seeing a building like Memorial Hall in Cambridge, another might be seeing a building like Memorial Hall in China (if there were one), another might be seeing a building like Memorial Hall in Switzerland, and so on, and these sense data, although "similar," would not form the right kind of "bundle" to constitute a single building. So the sense-datum theorist says, "If people go to the same place, then . . . (OOPS! I used the word *place*)." And, in fact, the critics of the sense-datum theory pointed out that when phenomenalists stated the conditions under which people were supposed to have the sense data that constitute a given external thing, they invariably had to use not sense-datum language but material-object language. But James escapes *this* difficulty, at least, because he has not ruled out objective language, the language of two perceivers seeing the same thing, from the very beginning, as the phenomenalist has.[11] In sum, James's account of "reality" fits with his pragmatism inasmuch as the natural history, the genesis, of the notion of reality will turn out to be the same as the natural history of the notion of truth. And how could truth be shared if reality couldn't be shared?

A more serious objection is the following: consider a case in which an individual experiences something that he considers real (we suppose the individual is alone at the time), but later other people say he couldn't have seen any such thing. Is the individual simply "voted down"? (This is how a student once actually put this objection.) James has an easy answer to this objection: what is "shared" in James's sense is not just a matter of something like a "vote," but rather a matter of the whole course of future experience, of the "final opinion." But someone who is a realist about the past (as, I confess, I am) may still be troubled. How can the truth of a statement about the past be a function of *present and future* experience?

One answer—the answer C. I. Lewis would have given—would be that the individual might have been right even if the experiences people actually have later seem to "verify" that he was wrong: whether he was right depends not (merely) on what people in fact experience later, but on what they (counterfactually) *would* have experienced *if* they had looked, touched, and so on. This is a sensible answer, but I am convinced that it would not have been James's answer. I believe that the overwhelming weight of the textual evidence is that James had what is sometimes called an "inference license" view of counterfactuals. A counterfactual can indeed be true in the sense that experience—*actual* experience—licenses us to behave as if it were true; but James has no room for the idea that there are true statements about the past that we shall *never* know to be true.[12]

For better or for worse, I think James is committed to the view that statements about the past that do not square properly with present and future experience are simply not true. I confess that I find this kind of antirealism about the past a sure sign of a mistake, whenever and wherever it occurs; it could be argued, however, that what commits James to this mistake is not his "ontology" but his way of understanding counterfactuals (his "actualism," as one might term it).

Other Aspects of James's Radical Empiricism

I want to put one or two more pieces into this picture, and then I should invite you to reread the *Essays in Radical Empiricism,* for my purpose is to offer not a substitute for reading these essays, but an introduction to them. What becomes of the mind in James's picture? Obviously, there is not going to be any such thing as the "essence" of the mind in his picture. Indeed, James agrees with Hume that in a certain way the mind is a plurality, not a unity. There are, of course, long discussions of this issue in *The Principles of Psychology.* But we can bring out the disagreement with Hume—or one of the disagreements with Hume, for there are many[13]—by considering again James's example of viewing Memorial Hall. As we already saw, if I stand at a distance of 200 feet from Memorial Hall, the "Memorial Hall" that I see is, under one description, in my mind (and, if I believe in mind-brain identity, as Russell at times did, then the percept is in my brain). Under another description (another "external relation"), the "Memorial Hall" is 200 feet from my body. My mind "intersects" objects at a distance from me. In fact, as we shall see in a moment, one's mind can intersect as much of the pluriverse as one is able to conceive.

The point behind this last remark is that what I have so far left out of my account is that both reality and the part of the pluriverse we don't call reality contain things other than percepts. A respect in which James is unlike any empiricist before him (and much more like the phenomenologists who followed him) is in *putting conception on a plane with perception*. An object which is conceived (the "intentional object" of a thought, in the phenomenological sense) is also part of the pluriverse and may or may not be part of reality. Now this is a fantastic transformation of empiricism. James is certainly painting a metaphysical picture, there is no getting away from it. But the effect of this metaphysics is quite fascinating, because what it results in is a novel move away from positivism. Up to now, I have made James sound quite close to positivism, at least as far as thoughts about middle-sized dry goods are concerned. It sounds from what I have said so far as if this table consists of its perceptual aspects, its solidity, its spatiality, its color, although those perceptual aspects are (in the appropriate "context" or "external relation") not in my brain but at this point five feet or so in front of me. Thus it must seem that talk about the atoms of which the table consists must be construed as highly derived talk about what percepts you would have if you were to make certain experiments. James's view does not have that consequence, because although it is true that I cannot see or feel the atoms of which the table consists, I can *conceive* of them; I can "build out" the table with my conceptions of theoretical entities of all kinds. This may, by the way, be an idea that James gets from Kant. James never admits that he gets *anything* from Kant, but on a certain reading of Kant all representations are on a par—even sensations are, in a way, minimum representations. But I shall not speculate about sources; suffice it to say that, as I read these essays, when I conceive of the table as having atoms scattered through it, those atoms are also part of the pluriverse.

This aspect of James's theory is also a reason for describing it as proto-phenomenology. If we "bracket" the question of the truth of radical empiricism as a metaphysical theory of the stuff of the pluriverse—and I have intentionally used the phenomenological term "bracket"—then we at once open the door to Husserl's grand project of trying to describe experience without either presupposing or imposing anything like the traditional sense-datum theory, of describing it as it is actually *pregiven*.

In the last two sections of this essay I have distanced myself at certain points from James's views. A metaphysics in which reality consists of intentional objects which are in turn the "natures" of bits of "pure experience" is, I confess, too rich for my battered digestive system.

But what I hope to have brought out in this account is the *depth* of the problems James was dealing with. Even today, when the idea of "incorrigibility" has been given up, belief in something like the sense-datum theory is as strong as ever, if unacknowledged. (The theory is more powerful than ever precisely because it is unacknowledged.) Cognitive science is full of thinly disguised mixtures of sense-datum theory and identity theory. But James struck, I believe, the opening blow in the unfinished war against the sense-datum theory. Showing that at least one alternative exists—that the mere existence of illusions, errors, dreams, and the extreme phenomenon of hallucination does not, in and of itself, *force* one to accept anything like the traditional sense-datum theory—that the sense-datum theory is a *hypothesis* (a most peculiar one, I would add) and, for that reason, sense data cannot possibly be a *foundation* for empirical knowledge—this was, I believe, an epochal achievement. Others have continued the fight in different ways, and put yet other alternatives before us—I am thinking of Austin's *Sense and Sensibilia*—but it is time we were aware that this is part of what James was doing as well.

Those who defend the sense-datum theory of perception today (nowadays, sense data are usually renamed "perceptual states," or something like that, and are usually identified with brain states and/or functional states) may reply that they are not trying to do "foundationalist epistemology." They are only trying to do "philosophical psychology," they will say. But the very assumption that there must be such things as "perceptual states" (where this doesn't mean merely that the brain is involved in perception, but that seeing a rose and hallucinating a rose have a "similarity" which is *explained* by the idea that the two subjects are in "the same perceptual state") packs in the idea that there are *states* which are, in some way, also *appearances* and that those states are *inside* us; and this is just the picture from whose grip James was trying to free us.[14] It is amazing how hard it is to get back to the idea that we do, after all, normally perceive what is out there, not something "in here."

I believe that James was on the right track, and that Austin was on the right track, even if neither of them quite finished the job. I know that James is normally seen as an *inspiring* philosopher—often in a pejorative sense of the word. The purpose of this essay has been to suggest that he was also a deep thinker, who struggled with incredibly deep questions. His solutions may have been "crazy"—but as Wittgenstein remarked in a private note: "It is only by thinking even more crazily than philosophers do that you can solve their problems."[15]

18. Peirce the Logician

My topic in this essay is hardly one on which I can be said to have specialized knowledge or training. I am not a historian of logic, nor (although I regard Peirce as a towering giant among American philosophers) am I a "Peirce scholar." But I am a working logician who found himself at one time led, if only for a few months and if only out of a quite personal curiosity, to research the early history of mathematical logic, and thereby to discover just what Peirce's contribution to and stature in nineteenth-century logic was.

I shall not concern myself with the actual details of Peirce's system, although there are matters there that are of interest to students of Peirce's philosophy. (For example, Hans Herzberger has verified a claim that Peirce often makes, that in the Peircian "logic of relatives" all four- and higher-term relations are reducible to triadic relations, but that it is not possible in general to reduce a higher-degree relation to dyadic relations. This claim has metaphysical significance within Peirce's system because of its connection with "thirdness.")[1] Nor shall I concern myself with what is or has become esoteric in Peirce's logical work, as the method of existential graphs has become. Rather, my aim is to show that much that is quite familiar in modern logic actually became known to the logical world through the efforts of Peirce and his students.

My "Boolean" Motivation

What triggered my investigations was a certain admiration I have for George Boole, and a certain piece of disrespect to Boole and his followers on the part of W. V. Quine. I would not have fully appreciated Boole's mathematical mind if it had not been for a couple of accidents. In my twenties I knew, of course, that Boole was the inventor of "Boolean algebra" (which I knew from contemporary texts, not from nineteenth-century ones). I had learned that he had taken holy orders, and not knowing then what I know now about early nineteenth-century England, I pictured Boole much more as a clergyman than as a mathematician. I supposed that he might have been an amateur whose discovery of mathematical logic was rather the product of one good idea and some modest mathematical ingenuity than of real power.

Just as I turned thirty, however, I was working on Hilbert's 10th Problem with Martin Davis. In the course of a summer's research he and I (with some crucial help from Julia Robinson) succeeded in showing the unsolvability of the decision problem for exponential Diophantine equations (a result which Matyasevich improved a few years later to complete the "negative solution" of Hilbert's 10th Problem—that is, the proof that the decision problem for ordinary Diophantine equations is unsolvable). The first proof of our result that Davis and I found used a bit of complicated mathematical analysis, but this was later eliminated when Robinson simplified the entire proof drastically and eliminated one unproved number-theoretic hypothesis that Davis and I had had to use. We had to use, in fact, the theory of the gamma function, which we learned from Whittaker and Watson and an old mathematics text—Boole's *Calculus of Finite Differences*,[2] a theory of the evaluation of indefinite sums and products that Boole developed on the basis of an ingenious generalization of the ideas of the differential and integral calculus. At this point I became aware that Boole was not a clerical amateur but a very high-powered mathematician.

During the summer Davis taught me something about modern "operator methods" in differential equations. These methods, which are based on the idea of a "ring of operators," go back directly to another idea of Boole's[3]—the idea of treating the symbol for differentiation as if it were the name of a strange kind of number. Indeed, Boole solved differential equations by exactly the method that was just then (in the late 1950s) beginning to work its way down into the more sophisticated introductory texts.

This made me interested in Boole in earnest, and a little reading soon convinced me that Boole had a remarkable mathematical program (which he shared with a certain school of British analysts) and that his discovery of mathematical logic was the direct result of that program. The program—that of the "Symbolic School" of British analysts—is today out of date, but in a certain sense it was the bridge between traditional analysis (real and complex analysis) and modern abstract algebra. In effect, Boole and his co-workers were struggling for the notion of an abstract ring, in the modern mathematical sense, that is, a structure with an addition and a multiplication. They could not quite come up with this idea, but they did see that they wanted to free the methods of algebra from an exclusive concern with their traditional content, the real and complex numbers. So they started to use algebraic methods beyond their ability to give those methods an interpretation. I do not mean to use these terms confusedly or vaguely, but rather formalistically: in fact, Boole was quite conscious of the idea of *disinterpretation,* of the idea of using a mathematical system as an algorithm, transforming the signs purely mechanically without any reliance on meanings. In connection with logic, this very important idea appears on the opening pages of Boole's *Laws of Thought.*[4]

Boole's work, then, was an extension of algebra beyond its previous bounds; the algebra of classes, the calculus of finite differences, and the contributions to the theory of differential equations were simply three parts of what Boole (and the Symbolic School generally) saw as a unified enterprise. Modern mathematical logic is something whose early history cannot be separated from the development of modern mathematics in the direction of abstractness.

Even before I came to appreciate Boole's power as a mathematician, I had known that, prior to Boole, logic had been in a straitjacket of sorts because of the fossilization of Aristotelian logic during the late Middle Ages. Almost all logic texts prior to Boole (and many after him) taught nothing but syllogistic logic, or syllogistic logic with insignificant extensions and improvements. All premises, in the inferences discussed, had exactly two "terms," or class names, in them: this was because only premises in the old "categorical forms" (*A,* or "All *S* are *P*," *I,* or "Some *S* are *P*," *E,* or "no *S* are *P*," and *O,* or "Some *S* are not *P*") were considered. After Boole introduced mathematical notation (as Leibniz had done earlier, but without issue), inferences could be studied which contained any number of terms and the premises and conclusions of which contained as many "ors," "ands," and "nots" (or class unions, class intersections, and complementations—Boole gave both interpretations) as you please.

It is true that the system was still very weak compared to modern quantification theory. Dyadic and higher-degree relations could not be symbolized, and there were no quantifiers. But the search for an improvement in the first respect, a logic or "algebra" of relations, began at once, and the quantifiers were invented thirty-two years after the appearance of Boole's *Mathematical Analysis of Logic*[5] (by

Frege;[6] also by Peirce's student O. H. Mitchell).[7] I assumed that everyone realized that with the appearance of a complete "algebra of classes" the dam was broken, and (given the mathematical sophistication
of the age) the subsequent development was inevitable. It seemed
inconceivable to me that anyone could date the continuous effective
development of modern mathematical logic from any point other
than the appearance of Boole's two major logical works, the *Mathematical Analysis* and the *Laws of Thought*.

Yet, in a widely used text by a philosopher I admire enormously, I
read that "logic is an old subject and since 1879 it has been a great
one."[8] In short, logic only broke out of its long stagnation with Frege.
In one pen stroke Quine dismisses the entire Boolean school—of
which Peirce was, in a sense, the last and greatest figure. In van Heijenoort's *Source Book*[9] I detect a similar bias (though not as extremely
stated): the Booleans are mentioned only for the purpose of unflat-
tering comparison with Frege and later authors. It is this biased
account, the "logic was invented by Frege" account, that I want to
rebut here. In the process, I can do honor to Peirce as well as to
Boole—and honoring one's intellectual heroes is one of the purest and
most self-sufficient of life's pleasures.

The Birth of the Quantifier

I do not know exactly what Quine meant by his remark; I suspect it
was meant simply as an appreciation of the great richness and power
of the two systems constructed by Frege (*Begriffsschrift* was very similar—except for the unattractive notation Frege used—to today's standard systems of second-order logic; the *Grundgesetze* system, which
Russell proved inconsistent, sketched the whole program of developing modern mathematics within higher predicate calculus, the program Russell repaired by inventing the theory of types). But to many
readers of Quine's *Methods of Logic* it has come to mean something
quite different. The impression which has unfortunately become
widespread is that Frege discovered the quantifier not only in the
sense of discovering it four years earlier than O. H. Mitchell (Peirce's
student and co-worker), but in the sense that it was Frege who, so to
speak, launched the whole mighty ship by himself. Reading the Heijenoort *Source Book* does little to dispel this impression. Certainly I
must have believed something like this; otherwise I would not have
been so surprised to discover the facts that follow.

When I started to trace the later development of logic, the first thing I did was to look at Schröder's *Vorlesungen über die Algebra der Logik.*[10] This book, which appeared in three volumes, has a third volume on the logic of relations (*Algebra und Logik der Relative,* 1895). The three volumes were the best-known logic text in the world among advanced students, and they can safely be taken to represent what any mathematician interested in the study of logic would have had to know, or at least become acquainted with, in the 1890s.

As the title suggests, the approach was algebraic (Boole's logic, as we saw, grew out of abstract algebra), and the great problem was to develop a logic of *Relative* (that is, relations). (The influence of the German word *Relativ* is, perhaps, the reason Peirce always wrote "relatives" and not "relations.") Peirce, although himself a member of the algebraic school (he criticized himself for this in his correspondence), had reservations about Schröder's close assimilation of logical problems to algebraic ones. "While I am not at all disposed to deny that the so called 'solution problems', consisting in the ascertainment of the general forms of relatives which satisfy given conditions, are often of considerable importance, I cannot admit that the interest of logical study centers in them," Peirce wrote.[11] And "Since Professor Schröder carries his algebraicity so very far, and talks of 'roots', 'values', 'solutions', etc., when, even in my opinion, with my bias towards algebra, such phrases are out of place . . ." But my purpose in consulting this reference work was narrower; I simply wished to see how Schröder presented the quantifier.

Well, Schröder does *mention* Frege's discovery, though just barely; but he does not *explain* Frege's notation at all. The notation he both explains and adopts (with credit to Peirce and his students, O. H. Mitchell and Christine Ladd-Franklin) is Peirce's. And this is no accident: Frege's notation (like one of Peirce's schemes, the system of existential graphs) repelled everyone (although Whitehead and Russell were to study it with consequential results). Peirce's notation, in contrast, was a typographical variant of the notation we use today. Like modern notation, it lends itself to writing formulas on a line (Frege's notation is two-dimensional) and to a simple analysis of normal-form formulas into a prefix (which Peirce calls the Quantifier) and a matrix (which Peirce calls the "Boolean part" of the formula).

Moreover, as Warren Goldfarb has emphasized in a fine paper on the history of the quantifier,[12] the Boolean school, including Peirce, was willing to apply logical formulas to different "universes of discourse," and Peirce was willing (unlike Frege) to treat first-order logic by itself, and not just as part of an ideal language (with a fixed universe of discourse, namely, "all objects," for Frege). In fact—and this may be surprising to others as it was to me—the term "first-order logic" is due to Peirce! (It has nothing to do with either Russell's theory of types or Russell's theory of *orders,* although the way Peirce distinguished between first-order and second-order formulas—by whether the "relative" is quantified over or not—obviously has something to do with logical type.) In summary, Frege tried to "sell" a grand logical-metaphysical scheme with a dubious ontology, while Peirce (and, following him, Schröder) was busy "selling" a modest, flexible, and extremely useful notation.

The success they experienced was impressive. While, to my knowledge, no one except Frege ever published a single paper in Frege's notation, many famous logicians adopted Peirce-Schröder notation, and famous results and systems were published in it. Löwenheim stated and proved the Löwenheim theorem (later reproved and strengthened by Skolem, whose name became attached to it together with Löwenheim's) in Peircian notation. In fact, there is no reference in Löwenheim's paper to any logic other than Peirce's. To cite another example, Zermelo presented his axioms for set theory in Peirce-Schröder notation, and not, as one might have expected, in Russell-Whitehead notation.

One can sum up these simple facts (which anyone can quickly verify) as follows: Frege certainly discovered the quantifier *first* (four years before O. H. Mitchell, going by publication dates, which are all we have as far as I know). But Leif Erikson probably discovered America "first" (forgive me for not counting the native Americans, who of course *really* discovered it "first"). If the effective discoverer, from a European point of view, is Christopher Columbus, that is because he discovered it so that it *stayed* discovered (by Europeans, that is), so that the discovery became *known* (by Europeans). Frege did "discover" the quantifier in the sense of having the rightful claim to priority; but Peirce and his students discovered it in the effective sense. The fact is that until Russell appreciated what he had done, Frege was relatively obscure, and it was Peirce who seems to have been known to the entire world logical community. How many of the people who think that "Frege invented logic" are aware of these facts?

The example of Löwenheim shows something else: *metamathematical* work (of a certain kind) did not have to wait for Russell and Whitehead to make Frege's work known (and to extend it and repair it). First-order logic (and its metamathematical study) would have existed without Frege. (Zermelo even denied that his *set-theoretic* work depended on Whitehead and Russell; he claimed to have been aware of the "Russell paradox" on his own.)[13]

The Peircian Influence on Whitehead and Russell

Still, I thought, Russell and Whitehead themselves certainly learned *their* logic from Frege. To check this I turned to Russell's autobiographical writings. The result was frustrating. In *My Philosophical Development*[14] Russell describes the impact that meeting Peano had upon his logical development. Strangely enough, he does not mention the quantifier, which seems so very central from our present point of view, at all. Peano taught Russell what was a commonplace in the Peirce-Schröder logical community, the difference in logical form between *all men are mortal* and *Socrates is a man*. And it is clear that one of the notations used in *Principia* for a universally quantified *conditional*—writing the variable of quantification *under* the sign of the conditional—came from Peano. But the quantifier as such is not something that Russell singled out for discussion (unless there is something in the unpublished *Nachlass* in the Russell Archives in Ontario). Even when Russell discusses his debt to Frege (in a peculiar way: Russell is unstinting in his praise of Frege's genius, but claims to have thought of the definition of number quite independently), he does not mention the quantifier. *Principia* is no more help on this score, although there is an indication in it that most of the specific notations were invented by Whitehead rather than Russell.*

Since I have mentioned Peano, I should remark that he was not only well acquainted with Peirce-Schröder logic, but he had actually corresponded with Peirce.

In desperation, I looked at Whitehead's *Universal Algebra*. This is a work squarely in the tradition to which Boole, Schröder, and Peirce belonged, the tradition that treated general algebra and logic as virtually one subject. And here, *before* Whitehead worked with Russell, there is no mention of Frege, but there *is* a citation of "suggestive papers" by Peirce's students O. H. Mitchell and Christine Ladd-Franklin.[15] The topic, of course, is the quantifier.

In sum, Whitehead certainly came to *his* knowledge of quantifica-

---

*Subsequent to writing this essay I discovered that, in "Whitehead and Principia Mathematica," *Mind* (1948), p. 137, Russell says that Whitehead contributed the notion for the universal quantifier.

tion through "Peirce and his students." On the other hand, the *axioms* in *Principia* are almost certainly derived from Frege's *Begriffsschrift;* Peirce gave no system of axioms for first-order logic, although his "existential graphs" are a complete proof procedure for first-order logic (an early form of natural deduction).

I have, if anything, minimized Frege's contribution and played up the Boolean contribution for reasons which I have explained. But to leave matters here would be as unjust to Frege and to a third tradition, the Hilbert tradition (proof theory), as Quine's unfortunate remark was to the Boolean tradition.

Frege's work is sometimes disparaged today (I mean Frege's logical achievement; Frege's stock as a *philosopher* has never been higher), though not, of course, by Quine. It is conceded that Frege was far more rigorous and, in particular, far more consistently free of use-mention confusions than other logicians; but such domestic virtue is no longer felt to be impressive. The central charge laid against his work (and that of Whitehead and Russell) is that what they called logic is not logic but "set theory," and that reducing arithmetic to set theory is a bad idea.

This raises philosophical issues far too broad for this essay. But let me just make two comments on this: (1) Where to draw the line between logic and set theory (or predicate theory) is not an easy question. The statement that a syllogism is *valid*, for example, is a statement of *second*-order logic. (*Barbara* is valid just in case $(F)\ (G)\ (H) \cdot ((Fx \supset Gx) \cdot (Gx \supset Hx) \supset (Fx \supset Hx))$, for example.) If second-order logic is "set theory," then most of traditional logic thus becomes "set theory." (2) The full intuitive principle of mathematical induction is definitely second-order in anybody's view. Thus there is a higher-order element in arithmetic whether or not one chooses to "identify numbers with sets" (just as Frege realized).

But, philosophical questions aside, Frege certainly undertook one of the most ambitious logical investigations in all history. Its enormous sweep made it (after its repair by Whitehead and Russell, and its translation into a notation resembling Peirce's) a great stimulus to all future work in the field. The Hilbert school certainly put it in the center of their proof theoretic investigations: Gödel's most famous paper, after all, bears the title "On Principia Mathematica and Related Systems, I."[16] That all its achievements could be imitated successfully by the Cantorians (Zermelo and von Neumann) does not take away either its priority or its influence. If Peirce and Schröder were the cutting edge of the logical world prior to Russell and Whitehead's *Principia Mathematica* (or *a* cutting edge—the Hilbert school was already under way), after the appearance of *Principia* their work lost its importance—or lost it except for one important thing: its influence on Hilbert, who followed Peirce in separating off first-order logic from the higher system for metamathematical study.

Principia in turn was to lose *its* cutting-edge position when interest shifted from the construction of systems (and the derivation of mathematics within them) to the metamathematical study of properties of systems. Nothing remains forever the cutting edge in a healthy science. But a fair-minded statement of the historical importance of the different schools of work, a statement that does justice to each without slighting the others, should not be impossible. Such a statement was given by Hilbert and Ackermann:

> The first clear idea of a mathematical logic was formulated by Leibniz. The first results were obtained by A. de Morgan (1806–1876) and G. Boole (1815–1864). The entire later development goes back to Boole. Among his successors, W. S. Jevons (1835–1882) and especially C. S. Peirce (1839–1914) enriched the young science. Ernst Schröder systematically organized and supplemented the various results of his predecessors in his *Vorlesungen über die Algebra der Logik* (1890–1895), which represents a certain completion of the series of developments proceeding from Boole.
>
> In part independently of the development of the Boole-Schröder algebra, symbolic logic received a new impetus from the need of mathematics for an exact foundation and strict axiomatic treatment. G. Frege published his *Begriffsschrift* in 1879 and his *Grundgesetze der Arithmetik* in 1893–1903. G. Peano and his co-workers began in 1894 the publication of the *Formulaire des Mathématiques*, in which all the mathematical disciplines were to be presented in terms of the logical calculus. A high point of this development is the appearance of the *Principia Mathematica* (1910–1913) by A. N. Whitehead and B. Russell. Most recently Hilbert, in a series of papers and university lectures, has used the logical calculus to find a new way of building up mathematics which makes it possible to recognize the consistency of the postulates adopted. The first comprehensive account of these researches has appeared in the *Grundlagen der Mathematik* (1934–1939), by D. Hilbert and P. Bernays.[17]

If Quine had produced a statement like this in *his* book, I should not have had a topic for this essay!

19. The Way the World Is

This essay was originally presented as the introductory talk for a symposium entitled "The Way the World Is," held at Harvard University in September 1986. The other two participants were W. V. O. Quine and Nelson Goodman.

Immanuel Kant, writing two hundred years ago, told us that knowledge of the world is possible, but it does not go beyond experience. The words might have pleased Bishop Berkeley, who held that human knowledge does not go beyond *sensation,* but sensations are not what Kant meant by "experience." Kant's purpose, unlike Berkeley's, was not to deny the reality of matter, but rather to deny that things in themselves are possible objects of knowledge. What we can know—and this is the idea that Kant himself regarded as a kind of Copernican Revolution in philosophy—is never the thing in itself, but always the thing as represented. And the representation is never a mere copy; it always is a joint product of our interaction with the external world and the active powers of the mind. The world as we know it bears the stamp of our own conceptual activity.

If this is right, then the question immediately arises: What sense does it make to talk of "things in themselves" at all? A world of unknowable "things in themselves" seems a world well lost. And thus most philosophy that has followed Kant in insisting on our own conceptual contribution to constituting what we call "the world" has refused to follow Kant in postulating a world of Things in Themselves. In what may be called "post-Kantian" as opposed to merely neo-Kantian philosophy, the dichotomy of conceptual scheme and world is attenuated or abandoned.

The influence of this circle of ideas on American philosophy is attested to by the fact that all three of the participants in this symposium have tried to restate these ideas in their own languages.[1] For

W. V. O. Quine, the question is whether we can distinguish sharply between what is pure "fact" and what is our own legislation or "convention." And his famous answer is:

> The lore of our fathers is a fabric of sentences. In our hands it develops and changes, through more or less arbitrary and deliberate revisions and additions of our own, more or less directly occasioned by the stimulation of our sense organs. It is a pale grey lore, black with fact and white with convention. But I have found no substantial reasons for concluding that there are any quite black threads in it, or any white ones.

Nelson Goodman's denial of the conceptual scheme/noumenal world distinction is even more radical, as evinced by the following:

> Yet doesn't a right version differ from a wrong one just in applying to the world, so that rightness itself depends upon and implies a world? We might better say that "the world" depends upon rightness. We cannot test a version by comparing it with a world undescribed, undepicted, unperceived, but only by other means that I shall discuss later. While we may speak of determining what versions are right as "learning about the world," "the world" supposedly being that which all right versions describe, all we learn about the world is contained in right versions of it; and while the underlying world, bereft of these, need not be denied to those who love it, it is perhaps on the whole a world well lost.

And in the preface to one of my books *I* wrote:

> I shall advance a view in which the mind does not simply "copy" a world which admits of description by One True Theory. But my view is not a view in which the mind *makes up* the world, either (or makes it up subject to constraints imposed by "methodological canons" and mind-independent "sense-data"). If one must use metaphorical language, then let the metaphor be this: the mind and the world jointly make up the mind and the world. (Or to make the metaphor even more Hegelian, the Universe makes up the Universe—with minds—collectively—playing a special role in the making up.)

Yet there are differences in our three views. In the paragraph I quoted, Quine emphasizes that revisions of our "lore" are occasioned by "stimulation of our sense organs"—a traditional empiricist theme. And he identifies our versions or "lore" with a "fabric of sentences"—

identifying what we know with what we can express *discursively*. Quine's world-view is one in which knowledge, while not restricted to technical science, *aspires to be* science. If science and common sense are continuous, in Quine's view, still it is science that best represents our cognitive ideals. Ethics, the arts, religion are all for Quine—as they were for Rudolf Carnap and the Vienna Circle—non-cognitive.

Quine is famous for raising a problem that has exercised philosophers all over the world—so-called Continental philosophers as well as so-called analytic ones: the problem of the Indeterminacy of Translation. Imagine that you are trying to learn a "jungle language" (this is a famous thought experiment of Quine's). You have learned the native words for "yes" and "no." You try out a new native word you have picked up, the word *gavagai*. You say *gavagai* whenever you see a rabbit, and your friendly native informant says "yes" in the jungle language. When you point to anything other than a rabbit and say *gavagai* the native says "no" in the jungle language. May you conclude that *gavagai* means "rabbit"?

Not so quickly! As Quine points out (and as anthropologists and linguists like Whorf and Sapir might also have pointed out), the native may "cut up the world" differently from the way we do. Consistent with the native's disposition to say *gavagai* when prompted by the sight of a rabbit and to deny *gavagai* when prompted by the sight of a non-rabbit, *gavagai* might, for example, mean "rabbithood exemplified," or "temporal slice of a rabbit," or "undetached rabbit parts."

Generalizing from this case, and on the basis of arguments too complex to review here, Quine concludes that the meaning of *gavagai* (and, indeed, of our own word *rabbit*) is "indeterminate," fixed only relative to one or another "translation manual." If meaning and reference are indeterminate, does the notion of what the native "really means" by *gavagai* make any sense, then? Quine forthrightly (though in the strange company of such thinkers as Derrida) answers "no." There is, Quine says, no "fact of the matter" as to what a word refers to. (Except, again, relative to the choice of a translation manual. But that choice is merely a pragmatic affair, a means of correlating one's speech dispositions with those of another linguistic community, not a means of discovering what the others "really mean.")

This skepticism about meaning might suggest cultural relativism, and in the hands of anthropologists and fashionable French philosophers it does often lead to extreme relativism, but not in the case of

Quine. Quine avoids the yawning abyss of relativism by pointing out that it is only what he calls the "analytic meaning" of utterances like *gavagai* and *rabbit* that is indeterminate. If we stop trying to analyze these utterances so finely, we will notice that *situationally* "unde-tached rabbit parts," "rabbit," and "temporal slice of a rabbit" come to the same thing. As unanalyzed *wholes* ("taken holophrastically," as Quine says), they come to the same thing. If we do not insist that a situation must have a determinate parsing into objects and relations, we can view them as tokening the same situation. And the proof that they token the same situation is that English speakers would assent to one just in the perceptual situations in which they would assent to the others. Similarly, if we do not inquire into the "ontology" of the Gavagese speakers, but content ourselves with seeing in what percep-tual situations they assent to *gavagai,* we will quickly see that these are just the same situations. "Gavagai," "rabbit," "rabbithood," and so forth do have determinate meaning *holophrastically,* Quine says (this is how he escapes from Derrida's radical linguistic idealism). This determinate holophrastic meaning is a characteristic—indeed the defining characteristic—of what Quine calls "observation sentences." It is the observation sentence that is the foundation of whatever objec-tivity there is.

What about theoretical sentences—say, sentences about neutrinos, or filterable viruses—or sentences too complex to be so invariantly linked to perceptual situations? All sentences, Quine replies, are part of a system whose objective cognitive function is the prediction and control of sense experience. Our lore is "a man-made fabric which impinges on experience only along the edges. Or, to change the fig-ure . . . a field of force whose boundary conditions are experience."[2]

What happens, then, if it turns out that there are "empirically equivalent systems of the world"? That is, two systems of sentences which are mutually incompatible, but which both predict the same observations? Even in the ideal limit, there might be two or more mutually *incompatible* systems which were ideal in the sense of pre-dicting *all* possible observations. Can we say that they would both be right? On the one hand, the fact that they both satisfy the objective constraint Quine recognizes, the constraint of enabling us to predict successfully our sensory inputs, suggests that the answer should be "yes"; on the other hand, Quine the logician is not willing to say of incompatible theories that *both* can be "true."

At any rate, Goodman's answer to the question of whether incompatible versions can both be true (or "right") is a forthright "yes." In a term suggested by Quine, Goodman's attitude is "ecumenical." Here is how Goodman opens his *Ways of Worldmaking*:

> Countless worlds made from nothing by use of symbols—so might a satirist summarize some major themes in the work of Ernst Casirer. These themes—the multiplicity of worlds, the speciousness of "the given," the creative power of the understanding, the variety and formative function of symbols—are also integral to my own thinking. (p. 1)

Three pages later, Goodman hits the pluralistic note again:

> Since the fact that there are many different world-versions is hardly debatable, and the question how many if any worlds-in-themselves there are is virtually empty, in what non-trivial sense are there, as Cassirer and like-minded pluralists insist, many worlds? Just this, I think: that many different world-versions are of independent interest and importance without any requirement or presumption of reducibility to a single base. The pluralist, far from being anti-scientific, accepts the sciences at full value. His typical adversary is the monopolistic materialist or physicalist who maintains that one system, physics, is preeminent and all-inclusive, such that every other version must eventually be reduced to it or rejected as false or meaningless. If all right versions could somehow be reduced to one and only one, that one might with some semblance of plausibility[3] be regarded as the only truth about the only world. But the evidence for such reducibility is negligible, and even the claim is nebulous since physics itself is fragmentary and unstable and the kind and consequence of reduction are vague. (How do you go about reducing Constable's or James Joyce's world-view to physics?) (pp. 4–5)

Here Goodman is anticipating at least three different points, which he goes on to develop at length, both in *Ways of Worldmaking* and in his other books. First, he insists that incompatible versions can both be right (and can even both be "true," in the case of a discursive version). Physicists have been familiar with a number of cases in which the facts admit of what are, at least if taken literally, incompatible descriptions, of which the most famous is the possibility of describing the world either in terms of particles interacting at a distance or in terms of wavelike "fields" interacting with particles. Mathematicians are familiar with the possibility of identifying mathematical objects such as numbers or functions with sets, and of doing this in equally satisfactory but incompatible ways. Two centuries ago, Kant was already aware of the possibility of regarding geometrical points either as individuals (as genuine parts of space) or as "mere limits." We can make different choices (these are the "more or less arbitrary revisions" that Quine spoke of in the first of the quotations I gave), and the results may be equally "true." Or so says Goodman, and I would agree with him on this. Second, as the reference to Joyce indicates, the versions Goodman is speaking of include *artistic* versions of the world. A novel, like Joyce's *Ulysses,* may not be "true" but it may nonetheless, Goodman says, be *right*—may enable us to reorder our experience in ways that are "fitting" and "revelatory." And insofar as it does this, art, according to Goodman, contributes to *understanding,* not just to pleasure. And third, as the reference to Constable indicates, Goodman puts nonverbal versions—paintings, musical compositions, statues, dances, and so on—on a par with verbal versions, as far as contributing to understanding goes. Here is how he ends *Ways of Worldmaking,* in fact:

> Whether a picture is rightly designed or a statement correctly describes is tested by examination and reexamination of the picture or statement and what it refers to in one way or another, by trying its fit in varied applications and with various other patterns and statements. One thinks again of Constable's intriguing remark stressed by Gombrich,[4] that painting is a science of which pictures are the experiments. Agreement on or among initial untested judgements, and their survival upon testing, is rather rare for either designs or statements. Furthermore, rightness of design and truth of a statement are alike relative to system: a design that is wrong in Raphael's world may be right in Seurat's, much as a description of the stewardess's motion that is wrong from the control tower may be right from the passenger's seat; and such relativity should not be mistaken for subjectivity in either case. The vaunted claim of community of opinion among scientists is mocked by fundamental controversy raging in almost every science from psychology to astrophysics. And judgements of the Parthenon and the Book of Kells have hardly been more variable than judgements of the laws of gravitation. I am not claiming that rightness in the arts is less subjective, or even no more subjective, than truth in the sciences, but only suggesting that the line between artistic and scientific judgements does not coincide with the line between objective and subjective, and that any approach to universal accord on anything significant is exceptional. (pp. 139–140)

My own thinking has been deeply influenced by the work of both these two brilliant and creative philosophers. To indicate the direction in which I hope to go, building on insights from both Quine and Goodman, I shall quote from the opening chapter of a recent book of mine:

Many thinkers have argued that the traditional dichotomy between the world "in itself" and the concepts we use to think and talk about it must be given up. To mention only the most recent examples, Davidson has argued that the distinction between "scheme" and "content" cannot be drawn, Goodman has argued that the distinction between "world" and "versions" is untenable, and Quine has defended "ontological relativity." Like the great pragmatists, these thinkers have urged us to reject the spectator point of view in metaphysics and epistemology. Quine has urged us to accept the existence of abstract entities on the ground that these are indispensable in mathematics, and of microparticles and spacetime points on the ground that these are indispensable in physics; and what better justification is there for accepting an ontology than its indispensability in our scientific practice? he asks. Goodman has urged us to take seriously the metaphors that artists use to restructure our worlds, on the ground that these are an indispensable way of understanding our experience. Davidson has rejected the idea that talk of propositional attitudes is "second class," on similar grounds. These thinkers have been somewhat hesitant to forthrightly extend the same approach to our moral images of ourselves and the world. Yet what can giving up the spectator view in philosophy mean if we don't extend the pragmatic approach to the most indispensable "versions" of ourselves and our world that we possess? Like William James (and like my teacher Morton White) I propose to do exactly that.[5]

The fact that my thinking has been greatly influenced by the work of my Harvard colleagues Quine and Goodman will, at this point, probably not come as news to very many readers. What, however, may still come as news to a surprising number of analytic philosophers is the extent to which the views of all three of us have been shaped by a continuous tradition of American thought—one that can be traced from its beginnings in the debates at Harvard between Royce and James, as well as in the work of Peirce and Dewey, through the writings of our teacher C. I. Lewis, up to and including some of the most recent developments in American professional philosophy.[6]

20. The Greatest Logical Positivist

In his book *Quiddities,* W. V. O. Quine, "the most distinguished and influential of living philosophers" (P. F. Strawson's description of Quine, on the dust jacket) presents a collection of loosely connected essays in a format inspired by Voltaire's *Philosophical Dictionary*— and the result is a remarkable addition to English literature.[1] Quine is not only a great philosopher but also a master of the English language and a genuine polymath, and the "dictionary" format—more than eighty articles ranging from A (Alphabet) to Z (Zero), and including entries on Belief, Communication, Free Will, Idiotisms, Latin Pronunciation, Longitude and Latitude, Marks, Prizes, Tolerance, and Trinity—affords Quine ample opportunity to write (and, he tells us in the Preface, to have "more than half the fun") about "lowlier themes" than philosophy (which occupies less than half the book). Apart from philosophy, the subjects most fully represented in the book are mathematics, logic, and language (including English etymologies, stylistics, and the philology of the Romance languages), but there are also many short essays in which Quine pokes fun or grumbles good-naturedly at various pet peeves. (The essays on Artificial Languages, Extravagance, Mathematosis, Usage and Abusage are wonderful examples.)

Perhaps the most charmingly lighthearted essay in the book is the one titled "Misling." Many people have been misled to pronounce *misled* as "mizzled." "But the verb *misle* that is born of that misconception is too pat to pass up, descriptive as it is of the very circumstance that engendered it," Quine tells us. "Perhaps we can press it into service as a mild word for the restrained sort of deception, not quite actionable as fraud even in Ralph Nader's day, that has a respected place in enlightened modern merchandising." (The discussion of examples of misling that follows must delight anyone who is not suffering from terminal melancholia.) Although Quine steers clear of political themes for the most part, there is even one beautifully formulated statement of his own conservative creed—the essay on Freedom. An added charm is the not quite self-deprecating humor exhibited by some of the best remarks in the book, as when Quine writes (in the essay on Communication): "Examples taper off to where communication is less firmly assured, as when Hegel writes 'Truth is in league with reality against consciousness,' or I write, 'Logic chases truth up the tree of grammar.' I am confident that I grasp and appreciate this message of Hegel's, and that there are philosophers of logic who grasp mine. But mere acknowledgment, however sincere—'I dig you,' or 'I read you. Roger and over'—is not conclusive evidence of successful communication. The Latin pupil gets low marks who says 'Oh, I know what it means but I can't quite put it into words.'"

In spite of the immense range of learning Quine displays, there are very few errors that I could detect. The most surprising is the totally wrong statement about quantum physics which constitutes the last paragraph of the essay on Discreteness. Time in quantum mechanics is not discrete, and Planck's constant, in any case, is not in units of time. Less surprising, but still erroneous, is the listing of Erret Bishop as someone who "worked at it [constructive mathematics] with standard logic" (p. 36). Not only is there very little error in this book, but there is much that was discovered by Quine himself (although Quine modestly refrains from saying so), including the beautiful combinatorial equivalent to Fermat's Last Theorem on p. 62.

If Quine had "more than half the fun" writing the nonphilosophical essays in this Dictionary, still the philosophical essays—perhaps because of their very informality—give a remarkably good picture of how Quine pictures the universe, and I must devote much more than half of this review to them. Quine is often thought to have destroyed logical positivism, with his rejection of the analytic-synthetic distinction and his likening of philosophy to natural science rather than to pure logic, and indeed, a generation of young "scientific realist" philosophers has been inspired by him to denounce logical positivism root and branch. But reading these essays, I must say that I am inclined to class Quine as the last and greatest of the logical positivists, in spite of his criticisms of the movement. Not only is the reverential appraisal of the philosophical achievements of modern logic still there—"Gottlob Frege, however, seems to have been the first to offer a coherent account of what [the numbers] are," Quine writes in

the essay on Natural Numbers—but so, I seem to detect, is something
of the positivist picture of the world as a system of "posits."

The External World as a Construction

The greatest work produced during the existence of the Vienna Circle
was Carnap's *The Logical Construction of the World*, and Quine
describes Carnap's views very sympathetically. Carnap, Quine tells us
in the essay on Things, "gave us a masterful scheme or caricature . . .
of how this law or maxim ["posit the simplest and laziest of all worlds
compatible with our observations"] governs *our conceptual construction of the world*" (emphasis added). Physical objects are, fundamentally, *constructions*. Our purpose in introducing them is to store up
"observation categoricals" in a logically compact form; "observation
categorical" is Quine's technical term for a general if-then assertion
whose antecedent and consequent describe observable situations, for
example, "Whenever there is a fire at a place and one's wristwatch
shows ten o'clock, then there is smoke at that place when one's wristwatch shows ten minutes after ten."

Quine is not saying that our sole aim is to make predictions. We
want and need correct observation categoricals, of course. But we
also want and need a tidy system. What we want is a system of generalizations from which as many correct observation categoricals
(and as few incorrect ones) as possible can be derived. In short, we
also want both simplicity and generality.

This desire is, I think, what Quine means when he says that we
want not just successful prediction but *satisfaction of pure intellectual
curiosity*. ("This is not to say that prediction is the *purpose* of science . . . an overwhelming [purpose] is satisfaction of pure intellectual
curiosity," p. 162.) This quotation from the essay on Prediction might
seem to say that we want to make true statements about the way the
world really is; but a look at some of the other articles (Reification,
Truth, Reference) quickly dispels the illusion that Quine possesses any
notion at all of "how the world really is" that transcends the (traditional positivist) idea of a simple system of general laws that leads to
successful prediction. There is, to be sure, one other desideratum
besides generality, simplicity, and predictive power: we inherit a body
of past doctrine, and, like William James, Quine attaches value to
"minimum mutilation" of this past doctrine; but this is an *internal*
constraint on the acceptability of a construction of the world. The
world, as Quine views it, seems to be a human construction.

Truth

Quine's view of truth is (fundamentally) Alfred Tarski's (as well as Carnap's). There is no general philosophical problem about truth, according to these thinkers. If we list all the sentences of the form *"S" is true if and only if S,* for example, *"Snow is white" is true if and only if snow is white, "There are infinitely many prime numbers" is true if and only if there are infinitely many prime numbers, "Australia is a continent" is true if and only if Australia is a continent,* we will have succeeded in stating for *each* sentence of the English language a condition for its membership in the set of true sentences which we understand as well as we understand the sentence itself. Moreover—this is the technical part of Tarski's theory—Tarski's work shows how, after we have formalized English, this infinite set of, so to speak, axioms for the property of truth in English can be captured by a finite definition in an appropriate "metalanguage."

To this there is an objection—or at least a question—which I would put thus: when you say that I understand " 'Snow is white' is true" just as well as I understand "Snow is white," what do you mean by *understand?* If Quine were to answer, "To understand a sentence is to know the conditions under which it is *true,*" obviously no progress would have been made. But Quine's account of understanding does not use the notion of truth (which is how circularity is avoided). To understand an observation sentence is to be conditioned in such a way that appropriate sensory stimulations will prompt one's assent to the sentence. And to understand a non-observation sentence is to master its role in the system. On this picture, cognitively meaningful speaking or thinking is simply an attempt to get someone—myself or someone else—to change his dispositions-to-predict. Calling a sentence that someone (myself or someone else) utters (or thinks) "true" is just an indication that I would currently include that sentence in the system I use to predict.

Indeterminacy of Translation

Quine's most famous doctrine is, of course, that of the indeterminacy of translation, a doctrine that is widely misunderstood. The articles in this "dictionary" hint at the doctrine, but they do not explicitly state or defend it. In *Word and Object* Quine explained the doctrine with the aid of a thought experiment which has been endlessly quoted and discussed. Imagining a "jungle language" in which the natives say (or at least "assent to") *gavagai* whenever they see a rabbit, Quine argued that one could translate the native utterance either as "Rabbit!" or as "Rabbithood!"

A point which many critics missed is that Quine was arguing at least as much for the determinacy of translation in the case of observation sentences as for indeterminacy. True, Quine wants us to see that the use of a sentence need not fix its *exact* translation into another language, or even determine what objects the sentence is about. But he also wants us to see that there is an important sense in which (considered *just* as observation sentences, apart from their contribution to inferences) the *English* sentences "That is a rabbit" and "That is rabbithood exemplifying itself" have the *same* meaning; they correspond to exactly the same perceptual stimuli. "Taken holophrastically" (that is, as unanalyzed wholes), why should we regard "That is a rabbit" and "That is rabbithood exemplifying itself" as differing in meaning at all? We *do* know what *gavagai* means, according to Quine: it means "Rabbit!" *and* it means "Rabbithood!" Quine does not discuss these technical issues in *Quiddities,* but such a belief in the determinacy of meaning of the observation sentence is what is behind his insistence (in the essay on Communication) that statements about "tangible, visible, and audible reality" are "unfailing vehicles of communication."

When it comes to exact word-for-word translation—the sort of translation we need to determine whether a sentence commits the speaker to belief in the existence of universals ("rabbithood") or not—and when it comes to non-observation sentences, things do become much more indeterminate on Quine's view, though still not completely so. Here Quine is drawing a conclusion deeply disturbing to positivists from positivist premises. If we construct the world by making up a system of posits that helps us to predict our sensations, then why should we suppose that the sentences which comprise that system of posits are associated with such suspiciously nonempirical entities as "meanings" or "ideas"? (Quine ends the essay on Ideas by writing, "The idea idiom is an entrenched and consequently useful element of our vernacular. In daily discourse we cannot easily do without it, nor need we try. But it is a snare to the philosopher or scientist who admits it to his theory . . . There is no place in science for ideas.") To say that a sentence in one language has the same "meaning" as a sentence in another is to say that their roles are similar; but we should not expect similarity of role to be a precise or well-defined notion. Sameness of meaning is a useful notion in everyday life, but it has no role to play in our "first class" scientific theory of the world. Or as Quine writes, ending his essay on Communication, "We get an exaggerated idea of how well we have been understood, simply for want of checkpoints to the contrary. The miracle of communication, in its outer reaches, is a little like the miracle of transubstantiation: what transubstantiation?" (p. 29).

Here is a little bit of evidence in support of Quine's claim. When I visited China in 1984 I lectured on Quine's views at Fudan University in Shanghai, and sophisticated Chinese told me that they did not think the Chinese word *mo* (cat) could be determinately translated into English as "cat/cathood." What they claimed was that "Are you saying that there is a cat or that there is cathood exemplifying itself?" is the wrong question to put to a Chinese speaker. There is no special suffix in Chinese to distinguish "mo" from "mohood" (*mo* is used both in contexts in which we would translate it as "cat" and in contexts in which we would translate it as "cathood"), nor are there articles in Chinese. "Cat there" and "Cathood there" would go into the same sentence in Chinese.

Of course, one could say that the Chinese word *mo* is ambiguous. But is the fact that one language has two words where another language has one *really* a proof of the existence of an ambiguity in the one word? Quine is arguing that such questions are bad questions. The Chinese conceptual scheme works as well as ours at producing those "observation categoricals," but the sentences are not exactly isomorphic to our sentences; the consequence of the failure of isomorphism is that our "parochial" ontology of particulars and universals can be projected onto the Chinese utterances in more than one way. There is no "fact of the matter" as to whether the Chinese speaker is really talking about the cats or the cathood.

This conclusion was unwelcome to Quine's fellow positivists (and to analytic philosophers generally) because analytic philosophy was conceived of as "analysis of meaning," and Quine is telling us that the notions of "meaning" and "analysis of meaning" are hopelessly vague. If analytic philosophy has become more of a style than a school since Quine published *Word and Object,* that is in large part the consequence of the corrosive effect of his views on the whole notion of "analysis."

The role of the positivist premises in Quine's argument is most easily seen by contrasting his view with a more standard "realist" view of language. A realist who sees objects as just "there" independent of language naturally expects that different languages will have "names" for at least the more salient features of the external world, and expects there to be a fact of the matter as to which words in a language "correspond" to which mind-independent objects. Someone like Quine, who sees objects as constructions within language, does not expect the ontologies of different languages to line up exactly. A philosopher of this second kind—call him a "linguistic idealist"—may either regard the ontologies of different discourses as incommensurable (the line of thinking of a Kuhn or a Saussure or a Derrida) or, like Quine, regard the attribution of an ontology to a discourse as a useful but sloppy bit of projection.

Quine and Realism

That Quine's perspectivalism about meaning flows from his positivist picture of knowledge and language does not mean that his arguments can safely be ignored by philosophers of a more realist persuasion. Quine's writing has sensitized philosophers to problems which had been long ignored, and lost innocence is impossible to recapture. Realists tend to assume that it is possible to draw a sharp line between "the facts" and "what we project onto the facts" (or between "the facts" and "our conventions"). What Quine's work suggests is that no such line can be drawn. We cannot translate the Chinese word *mo* just any which way. (To translate *mo* as "rabbit" would be simply wrong.) But it does not follow that there is a fact of the matter as to whether *mo* "corresponds" to rabbits or to rabbithood. (From within Chinese it is easy to say what *mo* corresponds to, of course: "mo" corresponds to mo.) The notion of "correspondence" on which traditional realism leans has proved to be a weak reed.

   Some facts are, if not totally independent of mind and language, at least independent of any particular conceptual scheme on Quine's view. These are the facts expressed by observation sentences (taken holophrastically). These are not so much "preanalytic" facts as "disanalyzed" facts; when we take an observation sentence holophrastically what we are doing is subtracting whatever in it is peculiar to the particular language in which it is expressed, to arrive at a fact which is to the maximum degree independent of conceptual scheme. That criterion of what is "absolute"—namely, what is to the maximum degree independent of conceptual scheme—has been thought by Bernard Williams (in his recent *Ethics and the Limits of Philosophy*) to delimit science, and to distinguish science from ethics. In Quine's view, Williams is wrong. It is not total science that is "to the maximum degree independent of conceptual scheme," but only the observation sentences and observation categoricals.

Criticisms

Quine's views have provoked an enormous variety of responses. My own work has been deeply influenced by Quine's rejection of a sharp convention/fact distinction and by his insistence that the notion of "sameness of meaning" that we actually possess is constituted by our actual practice of translation and interpretation; meanings are not to be seen as Platonic objects which somehow *explain* translation and interpretation. But that does not mean that I can accept the whole of Quine's view, although I enormously admire his willingness to push his view to the limits, and to bring out and emphasize controversial or paradoxical consequences of his view rather than try to sweep them under the rug.

Here I should like to mention three points on which I disagree with Quine.

(1) *The privileged status of observation sentences.* It seems to me that Quine's increasing insistence on the determinacy of the meaning of observation sentences (taken holophrastically) represents a backing away from his own insight that it is impossible to draw a sharp fact/convention distinction. Quine put this insight very beautifully some years ago when he wrote that the lore of our fathers is a pale grey lore, "black with fact and white with convention," and went on to add that he found "no substantial reasons for concluding that there are any quite black threads in it, or any white ones."[2] Although Quine would not agree that this is what he is doing, it is as if he were now *telling* us what the real facts are (telling us that they are expressed by the true observation sentences, taken holophrastically, and that everything else is the product of convention).

In fact, Quine's claim that observation sentences are "unfailing vehicles of communication" is not right. Thus, imagine that we come across a jungle language (call it Natool) and succeed in working out a successful translation scheme. Suppose the sentence *Hu bosarka* turns out to have the translation "She is a witch." Suppose further that only women with moles on their noses are called witches. Then

Hu bosarka might well turn out to be conditioned to the same stimuli as our English sentence "She has a wart on her nose"; but it would not have the same meaning, not even "taken holophrastically." The Natool speaker who says of a woman *Hu bosarka* is not making the same claim in any sense as the claim an English speaker makes when he says of the same woman "She has a wart." In fact, what the Natool speaker is claiming is *false* while what the English speaker is claiming is *true*. Quine is right to suppose that sometimes two sentences which consist of totally nonequivalent parts can make the same claim taken as wholes, but wrong to suppose that whenever two sentences are conditioned to the same stimuli they can be regarded as in some ("holophrastic") sense equivalent in meaning. Quine's retrograde motion here testifies to the enormous strength of the urge to find some level of foundational "facts."

(2) *Quine's view of truth and understanding.* The combination of a Tarskian theory of truth and a positivist theory of understanding leads, as I said, to the picture of cognitively meaningful speaking and thinking as an attempt to get someone—myself or someone else—to change his dispositions to predict, or better, to change the complex system which he employs to generate those dispositions to predict (or their linguistic counterparts, the "observation categoricals"). The distance of such a view from our commonsense picture is enormous. Consider a sentence about the past: on the commonsense view, when I say "Caesar crossed the Rubicon" I am making a true assertion, and calling the sentence true is ascribing a genuine property to the sentence, not merely making a noise which is equivalent to the original noise according to the rules of some system. On Quine's view, I get the feeling, uttering a sentence about the past is making a move in a game whose real point is to predict the *future*. I share Quine's dissatisfaction with traditional "realist" philosophy; but the right alternative cannot be such a radical positivism as this.

(3) *Quine's emphasis on prediction.* Quine's devotion to empiricism comes out most strongly in his emphasis on successful prediction as the sole ultimate "evidence" for anything. Mathematical statements, for example, are only justified insofar as they help to make successful predictions in physics, engineering, and so forth, on Quine's view. I find this claim almost totally unsupported by actual mathematical practice. As I have argued elsewhere, we have many more cognitive interests than prediction, and, correspondingly, many more kinds of justification than are included in this narrow notion of "evidence."

Discussion of these issues will certainly continue; in the meantime, anyone who wants to encounter a great philosophical mind in a less technical mood, and to get some feeling for Quine as the peerless companion, raconteur, and amused commentator on the passing show that his friends know him to be, cannot do better than read this book. I began by quoting what Strawson says about the author on the jacket of *Quiddities;* I cannot end with a more fitting tribute than the one Colin McGinn paid to Quine in the *Journal of Philosophy:* "Quine pursues philosophical vision with an uncompromising consistency of purpose that makes his doctrines impossible to ignore. You either go with him or define your position in reaction to his. And this is one mark of a great philosopher."

21. Meaning Holism

W. V. O. Quine's argument for meaning holism in "Two Dogmas of Empiricism" is set out against the meaning theories of the positivists. Sentences, he insists, do not have their own "range of confirming experiences." Assertibility depends upon trade-offs between such desiderata as preserving the observation reports to which we are prompted to assent, preserving past doctrine, and securing or preserving simplicity of theory. The idea that the meanings of individual sentences are mental or Platonic entities must be abandoned. Instead, we must recognize that it is a body of sentences, and ultimately our whole system of evolving doctrine, which faces the "tribunal of experience as a corporate body."

A literal-minded philosopher might object that even on Quine's account a sentence *does* have a "range of confirming experiences"; it is confirmed by each experience which confirms at least one total body of theory which contains the sentence. But this reply is pure legalism. It concedes the point that is really at issue: that it is *not by reflecting on some object, say a rule, associated with the individual sentence* that the scientist or the man of common sense is able to determine (in an arbitrary situation) what does and what does not confirm or "infirm" that sentence. Frege taught us that words have meaning only in the sense of making a systematic contribution to the truth-conditions of whole sentences. Quine argues that to the extent that there are "procedures" for deciding what is and what is not assertible, such procedures are associated with the entire language, not with any single sentence. Individual sentences are meaningful in the sense of making a systematic contribution to the functioning of the whole language; they don't have "meanings," in the form of isolable objects, properties, or processes which are associated with them individually and which determine individual assertibility conditions.

This is, perhaps, clear in the case of theoretical sentences. But nonobservation sentences in ordinary language, and even observation sentences, exhibit similar features. For Quine, an observation sentence is not one which is formed from a privileged set of nonlogical names and predicates ("observation terms"), as for Carnap—Quine knows no "observational/theoretical dichotomy" of that sort—but, rather, one which is intersubjectively conditioned to certain "sensory stimulations." These sensory stimulations—the ones that "prompt assent" to the sentence and the ones that prompt dissent from it (or the ordered pair of these two sets)—constitute the "stimulus meaning" of the observation sentence in the relevant community. This— the "stimulus meaning"—*is* something associated with the individual sentence. But it cannot be called the *meaning* of the individual sentence, Quine argues, for at least two reasons. One, the more technical reason, is that even in the case of the simplest sentences ("Lo, a P") the "meaning" of the sentence is supposed to determine the extensions of the predicates out of which the sentence is built, and sentences built out of predicates which are not even coextensive can have the same stimulus meaning ("Lo, a rabbit" and "Lo, an undetached rabbit-part"). The other is that an observation sentence is sometimes assertible when it does not *appear* (to theoretically uncorrected sense experience) to be true. The stimulus meaning determines the *normal* confirmatory situation and the normal disconfirmatory situation; but in abnormal situations the decision to accept or reject the sentence is based on holistic considerations (on care for the value of overall theory). To take stimulus meaning to be meaning *simpliciter* would be to oversimplify our account of the functioning of even the observation sentences.

Meaning and Change of Meaning

I have described Quine's argument in the form which I myself find most convincing. In what follows I shall make use of a distinction Quine did not himself introduce: the distinction between holism with respect to meaning and holism with respect to belief fixation. In this essay, I shall not attempt to say when my arguments reproduce Quine's, when they merely parallel Quine's, and when they are completely my own; one of the things I hope to learn from this exchange is to what extent the considerations that lead *me* to embrace the doctrine of meaning holism are acceptable to Quine.

My intention in describing Quine's arguments in this particular way is to focus on two ways in which philosophers are tempted to counter it. One way is obvious: to deny holism even with respect to belief fixation. The other way is to concede that Quine's holistic account of belief fixation is correct, while maintaining that an ontology of "meanings" is still scientifically or philosophically necessary and useful. In this section I shall consider only the first way; the remainder of the essay will concern the second.

Those philosophers who have taken the first way (for example, Carnap in his debate with Quine on these issues) generally concede that Quine's account, or one like it, is correct in theoretical science. They are thus led to draw a more or less sharp boundary between theoretical science and observational statements (or, in the case of some philosophers, "ordinary language"). Rather than concede that the notion of a "meaning" is not helpful (at least not in the case of theoretical sentences and/or "theoretical terms"), these philosophers typically take the meaning of such sentences and terms to be in one way or another a function of the *theory* in which those sentences and terms occur. (Various devices from set theory, for example the Ramsey sentence and the Hilbert epsilon operator, have been used to formalize this approach.) The theory, for this purpose, is not the mere formal system, but the system *together* with the interpretation of the observation terms and the interpretation of the logical terms. Theories, on this view, are "partially interpreted calculi."[1]

The most serious problem with such a theory of meaning is the number of *meaning changes* it makes it necessary to postulate.[2] Suppose someone asks, "Were electrons flowing through such-and-such a crystal at such-and-such a time?" It may easily happen that, by the time the question is answered, the theory in which the term "electron" occurs has been modified as a result of ordinary inductive and abductive inference. If so, the sentence "Electrons were flowing through the crystal at that time" that the scientist utters today does not have the *meaning* that it had at the time of the original question. Evidently a distinction central to the traditional theory of meaning, the distinction between *discovering the answer to a question* (by employing the appropriate method of belief fixation) and *changing the meaning of the question,* has been abandoned (or altered beyond recognition).

Not only is it the case that this proposal (to take the meaning of the theoretical term or statement to be the theory or a suitable function of the theory) involves an unmotivated departure from our preanalytic use of the notion of *meaning;* it has the effect of robbing that notion of all epistemological interest. If I want to know whether electrons are flowing through a certain crystal, I want the best scientific answer that can be discovered; I do not care whether discovering that answer requires modifying the current theory of electrons. Whether an answer is rationally supportable is epistemologically important; whether it "changes the meaning of the question" is no longer of any epistemological interest, if *any* change in the theory is going to count as a "change in the meaning of the question." If meanings are not invariant under normal processes of belief fixation, then concern with meanings loses its *raison d'être.*

In the case of observation terms, anti-holists have usually taken the meaning to be given by the "ordinary" criteria for the application of the terms. The word "water," for example, would be governed by some such rule as this: *apply "water" to anything which is liquid, colorless, tasteless, odorless, quenches thirst, does not poison the drinker,* and so on. Carnap is not completely consistent here: he speaks of "P-Postulates" (Physical Postulates) such as "Water is H_2O" as (indirectly and incompletely) *fixing the interpretation* of "H_2O," but he could not have been unaware that they *also* have the effect of making the assertibility conditions for "this is water" dependent on physical theory. Be this as it may, he often writes as if they did *not* have this effect: as if the assertibility conditions associated with observation terms were in no way *altered* by the incorporation of those terms into a scientific theory.

Ordinary language philosophers who have taken a similar line (I am thinking of Norman Malcolm, and, with less confidence, Michael Dummett) tend to compartmentalize the language: the presence of water in a physical theory ("Water is H_2O") is held to involve a different use (that is, a different *sense*) from the "ordinary use." (This compartmentalization is often ascribed to Wittgenstein; incorrectly, in my opinion.)

This compartmentalization theory seems to me to be simply wrong. Our language is a cooperative venture; and it would be a foolish layman who would be unwilling *ever* to accept correction from an expert on what was or was not water, or gold, or a mosquito, or whatever. Even if I drink a glass of "water" with no ill effects, I am prepared to learn that it was not really water (as I am prepared to learn that a ring that seems to be gold is really counterfeit); we do not and should not treat scientists' criteria as governing a word which has different application-conditions from the "ordinary" word *water*, in the sense of having *unrelated* (or only weakly related) application-conditions.

There are, to be sure, respects in which the ordinary use of the word "water" differs from the use in, say, physics. In physics "water" means chemically pure water; in ordinary language, things are more complicated. On the one hand, "water," in the ordinary sense, may have impurities; on the other, tea and coffee are *not* "water." What sort of or degree of departure from ideally "pure" taste, color, or odor disqualifies H_2O-cum-impurities from being "water" in an ordinary context is interest-relative and context-sensitive. But this is not to say that "water," in ordinary language, is an *operationally defined* word, pure and simple.

A thought experiment may be of assistance here. Let us suppose there exists a liquid which is colorless, tasteless, odorless, harmless, but does *not* satisfy the need for water. (For all I know, there may actually be such liquids.) Call this liquid "grook." Let us suppose that a mixture of 50 percent grook and 50 percent water will pass all the lay tests for being water, *excluding* "sophisticated" tests (such as distilling the liquid, or measuring its exact boiling point or freezing point with a thermometer). On the theory that "water" means "odorless, transparent, tasteless liquid which quenches thirst and is not harmful to drink," grook plus water just *is* water, "in the ordinary sense." But this is plainly wrong; even a layman, on being told by a scientist that what he is drinking is a mixture of a liquid which is indistinguishable in composition from paradigm examples of "water" and a liquid which does *not* occur as a part of typical water, will say that what he is drinking is *not* water (although it *is* 50 percent water). Ordinary language and scientific language are different but *interdependent*.

Why "Sophisticated Mentalism" Appears to Be an Option

If denying the holistic character of rational belief fixation (or restricting it to "science") is a hopeless move, there is another option available to the philosopher who wishes to defend the psychological reality and philosophical importance of meanings (as independent entities), and that is to challenge the step from that holistic character to what I have called "meaning holism." The general idea which defines this option is easy to describe: *postulate "meanings" as psychological enti-*

ties (*not,* at most times, available to consciousness—this is the difference between contemporary mentalism and the "naive mentalism" of the older empiricists). Let these entities be, in some way, *associated with individual words, morphemes, and sentences* (so that meanings will be *non*-holistic). Account for the holistic character of *belief fixation* by *postulating that the step from the meaning of a sentence to its assertibility conditions involves "top down processing"*—that is, the use of general intelligence and available information.

This option appears to be open simply because the identification of "meanings" with assertibility conditions (or with rules which determine assertibility conditions) is only evident to a philosopher who wishes to retain the verifiability theory of meaning in some form. Quine himself does, and he is willing to pay the price: to the extent that there are processes (he is leery of talk of "rules," "inductive logic," "confirmation theory," or vague notions of "justification," "coherence," and the like) which guide us in deciding when to accept and when to reject sentences, these processes are *associated with the whole language,* in his view, and not associated with individual sentences in a piecemeal fashion. That is why I call him a "meaning holist": because in *his* view the acceptance of his doctrine is just a further step in the direction of seeing the "unit of empirical significance" as something larger than the *word.* Prior to Quine we had already been forced to see the sentence and not the word as the primary unit; since Quine we are (he holds) forced to see the *whole language* as "the unit of empirical significance."

If the verifiability theory is wrong, even in its holistic version (and I myself cannot accept it in *any* version), then there would appear to be a serious gap in Quine's argument. Why should the meaning of a sentence be *directly* tied to its conditions of assertibility, to the experiences which confirm it and the experiences which "infirm" it? Perhaps the holistic character of all "top down" processing infects the step *from* meanings (whatever they are) *to* the knowledge that certain experiences confirm a sentence (in a particular context) and others "infirm" it. Or so one might suppose.

Quine himself dismisses the idea that "meanings" can have explanatory value as out of date and "obscure." But since he wrote "Two Dogmas" and "On What There Is" there has been a New Wave in psychology, a wave of talk about concepts, "contents," and "mental representation." and even if this talk has not resulted in a single *theory* of these entities, it has had the effect of making them no longer seem "obscure." What we countenance in present-day intellectual life is (as perhaps it always was) a matter of what is in vogue and not of what is intelligible. Quine (and Wittgenstein) were hostile to mentalism, it is said, because they knew only the mentalism of the eighteenth-century empiricists (and because they are "behaviorists," it is sometimes said). Even those who do not make the error of reading Quine or Wittgenstein as simple behaviorists often suppose that their arguments have weight only against naive mentalism; *sophisticated* mentalism is thought to be at a higher level in the evolution of thought than the reflections of even the greatest giants of the century's philosophy could reach. If, as I have argued, there *is* a gap in Quine's argument, then there is certainly room for "sophisticated mentalism" as a *program:* our question must be whether there is reason to hold out any hope for the success of such a program.

Three Constraints on Any Theory of "Meanings"

If *all* that was wanted to carry out the "sophisticated mentalist" program were any entities at all which are (1) "psychologically real," (2) associated with individual sentences, and (3) involved in the "processing" of those sentences, then things would be easy. There would be a great many possible choices of entities to play the role of "meanings." For example, *the sentences themselves* have all three properties listed: so one could simply take each sentence as its own "meaning"! But this clearly will not do.

Why it will not do is obvious: it is part of our preanalytic use of the notion of "meaning" that different sentences can have the *same* meaning and that the same sentence can have different meanings. A theory which gave up beliefs about meaning as central as these could not be regarded as having anything to do with our preanalytic notion of "meaning" at all. A proposal which conceded that our preanalytic notion has to be scrapped, and which simply recommitted the *noise* "meaning" to a new use, would, in effect, grant Quine's point.

It is, then, a constraint on any theory of "meanings" that different meanings should, in general, be assigned to sentences which we preanalytically *suppose* to differ in meaning and that the same or closely similar meanings should be assigned to sentences which we preanalytically suppose to be alike in meaning. In short, "meanings," whatever they may be, must have the right powers of *disambiguation*.

This constraint operates in Quine's own argument against a proposal he himself raises only to reject: the proposal to take the *stimulus meaning* to be the *meaning,* in the case of observation sentences. As mentioned in earlier chapters, Quine points out that *gavagai* (a word in a "jungle language") could mean "undetached rabbit part" or could mean "rabbit"—assuming there were a "fact of the matter" as to what *gavagai* means—without altering in stimulus meaning. Indeed, if talk of "undetached rabbit parts" became common in English, then "Lo, an undetached rabbit part" might become an English observation sentence with exactly the same stimulus meaning as "Lo, a rabbit"—but we want a theory of meaning or of meanings to disambiguate these two sentences, if only because we accept "rabbits are not the same things as undetached rabbit parts" as a *true* sentence.

Here is another example to the same effect: as we actually use the word "tiger," it is not *analytic* that tigers have stripes. (Many people incorrectly suppose that albino tigers have no stripes: actually the stripes are still visible, though fainter; but the mistake shows that we understand "tiger" so that a stripeless tiger is not *ruled out.*) Assume that a totally stripeless tiger would, however, cause one to hesitate and ask an expert (if only because the nonexperts couldn't be sure that it wasn't a stripeless *leopard*). Then the stimulus meaning of "Lo, a tiger" could be exactly the same as the stimulus meaning of "Lo, a striped tiger"; but again there is (speaking intuitively) a "difference in meaning." In fact, it is quite easy to see that stimulus meaning is highly insensitive to exactly what we take to be the "meaning" of the terms in an observation sentence, provided only that the various alternative "meanings" that are offered are *known* to pick out the same classes by all the members of the speech-community.

Again, if all the members of the speech-community become adept at recognizing tigers without relying on the presence or absence of *stripes,* then the stimulus meaning of "Lo, a tiger" will change: but this is not what we think of as the word "tiger" *changing its meaning.* What this illustrates is that stimulus meanings *are not invariant under normal processes of belief fixation.* And, as I argued earlier, a notion of "meaning" according to which normal processes of belief fixation (including inductive inference) change the "meanings" of the questions we are trying to answer is not only a poor explication of the preanalytic notion, but one which robs the notion being "explicated" of all epistemological significance.

The constraint just mentioned—*invariance of meanings under normal processes of belief fixation*—rules out another proposal I have occasionally encountered: the proposal to take the meaning of a sentence to be its "canonical" method of verification. In the case of observation sentences this would seem closely related to, if not the same as, the proposal to take the stimulus meaning as the meaning; but let us consider a different kind of sentence, a sentence about the past, say, "A couple with six children lived here two hundred years ago." If this has a "canonical" method of verification today, it involves the consultation of certain kinds of written records. Prior to the invention of writing, one would have had to rely on oral traditions passed down and preserved by the elders of the tribe. So "canonical method of verification" is not even invariant under technological change, let alone the normal process of belief fixation.

The last constraint I shall impose has been implicit rather than explicit in the discussion so far: it is simply that "meanings" should be implicitly known (or "associated" with the relevant words and sentences) by *every* speaker who counts as *fully competent in the use of the language.* This might be called the constraint of *publicity:* it requires that meanings should be public. Alternatively, one might think of this as a constraint of *psychological reality;* a theory in which "meanings" are known only to experts could not be a *mentalistic* theory, since the guiding idea of mentalism is that "meanings" are psychological entities which play an explanatory role in accounting for the competence of the native speaker. If we took the "meaning" of *electron* to be the theory of electromagnetism, for example, then we might be able to account for the competence of experts (ignoring the problem with invariance under belief fixation, which has already been discussed), but we could not account for the competence of the average speaker, since the average speaker does not know this theory. So whatever the meaning of *electron* may be for an average speaker, it cannot be the sophisticated physical theory.

We can now make the question we are investigating more precise: has "sophisticated mentalism," in its various forms, been able to come up with entities which have psychological significance and which could be taken to be "meanings" without violating at least one of the three constraints just listed? The question is not whether we are *allowed to talk* of words and sentences "having meaning" or "not having meaning," "having the same meaning" or "not having the same meaning," and so on, in normal contexts (in which it is clear why the question arises and what one is going to do with the answer); of course we are. The question is whether the idea that meanings are *objects,* isolable events, states, processes, or what have you, with some sort of explanatory role in a theory, has the slightest foundation.

Twin Earth Cases and the Linguistic Division of Labor

Readers familiar with my essay "The Meaning of 'Meaning'"[3] will notice that there is one very famous constraint on the notion of meaning which I have *omitted:* that is the traditional requirement that the "meaning" of a term (its Fregean sense) should fix its extension. In "The Meaning of 'Meaning'" I argued that, in fact, *no* theory can make it the case that "meanings" are "in the head" and simultaneously make it the case that "meanings" determine external-world reference.

To establish this point—the point that although "concepts," as we have thought of them ever since the seventeenth century, are supposed to be "individualistic" entities, entities that one isolated individual (or a brain in a vat) can "have," and simultaneously supposed to fix external-world reference, in fact this is impossible—I employed two different sorts of cases. On the one hand, I described cases in which two groups of speakers are in the same mental states, in all respects one might think relevant to a mentalistic theory of meaning, although the reference of some term changes upon going from one community to the other. For example, imagine that "water" (the liquid so called) is actually a mixture of 50 percent H_2O and 50 percent grook on Twin Earth. Let the year be 1750 on both earth and Twin Earth (so that earth textbooks do not yet contain the statement that "water is H_2O" and Twin Earth textbooks do not yet contain the statement that "water is 50 percent H_2O and 50 percent $C_{22}H_{74}$ . . . [the chemical formula for grook]"). Although there will be differences between earth and Twin Earth "water" (Twin Earth people will need twice as much "water" a day, on the average, as earth people, unless we modify their bodies so that they need less H_2O), we may suppose that these differences are noticed only by a few experts; or let both societies be prescientific village societies. Then the things that Twin Earth speakers will tell you about "water" will be exactly the things that earth speakers will tell you about "water"; what they have noticed about "water" will be just what earth speakers have noticed about water; and so forth. In short, the conceptual content of the word "water," for an average speaker, will be the same on earth and on Twin Earth.

What such "Twin Earth cases" show is that what we intend to refer to when we use such a word as "water" is whatever liquid has the same composition as . . . (here one can substitute almost any of the local paradigms without affecting what we call the "meaning"). In short, the reference is partly fixed by the substance itself (through the use of examples). The word "water" has a different extension on earth and on Twin Earth because the *stuff* is different, not because the brains or minds of Twin Earth speakers are in a different state from the brains or minds of earth English speakers in any psychologically significant respect.

The second kind of case I used is the case of words such as "elm" and "beech." Here the average speaker knows that the species are distinct, but cannot tell you *how.* The conceptual content associated with the words "elm" and "beech" is practically the same; but the extensions are determined by criteria known to experts with whom the average speaker is in a cooperative relation. In short, extensions cannot be determined by (individualistic) "concepts" because extensions depend upon other people. Because of both of these sorts of cases, if we are going to be mentalistic, then we have to omit the traditional requirement that "sense fixes reference." However, this weakens the constraint that "meanings" can do what we preanalytically suppose they can do in the way of disambiguating words and sentences. Jerry Fodor has recently proposed the name "contents" for "meanings" which *are* (according to sophisticated mentalism as practiced at MIT) "in the head." Fodor concedes that "elm" and "beech" have the same "content" (for a speaker like *me,* at any rate), and abandons the traditional idea that the content is what fixes the reference. But notice that it was *also* a traditional idea that "elm" and "beech" differ in *meaning.* Even at this early stage in our discussion, the danger appears on the horizon that we shall find ourselves rescuing the noise "meaning" by merely recommitting it to something there is no good reason to call by that name.

The Analytic and the Synthetic

One philosophically central strand in the complex network of traditional assumptions about meaning is the idea that there are some sentences which are *true* by virtue of what they mean, and *simply* by virtue of what they mean—the analytic sentences. If we are to see why it is impossible to fulfill the desire to have a notion of meaning which obeys our three constraints, it is well to begin by unraveling this strand (as Quine did in "Truth by Convention" and "Two Dogmas of Empiricism").

If S is true simply by virtue of what S means, and meanings are invariant under scientific and commonsensical belief fixation, then the status of S must likewise be so invariant. S must be an *unrevisable* truth (Quine tends to assume the converse—that any unrevisable truth would have to be analytic, but this is a hangover from empiricism).[4] If the technical notion of meaning obeys our first constraint—if the lines it draws correspond, at least in general, to preanalytic uses of the notion of "meaning"—then the analytic sentences must be ones which it is not counterintuitive to classify as such, at least in the majority of cases. In particular, then, such traditional examples as "A bachelor is an unmarried man," "A vixen is a female fox," and (perhaps) "Force is mass times acceleration" must turn out to be analytic, and hence to be unrevisable under normal processes of induction, theory construction, and so on. But these sentences are *not* so invariant.

Consider first "Force is mass times acceleration." Many physicists say this is "true by definition," that is, analytic. But I am sure they would also say "The force on a body is the vector sum of all the individual forces acting on the body" is "true by definition." Together, however, these two "definitions" imply that "The vector sum of the individual forces acting on a body is equal to the acceleration vector of the body multiplied by the mass." This last principle hardly *looks* analytic. Kant might have considered it a "synthetic *a priori* truth"—it justifies the rule that, if the known individual forces are not sufficient to account for a body's state of acceleration, one should always postulate unknown individual forces, and one might regard this as a "regulative principle" in physics—but is there any reason to regard it as correct by virtue of *meaning*? (In fact, it is *given up* in quantum mechanics—the effect on a body of the sum of the individual forces is, in general, *statistical* and not deterministic.)

The argument I have just used against calling either of these "force is . . ." statements analytic resembles an argument Reichenbach used against the Kantian notion of a synthetic *a priori* truth. In *Theory of Relativity and A Priori Knowledge* (1922) Reichenbach listed a number of statements (the general reliability of induction, normal causation, Euclidean geometry, and so on) each of which Kant would have regarded as synthetic *a priori*, and each of which can be held immune from revision (the Duhem thesis!), but which *collectively imply state-*

ments that are empirically testable, and that Kant would, therefore, have had to regard as *a posteriori.* In short, given that it is part of Kant's theory that the *a priori* truths are a *deductively closed class,* Kant's intuitions about what is *"a priori"* are in deep trouble. Similarly, given that the *analytic* truths are supposed to be a deductively closed class, or at least not to imply any *testable* statements (otherwise the conjunction of analytic *truths* could imply something *false*), some physicists' intuitions about what is "true by definition" are incoherent.

In general, if we call *any* truth which contains law-cluster concepts[5]—terms which are implicated in a number of scientific laws—"analytic," we are in trouble. "Momentum is mass times velocity" may have originally entered physics as a "definition" and the law of the conservation of momentum may have originally entered as a "law," but in the actual history of later physics they functioned on a par, and when it was discovered that (in the presence of Special Relativity) one could not have both, it was the former statement that was the one revised and not the latter. The attempt to draw an analytic/synthetic distinction not only does not assist us in understanding belief fixation in the exact sciences; it positively distorts the picture.

What of less scientific examples? As long as being an unmarried (or never-been-married) male adult person is the only known and generally employed criterion for being a bachelor, then the word "bachelor" will continue to function (in purely referential contexts) as virtually an abbreviation of the longer phrase "male adult person who has never been married." And similarly, unless "vixen" becomes an important notion in scientific theory, and various important laws about vixens are discovered, that word will continue to be used virtually as an abbreviation for "female fox." But either or both of these situations may change *as a result of empirical discovery,* with no stipulative redefinition of these words, and no unmotivated linguistic drift, being involved.[6]

In any case, the fact is that very few one-criterion words exist. It is not only such "theoretical" terms as *force* and *momentum* that lack "analytic" definitions; natural kind words such as *tiger* and *leopard* and *water* lack them as well. We are left with no standards, except pragmatic and context-sensitive ones, for deciding which of our beliefs about tigers, or leopards, or water are to count as somehow connected with the "meaning" of these terms. Even the belief that tigers are animals is not immune from revision (they might turn out to be robots remotely controlled from Mars). We can make the decision I once recommended in the case of the one-criterion words,[7] to look for beliefs which are *relatively* central, relatively immune from revision (barring revolutionary discoveries), thereby very much weakening the constraint that meanings should be invariant under belief-fixation (we shall have to in any case); but then the whole problem of what to count as "sameness of meaning" rearises as the problem of what to count as *sufficient similarity* in such central beliefs. The impossibility of a notion of "meaning" which agrees at all with our preanalytic intuitions about sameness and difference of meaning *and* which is invariant under belief-fixation dooms the notion to be exactly what it is: a vague but useful way of speaking when (by intuition and by experience) we correlate words and phrases in different languages and discourses.

A Little Bit of Indeterminacy

Quine is famous for the thesis of the "indeterminacy of translation." This is an immense thesis, connected with views on the rootlessness of reference and the notion of a "fact of the matter." I shall confine myself for the moment to just a little bit of indeterminacy, the little bit that follows more or less directly from the considerations just reviewed. In particular, I will for the most part not consider the indeterminacy of *reference* as opposed to *meaning*.

Let us consider an actual case in which translators disagree. *Eudaemonia* is standardly translated as "happiness." John Cooper, however, proposes that it would be more faithful to the meaning of the word in Aristotle's *oeuvre* to render *eudaemonia* as "human flourishing." What shall we say about this? The difficulty is that there seems nothing to be right or wrong about. One can ask whether Cooper's translation of any reasonably long chunk of Aristotle's text, or even of a key paragraph, "brings out the sense of the whole"; but (assuming that "happiness" and "human flourishing" *are* coextensive in Aristotle's *theory*) a translation might undeniably bring out the sense of the whole *either* by translating *eudaemonia* as "happiness" (with appropriate glosses, footnotes, compensatory adjustments in the translation of other words) *or* by translating *eudaemonia* as "human flourishing."

To see the relevance of my discussion of the analytic/synthetic distinction to this case, observe that the difference between the two translations is that one makes it in effect "analytic" that "*eudaemonia* is happiness" and "synthetic" (perhaps synthetic *a priori*) that "*eudaemonia* is human flourishing," while the second has it the other way around. But *eudaemonia* is not the sort of word that has an analytic definition, least of all in a philosopher's writing.

The case may seem highfalutin, but it does not really differ from the question: is it or is it not *part of the meaning* of "leopard" that leopards are typically spotted? We have an enormous number of "central" beliefs about almost anything; there is no general rule which decides in each case which of these to take as part of the meaning of a word in a given context and which to take as "collateral information" that will, given what speaker and hearer know, surely be conveyed by the use of the word. (Grice's distinction between what a word "literally means" and what is a "conversational implicature" is just what we *can't* draw in any systematic way.)

Let me move to a different example: I imagine (perhaps wrongly, but if so let this be more "science fiction") that all the cats in Thailand (formerly "Siam") are of the breed we call "Siamese." A person growing up in Thailand has a quite different stereotype of a cat from the one we have! In fact, the idea *he* normally associates with the Thai word *meew* (the Thai word that dictionaries translate as "cat") is just the stereotypical idea of a "Siamese cat." If sophisticated adult speakers of Thai *know* that there *are* other breeds of *meew*, then that is, perhaps, a good reason in this case for assigning the set of cats as extension to *meew*; it is certainly sufficient justification for *not* assigning the set of just *Siamese* cats as the extension the word standardly has in the Thai language.

I am myself the son of a translator, and I learned at my father's knee the elementary fact that no translator worth his salt would stick to the "dictionary translation" in all contexts. Undoubtedly, a good translator would sometimes render *meew* as "Siamese cat," sometimes as "cat," sometimes as "puss," sometimes as "tom cat," sometimes as "tabby," and so forth, depending on the situation; and there is no general rule determining when one translation is better and when another is better.

Let us, however, "stipulate" that *meew* has as its extension *the set of all cats* in *all* contexts in which we are interested. It is (we have just stipulated) coextensive with "cat" and not coextensive with "Siamese cat." Even so, does it have the same *meaning* as "cat"? Why or why not?

If such facts as the fact (or putative fact) that "leopards are typically spotted" and "tigers are typically striped" count as part of the *meaning* of the natural kind words "leopard" and "tiger," then the fact that "cats typically look thus and so . . ." must, by parity of reasoning, be counted as part of the meaning of "cat." And if the Siamese stereotype is different from the European stereotype, should that, then, not count as a meaning difference? But things are not so simple. Stereotypes are not just images (or "perceptual prototypes," in psychological jargon) but beliefs stated in words ("aluminum is a metal"). Thus, knowing what someone's stereotype of something is *presupposes* that we understand his language; a theory which takes the notion of a "stereotype" as basic cannot *explain* interpretation.

But we are going to ignore that for the time being; we "stipulate" that we have some kind of holistic understanding of what the Thai speaker believes (as in the case of Aristotle). We may even suppose that some psychologist has come up with a reasonable and operationally meaningful criterion for determining whether a feature of something is "stereotypical" for a given subject, at least in the case of features that can be *pictured* (stripes on a tiger, spots on a leopard, whiskers on a cat, and so on).

To count *every* difference in "stereotype" (in such a sense) as a difference in *meaning* would depart totally from actual practice in disambiguation. Not only would it turn out that *meew* does *not* have the same meaning as "cat" (even when it has the same extension), and that *gorbeh* in Persian does not have the same meaning as "cat," but worse, if Tom next door does not (by the psychological criterion) use the whiskers of a cat (or the milk drinking) as part of his *stereotype* and Dick does, then the meaning of the word is different for Tom and for Dick. Of course, many "folk philosophers" *say* just this: "no word has quite the same meaning for two different people"; but that is *not* how we actually *use* the notion of "meaning" when we *aren't* being folk philosophers. In fact, all the sophisticated mentalists I know *attack* the idea that meanings simply *are* stereotypes (and rightly so; can we even make sense of the notion of a "stereotype" in the case of such words as *mind, esprit, Geist?*); but if someone were so ill-advised as to hold this view, we should just advise him to *drop* the word "meaning" and to talk about the role of stereotypes in communication. (Of course, they aren't invariant under belief fixation, even barring scientific revolutions: they don't determine paraphrase relations, . . .)

Suppose, on the other hand, we go to the opposite extreme and decide that stereotypes have *nothing to do* with the meaning of natural kind words. Then the stereotypical stripes have nothing to do with the meaning of "tiger," the stereotypical spots have nothing to do with the meaning of "leopard," and so on. What about the knowledge that "tigers are *animals*"? It is not more *analytic* that tigers are animals than that tigers are striped (although it is more permanent; tigers could *in fact* evolve to the point of losing their stripes, though not to the point of ceasing to be animals). Should we count some very *central* stereotypical features ("animal, vegetable, and mineral," perhaps?) as part of the meaning, and not the less central ones? Even if we could decide on what counts as a sufficiently "central" feature, it seems that on such a theory there would be no difference in the "content" (the meaning, apart from the actual *extension*) of the words "leopard" and "tiger." It seems to me that a theory of "meanings in the head" that gives up the idea that "tiger" and "leopard" have different "content" has, in effect, conceded Quine's point that no psychologically useful notion of meaning exists (at least not in the case of natural kind words). This has, in fact, been proposed by Dretske, who would treat "tiger" and "leopard" as names with an extension but no "content." But what goes for natural kind words goes for many verbs as well (consider the verb "breathe"). If so many words have no "meaning" (content), then the notion of meaning cannot play the fundamental explanatory role that mentalists want it to play.

The course we actually follow in disambiguation is a middle one between the extremes just described. In the first place, when two words have exactly the same *extension* we tend to treat them as synonyms *regardless* of what is "in the head." This is why mentalistic theories of an MIT type are in trouble from the start: they try to *factor out* extensions; but extensions are what most strongly guide us in interpretation, especially when there is no specific context to guide us. (Yes, I know all about "creature with a heart" and "creature with a kidney" having a different meaning but the same extension; but the *parts* of these phrases don't even have the same *extensions*.)

In the second place, when we consider factors beyond the extension, we *do* consider stereotypes (those stripes *are* somehow connected with the meaning of "tiger"), but what we are concerned with is not *identity* of stereotype (however that might be defined) but *sufficient similarity*. And there is no general rule for deciding when two stereotypes are sufficiently similar; it depends on the particular context, including the reasons why someone wants to know what a word means and what he is going to do with the answer.

To sum up: I have not argued that meaning is indeterminate even in typical contexts (although Quine would so argue, and in cases such as the highfalutin one I described it *is* indeterminate). What I have argued is that *when* meaning is determinate it is *no one thing* that makes it so. The "standard meaning" of *meew* in Thai and of *gorbeh* in Farsi is "cat"—not because the *same* entity is in the heads of Thai, Persian, and English speakers, but notwithstanding the fact that there are psychological differences. The sameness of meaning is the reasonableness of ignoring the difference in the psychological processes.

Mentalism: Sophisticated and Naive

The form of mentalism associated with Noam Chomsky and Jerry Fodor depends on the notion of a "mental representation." As developed by Fodor,[8] the theory postulates an internal code, a "language of thought"—call it *Mentalese*. It further postulates that "all concepts are innate," that is, that Mentalese has the resources to express all the "contents" a human mind could understand. Although I much admire Fodor's articulate and scientifically informed writing and his philosophical ingenuity, I have to say (as John Haugeland once put it) that "one philosopher's *modus ponens* is another philosopher's *modus tollens*": the very fact that *artichoke* and *carburetor* have to be innate notions, if Fodor's theory is right, shows (me) that some of his premises must be wrong. It also seems to me that the empirical fact is that our "concepts" are *not* "universal" in the way that I am told syntactic categories are: the fact that French, English, and German have the very different concepts *esprit, mind,* and *Geist* (at least sensitive translators judge them to be quite different) rather than some one "universal concept" is evidence *against* the Innateness Hypothesis at the level of semantics. But let us assume that Harvard is wrong and MIT is right, and the mind does, as it were, express things twice: once in the public language (when a verbalized thought occurs either in my speaking or in interior monologue), and again in Mentalese. How does this help the notion of meaning?

The answer is that it does not help at all. Mentalese, if it exists, must have much the same character as any other language (apart from having an unthinkably huge vocabulary). Belief fixation must be just as *holistic* in Mentalese as it is in public language. For the holistic character of belief fixation is no accident: it is required by rationality. Mentalese cannot, any more than scientific language, obey the two Dogmas of empiricism: individual "words" in Mentalese cannot, in general, have operational definitions if Mentalese is to be an adequate vehicle for *general intelligence*. Here I am not disagreeing with Fodor; in his writings Fodor visualizes reasoning in Mentalese as generally abductive and holistic. But then, what reason is there to think that there is a precise, context-independent, more-than-merely-pragmatic notion of "sameness of meaning" that we possess or could construct *for Mentalese?*

Even if Mentalese existed, and we could "eavesdrop" on a person's Mentalese, how would that help with the problem of whether "meew" in Thai has the same meaning as "cat" in English? Dictionaries will still give "cat" as the translation of *meew* whether the corresponding "mental representation" (the hypothetical Mentalese word-analogue-in-the-brain) is the same or different. Again, let us suppose that most adult English speakers know that *brass* and *gold* are both shiny yellow metals, and that gold is precious and does not tarnish. An immature speaker may well not learn all these facts at once. Suppose a child knows that gold is a shiny yellow metal, but has not yet learned any more about it. Suppose a second child has the same information about *brass*. If at *that* stage the Mentalese representations are *different,* then (since the total "content" must be the same on any theory, if there is nothing the one child believes about *gold* that the other does not believe about *brass*), *difference* in "mental representation" has no relation to difference in "content."

Now suppose the contrary, that when the beliefs are not yet different, the representations are the *same* (or belong to some computationally defined equivalence class). What happens as the first child learns that gold is precious and does not tarnish?

If the Mentalese word correlated to *gold* does not change, then *it* will become associated with different "collateral information" and with a different "stereotype" as a result of normal belief fixation, just as English words will. In that case, we are no better off with respect to having a scientifically useful and explanatory notion of meaning (or even "content") for Mentalese than we are for English. If, on the other hand, the "mental representation" *does* change as the stereotype changes (and learning that gold is precious and does not tarnish is run-of-the-mill stereotype change), then it would be extremely odd if the "mental representations" associated with *meew, gorbeh,* and *cat* were not all different. In *that* case, sameness-or-difference-of-mental-representation would be a useful neurophysiological criterion for stereotype-sameness-or-difference, but, as we have already seen, stereotypes are not *meanings*.

I don't have the impression that Fodor now disagrees with this. He has recently denied ever holding the view that sameness-of-content is a computational relation in the case of Mentalese (that is, that one can effectively decide when Mentalese "words" have the same "content"); and, in a recent article,[9] he expresses doubt that there are type-type identities between *propositional* "contents" and syntactically defined types of sentences in Mentalese. "Contents" are not the *same* as "mental representations," and are, indeed, in a rather mysterious relation to them. So what is left of the claim that we can *now* see how "contents" could be scientifically well-defined explanatory entities?

It is instructive to see how analogous (what I view as) the collapse of MIT mentalism into total obscurity is to the collapse of the naive mentalism of Locke and Hume. If Locke's "ideas" are *not* taken to be *images* (they weren't taken to be images by Locke himself, of course), then (in the context of Associationist Psychology) it is totally unclear *what* they are. So Hume took them to be images. But (as, for example, Frege pointed out—and Kant had already seen) to think a thought just *isn't* the same thing as running a sequence of pictures through one's mind. So the theory can't explain what we want explained; what one informally explains in terms of "thinking thoughts" can't be scientifically explained in terms of "having a vivid sequence of images," because the causal powers of images are all wrong.

But now it turns out that even if we accept Fodor's *modus ponens*, even if we *buy* Mentalese and all that, we are in the same boat. There is simply no reason to believe that what we informally explain by saying "*meew* means *cat* in Thai" can be explained by R*(meew)* = R*(cat)*, where R is the function that carries a word onto its hypothetical "underlying" Mentalese counterpart. The similarity relations between psychological objects (perceptual prototypes, "mental representations," "canonical methods of verification," and so on) just don't correspond in any way to *semantic* relations. Nor can they, given that psychological objects are so extremely changeable under belief fixation, while the principles underlying interpretation (for example, the "principle of charity") have as their *raison d'être* precisely keeping "meanings" *invariant* under a lot of belief fixation. To say, "Well, perhaps *sentences in Mentalese* aren't invariant under belief fixation to the extent that intuitive 'meanings' are, but their *contents* are" is to talk about the we-know-not-whats of we-know-not-what. After Quine, one can no longer get away with this sort of talk.

Other Folks, Other Strokes

The MIT attempt to revive mentalism has the virtues of scientific sophistication (Chomsky's work in syntax is world-famous; Fodor has done extremely interesting experimental work in psycholinguistics) and serious scientific ambition. The aim is to sketch a way in which rehabilitated meanings (or "contents") could play a serious explanatory role. Even the willingness to entertain extravagant hypotheses and to accept the counterintuitive consequences is a virtue as well as a vice. The other well-known brand of modern mentalism, associated with the names of Paul Grice and Stephen Schiffer, has (up to now) a less scientific flavor, but also less extravagant claims to make.

In a given situation, what I mean to convey by an utterance of a sentence may deviate widely from what anyone would regard as a standard reading of the sentence. If I am asked about the intelligence of a student, and I reply "He knows how to spell his name correctly" with the intention of conveying the belief that the student is stupid, then "The student is stupid" is what *I* mean (or part of what I mean) by the sentence on that occasion, but it certainly isn't what the sentence means in English. In the terminology applied by advocates of "intention based semantics," "The student is stupid" is (part of) the *speaker's meaning* on that occasion, as opposed to the *sentence meaning*.

This distinction is certainly an important one. The program of Grice and Schiffer is to develop a theory of speaker's meaning, and then later (they hope) to use that theory as the basis of a theory of what sentences mean in a language or in a speech community. I cannot elaborate further here: as is well known, Grice has an elaborate theory of what might be called *dialogic intentions* (intentions in a situation in which there is a complex mutual recognition of intentions) and an elaborate theory of maxims governing conversation which aid in the mutual recognition of those intentions. When I say that speakers' meaning is a function of intentions, it is to these mutually recognizable dialogic intentions that I refer. That Grice has a great deal to teach us about communication, I do not doubt. It is the idea that any of this rehabilitates mentalism that seems misguided to me.

If I say "That chair is comfortable" to someone, then my intention is usually to get that someone to believe that some contextually definite chair is comfortable. In such a situation, I can say something of the form, "My intention in uttering that particular utterance of P was to get so-and-so to have the belief that P." In short, I can use the sentence P again to say what the speaker's meaning of P was on that occasion. If this were the *only* way of doing this, then Grice's theory would be of no interest.

I can, however, answer other questions about the beliefs I would like my hearer to acquire (by recognizing my dialogic intentions), and so can any sophisticated speaker. If Mrs. Shayegan (a Farsi speaker) says that there is a *gorbeh* on the chair, I can ask her whether she intends to convey the belief that there is a generic cat on the chair or the belief that there is a Persian cat on the chair; in the latter case, the speaker's meaning is (in part) *there is a Persian cat on the chair* even though the standard sentence meaning (relying on dictionaries) might be *there is a cat on the chair.*

To say what the "speaker's meaning" is (assume Mrs. Shayegan speaks *only* Farsi) I have to *translate* her answers, however. Without a notion of sentence meaning, all I have is her dispositions to assent and dissent from various questions put to her in Farsi. Such Rylean dispositions (complex dispositions to speech behavior) cannot be regarded as expressing the same "intentions" and the same "beliefs" unless we *already* have a practice of translation in place. To regard such intentions and beliefs as well-defined entities underlying (and ultimately explaining) translation is to reify meanings under another name.

Grice will now tell me, with some exasperation, that he is not now, never has been, and does not intend to be Gilbert Ryle. His "beliefs" and "intentions" are *not* "multi-tracked dispositions" in Ryle's sense. But that is precisely the problem! *What* they are is not one bit clearer than what "meanings" are.[10]

Michael Dummett, whose attacks on metaphysical realism have had a profound influence on my own thinking, would revive mentalism by restricting the holism of belief-fixation to *science.* He supposes that ordinary language sentences have definite verification conditions associated with them by a systematic and "surveyable" procedure. I have already discussed this approach, which seems to me radically misguided.

John Searle supposes that there are mental states which are, on the one hand, constituted or, as he says, "internally caused" by the chemistry and physics of the brain and which *intrinsically refer to external things*.

And Quine is *wrong* in thinking that "meanings" are *obscure?*

Quine, Wittgenstein, Davidson

I have taken Quine not to be rejecting our ordinary talk about what words mean, but as insisting upon the informal (and unformalizable) character of our decisions of "synonymy." It is not saying that *cat* and *gorbeh* are "synonyms" that Quine attacks, but the idea that our account of such statements can be an informative one if it posits independent objects called "meanings."

This reading of Quine is based not only on many conversations with Quine but also on many conversations with Burton Dreben, who has long insisted on the deep similarities between central parts of the philosophies of Quine and Wittgenstein. As far as Wittgenstein is concerned, the relevant reading is well expressed in a recent paper by Warren Goldfarb.[11] Commenting on Section 20b in the *Investigations* (in which Wittgenstein tells his interlocutor not to think of the meaning as if it were a shadow sentence, and remarks curtly that what it comes to for two expressions to have the same meaning is that they have the same use), Goldfarb writes:

> It might be objected that this is false, and that, indeed, no two sentences have (exactly) the same use, since there will inevitably be some occasions where one would be employed but not the other. I take Wittgenstein to be aware of this (although it does not come out in section 20); the reply is not simply that he means "more-or-less the same use". To ascribe sameness of sense to two sentences is to say that they have features of their application in common. What features might be essential to the ascription is not given beforehand; for that depends on our aims in the classification, on the reasons we are talking—in the particular context—of sense at all. I would argue that there is no general notion of use; and I would claim that Wittgenstein agrees. For these sorts of reasons, I read his notorious "definition" of meaning as use (section 43) not as a definition, not as

explanatory, and certainly not as suggesting a "use-based theory of meaning". (My reading is closely connected to my taking Wittgenstein not to be a behaviorist. It should be clear that if he is not, then little can be made of talk of use simpliciter.) Given that invoking use by itself carries little information, I take his remark in section 43 to be, by and large, a denial of the possibility and the appropriateness of theorizing about meaning.

If this reading is correct, as I believe it to be, then it is striking that two of the very greatest analytic philosophers of the twentieth century have so powerfully argued against the same error (and even more striking how persistent the error is, in spite of the criticism directed against it).

If I have not discussed Donald Davidson in connection with mentalism, it is because the theories of meaning that he speaks of presuppose translation-practice. This is the reason why Quine is not hostile to Davidson's enterprise. (But this point seems not to have been grasped at Oxford.)

Does Quine Go Too Far?

Where I do *not* follow Quine is in his doctrine of the almost total indeterminacy of *reference* (and of *meaning* even when the context is specified). Quine's argument is long and subtle, and I will not attempt to sketch it. Suffice it to say that it moves from such premises as "No change without a physical change" (which I accept, as I think Quine intends it) and "All facts are physical facts" (which I do *not* accept—the relation between these two premises is obscure to me), to the conclusion that there is "no fact of the matter" about meaning or reference.

Quine's argument is so abstract that it applies to all of mentalistic talk (talk about beliefs and desires) as well as to meaning talk, whether scientific or informal. The idea is that if the negation of a statement could be incorporated into a theory which is compatible with the same *trajectories of bodies* as the theory which contained the original statement, then the statement has only a theory-relative truth-value. "*Gorbeh* means *cat*" may be true relative to our present mentalistic linguistic "theory," but there is an empirically equivalent theory relative to which that statement is *not* true, and there is no "fact of the matter" as to which of these empirically equivalent theories is correct.

This is another case in which "another philosopher's *modus ponens* is my *modus tollens*." Even if the extreme counterintuitiveness of the conclusions did not force me to reject one of the premises, the fact is that Quine's argument for the indeterminacy of mentalistic talk applies equally well to *philosophy*. A philosophy based on St. Thomas might well be compatible with every "trajectory of bodies" that Quine's philosophy accommodates, and imply that there is a fact of the matter about translation, that meanings exist, that Quine's use of "fact of the matter" is incoherent, and so on. Can Quine consistently hold that there is no fact of the matter about any of *these* things? But my purpose in this essay is to discuss not Quine's scientism, but his meaning holism. And the latter, though not the former, seems to me to be a revolutionary contribution to thinking about talking and thinking.

22. Nelson Goodman's *Fact, Fiction, and Forecast*

Fact, Fiction, and Forecast has achieved the paradoxical status of a contemporary classic. It is a classic by virtue of being one of the few books that every serious student of philosophy in our time *has* to have read; it is contemporary not just because it is by a contemporary philosopher but because it speaks to what are still among the most widely discussed issues in philosophy.

Goodman totally recasts the traditional problem of induction. For him the problem is not to guarantee that induction will succeed in the future—we have no such guarantee—but to characterize what induction *is* in a way that is neither too permissive nor too vague. The central difficulty, which Goodman was the first to highlight, is the projection problem: what distinguishes the properties one can inductively project from a sample to a population from the properties that are more or less resistant to such projection? Goodman's celebrated argument, which he uses to show that all predicates are not equally projectible, depends on his invention of the strange predicate "grue." He defines something as grue if it is either observed before a certain date and is green, or is not observed before that date and is blue. There is something very much like a work of art about this piece of philosophical invention, but why? It isn't just that it has the aesthetic virtues of elegance, novelty, and simplicity. Perhaps what makes the argument so stunning is the rarity in philosophy of proofs that really are proofs. However, Goodman doesn't present his argument as a proof, but rather as a puzzle. Perhaps *that* is the artistry—that, and the fact that an elegant proof is conveyed by means of a simple example.

What did Goodman show? In his contribution to a widely read discussion, Jerry Fodor claimed it was that an innate ordering of hypotheses is needed for induction.[1] But that is *not* what he showed; in fact, it isn't even right. There are models for induction in which no innate ordering of hypotheses or predicates is presupposed; Goodman's own model is one such. Hypotheses are ordered in a way that changes in the course of cultural and scientific history in his model. Even the principles Goodman uses to order hypotheses in the light of past inductive practice, for example, the principle of "entrenchment," are not innate in his view but are arrived at by philosophical reflection on the practice of our community.

Catherine Elgin recently suggested to me that there is a strong resemblance between Goodman's views and those of the later Wittgenstein, at least on one reading.[2] Such a comparison is more to the point than any attempt to relate Goodman's ideas to those of Noam Chomsky. Like Wittgenstein, Goodman doesn't believe in looking for guarantees, foundations, or the Furniture of the Universe. (He goes even further than Wittgenstein in his rejection of traditional philosophy, describing himself in his most recent writing as a "relativist" and an "irrealist.") What we have in Goodman's view, as, perhaps, in Wittgenstein's, are practices, which are right or wrong depending on how they square with our standards. And our standards are right or wrong depending on how they square with our practices. This is a circle, or better, a spiral, but one that Goodman, like John Dewey, regards as virtuous.

I referred to Goodman's celebrated argument as a proof. What he proved, even if he did not put it that way, is that inductive logic is not formal in the sense that deductive logic is. The *form* of an inference, in the sense familiar from deductive logic, cannot tell one whether that inference is inductively valid.

In order to "solve" Goodman's problem one has therefore to provide some principle capable of selecting among inferences that do not differ in logical form, that is, on the basis of the particular predicates those inferences contain. Philosophers who dislike Goodman's proposal, because of its dependence on the actual history of past inductive projections in the culture, have come up with a number of "solutions" that *don't* work. For example, some philosophers think that a valid inductive inference must not contain any disjunctive predicates. However, this fails because, from the point of view of logic, being disjunctive is a *relational* attribute of predicates: whether a predicate is disjunctive is relative to the choice of a language. If one takes the familiar color predicates as primitive, then Goodman's predicate "grue" *is* a disjunctive predicate; if one takes the unfamiliar predicates grue and bleen as primitive, however, then being green may be defined as being grue and observed prior to time t or being bleen and not observed prior to time t. Thus the predicate grue is disjunctive in a language with normal color predicates as primitive, while the normal color predicates are disjunctive in a language having as primitive the nonstandard predicates (call them "gruller" predicates) that Goodman invented. No predicate is disjunctive or nondisjunctive in itself.

What I have just described is the situation as it looks to a logician. Rudolf Carnap proposed that over and above this way in which a predicate can be disjunctive or nondisjunctive, that is, relative to a language or a choice of primitives, a predicate can be intrinsically disjunctive or nondisjunctive. In effect, he postulates a metaphysical pointer than singles out, we know not how, certain predicates as qualitative, that is, as kosher from the point of view of induction. However, even if we rule out predicates like grue, which are, in Carnap's view, nonqualitative, problems still remain, at least in his systems of inductive logic. For example, we will get abnormal degrees of confirmation for certain hypotheses if we take the magnitude "the square of the length" as primitive instead of the magnitude "length."[3] Yet both "length" and "length squared" are qualitative, according to Carnap. To justify the choice of the standard primitive magnitude, length, he therefore postulated that some qualitative magnitudes, including length, are intrinsically fundamental. Logical Heaven itself tells us which predicates to take as primitive in our theories! These Carnapian views do not solve Goodman's problem; they merely turn logic into metaphysics.

A more radical solution proposed by Wesley Salmon—and several other philosophers have made similar proposals—is that *ostensively defined* primitive predicates are what is needed for inductive logic: "Ostensive definability is the basis for distinguishing normal from pathological predicates."[4] However, ostensively definable predicates are all *observational* predicates, and the proposal to rule out all non-observational predicates is unmotivated and too severe.

Unmotivated: Call a bacillus "S-shaped" if it looks so under a microscope. Then "is an S-shaped bacillus" isn't observational but perfectly projectible. If one weakens "ostensively definable" by allowing oneself to use instruments, then, as Goodman points out, grue is ostensively definable: all one has to do is build a measuring instrument that flashes a red light if the time is before t (imagine that the measuring instrument contains an internal clock) and the instrument is scanning something green or if the time is later than t and the instrument is scanning something blue.[5] Using such an instrument, one can tell whether or not something is grue without knowing what time it is, by seeing whether or not the red light is flashing. Critics might object that such an instrument is really measuring the time, but there is a sense in which any measuring instrument that contains internal moving parts and whose correct functioning depends on those parts moving at the appropriate rate may be said to contain an internal clock. The point is that unless we rule out the use of mechanical aids to observation altogether, then we cannot rule out grue for the reason given.[6]

Too severe: If only ostensively definable predicates are projectible, then how do we make inferences to the unobservable? One strength of Goodman's account is that it includes a mechanism by which new predicates, including nonobservation predicates, can acquire projectibility. These mechanisms, which are similar to what Hans Reichenbach called "cross induction," depend upon a relation between one hypothesis and another, called by Goodman an "overhypothesis," that contains higher-level predicates than the first. For example, "all the marbles in any bag are the same color" is an overhypothesis of "all the marbles in this bag are red." But if the higher-level predicates we are allowed to use are all ostensively definable (as on Salmon's proposal), then an underhypothesis of a projectible hypothesis will always be about observables because the overhypothesis is; so the objector can't use Goodman's mechanisms to transfer projectibility from projectible observation predicates to nonobservation predicates, and thus Goodman's critics have failed to come up with any alternative mechanisms to do the job.

In any case, we don't want to rule out grue completely. Sometimes it is projectible, and Goodman's discussion allows for this explicitly.

The failure of these attempts to evade Goodman's problem does not show that our ordering of predicates must be based on entrenchment, but his choice of entrenchment accords with his metaphilosophy. Entrenchment depends on the frequency with which we have actually inductively projected a predicate in the past; whether Goodman is writing about art or induction, what he prizes is congruence with actual practice as it has developed in history. This may seem paradoxical in a philosopher who also prizes novelty and who is a friend of modernity, but Goodman sees no conflict here. In his view, what makes it possible to value and operate within both inherited traditions and novel activities and versions is the truth of pluralism. This pluralism is only hinted at in *Fact, Fiction, and Forecast,* for instance, in the clear statement that which predicates are projectible is a matter of the contingent history of the culture, but it has become the dominant theme in Goodman's most recent work.[7] Even if the choice of entrenchment as the primary source of projectibility is congruent with Goodman's metaphilosophy, that does not mean he excludes the possibility of any other solution to the projectibility problem *a priori.* Few philosophers are less aprioristic than Goodman. What he insists upon, and all that he insists upon in this connection, is that *any* proposed solution be judged by its ability to systematize what we actually do.

In this connection as in others, it is important to recognize that Goodman is not interested in formalisms that we can't use. This pragmatism, in the best sense of the term, is apparent in his work on counterfactuals—another vexed area of contemporary philosophy in which Goodman's work, although negative in its upshot, has set the agenda for the subsequent discussion. Recent workers on the problem, for example, David Lewis, have produced formalistic schemes that presuppose a given totality of "possible worlds" and a "similarity metric" that measures their similarity.[8] Such "solutions" to the problem of counterfactuals are not solutions at all in Goodman's view, since we are not given any principles for telling which possible worlds are more or less similar to the actual world. Relying on intuition for the answer is no improvement on relying on intuition to tell us that the counterfactual we are interested in is right or wrong in the first place. Moreover, there aren't any "possible but not actual" worlds. Carnap's formalized inductive logics, mentioned earlier, are in the same boat. Goodman respects formal logic, but not when it dresses up a problem in a way that has no payoff in practice. He deplores the current love of formalism for formalism's sake.

This brings me to perhaps my most important remark about Goodman's philosophical methods and attitudes. Although he starts as, say, Rorty does, by rejecting certainty and the idea of an ontological ground floor independent of our theorizing and, even more like Rorty, by rejecting the most fashionable problems of philosophy, he is totally free of the "now philosophy is over" mood that haunts much of twentieth-century philosophy.[9] If there isn't a ready-made world, then let's construct worlds, says Goodman. If there aren't objective standards, then let's construct standards! Nothing is ready-made, but everything is to be made.

Goodman's prodigious output and enormous breadth of interest—he has written on the theory of constructional systems, on nominalistic foundations for mathematics, on the general theory of signs, and on the philosophy of psychology, as well as on aesthetics and on the tasks of philosophy today—illustrate how far he is from sharing the view that philosophy is over. So does the constructive nature of much of his writing. Most philosophers are people with theses to defend; Goodman is a man with methods and concepts to "sell" (his word). But, he would remark, if there is no ready-made world, the line between a thesis and a construction dissolves.

As I already remarked, it is a mistake to see Goodman as providing support for any doctrine of innate ideas. It is not that he is uninterested in psychology; he has worked in it most of his life. The real problem, in his view, isn't what is innate; the real problem has to do with cultural evolution. We are world-makers; we are constantly making "new worlds out of old ones." What we see, perceive, touch, is all in flux—a flux of our own creation. The real psychological question is how we shape this flux and how we maneuver in it. In thinking about Goodman, I keep coming back to his optimism, or perhaps I should say his energy. He doesn't believe in progress in any sense that implies things are getting better, or must in the future. But he does believe that novelty can be exciting and good as well as boring and bad; he finds construction and creation exciting and challenging. He believes, in short, that there is a great deal we can do, and he prefers concrete and partial progress to grand and ultimately empty visions.

Notes
Credits
Index

Notes

Introduction

1. This is the first of two volumes of Putnam's philosophical papers to be published by Harvard University Press. The present volume contains recent essays in the areas of metaphysics, value theory, and American philosophy; the forthcoming volume will collect Putnam's recent work in the areas of history of philosophy, philosophy of science, and philosophy of mind and language.

2. "Before Kant it is perhaps impossible to find *any* philosopher who did *not* have a correspondence theory of truth . . . It is impossible to find a philosopher before Kant who was *not* a metaphysical realist, at least about what he took to be *basic* or unreducible assertions." Hilary Putnam, *Reason, Truth, and History* (Cambridge: Cambridge University Press, 1981), pp. 56–57.

3. "Kant offered a radically new way of giving content to the notion of equality, a way that builds liberty into equality . . . That the truths of religion— which for Kant are the most important truths—should be by their very nature *problematic* is a good thing, not a bad one . . . What Kant is saying, to put it positively, is that we have to think for ourselves . . . and that fact is itself the most valuable fact about our lives. *That* is the characteristic with respect to which we are all equals. We are all in the same predicament, and we all have the potential of thinking for ourselves with respect to the question of How to Live . . . Freedom of thought is essential, because the fundamental characteristic with respect to which we are equal, our so to speak 'respect of equality,' is precisely our need for, our capacity for, free moral thinking." Hilary Putnam, *The Many Faces of Realism* (LaSalle, Ill.: Open Court, 1987).

4. Hilary Putnam, *Representation and Reality* (Cambridge, Mass.: MIT Press, 1989), pp. 108, 133.

5. It will emerge in the course of this introduction that there are good reasons to be more cautious than I am allowing myself to be here about referring to Putnam's internal realism as a "metaphysical position."

6. Putnam, *Reason, Truth, and History,* p. 60. Chapter 2 of the present volume offers important clarifications of certain aspects of Putnam's "internal realism."

7. Putnam takes the terminology of "an absolute conception" from David Wiggins's *Truth, Values, Needs* (London: Basil Blackwell, 1988) and Bernard Williams's *Ethics and the Limits of Philosophy* (Cambridge, Mass.: Harvard Uni-

versity Press, 1985, pp. 138–139). Putnam criticizes Williams's notion of the absolute conception in Chapter 11 of the present volume on the grounds that it presupposes an incoherent theory of truth as correspondence to a preexisting unconceptualized reality.

8. This phrase actually stems from David Wiggins. Putnam appropriates it approvingly in Chapter 15 of the present volume and then clarifies the polemical character of his appropriation of Wiggins's phrase in Chapter 16: "Whereas Bernard Williams and David Wiggins claim that truth in morality is one thing (truth 'humanly speaking') and something else ('absolute truth') in science, pragmatism urges that truth humanly speaking is all we've got."

9. I am here partly paraphrasing and partly quoting phrases from the concluding paragraph of Chapter 11 of this volume. Putnam, in turn, is partly paraphrasing and partly quoting remarks from John Dewey's *Logic*.

10. From the penultimate paragraph of Chapter 10 of this volume.

11. Putnam, *The Many Faces of Realism*, p. 44.

12. Ibid.; see the passage quoted in note 3.

13. Ibid., p. 48.

14. Ibid., p. 52.

15. Putnam also challenges certain prevalent assumptions concerning the place of rules in the scheme of Kant's moral philosophy: "The central purpose of Kant's ethical writing, in fact, is not to issue detailed rules at all, but to give us a normative picture of the activity of arriving at such rules." (Chapter 13.)

16. In particular, Putnam argues that Kant does not view the categorical imperative and the principle that we should seek to bring about the greatest possible happiness as simply incompatible moral principles: "In Kant's picture there are two principles which guide us in arriving at moral rules: the formal (categorical) imperative, which directs us to act so that the maxim of our action might be one to which others could be imagined as consenting, and the principle of the highest good, identified first with my own private virtue and happiness and eventually with the happiness of all mankind in a world governed by just institutions." (Chapter 13.)

17. Ibid. Putnam goes on to clarify this point by explaining Kant's concern to be that the principle of the highest good remain always subordinate to the categorical imperative: "The formal imperative always takes precedence, for Kant, over the material imperative (to seek the highest good). Our duty is not to pursue a utopian vision by manipulative, dishonest, or cruel means, but to pursue an idealistic vision by moral means."

18. Although Putnam does qualify this claim with the concession that "Aristotle's picture is strong precisely where Kant's picture is weak." Specifically: "Where Kant's picture is defective, the problem lies with Kant's dualistic picture of happiness . . . the dualism of a transcendental and empirical self results in a portmanteau conception of happiness, happiness as moral 'gratification' *plus* satisfaction of the 'inclinations.'" (Ibid.)

19. The remark of Kant's that Putnam particularly builds on here is to be found in the *Critique of Pure Reason*, A141/B180–181, where Kant remarks that the "schematism of our understanding in its application to appearance" is "an

art concealed in the depths of the human soul, whose real modes of activity nature is hardly likely ever to allow us to discover, and to have open to our gaze."

20. Putnam, *Representation and Reality*, p. 108.

21. The inability of any form of physicalism or materialism to account for intentionality plays an important supporting role in the arguments of a number of the essays in this volume. See, in particular, Chapter 5 of this volume.

22. This essay appears in *Exploring the Concept of Mind*, ed. Richard M. Caplan (Iowa City: University of Iowa Press, 1986), pp. 31–50.

23. Ibid., p. 39.

24. Ibid.

25. Perhaps most noteworthy in this regard is Chapter 11.

26. *Critique of Pure Reason*, A51/B75.

27. *Critique of Pure Reason*, A838–839/B866–867. I have emended Kemp Smith's translation slightly.

28. I am indebted to Georg Picht's essay "Philosophie oder vom Wesen und rechten Gebrauch der Vernunft" for drawing my attention to these passages in the *First Critique*. Although my reading of these passages has been influenced by Picht's essay, it also departs from his interpretation in a number of respects. The essay appears in *Hier und Jetzt, Band I* (Stuttgart: Verlagsgemeinschaft Ernst Klett, 1980); see especially pp. 11–12.

29. Quine's work is discussed in Chapters 20 and 21 of this volume. This feature of his work comes under fire in Chapter 20.

30. Consider, for example, the following remarks from Quine's essay "Has Philosophy Lost Contact with People?" in his *Theories and Things* (Cambridge, Mass.: Harvard University Press, 1981), p. 193: "What I have been discussing under the head of philosophy is what I call scientific philosophy . . . By this vague heading I do not exclude philosophical studies of moral and aesthetic values. Some such studies, of an analytical cast, can be scientific in spirit. They are apt, however, to offer little in the way of inspiration or consolation. The student who majors in philosophy primarily for spiritual comfort is misguided and is probably not a very good student anyway, since intellectual curiosity is not what moves him.

"Inspirational and edifying writing is admirable, but the place for it is the novel, the poem, the sermon, or the literary essay. Philosophers in the professional sense have no peculiar fitness for it. Neither have they any peculiar fitness for helping to get society on an even keel, though we should all do what we can."

31. Putnam, *Mind, Language, and Reality* (Cambridge: Cambridge University Press, 1975), pp. 132–133.

32. *Critique of Pure Reason*, A840a/B867a. I prefer the Mueller translation here. Kemp Smith renders the passage as follows: "By 'cosmical concept' [*Weltbegriff*] is here meant the concept which relates to that in which everyone necessarily has an interest."

33. This is again the Mueller translation. Kemp Smith puts it: "to be found in that reason with which every human being is endowed."

34. Ibid., Avii. First sentence of the *Critique of Pure Reason*.

35. Ibid., A295/B352.

36. As, for example, in the penultimate paragraph of Chapter 10, in which Putnam adduces the metaphysical realist's notion of "a concept-independent, perspective-independent reality" as an instance of "transcendental illusion."

37. *Critique of Pure Reason*, A247–248/B353–355.

38. Ibid., A297/B353.

39. Ibid., A838/B866. "Es gibt aber noch einen *Weltbegriff* [conceptus cosmicus], der dieser Bennennung jederzeit zum Grunde gelegen hat."

40. Ibid., A839/B867.

41. Putnam, *Realism and Reason* (Cambridge: Cambridge University Press, 1983), p. 211; emphasis mine.

42. "An Interview with Hilary Putnam," *Cogito*, 3 (Summer 1989), pp. 85, 90.

43. Putnam has recently evinced interest in Kierkegaard on a number of occasions, as, for example, in the following pertinent remark: "I admire Kierkegaard for his insistence on the priority of the question, 'How shall I live?'" (ibid., p. 90). See also his remarks on Kierkegaard in "Bringing Philosophy Back to Life," in *U.S. News and World Report*, April 25, 1988, p. 56. For a brief comparison of Kierkegaard and James, see Putnam's remarks in Chapter 16.

44. The latter half of this formula is explicitly articulated at one point in Putnam's writing: "If science is a philosophy, it suffers from being all metaphysics and no ethics; and metaphysics without ethics is blind" (*Meaning and the Moral Sciences*, p. 92). Putnam elsewhere explicitly invokes Kant in this connection: "I admire Kant, not just for his undoubted genius, but for his breadth of vision—his concern with religious and social as well as theoretical, epistemological and metaphysical questions, and his ability to integrate all of those concerns." "An Interview with Professor Hilary Putnam," *Cogito*, 3 (Summer 1989).

Wolfgang Stegmüller finds himself admiring in Putnam precisely what Putnam says here that he admires in Kant. In the middle of a chapter devoted to an exposition of Putnam's work, Stegmüller writes: "In the final analysis he [Putnam] is perhaps the only philosopher of the present time who still has something like a *complete perspicuous overview*" (*Hauptstroemungen der Gegenwartsphilosophie*, Band II [Kroener Verlag, 1987], p. 345; my translation).

45. *Realism and Reason*, p. vii.

46. See, for example, Lecture III of *The Many Faces of Realism*.

47. See Chapter 7 of the present volume.

48. See Chapter 15 of the present volume.

49. See, for example, "Dreaming and 'Depth-Grammar,'" in *Mind, Language, and Reality*. The paper is an attack on a claim put forward in a book by Norman Malcolm, a famous student of Wittgenstein's, to the effect that waking testimony provides the sole criterion of dreaming, along with the further claim that if some further physiological criterion of when someone is dreaming were to be discovered, it would involve the creation of an entirely new concept, hence entailing a change in the meaning of the word "dreaming." Putnam argues that Malcolm's picture of language (as governed by criteria that stipulate strict rules for verifying the correct application of concepts) presupposes an artificially sharp separation of our semantical ability (our ability to speak intelligibly) from our overall reasoning ability (in particular, our ability to draw inductive inferences). Although Putnam makes it clear at the outset of the paper that his interest in

Malcolm's views is in part tied to their supposed connection with certain "famous arguments of Wittgenstein's," it remains an open question for him whether Malcolm's interpretation is "faithful to what Wittgenstein had in mind": "His arguments are . . . of interest in that they can be read as simple versions of some famous arguments of Wittgenstein's as he is interpreted by Malcolm. If this interpretation of Malcolm's is faithful to what Wittgenstein had in mind, then these famous arguments are bad arguments and prove nothing. But this relation to Wittgenstein's philosophy may, in the present years, be a further reason for finding Malcolm's book interesting to discuss" (p. 304).

50. "Analyticity and Apriority: Beyond Wittgenstein and Quine," in *Realism and Reason*. In this paper Putnam criticizes the interpretations of Wittgenstein put forward by Michael Dummett and Barry Stroud on the grounds that both the resulting views entail what Putnam takes to be a problematic conclusion, namely, that mathematical truth and necessity simply "arise in us" as an artifact of our human forms of life. It is worth pointing out that, at this point in his career, Putnam takes considerably more care at the outset of his essay to distinguish between Wittgenstein himself and the views of Wittgensteinians: "Just *what* Wittgenstein's contention is, in connection with philosophers' opinions, theories, and arguments on the topic of mathematical necessity, has been a subject of considerable controversy. Clearly he thinks the whole discussion is nonsensical and confused, and whether he offers any explanation at all of why we *think* there is such a thing as mathematical necessity and of what the difference is between mathematical and empirical statements, is a subject on which there seems to be a great deal of disagreement among his interpreters.

"I shall not attempt to do any textual exegesis here. I know what the (several) views of *Wittgensteinians* are, even if I do not know for sure which, if any, was Wittgenstein's; and what I shall try to show is that not even the most sophisticated of these "Wittgensteinian" views is tenable" (p. 115).

51. "An Interview with Hilary Putnam," p. 90.

52. Ibid., p. 90. Putnam goes on to qualify this remark by adding: "With the possible exception of [William] James" (pp. 90–91).

53. "I find myself entirely mystified by people who think that 'ordinary language philosophy' is a *position* . . . Wittgenstein did not employ *arguments*, in the traditional philosophical sense, at all" (*Mind, Language, and Reality*, p. 134).

54. *Realism and Reason*, p. 183.

55. Stanley Cavell, *Themes out of School* (San Francisco: North Point Press, 1984), p. 9.

56. "An Interview with Stanley Cavell," in *The Senses of Stanley Cavell*, ed. Richard Fleming and Michael Payne (Lewisburg, Pa.: Bucknell University Press, 1989), pp. 47–48. It is worth noting that this feature of Cavell's reading of Wittgenstein—namely, that on his view philosophy is not something that could coherently be thought of as coming to an end at some point in cultural time—is one that Putnam himself has had occasion to insist upon in seeking to distinguish Cavell's reading from that of certain other "Wittgensteinians": "Cavell's thought can . . . sound closer to that of some Wittgensteinians than it is. While there is a sense in which Cavell is a 'Wittgensteinian'—*The Claim of Reason* offers a powerful and sympathetic interpretation of some of the central ideas of Wittgenstein's

Philosophical Investigations, and references to Wittgenstein appear early and late in Cavell's writing—the 'end of philosophy' interpretation of Wittgenstein is foreign to Cavell's thought (and to Wittgenstein's as well, if Cavell reads him correctly). On an 'end of philosophy' reading of Wittgenstein, wanting to transcend our own human position is a kind of philosophical neurosis, and the only task that remains for philosophy is to 'cure' us. Once cured, we shall be able to live in the ordinary, untroubled by skeptical/metaphysical impulses, however disguised. But this is not Cavell's view at all" ("An Introduction to Cavell," in *Pursuits of Reason: Essays in Honor of Stanley Cavell,* ed. T. Cohen, P. Guyer, and H. Putnam [Lubbuck, Tex.: Texas Tech. University Press, 1990]).

57. The idea that the activity of philosophizing, as it is exemplified in Wittgenstein's work, is not one that ever comes to an end is something that Wittgenstein insists upon on a number of occasions. See, for example, *Zettel,* no. 447.

58. The later Wittgenstein's most celebrated work is titled *Philosophical Investigations* and is famous for offering a trenchant criticism of his own early work.

59. *Representation and Reality,* p. xii.

60. Wittgenstein, *Lectures on the Foundations of Mathematics,* ed. Cora Diamond (Ithaca, N.Y.: Cornell University Press, 1990), p. 84.

61. For an extended discussion of Wittgenstein's views on the relation between riddles and philosophical questions, see Cora Diamond's article "Riddles and Anselm's Riddle," *Aristotelian Society Proceedings, Supplementary Volume 51,* 1977.

62. Hence Wittgenstein has his interlocutor ask: "Where does our investigation get its importance from, since it seems to destroy everything interesting, that is, all that is great and important?" (*Philosophical Investigations,* no. 118).

63. Wittgenstein, *Philosophical Investigations,* no. 111.

64. *Representation and Reality,* p. xii. It is worth remarking that there is a point of considerable divergence between Putnam and Wittgenstein here as well, insofar as Putnam speaks of the philosopher's task lying in making the full *mystery* of the problems of philosophy manifest, while Wittgenstein says his ultimate aim is to make the problems (each time they arise) completely *disappear.*

65. Daniel Dennett's humorous publication, *The Philosophical Lexicon,* offers the following definition: "*hilary,* n. (from hilary term) A brief but significant period in the intellectual career of a distinguished philosopher. 'Oh, that's what I thought three or four hilaries ago.'" (*The Philosophical Lexicon,* American Philosophical Association, 1987, p. 11).

66. Richard Rorty has also compared Putnam with Russell: "Putnam is, among contemporary analytic philosophers, the one who most resembles Russell: not just in intellectual curiosity and willingness to change his mind, but in the breadth of his interests and in the extent of his social and moral concerns" (a quote from the dust jacket of *Realism and Reason*). The following remark of Putnam's about A. J. Ayer, from Chapter 3 of this volume, suggests that Putnam might have some reservations concerning Rorty's and Passmore's comparison: "Sir Alfred Jules Ayer has been somewhat of a paradox—always against the fashion, always rebellious, yet, also . . . old-fashioned in his philosophical demeanor. Although his views have changed considerably since he wrote *Language, Truth,*

and Logic, he continues to philosophize in the style and spirit of Bertrand Russell. If that style and spirit no longer speak to the concerns of practicing philosophers, that is, I suspect, a fact of cultural importance and not just an event for professional philosophers to note." The opposition quietly implied here between "practicing philosophers," on the one hand, and "professional philosophers," on the other, comes close to offering what amounts to an only slightly more tactful version of Thoreau's observation about professional philosophers in *Walden:* "There are nowadays professors of philosophy but not philosophers. Yet it is admirable to profess because it was once admirable to live."

67. John Passmore, *Recent Philosophers* (London: Duckworth, 1988), p. 104.

68. Ibid., p. 92.

69. Ibid., p. 97.

70. Stegmüller, *Hauptstroemungen der Gegenwartsphilosophie,* Band II, p. 345 (my translation).

71. Passages from the *Critique of Pure Reason* such as the following highlight the feature of Kant's conception of the "natural dialectic of human reason" echoed in the work of the later Wittgenstein (and *a fortiori* the latest Putnam): "The first step in matters of pure reason, marking its infancy, is *dogmatic.* The second step is *skeptical;* and indicates that experience has rendered our judgment wiser and more circumspect. But a third step, such as can be taken by a fully matured judgment . . . is now necessary, namely to subject to examination, not the facts of reason, but reason itself, in the whole extent of its powers . . . This is not the censorship but the *criticism* of reason, whereby not its present *bounds* but its determinate *limits,* not its ignorance on this or that point but its ignorance in regard to all questions of a certain kind, are demonstrated . . . Skepticism is thus a resting-place for human reason, where it can reflect upon its dogmatic wanderings and make survey of the region in which it finds itself . . . But it is no dwelling-place for permanent settlement" (A761/B789). The analogy between Wittgenstein and Kant (and Putnam) here depends upon a rejection of Saul Kripke's reading of Wittgenstein's work as proposing a "skeptical solution" (see his *Wittgenstein on Rules and Private Language*). Two essays that explicitly contest Kripke's reading, both of which influenced Putnam's understanding of Wittgenstein, are worth consulting in this connection: Cora Diamond's "Realism and the Realistic Spirit" in *The Realistic Spirit* (Cambridge, Mass.: MIT Press, 1991), and Stanley Cavell's "The Argument of the Ordinary: Scenes of Instruction in Wittgenstein and Kripke" (chap. 2 of *Conditions Handsome and Unhandsome* [Chicago: University of Chicago Press, 1990]).

72. See "The Availability of Wittgenstein's Later Philosophy," in *Must We Mean What We Say?* (New York: Scribner's, 1969). I discuss the relation in Wittgenstein between the voice of temptation and the voice of correctness in my article "Throwing Away the Top of the Ladder," *The Yale Review,* vol. 79, no. 3.

73. I find myself in these remarks either borrowing on or paraphrasing sentences about Wittgenstein which grew out of a conversation I had with Putnam and which occur in my introduction to "An Interview with Stanley Cavell," in *The Senses of Stanley Cavell* (Lewisburg, Pa.: Bucknell University Press, 1989), pp. 27–28.

74. *Philosophical Investigations,* no. 133. I have emended the translation.

75. I am here paraphrasing a remark from a passage of Stanley Cavell's which is one that Putnam either echoes or alludes to at a number of junctures in the essays collected here. It runs as follows: "We question what we cannot fail to know in order not to seek what it would be painful to find out. This, of course, does not suggest that skepticism is trivial; on the contrary, it shows how profound a position of the mind it is. Nothing is more human than the wish to deny one's humanity, or to assert it at the expense of others. But if that is what skepticism entails, it cannot be combatted through simple 'refutations'" (Cavell, *The Claim of Reason,* p. 109).

76. See, for example, Rorty's "Pragmatism and Philosophy," the introduction to his *Consequences of Pragmatism* (Minneapolis: University of Minnesota Press, 1982).

77. The remark comes from the concluding sequence of Gilson's William James Lectures, delivered at Harvard in 1936, reprinted as Gilson, *The Unity of Philosophical Experience* (New York: Scribners, 1965), pp. 305–306.

78. From Chapter 1, Part Two. Putnam's remark here about "when we are allowed to use words like 'know,' 'objective,' 'fact,' and 'reason'" echoes Wittgenstein's remark that "if the words 'language,' 'experience,' 'world' have a use, it must be as humble a one as that of the words 'table,' 'lamp,' 'door'" (*Philosophical Investigations,* no. 97). It is also worth contrasting the attitude toward our ordinary linguistic practice embodied in what Putnam calls Rorty's "philosophical revisionism" with the attitude expressed in the following passage from Wittgenstein: "Philosophy may in no way interfere with the actual use of language; it can in the end only describe it.

"For it cannot give it any foundation either.

"It leaves everything as it is" (*Philosophical Investigations,* no. 124).

79. Putnam, *Many Faces of Realism,* p. 13.

80. Ibid., p. 84. Putnam briefly explores the parallels between Wittgenstein and Husserl in Chapter 3 of the present volume.

81. Wittgenstein's remark can be found in Lecture XXV of *Wittgenstein's Lectures on the Foundations of Mathematics,* ed. Cora Diamond. Putnam invokes this remark in Part Two of Chapter 1. The context of the remark runs as follows: "If we then translate the words 'It is true . . .' by 'A reality corresponds to . . .'—then to say a reality corresponds to them would say only that we affirm some mathematical propositions and deny others . . . If this is all that is meant by saying that a reality corresponds to mathematical propositions, it would come to saying nothing at all, a mere truism: if we leave out the question of *how* it corresponds, or in what sense it corresponds.

"We have here a thing which constantly happens. The words in our language have all sorts of uses; some very ordinary uses which come into one's mind immediately, and then again they have uses which are more and more remote . . . So you forget where the expression 'a reality corresponds to' is really at home—what is 'reality'? We think of 'reality' as something we can *point* to. It is *this, that*" (pp. 239–240).

Wittgenstein summarizes the aim of this discussion of "reality" in the following aphorism from the *Remarks on the Foundations of Mathematics:* "Not empiricism and yet realism in philosophy, that is the hardest thing" (revised edition, Cambridge, Mass.: MIT Press, 1988, p. 325). Cora Diamond (in her essay cited in note 61) makes this remark the centerpiece of her interpretation of the later Wittgenstein. Partially because of the influence of Diamond's essay, an appeal to the sense of "realism" at play in this remark—in which realism can be understood as a posture Wittgenstein aspires to achieve—plays a critical role in Putnam's claim that his own "realism with a small 'r'" inherits an aspiration (to achieve a certain perspective on the ordinary) which he finds in Wittgenstein's later writings.

82. Putnam, *The Many Faces of Realism*, pp. 4–5.

83. I am drawing here on remarks from the second paragraph of Chapter 8 of this volume.

84. Wittgenstein, *The Blue and Brown Books* (New York: Harper and Row, 1965), p. 18.

85. Chapter 1 of this volume, Part Two, fifth paragraph.

86. Chapter 7, penultimate paragraph.

87. Rorty, *Consequences of Pragmatism*, pp. 176, 177.

88. Ibid., p. 177.

89. *Philosophical Investigations*, no. 309.

90. Ibid., no. 115.

91. Wittgenstein offers the following image for how in philosophy one can be held captive by oneself: "A human being is *imprisoned* in a room, if the door is unlocked but opens inwards, he, however, never gets the idea of *pulling* instead of pushing against it" (*Remarks on the Foundations of Mathematics*, original edition, p. 125).

92. Rorty, *Consequences of Pragmatism*, p. 181.

93. Contrast the preceding quotation from p. 181 of Rorty (about Nietzsche and Wittgenstein) with the following remark from Cavell: "Only masters of a game, perfect slaves to that project, are in a position to establish conventions which better serve its essence. That is why deep revolutionary changes can result from attempts to conserve a project, to take it back to its idea, keep it in touch with its history . . . It is in the name of the idea of philosophy, and against a vision that it has become false to itself, or that it has stopped thinking, that such figures as . . . Nietzsche . . . and Wittgenstein seek to revolutionize philosophy" (*The Claim of Reason*, p. 121).

94. Richard Rorty, *Philosophy and the Mirror of Nature* (Princeton, N.J.: Princeton University Press, 1979), p. 378.

95. Rorty, *Consequences of Pragmatism*, p. xxxi. Rorty amplifies the terms of his charge as follows: "Cavell switches with insouciance from the narrow and professional identification of 'philosophy' with epistemology to a large sense in which one cannot escape philosophy by criticizing it, simply because any criticism of culture is to be called 'philosophy' . . . He *takes for granted* that the 'philosophical problems' with which we infect the freshman by assigning Descartes and Berkeley are something the freshman really needs—not just so that he can understand history, but so that he can be in touch with himself, with his own humanity" (p. 181).

96. *Philosophical Investigations*, no. 255.

97. *Philosophical Investigations,* no. 133: "There is not *a* philosophical method, though there are indeed methods, like different therapies."

98. My translation from p. 410 of *The Big Typescript;* reprinted in *Revue Internationale de Philosophie,* 43 (1989), no. 169.

99. *Philosophical Investigations,* no. 131.

100. The penultimate paragraph of Chapter 1 offers an example of the temptation to latch onto a counterassertion: "In this situation it is a temptation to say, 'So we make the world,' or 'our language makes up the world,' or 'our culture makes up the world'; but this is just another form of the same mistake. If we succumb, once again we view the world—the only world we know—as a *product.* One kind of philosopher views it as a product from a raw material: Unconceptualized Reality. The other views it as a creation *ex nihilo.*"

101. Putnam, *Representation and Reality,* p. 6.

102. Ibid., p. 109.

103. *Philosophical Investigations,* no. 308.

104. I say "can *seem* to be a purely negative one" because, of course, the experience of attaining such elucidatory insight—loosening the grip of a picture that held one captive—can be a liberating one. An initial sense of deprivation often gives way to a sense of having attained new resources of self-understanding and a sense of newly won freedom outside the conditions that had formerly been imposed through one's attachment to a fantasy. It is an experience not of loss, but of conversion: a shifting of one's senses of significance and reality.

105. From the dust jacket for Stanley Cavell's *Conditions Handsome and Unhandsome.*

106. Putnam, *Realism and Reason,* p. 180.

107. Cavell, *Must We Mean What We Say?* p. 219.

108. Ibid., p. xviii.

109. Putnam, *Realism and Reason,* p. 180.

110. Ibid.

111. Ibid.

112. Ibid., p. 179. This topic is linked for Putnam with questions surrounding the relationship between philosophy and literature. This is also another connection in which he sees Cavell's work as helping to point the way: "For Cavell it is a matter of course that philosophy needs arguments (that is why it is impossible to assimilate his work to 'Continental philosophy' in the current French mode); but it is also a matter of course that argument without cultural vision is empty (which is why it is impossible to assimilate him to present-day 'analytic philosophy'). If a philosopher aims at getting across a vision of what our culture might be, what we might be, then he cannot express his thought in neat formulas (any philosophy that can be put in a nutshell belongs there). For Cavell, the fact that literature and argument have come to be seen as opposed is itself a cultural tragedy. The practice of seeing literature and argument as opposed is tragically mistaken, and not just because 'literature' (as usually conceived) and 'argument' (as usually conceived) can be mutually supportive; it is that seeing them as opposed (or as at best irrelevant to one another) leads us to have distorted conceptions of both argument and literature" ("An Introduction to Stanley Cavell").

113. From Chapter 7 of this volume.

114. Stanley Cavell, *The World Viewed* (Cambridge, Mass.: Harvard University Press, 1980), p. 112.

115. Chapter 1, Part Two, second paragraph.

116. Ibid., sixth paragraph.

117. Ibid., sixth paragraph.

118. Cavell, *Themes out of School*, p. 9.

119. Arnold Davidson, *London Review of Books,* December 20, 1984, pp. 17–18. The review is reprinted under the title "Beginning Cavell" in *The Senses of Stanley Cavell,* p. 234.

120. Ibid., p. 237.

121. "An Interview with Hilary Putnam," p. 90.

122. Cavell, *Must We Mean What We Say?,* p. 46.

123. Cavell writes that, when pressed to justify a claim at which it has arrived, "a critical position will finally rest upon calling a claim *obvious*" (ibid., p. 311). The integrity of such a procedure is rendered particularly suspect when a claim to obviousness is interpreted as a claim to certainty, as Cavell suggests has often happened in the history of modern epistemology: the "effect has been to distrust conviction rather than to investigate the concept of the obvious" (p. 312). Putnam's recent work explicitly declares that it seeks to restore our capacities for conviction from the corrosive effect of this history.

124. Ibid., p. 312. Hence also Wittgenstein's remark: "Philosophy simply puts everything before us, and neither explains nor deduces anything.—Since everything lies open to view there is nothing to explain. For what is hidden, for example, is of no interest to us" (*Philosophical Investigations,* no. 126).

125. From Chapter 11 of this volume.

126. Ibid.

127. See the third paragraph of "Taking Rules Seriously," Chapter 13 of this volume. In "An Interview with Hilary Putnam," Putnam remarks: "Part of Wittgenstein's appeal to me is that he is a writer as much as a philosopher" (p. 91).

128. Putnam, *Meaning and the Moral Sciences,* p. 86.

129. From Chapter 8 of this volume.

130. From Chapter 16 of this volume.

131. William James, *Pragmatism* (Cambridge, Mass.: Harvard University Press, 1978), p. 11.

132. Ibid.

133. In Chapter 16.

134. "An Interview with Hilary Putnam," p. 90.

135. Cavell, *The Claim of Reason,* p. 125.

136. From Chapter 1, Part Two.

137. Especially Chapters 11 and 12.

138. From Chapter 11 of this volume. The reference is to a passage in which Cavell describes C. L. Stevenson as suffering from "an amnesia of the very concept of justice" (*The Claim of Reason,* p. 283).

139. *Philosophical Investigations,* no. 19.

140. Putnam, *The Many Faces of Realism,* p. 85.

141. *Philosophical Investigations,* no. 217.

142. Putnam, *The Many Faces of Realism,* p. 91. It is therefore significant for

Putnam that Cavell's reflection on what is involved in the activity of imagining a form of life insists relentlessly upon a use of the first-person singular: "In philosophizing, *I* have to bring *my* own language and life into imagination. What *I* require is a convening of *my* culture's criteria, in order to confront them with *my* words and life as *I* pursue them and as *I* may imagine them; and at the same time to confront *my* words and life as *I* pursue them with the life *my* culture's words may imagine for *me:* to confront the culture with itself, along the lines in which it meets in *me*."

143. Saul Kripke, *Wittgenstein on Rules and Private Language* (Cambridge, Mass.: Harvard University Press, 1982), p. 146.

144. Chapter 1, Part Two, note 19.

145. See *Philosophical Investigations*, p. 230.

146. Cavell, *The Claim of Reason*, pp. 110–111.

147. Stanley Cavell, "Declining Decline: Wittgenstein as a Philosopher of Culture," in *This New Yet Unapproachable America* (Chicago: University of Chicago Press, 1989), p. 41.

148. Ibid., p. 41.

149. *Philosophical Investigations*, no. 241.

150. Cavell, *The Claim of Reason*, p. 32.

151. *The Brown Book*, p. 93.

152. Putnam, *The Many Faces of Realism*, p. 85.

153. Cavell, "The Argument of the Ordinary: Scenes of Instruction in Kripke and Wittgenstein," *op. cit.*

154. From Chapter 1, Part Two.

155. Cavell, *The Claim of Reason*, pp. 124–125.

156. Ibid., p. 125.

157. Ibid. Cavell continues: "The anxiety in teaching, in serious communication, is that I myself require education. And for grownups this is not natural growth, but *change*."

158. I would like to thank Steven Affeldt, Bill Bristow, Stanley Cavell, Cora Diamond, Mary Ellen Geer, and Lindsay Waters for their comments on earlier drafts of this introduction.

1. Realism with a Human Face

1. This is denied, however, by the so-called Many-Worlds Interpretation of quantum mechanics, which is discussed later in this chapter.

2. J. von Neumann, *Mathematical Foundations of Quantum Mechanics* (Princeton, N. J.: Princeton University Press, 1955). I interpret von Neumann's interpretation in my "Quantum Mechanics and the Observer," chapter 14 of *Realism and Reason* (Cambridge: Cambridge University Press, 1975), which is volume 3 of my *Philosophical Papers*.

3. In what follows, I am deliberately identifying states with their descriptions to simplify the exposition.

4. The defense to the objection described in the texts is von Neumann's. Bohr himself would have said that the transition $A \longrightarrow A^{\#}$ is a purely formal one,

which has no meaning apart from a particular experimental situation. If the experimental situation is that a measurement is made at time t to find out if the atom decayed or not, then the appropriate classical picture is that the atom was already in state A or in state B (that is, it had already emitted radiation or it had not) and the measurement finds out which; but this is *only* a "classical picture," albeit the one appropriate to *that* experimental situation. The question "But what state is the atom in at time t if *no* measurement is made?" is scientifically meaningless, in Bohr's view.

5. Hugh Everett, "'Relative State' Formulation of Quantum Mechanics," in B. S. De Witt and N. Graham, *The Many-Worlds Interpretation of Quantum Mechanics* (Princeton, N.J.: Princeton University Press, 1973).

6. More precisely, the Dirac equation, or whatever successor that equation may have when quantum mechanics and relativity theory are finally reconciled.

7. Strictly speaking, the states A and B would have to be replaced by appropriate states of the entire cosmological universe in this argument, on the Many-Worlds Interpretation.

8. Hans Reichenbach, *Philosophical Foundations of Quantum Mechanics* (Berkeley: University of California Press, 1948).

9. Actually, another problem remains with the Many-Worlds Interpretation: namely, the difficulty of interpreting the notion of probability if all possible worlds are equally "real."

10. This has been proposed by Itamar Pitowski. See his communication in *Physical Review Letters*, 48 (1982): 1299.

11. Strictly speaking, this sentence is paradoxical only on the supposition that (1) every Cretan other than the speaker tells at least one lie—otherwise the sentence is straightforwardly false; and (2) the speaker himself always utters the truth, with the possible exception of this one occasion—otherwise, if the first supposition holds, the sentence is straightforwardly true. It is to avoid these empirical suppositions that the paradox needs to be reformulated as it is above.

12. A. Tarski, "The Concept of Truth in Formalized Languages" (1933), reprinted in his *Logic, Semantics, Metamathematics* (Oxford: Oxford University Press, 1956), pp. 152–278.

13. Charles Parsons, "The Liar Paradox," in *Philosophy in Mathematics* (Ithaca, N.Y.: Cornell University Press, 1987).

14. For example, if I am sincerely convinced that I had eggs for breakfast, it makes sense to ask if I am right, but no sense to ask if I have a "justification."

15. Readers of *Reason, Truth, and History* (Cambridge: Cambridge University Press, 1981) will recognize that each of these principles played a role in the argument of that book.

16. Richard Rorty, *Consequences of Pragmatism* (Minneapolis: University of Minnesota Press, 1982), p. xxxvii.

17. See Ralph Barton Perry, *The Thought and Character of William James* (Boston: Little, Brown, 1935), vol. 2, p. 575. For a criticism of Perry's partial concession to Mussolini's view see Peter Skagestad's "Pragmatism and the Closed Society: A Juxtaposition of Charles Peirce and George Orwell," in *Philosophy and Social Criticism*, 2 (1986): 307–329.

18. *The Claim of Reason* (Oxford: Oxford University Press, 1979), p. 125.

19. Something like this view is ascribed to Wittgenstein in Kripke's *Wittgenstein on Rules and Private Language* (Cambridge, Mass.: Harvard University Press, 1982). In conversation, Stanley Cavell has suggested to me that this makes it sound as if Wittgenstein thought that truth and warrant are a matter of etiquette—wanting to find a justified (or a true) hypothesis is like wanting to use the same fork my "cultural peers" use, on such a story. But Wittgenstein would not have thought *this* is a description of *our* form of life at all.

20. Ludwig Wittgenstein, *Wittgenstein's Lectures on Mathematics*, ed. Cora Diamond (Oxford: Blackwell, 1971), Lecture 25. The remark "thises and thats we can point to" is from this lecture.

21. Hans Reichenbach, *Philosophy of Space and Time* (New York: Dover, 1958).

22. Morton White, *Towards Reunion in Philosophy* (Cambridge, Mass.: Harvard University Press, 1956).

2. A Defense of Internal Realism

1. Hartry Field, "Realism and Relativism," *Journal of Philosophy*, 79 (1982): 553–567.

2. I in no way mean to suggest that "*p* is true" is *synonymous with* "*p* is part of what I accept," on the redundancy theory of truth; but, on that theory of truth, "*p* is true" is just what one *says* (without thereby ascribing any substantive *property* to the assertion *p*) whenever *p* is part of what one accepts.

3. Gilbert Harman, *The Nature of Morality* (Oxford: Oxford University Press, 1977); John Mackie, *Ethics: Inventing Right and Wrong* (London: Penguin Books, 1977).

4. "Metaphysical Realism and Moral Relativism: Reflections on Hilary Putnam's *Reason, Truth, and History*," *Journal of Philosophy*, 79 (1982): 568–574. Harman writes, "We suppose that in the end the same basic principles underlie everyone's reasoning, in the way that the same grammar may underlie the speech of different speakers who have different vocabularies and different skills at speaking" (p. 570). I reply to this argument that the notion of an "underlying" principle which is here appealed to (like the Chomskian competence/performance distinction on which it seems to be based) is just the notion of a best idealization or best explanation, and that Harman owes us a reason to believe that *these* are physicalistic notions.

5. I argue that these notions are not physicalistic in "Why Reason Can't Be Naturalized" and "Beyond Historicism," chaps. 13 and 16 of Hilary Putnam, *Realism and Reason* (Cambridge: Cambridge University Press, 1975).

6. "Metaphysical Realism and Moral Relativism," pp. 569, 573. The phrase Harman uses is "a single causal and explanatory order."

7. The suggestion was first advanced (but only to reject it!) by G. H. Merrill.

8. I argue that vagueness is a phenomenon for which metaphysical realism has no successful account to offer in "Vagueness and Alternative Logic," chap. 15 of *Realism and Reason*.

3. After Empiricism

1. This essay was originally published in *Partisan Review*, 54 (1984): 265–275, as a discussion of Ayer's *Philosophy in the Twentieth Century* (London: Weidenfeld and Nicolson, 1982).

2. Where Ayer goes wrong is in charging Armstrong with denying that perception involves mental representation. Armstrong is a direct realist who denies that the *object* of perception is a mental representation. This, however, is not to deny the fact of consciousness (or the existence of mental representations) altogether. Armstrong's direct realism is reminiscent of the view of William James that I discuss in Chapter 17 of this volume.

3. A more detailed account of my objection to contemporary materialist appeals to the relation of "causal connection" is offered in Chapter 5 of this volume.

4. Is Water Necessarily H₂O?

1. The conference on "Levels of Reality" took place in the late 1970s; the proceedings were published in Italian but have never appeared in English. See Massimo Piattelli-Palmarini, *Livelli di realtà* (Milan: Feltrinelli, 1984).

2. See my paper "Possibility and Necessity," in Hilary Putnam, *Realism and Reason* (Cambridge: Cambridge University Press, 1975), esp. pp. 63–64.

3. I shall stick to high school chemistry because the actual quantum-mechanical picture of the structure of water is immensely complicated.

4. See my paper "The Analytic and the Synthetic," reprinted in Hilary Putnam, *Mind, Language, and Reality* (Cambridge: Cambridge University Press, 1975), pp. 33–69. This was originally published in *Scientific Explanation, Space, and Time*, ed. Herbert Feigl and Grover Maxwell (Minneapolis: University of Minnesota Press, 1962).

5. See my paper "Brains and Behavior," first published in *Readings in Analytical Philosophy*, 2nd series, ed. R. Butler (Oxford: Blackwell, 1963); reprinted in Putnam, *Mind, Language, and Reality*, pp. 325–341. See especially the footnote on p. 328.

6. Reprinted in Putnam, *Mind, Language, and Reality*, pp. 139–152.

7. This paper appeared originally in Keith Gundersen, *Language, Mind, and Knowledge*, vol. 7 of *Minnesota Studies in the Philosophy of Science* (Minneapolis: University of Minnesota Press, 1975), and was reprinted in Putnam, *Mind, Language, and Reality*, pp. 215–271.

8. On the last page of *Philosophy in the Twentieth Century* (New York: Random House, 1982), Ayer gives a thought experiment to *show* that it is logically possible that water is not H₂O: "Suppose that in some part of this world we came upon stuff which had the chemical composition H₂O but did not have the properties of falling as rain, allaying thirst, quenching fire, and so forth, perhaps even failed to appear in liquid form." I would reply that *this is conceivable but not possible*. If the question is, "What would you say if we actually discovered that composition is not what determines behavior," the answer is that *I would say*

that my view was wrong—I never claimed that it was *a priori*! If we discover that substances with identical composition can obey different laws, then our whole picture of the world—not just our philosophy—will have to be revised. A case that would be closer to my own reasons for becoming skeptical about "metaphysical possibility" is the following: suppose Ayer had stipulated that in the actual world water *is* H_2O and composition *does* determine behavior, but then went on to ask what I would say about a *possible* world in which composition does not determine behavior and some H_2O does not fall as rain, allay thirst, quench fires, and so forth? Would that *hypothetical* stuff still be water? Kripke would apparently answer "yes"; but this seems to me a case in which the answer is utterly arbitrary.

9. As I explained in "Possibility and Necessity," I would identify "possible situations" in a given context with states of affairs relative to some specified language (what Carnap calls "state descriptions"). This relativization of the notion of a possible situation to a language is something Kripke would reject.

10. Kripke appears to think that the only available notion of a criterion is of something that is exceptionless, unrevisable, and can be known *a priori*. I don't at all agree that this is the most illuminating use of the notion, but it would take us away from the topic to discuss this here.

11. And I don't claim that the condition of adequacy is *a priori* either!

12. For example, if the scientist tells a layman that 50 percent of the liquid in the glass he has just drunk is actually a (harmless) chemical that does not occur as a constituent of normal water, the layman will *not* say, "Well, it tasted like water and—you tell me—it didn't poison me, so it *is* water." The "man on the street" is not that instrumentalist. The chemist can convince the layman (sometimes) that something isn't water *even in the lay sense*, where this is not something that the layman could determine by "ordinary" nonscientific criteria. This is why I say that the lay sense and the scientific sense are *interdependent—different but interdependent*.

13. I believe that Nathan Salmon was the first to argue that this is the case, in "How *Not* to Derive Essentialism from the Theory of Reference," *Journal of Philosophy*, 76 (1979): 703–774.

14. Further examples occur in my paper "Possibility and Necessity."

15. It may be objected that the Greeks (who, of course, used the word *hydor,* which is cognate to our present *water*) did not have *our* concept of a physical law. That is, of course, true. But they did have an implicit notion that all samples of a pure substance must behave in the same way—that is what underlay Archimedes' search for a way to tell if the King's crown was gold: he assumed that if it was gold it would behave the same way under a density test as the known paradigms of gold. And the Greeks believed that the behavior of a substance depended upon its *ultimate* composition. These ideas were refined into something close to our present notions of a law and of a microstructure by the time of Newton—well *before* anyone knew that water is H_2O. The nineteenth-century chemists already had this criterion of substance-identity in place when they discovered that water is H_2O. (Philosophers of science who reject this account have a notorious tendency to describe this discovery as a case of meaning-stipulation.)

16. I ignore the thorny problem of "Meaning Postulates." On this, the *locus*

classicus is, of course, Quine's "Two Dogmas of Empiricism," in W. V. Quine, *From a Logical Point of View,* 2nd ed. (Cambridge, Mass.: Harvard University Press, 1961), pp. 20–46.

17. See G. E. M. Anscombe, "Causality and Determination," in *The Collected Papers of G. E. M. Anscombe,* vol. 2, *Metaphysics and the Philosophy of Mind* (Minneapolis: University of Minnesota Press, 1981), pp. 133–147.

18. I am not ascribing to Ayer the view that causal statements can be translated into regularity statements. The view I would ascribe to him—the Humean view—is compatible with the idea that there can be other elements in a causal description as well—for example, information about the epistemic status of certain regularities—but those elements are not "objective" in the sense of being independent of the evidence available to the speaker.

19. I should also list "material objects," because Ayer accepts an inference to these. It is not clear to me, however, whether their existence comes to more than the fact that *theories which posit them correctly predict sense experiences,* in Ayer's current view.

5. Is the Causal Structure of the Physical Itself Something Physical?

1. For example, Hilary Putnam (one of my former selves), "Reference and Understanding," in *Meaning and the Moral Sciences* (London: Routledge and Kegan Paul, 1978), pp. 97–122. In my present view, this is a correct account (of what goes on in us when we understand a language) at one level of description but not at another. It *is* the correct account at the computational level (describing the brain as if it were a computer), but not at the intentional level. In my present view, intentional predicates, for example, "is speaking a language," "means that there are a lot of cats in the neighborhood," "understands those words," are not reducible to computational or computational-cum-physical predicates any more than physical predicates are reducible to phenomenal ones. See, for example, my *Representation and Reality* (Cambridge, Mass.: MIT Press, 1988).

2. Richard Boyd, "Materialism without Reductionism: What Physicalism Does Not Entail," in *Readings in the Philosophy of Psychology,* ed. Ned Block (Cambridge, Mass.: Harvard University Press, 1980), pp. 67–106.

3. Hilary Putnam, *Reason, Truth, and History* (Cambridge: Cambridge University Press, 1981), chap. 2 and appendix.

4. Review of work cited in note 3, in *Philosophy and Phenomenological Research,* 45 (June 1985): 644–649.

5. David Lewis, "Putnam's Paradox," *Australasian Journal of Philosophy,* 62 (September 1984): 221–236.

6. Donald Davidson, "A Coherence Theory of Truth and Knowledge," in *Truth and Interpretation,* ed. E. Le Pore (Oxford: Blackwell, 1986), pp. 307–319.

7. In Michael Devitt, *Realism and Truth* (Princeton, N.J.: Princeton University Press, 1984). See esp. p. 189.

8. Clark Glymour, "Conceptual Scheming or Confessions of a Metaphysical Realist," *Synthese,* 51 (1982): 169–180.

9. Some readers have found this paragraph unclear. The problem I am point-ing out is the following: Suppose we grant Devitt and Glymour that the words "causal connection" stand in the relation C (causal connection) to C itself (this would, by the way, require a change in the axioms of set theory). Then (given the changed set theory) model theoretic arguments will show that there are infinitely many other relations C', C'', . . . such that the words "causal connection" stand in each of those relations to the relation itself (that is, being connected to R by R is not a *distinguishing* characteristic of C). The crucial assumption that Devitt and Glymour are making about C is not that C has this formal characteristic, but that C is capable of fixing reference (while C', C'', . . . are not). But this assumed fact that one relation is *intrinsically* capable of fixing reference is just what I find unintelligible.

10. J. L. Mackie, *The Cement of the Universe* (Oxford: Oxford University Press, 1974), pp. 60–64.

11. Nelson Goodman, *Fact, Fiction, and Forecast,* 4th ed. (Cambridge, Mass.: Harvard University Press, 1982), chap. 1.

12. W. V. Quine, *Ontological Relativity and Other Essays* (New York: Colum-bia University Press, 1969), chap. 5.

13. W. V. Quine, *Word and Object* (Cambridge, Mass.: MIT Press, 1960), pp. 33–34.

14. More precisely, it is to say that the word "cat" belongs to a certain recur-sively defined set of ordered pairs that includes the pair consisting of the word spelled 'c'-'a'-'t' and the set of cats. The statement *'cat' refers to cats* is a logical consequence of *'cat' is spelled 'c'-'a'-'t' and the set of cats is the set of cats* when the "disquotational" definition of reference is applied. Note that this is not at all a correct logical consequence of the intuitive notion of "reference."

6. Truth and Convention

1. See Hilary Putnam, *Reason, Truth, and History* (Cambridge: Cambridge University Press, 1981).

2. This example comes from Hilary Putnam, *The Many Faces of Realism,* Carus Lectures (LaSalle, Ill.: Open Court, 1987).

3. ". . . (dem) mathematischen Punkte, der einfach, aber kein Teil, sondern bloss die Grenze eines Raumes ist" (Immanuel Kant, *Kritik der reinen Vernunft,* B470); note also the flat statement "Nun besteht der Raum nicht aus einfachen Teilen sondern aus Räumen" (ibid., B463). Both remarks occur on the "Antith-esis" side of the Second Antinomy.

4. W. V. Quine, "On What There Is" (1953), in Quine, *From a Logical Point of View,* 2nd ed. (Cambridge, Mass.: Harvard University Press, 1961).

5. See Donald Davidson, *Truth and Interpretation* (Oxford: Oxford Univer-sity Press, 1984).

6. For example, even the truth-functional connectives are not preserved if we "translate" (1) as (2).

7. See Donald Davidson, "The Very Idea of a Conceptional Scheme," col-lected in Davidson, *Truth and Interpretation.*

7. Why Is a Philosopher?

1. Richard Rorty. See Richard Rorty, *Philosophy and the Mirror of Nature* (Princeton, N.J.: Princeton University Press, 1979) and Rorty, *Consequences of Pragmatism* (Minneapolis: University of Minnesota Press, 1982).

2. See Hilary Putnam, *Reason, Truth, and History* (Cambridge: Cambridge University Press, 1982) and Putnam, *Realism and Reason* (Cambridge: Cambridge University Press, 1983).

3. See Michael Foucault, *The Order of Things* (New York: Vintage Books, 1970), especially the concluding discussion of the human sciences.

4. See the works cited in note 1.

5. For a more detailed discussion see Hilary Putnam, *Reason, Truth, and History,* especially chap. 5, and "Why Reason Can't Be Naturalized," in *Realism and Reason.*

6. On this, see "The Meaning of 'Meaning,'" in Hilary Putnam, *Mind, Language, and Reality* (Cambridge: Cambridge University Press, 1975); see also "Explanation and Reference" in the same volume.

7. See Saul Kripke, *Naming and Necessity* (Cambridge, Mass.: Harvard University Press, 1982; lectures given at Princeton University in 1972).

8. See my paper "Models and Reality" in Hilary Putnam, *Realism and Reason* (first published in *Journal of Symbolic Logic,* 45 [1980]: 464–482).

9. See W. V. Quine, *Ontological Relativity and Other Essays* (New York: Columbia University Press, 1969).

10. Edward N. Lee, "Hoist with His Own Petard," in *Exegesis and Argument: Studies in Greek Philosophy Presented to Gregory Vlastos,* ed. E. N. Lee, A. P. D. Mourelatos, and R. M. Rorty (Assen: Van Gorcum, 1973).

11. See the essay titled "Realism and Reason" in Hilary Putnam, *Meaning and the Moral Sciences* (London: Routledge and Kegan Paul, 1976).

12. See Michael Dummett, "What Is a Theory of Meaning? II," in *Truth and Meaning,* ed. G. Evans and J. McDowell (Oxford: Oxford University Press, 1976).

8. The Craving for Objectivity

1. Stanley Cavell, *The Claim of Reason* (Oxford: Oxford University Press, 1979).

2. See A. I. Sabra, "Avicenna on the Subject Matter of Logic," *Journal of Philosophy,* 77 (November 1980): 748–763.

3. Edward N. Lee, "Hoist with His Own Petard," in *Exegesis and Argument: Studies in Greek Philosophy Presented to Gregory Vlastos,* ed. E. N. Lee, A. P. D. Mourelatos, and R. M. Rorty (Assen: Van Gorcum, 1973), pp. 225–261. The quotations are from pp. 247–250.

4. See Donald Davidson, "On the Very Idea of a Conceptual Scheme," *Proceedings and Addresses of the American Philosophical Association,* 47 (1974): 5–20. Collected in Davidson, *Truth and Interpretation* (Oxford: Oxford University Press, 1984).

5. Thomas Kuhn, "Reflections on My Critics," in *Criticism and Growth of*

Knowledge, ed. Imre Lakotas and Alan Musgrave (Cambridge: Cambridge University Press, 1970), pp. 231–278. Kuhn writes that his *Structure of Scientific Revolutions* (Chicago: University of Chicago Press, 2nd ed., 1970) does contain a preliminary codification of good reasons for theory choice. "These are . . . reasons of exactly the kind standard in philosophy of science: accuracy, scope, simplicity, fruitfulness, and the like" (p. 231).

6. See Richard Rorty, *Philosophy and the Mirror of Nature* (Princeton, N.J.: Princeton University Press, 1979).

7. Thomas Kuhn, "A Formalism for Scientific Change," paper delivered to the Fifth International Congress of Logic, Methodology, and Philosophy of Science, August 28, 1975. Reprinted as "Theory-Change as Structure-Change," *Erkenntnis,* 10 (July 1976): 179–199. See Joseph D. Sneed, *The Logical Structure of Mathematical Physics* (Boston: Dordrecht, 1971), and Wolfgang Stegmüller, *Theorie und Erfahrung* (Berlin: Springer Verlag, 1973).

8. Paul de Man, "Dialogue and Dialogism," paper delivered by de Man to the Modern Language Association, New York, December 29, 1981; published in *Poetics Today,* 4 (1983): 99–107. Both my quotations are from p. 105.

9. Beyond the Fact/Value Dichotomy

1. See Frank Plumpton Ramsey, Epilogue ("There Is Nothing to Discuss") in *Foundations of Mathematics,* ed. R. B. Braithewaite (New York: Harcourt Brace, 1931), pp. 291–292.

2. Hilary Putnam, *Reason, Truth, and History* (Cambridge: Cambridge University Press, 1981).

3. See Richard Rorty, *Philosophy and the Mirror of Nature* (Princeton, N.J.: Princeton University Press, 1979).

10. The Place of Facts in a World of Values

1. See Jacques Ellul, *The New Demons* (New York: Seabury Press, 1975).

2. I quote here from an unpublished paper.

3. See the Epilogue in Frank Ramsey, *The Foundations of Mathematics,* ed. R. B. Braithewaite (New York: Harcourt Brace, 1931), pp. 291–292.

4. Yehuda Elkana, "Science as a Cultural System," three (unpublished) lectures delivered to the Boston Colloquium in the Philosophy of Science, Fall 1976.

5. I have discussed emotivism rather than relativism (the view that moral facts are objective but relative to a "cultural framework") in these pages; but the reader will note that the poor man in this example would not be helped by this distinction. Tell him his duties are relative to the cultural framework he chooses (the framework of conventional morality or the Mafia framework) if you please; you are still saying that it's all "a choice of a way of life." The way in which recent forms of relativism continue to suffer from the problems that plagued emotivism is something I take up in the next chapter of this volume.

6. Iris Murdoch, *The Sovereignty of Good* (New York: Schocken Books, 1975).

7. Kripke's remarks were made at the Oxford International Symposium held at Christ Church College, Oxford, October 1976.

8. Reprinted as "Causality and Determination" in *Causation and Conditionals*, ed. Ernest Sosa (Oxford: Oxford University Press, 1970). It has also been reprinted in *The Collected Papers of G. E. M. Anscombe*, vol. 2, *Metaphysics and the Philosophy of Mind* (Minneapolis: University of Minnesota Press, 1981).

9. See Hilary Putnam, "Realism and Reason," presidential address to the American Philosophical Association (Eastern Division), December 1976, reprinted in Putnam, *Meaning and the Moral Sciences* (London: Routledge and Kegan Paul, 1977).

11. Objectivity and the Science/Ethics Distinction

1. Hilary Putnam, "The Corroboration of Theories," in *The Philosophy of Karl Popper*, ed. P. A. Schilpp (LaSalle, Ill.: Open Court, 1974).

2. W. V. Quine, "Two Dogmas of Empiricism," in Quine, *From a Logical Point of View*, 2nd ed. (Cambridge, Mass.: Harvard University Press, 1961).

3. Vivian Walsh, "Philosophy and Economics," in *The New Palgrave: A Dictionary of Economics*, vol. 3, ed. J. Eatwell, M. Milgte, and P. Newman (London: Macmillan Press, and New York: Stockton Press), 1987.

4. W. V. Quine, "Carnap on Logical Truth," in P. A. Schilpp, *The Philosophy of Rudolf Carnap* (LaSalle, Ill.: Open Court, 1963).

5. Hilary Putnam, *Reason, Truth, and History* (Cambridge: Cambridge University Press, 1981).

6. Bernard Williams, *Ethics and the Limits of Philosophy* (Cambridge, Mass.: Harvard University Press, 1985).

7. The philosopher whose views are closest to those of Williams is, perhaps, David Wiggins. See Wiggins, *Needs, Values, Truth* (Oxford: Oxford University Press, 1987).

8. Morton White, *Towards Reunion in Philosophy* (Cambridge, Mass.: Harvard University Press, 1956).

9. Iris Murdoch, *The Sovereignty of Good* (London: Routledge and Kegan Paul, 1971).

10. John McDowell, "Are Moral Requirements Hypothetical Imperatives?" *Proceedings of the Aristotelian Society*, suppl. vol. 52 (1978): 13–29. See also McDowell, "Virtue and Reason," *Monist*, 62 (1979): 331–350.

11. Stanley Cavell, *The Claim of Reason* (Oxford: Oxford University Press, 1979), chap. 10, "An Absence of Morality."

12. This argument is due to Kripke (in unpublished lectures).

13. David Lewis, *Counterfactuals* (Cambridge, Mass.: Harvard University Press, 1976).

14. Hilary Putnam, *The Many Faces of Realism* (La Salle, Ill.: Open Court, 1987).

15. See Putnam, *Reason, Truth, and History*.

16. See the following writings of mine: *Meaning and the Moral Sciences* (Lon-

don: Routledge and Kegan Paul, 1978); "Models and Reality," *Journal of Symbolic Logic*, 45 (1980): 464–482 (reprinted in *Realism and Reason); Reason, Truth, and History; Realism and Reason* (Cambridge: Cambridge University Press, 1983); "Information and the Mental," in *Truth and Interpretation,* ed. Ernest Lepore (Oxford: Oxford University Press, 1986); *The Many Faces of Realism; Representation and Reality* (Cambridge, Mass.: Bradford Books, a division of MIT Press, 1988); "Model Theory and the Factuality of Semantics," in *Reflections of Chomsky,* ed. Alexander George (Oxford: Blackwell, 1989).

17. Bernard Williams, *Descartes: The Project of Pure Enquiry* (Harmondsworth, Middlesex: Penguin Books, 1978).

18. For example, the argument of my *Representation and Reality.*

19. Israel Scheffler, "Teachers of My Youth," (unpublished; copyright I. Scheffler, 1987).

12. How Not to Solve Ethical Problems

1. Bernard Williams made this remark in a talk broadcast on the BBC some years ago.

2. *The Division of Labor in Society,* trans. George Simpson (The Free Press, 1933), pp. 408–409.

13. Taking Rules Seriously

1. I am referring here to Richard Wollheim's response to Nussbaum's article: Wollheim, "Flawed Crystals: James's *The Golden Bowl* and the Plausibility of Literature as Moral Philosophy," *New Literary History,* 50 (1983): 185–192; as well as to D. D. Raphael's contribution, "Can Literature Be Moral Philosophy?" (ibid., pp. 1–12). It is perhaps worth remarking that Cora Diamond offers some extremely penetrating observations on this general topic of the relation between literature and moral philosophy in her remarks on D. D. Raphael's piece in Diamond, "Having a Rough Story about What Moral Philosophy Is" (ibid., pp. 155–170; also reprinted in her volume of collected papers entitled *The Realistic Spirit,* forthcoming from MIT Press).

2. Richard Kuhns, "The Strangeness of Justice: Reading *Michael Kohlhaas,*" *New Literary History,* 50 (1983): 73–92.

14. Scientific Liberty and Scientific License

1. Doris Lessing, *The Golden Notebook* (New York: Simon and Schuster, 1982).

2. Ludwig Wittgenstein, *Philosophical Investigations,* 3rd ed., trans. G. E. M. Anscombe (New York: Macmillan, 1953), § 217.

3. Richard T. Herrnstein and James Q. Wilson, *Crime and Human Nature* (New York: Simon and Schuster, 1985).

4. Hilary Putnam, "Reductionism and the Nature of Psychology," *Cognition,* 2 (1973): 131–146.

15. Is There a Fact of the Matter about Fiction?

1. This essay was written before Davidson's articles "What Metaphors Mean" and "A Nice Derangement of Epitaphs" appeared, and therefore I do not take any subsequent revisions of his views into account here.

16. William James's Ideas

1. See, in particular, Hilary Putnam, *Reason, Truth, and History* (Cambridge: Cambridge University Press, 1981); *The Many Faces of Realism* (LaSalle, Ill.: Open Court, 1987); and the final chapter of *Representation and Reality* (Cambridge, Mass.: Bradford Books, a division of MIT Press, 1988). I also touch briefly on this issue in Chapter 9 of the present volume.

2. This remark presupposes a controversial answer to the question: which particular aspects of Russell's work was the early Wittgenstein primarily reacting to? However, we know from Wittgenstein's *Notebooks: 1914–1916* that he was familiar with (and perhaps even at one point sympathetic to) Russell's views on neutral monism.

3. I do go into these matters in Chapter 17.

17. James's Theory of Perception

1. In *The Analysis of Mind* (London: George Allen and Unwin, 1921), Russell writes: "The view that seems to me to reconcile the materialistic tendency of psychology with the antimaterialistic tendency of physics is the view of William James and the American new realists, according to which the 'stuff' of the world is neither mental nor material, but a 'neutral stuff,' out of which both are constructed. I have endeavored in this work to develop this view in some detail as regards the phenomena with which psychology is concerned" (p. 6). Russell then continues: "Their views [the 'new realists'], which are chiefly held in America, are in large measure derived from William James, and before going further it will be well to consider the revolutionary doctrine which he advocated. I believe this doctrine contains important new truth, and what I shall have to say will be in a considerable measure inspired by it" (ibid., p. 22).

2. In "William James's Ideas" (Chapter 16 of this volume) Ruth Anna Putnam and I argue that what James is offering is, in fact, a complex "imperfect procedural conception" of truth.

3. Ernest Mayr, *Evolution and the Diversity of Life* (Cambridge, Mass.: Harvard University Press, 1976).

4. *Essays in Radical Empiricism* (Cambridge, Mass.: Harvard University Press, 1976), p. 17.

5. I take it, rather, that the "we" in James's writing is supposed to include the

great majority of all human beings; and, in fact, there is no evidence that he is restricting it (and some evidence that he is not restricting it) to human beings. His famous images of cosmic struggle between good and evil, which will go on until "the last man" and which may well involve supernatural beings, if there are supernatural beings, or at any rate beings of other orders of reality (since belief in such higher orders of reality is regarded as something positive in many of James's writings, including *The Will to Believe* and *The Varieties of Religious Experience*) suggest that the relevant community is at least as inclusive as (and potentially more inclusive than) the entire human species.

6. Peter Strawson, "Perception and Its Objects," in *Perception and Identity: Essays Presented to A. J. Ayer,* ed. G. F. McDonald (Ithaca, N.Y.: Cornell University Press, 1979).

7. The answer given by the sense-datum theory is probably the answer that the man on the street accepts today, without being aware that this theory became the "obvious" one at a particular historical moment. Here Foucault is right; there is something fascinating in the phenomenon of a philosophy seeping down to the layman—the layman who thinks of himself as *anti*-philosophical, and in the way Western culture is deeply imbued not with one philosophy but with these changing philosophies.

8. See n. 1.

9. Quoted in the Editor's Introduction to William James, *Essays in Radical Empiricism,* ed. Frederick Burkhardt and Fredson Bowers (Cambridge, Mass.: Harvard University Press, 1976), p. xxvi.

10. An idea which also figures in Wittgenstein's later philosophy! See, for example, *Philosophical Investigations* (New York: MacMillan, 1953), §208.

11. Of course, James differs from the phenomenalist in another respect: he is not trying to *translate* material-object language into a different language.

12. This is how I would read the following passage from Lecture VI in James's *Essays in Radical Empiricism,* p. 141: "The stream of time can be remounted only verbally, or verified indirectly, by present prolongations or effects of what the past harbored. Yet if they agree with those verbalities and effects, we can know that our ideas of the past are true."

13. James's belief in the reality of "experienced relations," and the doctrine that one "pure experience" can be (irreducibly) *about* another "pure experience," are important disagreements with Hume. If James and Hume both have "bundle theories" of the mind, James at least has more "glue" available in his philosophy to hold such bundles together.

14. The presupposition is made less tenable, not more tenable, by identifying the "perceptual states" in question with brain states; for a moment's thought suffices to see that if "perceptual states" are supposed to correspond to *appearances,* then they *cannot* be identical with brain state *types* (two *type* brain states which are "adjacent" in a perceptual dimension will always have realizations which are much less than a threshold apart; in such a case, one will not be in the same (perceptual) brain state, but there will be no difference in the way things *appear* to one.

Although it is more difficult to argue that "token-token identity" is also a hopelessly confused idea, I believe that in fact it is.

15. Ludwig Wittgenstein, *Culture and Value,* ed. G. H. von Wright with Heikki Nyman, trans. Peter Winch (Chicago: University of Chicago Press, 1977).

18. Peirce the Logician

1. Hans Herzberger, "Peirce's Remarkable Theorem," in *Pragmatism and Purpose,* ed. L. W. Sumner, essays presented to Thomas A. Goudge (Toronto: University of Toronto Press, 1981), pp. 41–56.

2. George Boole, *Treatise on the Calculus of Finite Differences* (Cambridge: Macmillan and Co., 1860; reprinted, New York: Dover, 1960).

3. George Boole, *Treatise on Differential Equations* (Cambridge: Macmillan and Co., 1859).

4. George Boole, *An Investigation into the Laws of Thought* (Cambridge: Macmillan and Co., 1854; reprinted, New York: Dover, 1951).

5. George Boole, *The Mathematical Analysis of Logic* (Cambridge: Macmillan and Co., 1847; reprinted, Oxford: Blackwell, 1948).

6. Gottlob Frege, *Begriffsschrifft, eine der arithmetischen nachgebildete Formelsprache des reiner Denkens* (Halle: Louis Nebert, 1879).

7. O. H. Mitchell, "On a New Algebra of Logic" (1883), in *Studies in Logic by Members of the Johns Hopkins University,* ed. C. S. Peirce (Boston: Little, Brown, 1883).

8. W. V. Quine, *Methods of Logic,* 1st ed. (New York: Holt, Rinehart and Winston, 1950).

9. J. van Heijenoort, *From Frege to Gödel: A Source Book in Mathematical Logic* (Cambridge, Mass.: Harvard University Press, 1967).

10. Ernst Schröder, *Vorlesungen über die Algebra der Logik* (Leipzig: Druch and Verlag von B. G. Tenbner, 1890).

11. C. S. Peirce, *The Collected Papers of C. S. Peirce,* vols. 1–4, ed. C. Hartshorne and P. Weiss (Cambridge, Mass.: Harvard University Press, 1931–1935); vols. 7–8, ed. A. W. Burks (Cambridge, Mass.: Harvard University Press, 1958); vol. 3, paragraph 519.

12. Warren Goldfarb, "Logic in the Twenties: The Nature of the Quantifier," *Journal of Symbolic Logic,* 49 (1979): 351–368.

13. Ernst Zermelo, "Neuer Beweis für die Möglichkeit einer Wohlordnung," *Mathematishen Annalen,* p. 65 n. 9.

14. Bertrand Russell, *My Philosophical Development* (New York: Simon and Schuster, 1959).

15. A. N. Whitehead, *A Treatise on Universal Algebra with Applications* (1898), vol. 1 (Cambridge: Cambridge University Press, 1898).

16. Kurt Gödel, "Über Formel unentscheidbare Sätze der Principia Mathematica und Verwandter Systeme," I, *Monatschrifte für Mathematik und Physik,* 37 (1931): 349–360. Reprinted in van Heijenoort, *From Frege to Gödel,* pp. 596–616.

17. David Hilbert and W. Ackerman, *Grundzüge der theoretischen Logik,* 2nd ed. (Berlin: Springer, 1938); published in English as *Principles of Mathematical Logic* (New York: Chelsea, 1950).

19. The Way the World Is

1. The sources of the three following quotations are: W. V. O. Quine, "Carnap and Logical Truth," in *The Philosophy of Rudolf Carnap*, ed. P. A. Schilpp (LaSalle, Ill.: Open Court, 1963), pp. 385–406; Nelson Goodman, *Ways of Worldmaking* (Indianapolis, Ind.: Hackett, 1978), pp. 3–4; Hilary Putnam, *Reason, Truth, and History* (Cambridge: Cambridge University Press, 1981), p. 11.

2. The quote is from Quine's "Two Dogmas of Empiricism," chap. 2 of his *From a Logical Point of View* (Cambridge, Mass.: Harvard University Press, 1953), p. 42.

3. "But not much, for no one type of reducibility serves all purposes," Goodman adds in a footnote at this point.

4. E. H. Gombrich, *Art and Illusion* (New York: Bollingen Foundation, distributed by Pantheon Books, 1960), p. 33 and elsewhere.

5. Hilary Putnam, *The Many Faces of Realism* (LaSalle, Ill.: Open Court, 1987), p. 21.

6. It is partly in the service of underscoring this point that James Conant and I have chosen to collect this particular essay along with separate pieces on James, Peirce, Quine, and Goodman in a single section of the present volume under the rubric "Studies in American Philosophy."

20. The Greatest Logical Positivist

1. This essay is a review of W. V. O. Quine, *Quiddities* (Cambridge, Mass.: Harvard University Press, 1987). All page references are to this volume.

2. W. V. O. Quine, "Carnap on Logical Truth," *Synthese*, 12 (1960): 374. Reprinted in *The Philosophy of Rudolf Carnap*, ed. P. A. Schilpp (LaSalle, Ill.: Open Court, 1963).

21. Meaning Holism

1. See Frederick Suppe, ed., *The Structure of Scientific Theories* (Urbana, Ill.: University of Illinois Press, 1974), for a good description of the rise and fall of the "partially interpreted calculus" account of scientific theories.

2. See Jane English's excellent paper, "Partial Interpretation and Meaning Change," reprinted in *The Philosopher's Annual,* vol. 2, ed. Boyer, Grim, and Sanders (Alascadero, Calif.: Ridgeview, 1979).

3. "The Meaning of 'Meaning'" is reprinted in Hilary Putnam, *Mind, Language, and Reality* (Cambridge: Cambridge University Press, 1978).

4. See Hilary Putnam, "Two Dogmas Revisited," in *Contemporary Aspects of Philosophy*, ed. Gilbert Ryle (Boston: Oriel Press, 1976) for an elaboration of this point. This paper was reprinted in Putnam, *Realism and Reason* (Cambridge: Cambridge University Press, 1982).

5. This is a good opportunity to refute the suggestion (made by Saul Kripke in *Naming and Necessity* [Cambridge, Mass.: Harvard University Press, 1980]) that I once thought it was *analytic* that most (or even *some*) of the laws connected with a law-cluster word must be true for the word to have an extension. I wrote

in 1960 that "I mean not only that *each* criterion can be regarded as synthetic, but also that the cluster is *collectively* synthetic, in the sense that we are free in certain cases to say (for reasons of inductive simplicity and theoretical economy) that the term applies although the whole cluster is missing. This is completely compatible with saying that the cluster serves to fix the meaning of the word. The point is that when we specify something by a cluster of indicators we assume that people will *use their brains*. That criteria may be over-ridden when what good sense demands is the sort of thing we may regard as a 'convention associated with discourse' (Grice) rather than as something to be stipulated in connection with the individual words" (*Mind, Language, and Reality* [Cambridge: Cambridge University Press, 1975], p. 328). That the cluster which "fixes the meaning" may change without our saying that the "meaning" has changed was pointed out in my 1957 paper "The Analytic and the Synthetic," reprinted as chap. 2 of *Mind, Language, and Reality.*

6. Suppose, for example, we discovered that vixens are telepathic. If we thought that they were the only telepathic animals, then "vixens are telepathic animals" might come to be even more central than "vixens are female foxes." And if we then discovered a male telepathic fox, we might very well say "a few male foxes are vixens."

7. In Putnam, "The Analytic and the Synthetic."

8. See Jerry A. Fodor, *The Language of Thought* (Cambridge, Mass.: Harvard University Press, 1975). Noam Chomsky has never committed himself to the possibility of finding "psychologically real" entities which have enough of the properties we pretheoretically assign to "meanings" to warrant an identification. The "representations" and "innate ideas" of which Chomsky writes are deep *syntactic* structures and *syntactic* universals; Fodor's program is thus not identical with Chomsky's, but rather is a daring extension of it.

9. Jerry A. Fodor, "Cognitive Science and the Twin-Earth Problem," *Notre Dame Journal of Formal Logic,* 23 (1982): 98–118.

10. To say, as Schiffer did in "Intention Based Semantics" (*Notre Dame Journal of Formal Logic,* 23 [1982]: 119–156) that Gricean beliefs and intentions are functional states of the organism-cum-environment is no help at all. Given the informal and context-sensitive nature of our interpretative practice, we have no reason to think that even *one* such state could be defined in finitely many words, that it would not be infinitely disjunctive, that the disjunction would not fail to be effectively specifiable (as in the phenomenalism case), and so forth. (Schiffer now agrees with this criticism; see his *Remnants of Meaning* [Cambridge, Mass.: MIT Press, 1987.])

11. "I Want You to Bring Me a Slab," *Synthese,* 56 (September 1983): 265–282.

22. *Nelson Goodman's* Fact, Fiction, and Forecast

1. See Fodor's and Chomsky's comments in *Language and Learning,* ed. Massimo Piatelli-Palmarini (Cambridge, Mass.: Harvard University Press, 1980), pp. 259–261, for example.

2. The reading Elgin has in mind is due to Saul Kripke; see his *Wittgenstein on Rules and Private Language* (Cambridge, Mass.: Harvard University Press, 1982).

3. For example, in Carnap's systems, relative to the evidence "x has length between 0 and 1," the degree of confirmation of the hypothesis "x has length between 0 and ½" is 0.5 if "length" is primitive, but 0.25 if "length squared" is primitive. This is so because the hypothesis can be rewritten as "the square of the length of x is between 0 and ¼."

4. From Wesley C. Salmon, "Russell on Scientific Inference," in *Bertrand Russell's Philosophy*, ed. G. Nakhnikian (New York: Barnes and Noble, 1974), p. 10.

5. I have here shifted from Goodman's definition of grue to one proposed by Stephen Barker and Peter Achinstein, which can be used to make the same points.

6. See Goodman's discussion in Goodman, *Languages of Art*, 2nd ed. (Indianapolis, Ind.: Hackett, 1976), pp. 100–101.

7. See especially Goodman's *Ways of Worldmaking* (Indianapolis, Ind.: Hackett, 1978).

8. See David Lewis, *Counterfactuals* (Cambridge, Mass.: Harvard University Press, 1973).

9. See Richard Rorty, *Philosophy and the Mirror of Nature* (Princeton, N.J.: Princeton University Press, 1979). I criticize the "now philosophy is over" aspect of Rorty's view in Part Two of the opening chapter of this volume.

Credits

Chapter 1

Part One: An earlier version was delivered as an Albert Einstein lecture to the Israel Academy of Science. Both Part One and Part Two were delivered as Kant Lectures at Stanford University, Fall 1987. Part Two: Originally appeared as "After Metaphysics, What?" in *Metaphysik nach Kant?* ed. Dieter Henrich and Rolf-Peter Horstmann (Stuttgart: Klett-Cotta, 1988). An earlier version was presented at a conference on "Newton and Realism" that took place at Tel Aviv University and at the Van Leer Jerusalem Foundation under the sponsorship of the Institute for History and Philosophy of Science of Tel Aviv University, April 1987.

Chapter 2

Presented to the American Philosophical Association, 1982 meeting of the Eastern Division, for a symposium on "Reason, Truth, and History" with co-symposiasts Hartry Field and Gilbert Harman.

Chapter 3

Originally published in *Post-Analytic Philosophy*, ed. John Rajchman and Cornel West (New York: Columbia University Press, 1985), pp. 20–30. An earlier version appeared as "After Ayer, After Empiricism" in *Partisan Review*, 5 (1984): 265–275.

Chapter 4

Originally written for the Library of Living Philosophers volume entitled *The Philosophy of A. J. Ayer,* ed. Lewis Edwin Hahn (Peru, Ill.: Open Court, forthcoming).

Chapter 5

Originally published in *Midwest Studies in Philosophy*, vol. 9, *Causation and Causal Theories*, ed. Peter A. French, Theodore E. Uehling, Jr., and Howard K. Wettstein (Minneapolis: University of Minnesota Press, 1984). Copyright © 1984 by the University of Minnesota.

Chapter 6

Originally published in *Dialectica*, 41 (1987): 69–77.

Chapter 7

Originally appeared as "Pourquoi les Philosophes?" in *L'Encyclopédie Philosophique Universelle*, ed. André Jacob (Paris: Presses Universitaires de France, 1986).

Chapter 8

Originally published in *New Literary History*, 15 (1984): 229–240.

Chapter 9

Originally published in *Crítica*, 14 (1982): 3–12.

Chapter 10

Originally published in *The Nature of the Physical Universe: 1976 Nobel Conference*, ed. Douglas Huff and Omer Prewett (New York: John Wiley and Sons, 1979), pp. 113–140.

Chapter 11

To appear in *The Quality of Life*, ed. Martha Nussbaum and Amartya Sen (Oxford: Oxford University Press, forthcoming).

Chapter 12

Presented as the Lindley Lecture, University of Kansas, March 10, 1983.

Chapter 13

Originally published in *New Literary History*, 15 (1983–1984): 77–81.

Chapter 14

Originally published in *Grazer Philosophische Studien*, 13 (1987): 43–51.

Chapter 15

Originally published in *Poetics Today*, 4 (1983): 77–81.

Chapter 16

Originally published in *Raritan*, 8 (Winter 1989): 17–44.

Chapter 17

Forthcoming in the proceedings of the conference on "Frontiers in American Philosophy" held at Texas A & M University, June 1988.

Chapter 18

Originally published in *Historia Mathematica*, 9 (1982): 290–301.

Chapter 19

Presented as the introductory talk for a symposium at Harvard University entitled "The Way the World Is," Emerson Hall, September 5, 1986, for Harvard's 350th anniversary celebration.

Chapter 20

First appeared as a review of W. V. O. Quine's *Quiddities* in *London Review of Books,* vol. 10, no. 8 (April 21, 1988): 11–13.

Chapter 21

Originally published in *The Philosophy of W. V. Quine,* ed. Lewis E. Hahn and Paul A. Schilpp (LaSalle, Ill.: Open Court, 1986), copyright 1986 by the Library of Living Philosophers.

Chapter 22

Originally published as the foreword to Nelson Goodman, *Fact, Fiction, and Forecast,* 4th ed. (Cambridge, Mass.: Harvard University Press, 1983), pp. vii–xvi.

Index